||| || ||||||||||||||||||||||||||||||||||| ||| ||| |||
KU-180-679

ABERDEEN
CITY LIBRARIES
www.aberdeencity.gov.uk/libraries

Return to ....
or any other Aberdeen City Library
Please return/renew this item by the last day shown. Items may also be renewed
by phone or online

2 5 OCT 2014
1 4 JAN 2015
2 3 FEB 2015

X000 000 030 6324

ABERDEEN CITY LIBRARIES

The Necromancer created by:
Matt Hawkins, Joshua Ortega and Francis Manapul

for Top Cow Productions, Inc.
Marc Silvestri -CEO
Matt Hawkins -president and COO
Rob Levin -VP-editorial
Filip Sablik -VP-marketing & sales
Chaz Riggs -production manager
Phil Smith -managing editor
Joshua Cozine -assistant editor
Shelldon Mitchell -production assistant
Adrian Nicita -webmaster

for more info check out:
www.topcow.com

to purchase more books from
Top Cow check out:
www.topcowstore.com

this editon
Edited and Designed by:
Phil Smith

for **Image** Comics

Erik Larsen
Publisher

Eric Stephenson
Executive Director

To find the comics shop
nearest you call
1-888-COMICBOOK

The Necromancer **Book I** trade paperback,
2007 - FIRST PRINTING.
ISBN-13: 978-1-58240-648-0
Published by Image Comics Inc. Office of Publication: 1942
University Ave., Suite 305 Berkeley, CA 94704. $14.99 US,
$17.61 CAN. The Necromancer. © 2007 Top Cow
Productions, Inc.. All rights reserved. "The Necromancer,"
The Necromancer logos, and the likeness of all featured char-
acters are trademarks of Top Cow Productions, Inc. The char-
acters, events and stories in this publication are entirely fiction-
al. With the exception of artwork used for review purposes,
none of the contents of this book may be reprinted in any form
without the express written consent of Top Cow Productions,
Inc.
PRINTED IN CANADA.

TABLE OF CONTENTS

——————FOREWORD

Go West, Young Mage

You know what I love about *Necromancer*? More than anything else?

It's how cleverly and sweetly it lies to you. Draws you in with its superficial sweetness before digging the knife in deep and twisting it a hundred and eighty degrees.

Here's a story about an attractive, vivacious young cheerleader - Abigail van Alstine - and her glossy, prosperous friends, all drawn by Francis Manapul in heartbreakingly beautiful detail, to the point where their cuteness passes some hypothetical asymptote.

And it's a story we all know so well, from *Harry Potter* and elsewhere: a young wizard comes into his (or in this case her) power and ultimately - after triumphing over some serious obstacles - takes her place in a community of magic-users who will teach her the full extent of her gifts and the unsuspected sorcerous tradition in which she now, amazingly, has a place.

But the early *Harry Potter* books skewed that well-worn narrative very strongly towards wish fulfillment fantasy. So did *The Worst Witch in the School*, Diane Duane's *Young Wizards* books and even, despite the dark undercurrents, Diana Wynne Jones's superb *Witch Week*. You'd have to go all the way back to Ursula LeGuin's masterpiece, *A Wizard of Earthsea*, to find a take on the "hey look, I'm a wizard" story that's as scary, uncompromising and gut-churningly disturbing as the one that.Ortega and Manapul have served up for us here.

The first thing that happens after Abigail van Alstine discovers her flair for magic is that she loses her friends and family in an appalling orgy of violence which springs directly from her own spellcasting. The second is that she herself kills two innocent men. The third is that she's kidnapped and used by a necromantic cult which has infiltrated and suborned the US army.

Throughout the story - or rather the two back-to-back stories that are collected here, **Something in the Way** and **Lithium** - the darkness gathers and the stakes get higher. Not once does Ortega pull a punch. And neither does the art, because Manapul maintains the same lovingly detailed, fully rendered style throughout, even when what he's drawing shifts from high school football games and flirtatious encounters in bible study classes to beheadings and teen suicides.

The result is a story that grips you and forbids you to look away. There is the real sense of a soul, a life, in terrible peril, and of huge forces being mobilized to destroy her before she even gets a toe-hold in the new world she's discovered. And there's a climax which turns everything you were expecting on its head in a viscerally satisfying manner. I'm not going to apologise for that clichéd adverb, either - you'll see what I mean.

Joshua Ortega had already established his reputation in the field of prose fiction before starting to write comics. That's no guarantee of anything, of course: lots of guys find that transition - no matter which direction they make it in - really hard and problematic. It is hard, because narrative formulas that work brilliantly in prose can seem flaccid and under-cooked in a sequential art medium, and vice versa. But Ortega hits the water like that car in the James Bond movies that turns into a sub: when he runs out of road he turns his wheels into fins and keeps right on going.

It's true that he's ably abetted by his penciller and inkers, who bring cast and settings to life with spectacular bravura. Page layouts vary from a Dave Gibbons nine-panel grid™ used in some of the quieter moments to an almost Neal Adams-like explosion of jagged diagonals when the demon Berzelius makes the scene. But it's always organic and the effects are always locked smoothly and satisfyingly into the storytelling.

Actually, since I already started in with some tendentious comparisons, the other one that occurs to me here - young girl with magical heritage assembles group of friends to help her deal with unimaginable threat in small-town and high school settings - is Joss Whedon's immaculate *Buffy the Vampire Slayer.* I don't know of any higher praise than that.

So there you go. *The Necromancer.* A horror/fantasy story that's not afraid of its own terrifying implications.

But trust me when I say that you will be...

Mike Carey
Feb 2007

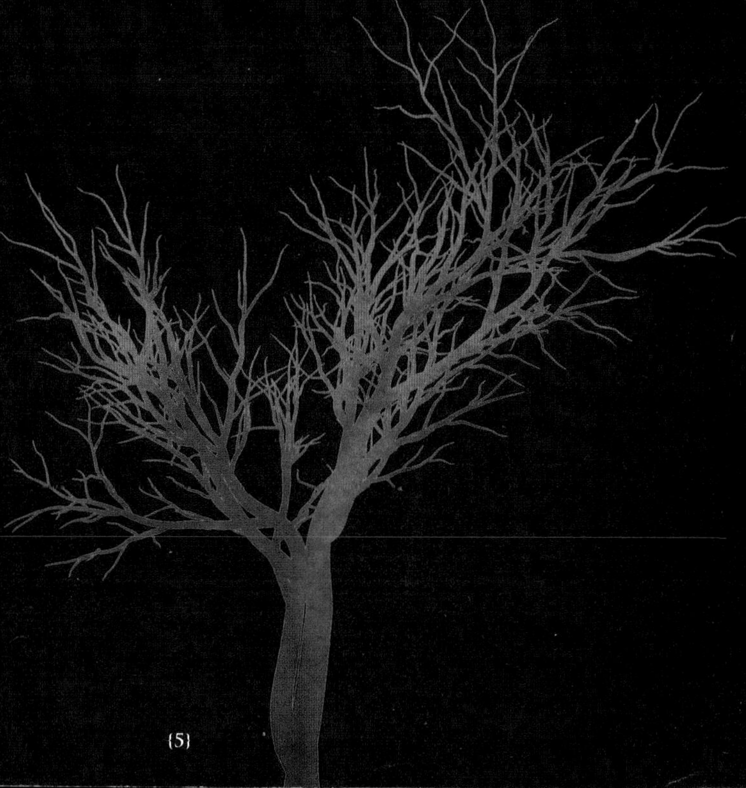

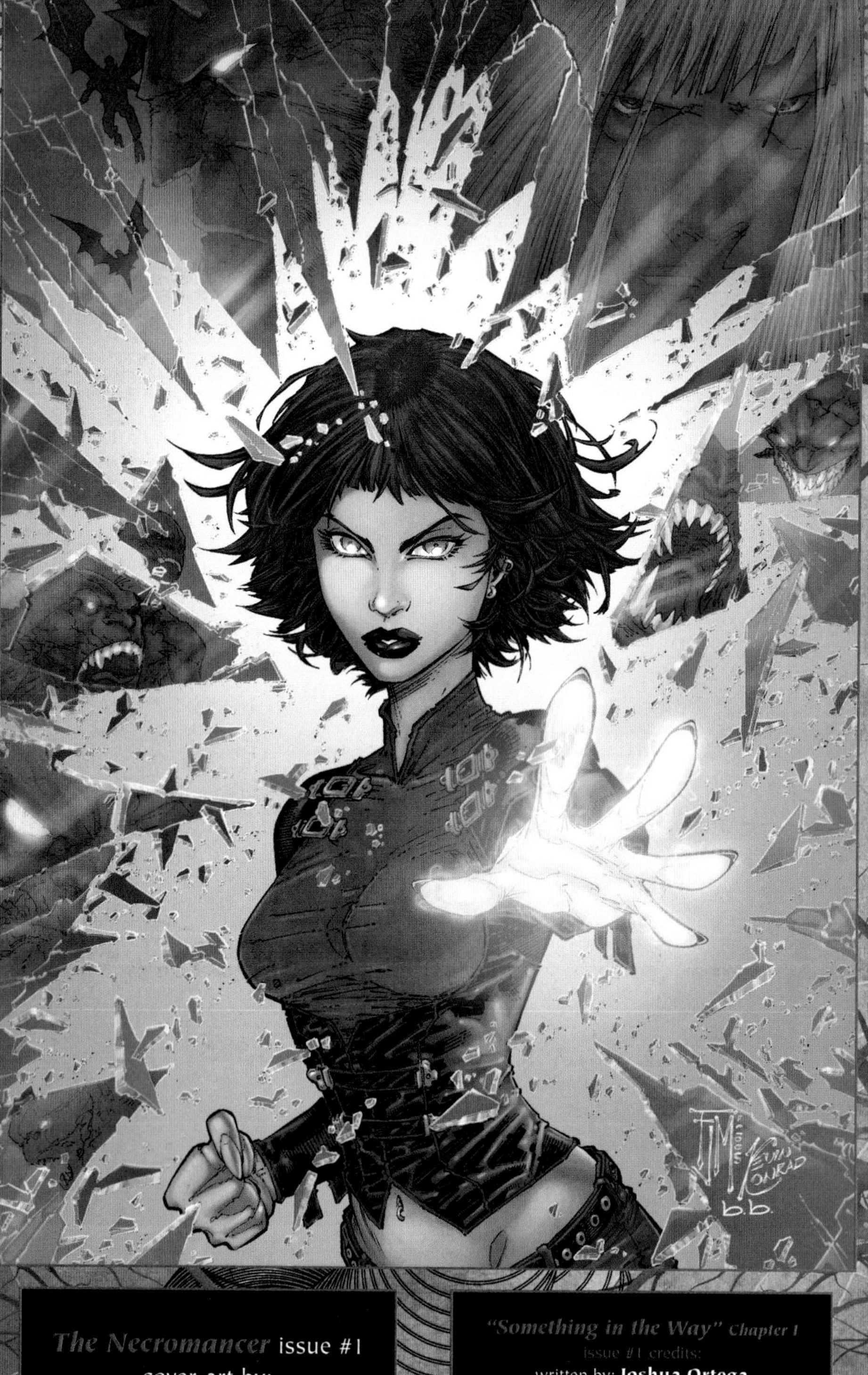

The Necromancer issue #1
cover art by:
Francis Manapul
Kevin Conrad
and
Brian Buccellato

"Something in the Way" Chapter 1
issue #1 credits:
written by: **Joshua Ortega**
pencils by: **Francis Manapul**
inks by: **Kevin Conrad, Rob Hunter, Jay Leisten, Scott Koblish, Rick Basaldua**
colors by: **Brian Buccellato**
letters by: **Troy Peteri**

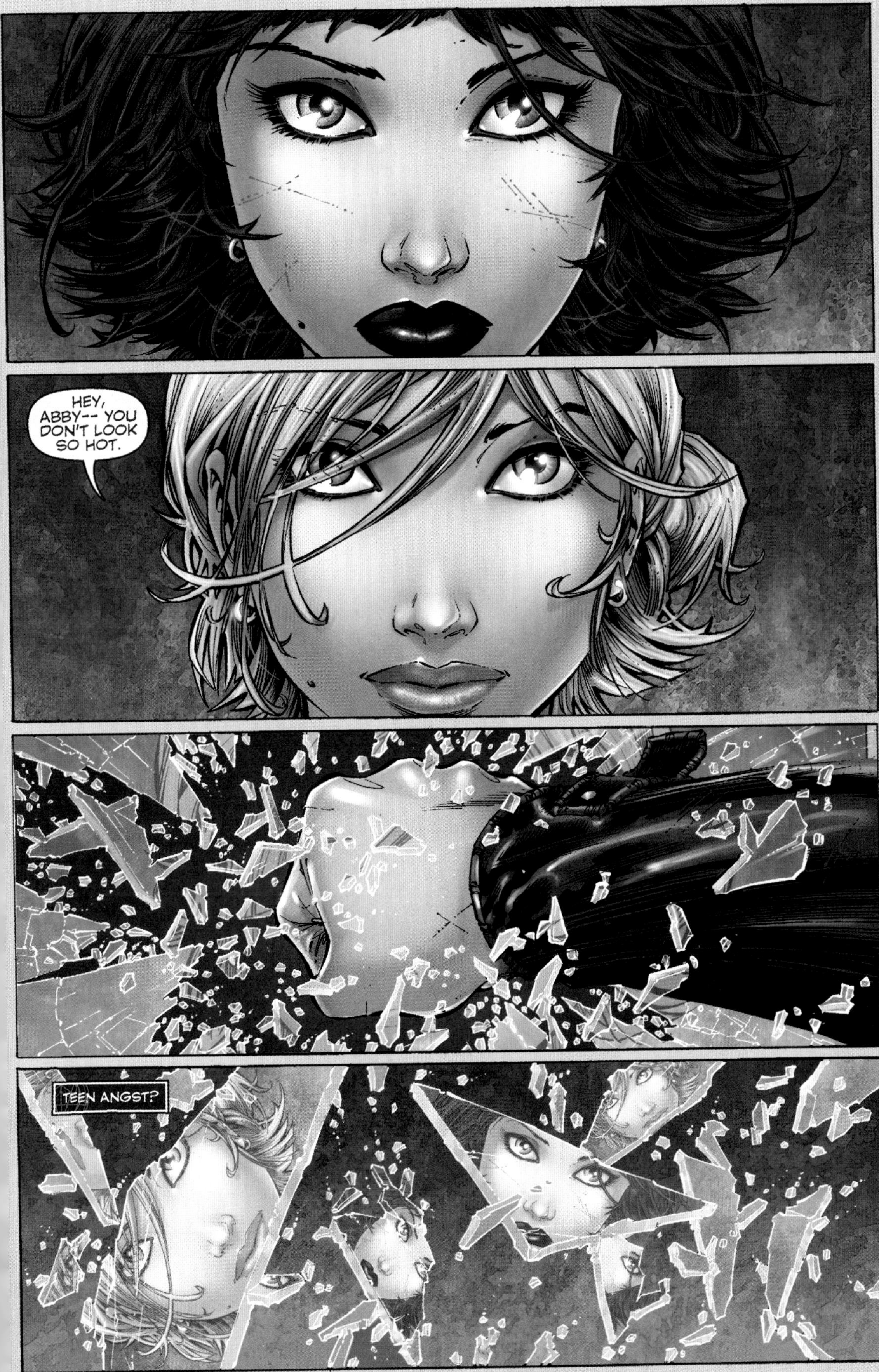
HEY, ABBY-- YOU DON'T LOOK SO HOT.
TEEN ANGST?

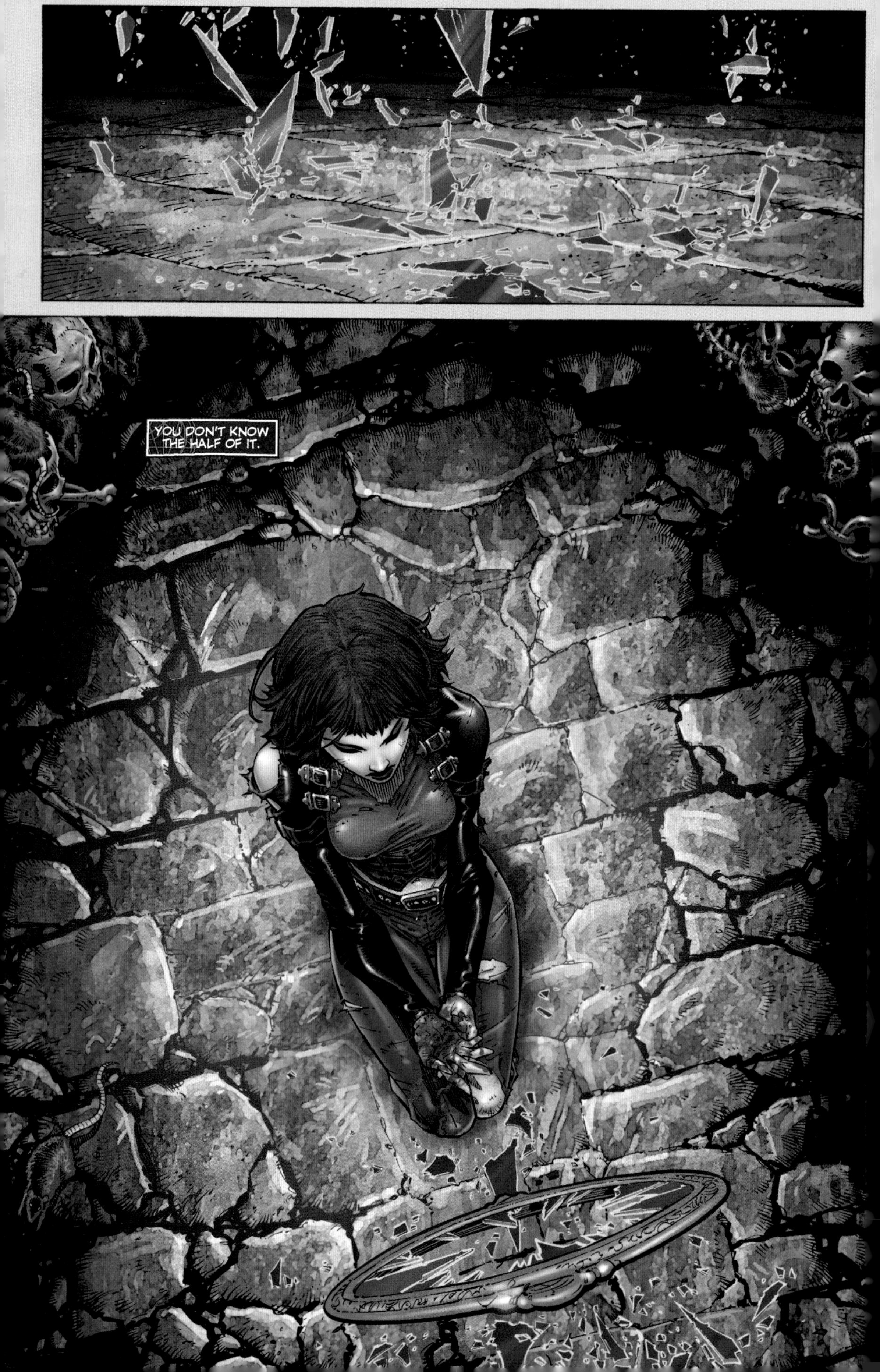
YOU DON'T KNOW THE HALF OF IT.

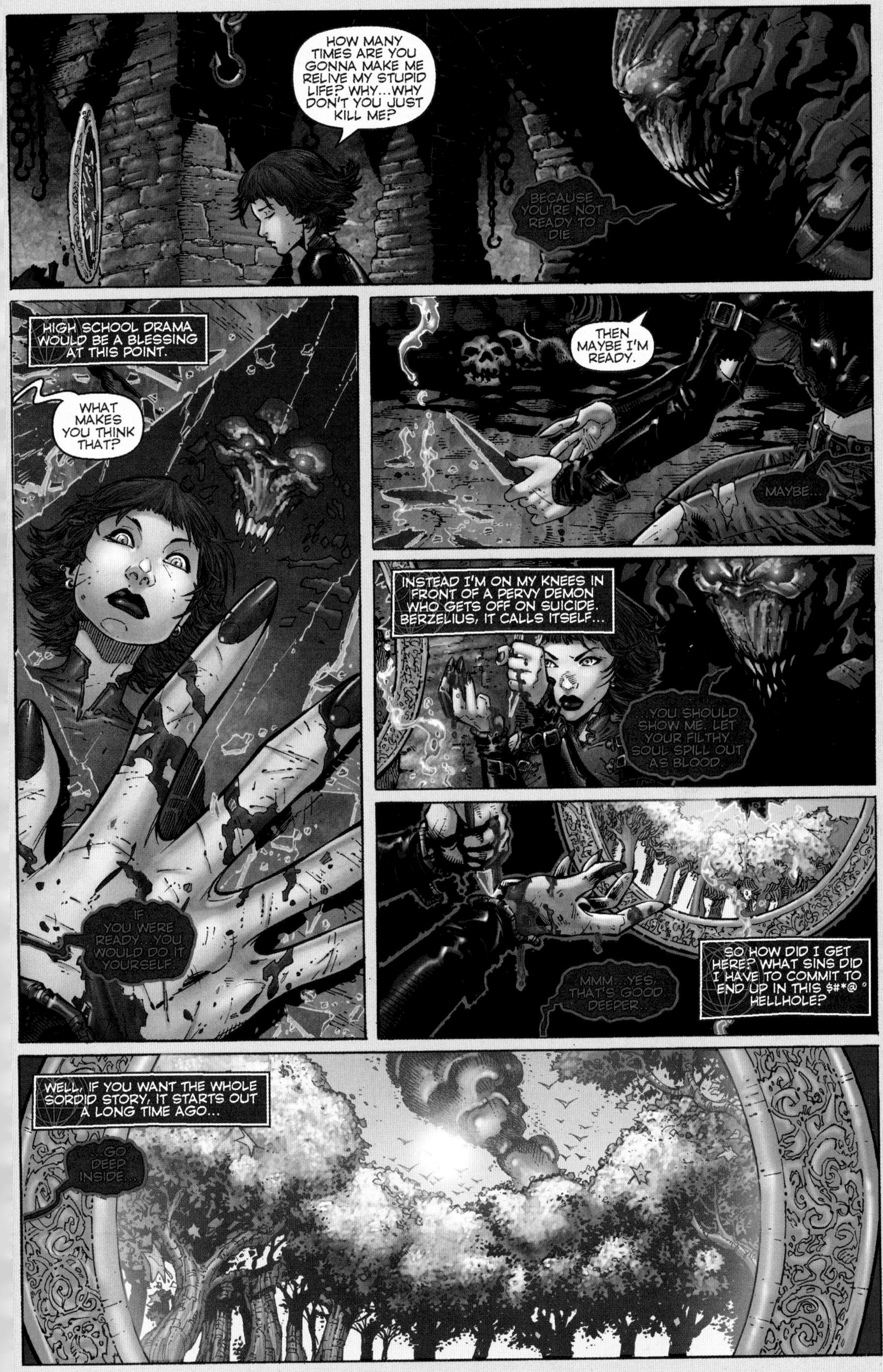
HOW MANY TIMES ARE YOU GONNA MAKE ME RELIVE MY STUPID LIFE? WHY...WHY DON'T YOU JUST KILL ME?
BECAUSE YOU'RE NOT READY TO DIE.
HIGH SCHOOL DRAMA WOULD BE A BLESSING AT THIS POINT.
WHAT MAKES YOU THINK THAT?
IF YOU WERE READY...YOU WOULD DO IT YOURSELF.
THEN MAYBE I'M READY.
MAYBE...
INSTEAD I'M ON MY KNEES IN FRONT OF A PERVY DEMON WHO GETS OFF ON SUICIDE. BERZELIUS, IT CALLS ITSELF...
YOU SHOULD SHOW ME. LET YOUR FILTHY SOUL SPILL OUT AS BLOOD.
MMM...YES, THAT'S GOOD. DEEPER...
SO HOW DID I GET HERE? WHAT SINS DID I HAVE TO COMMIT TO END UP IN THIS $#*@ HELLHOLE?
WELL, IF YOU WANT THE WHOLE SORDID STORY, IT STARTS OUT A LONG TIME AGO...
...GO DEEP INSIDE...

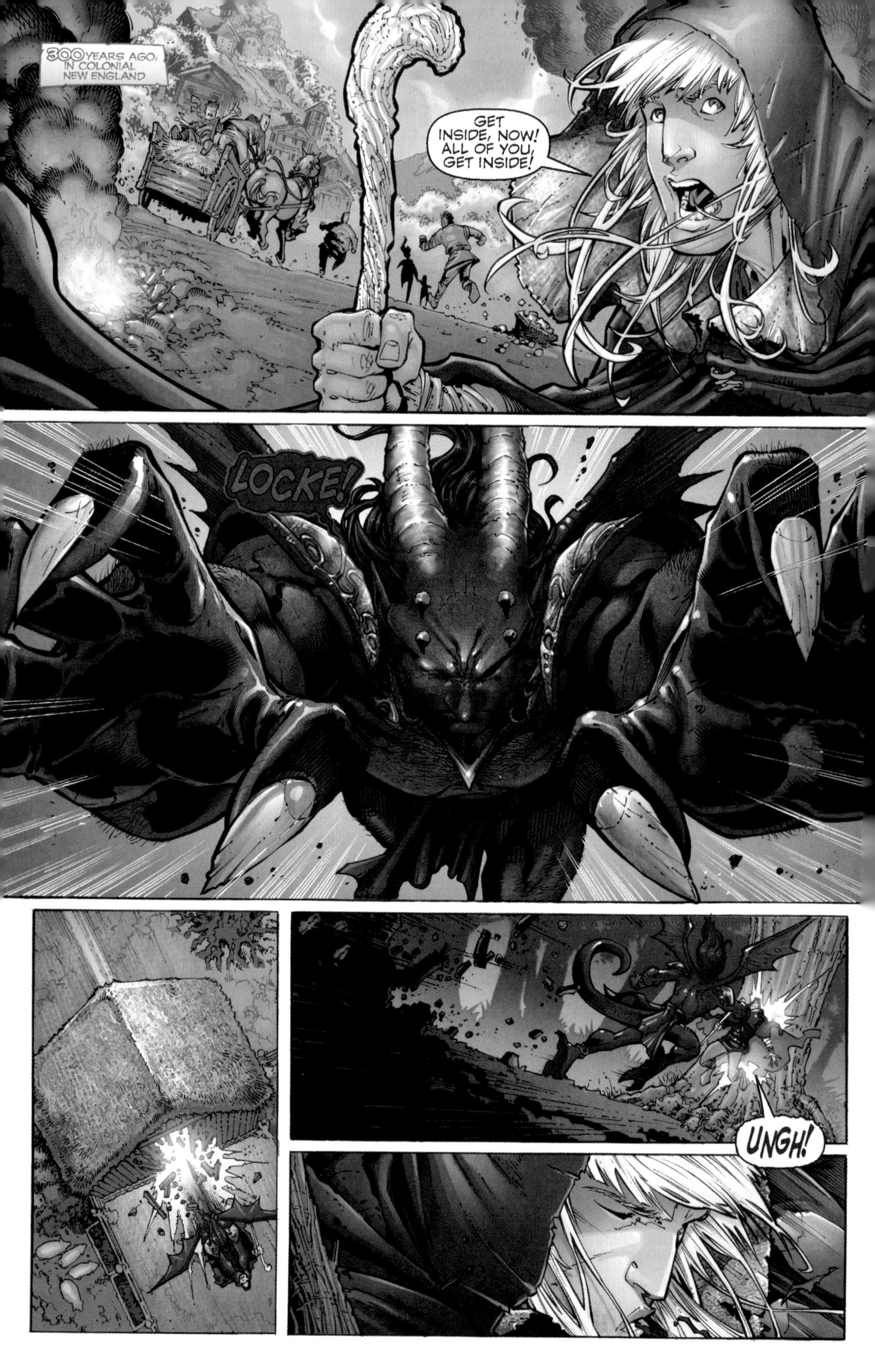
300 YEARS AGO, IN COLONIAL NEW ENGLAND
GET INSIDE, NOW! ALL OF YOU, GET INSIDE!
LOCKE!
UNGH!

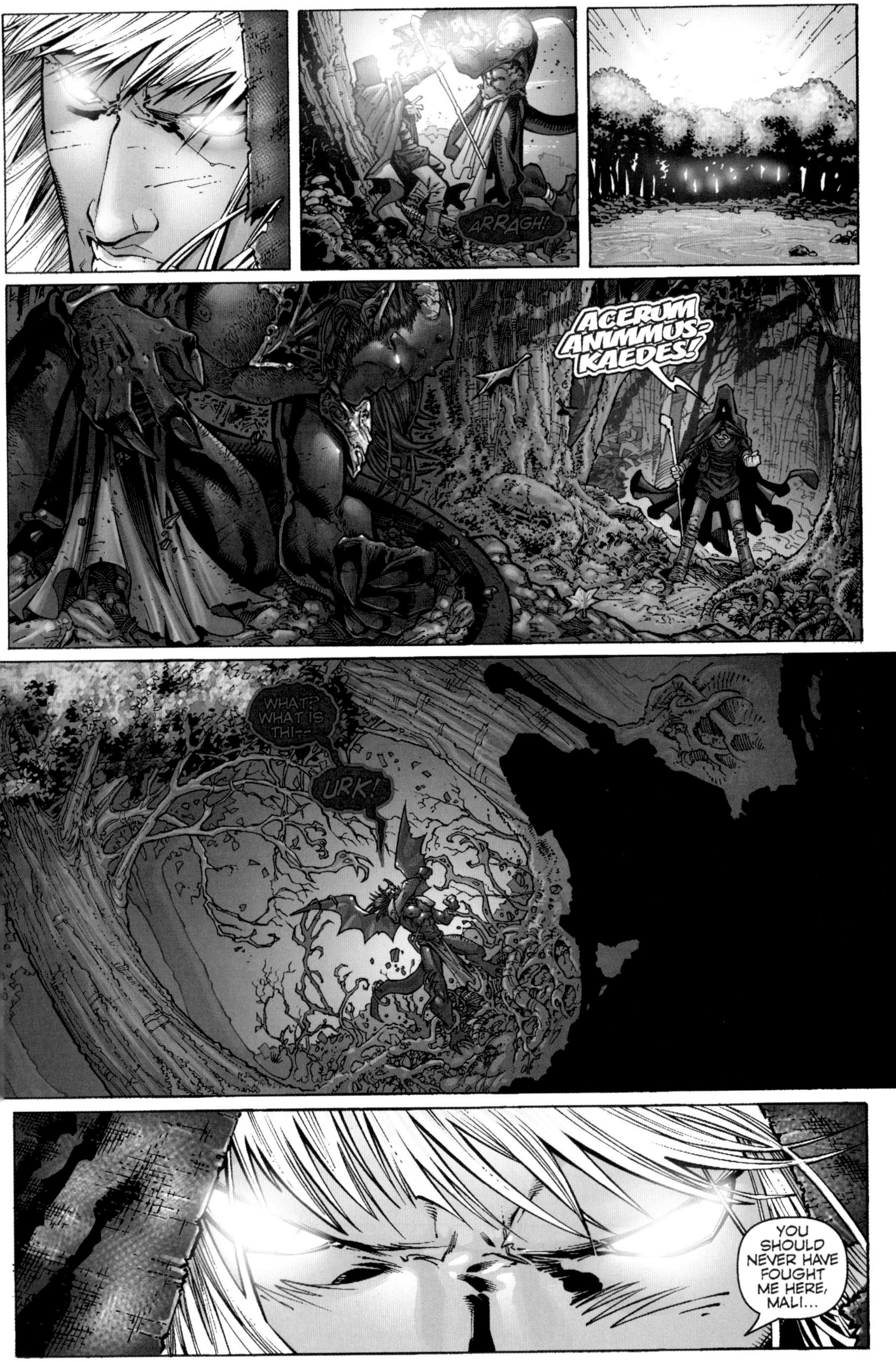
ARRAGH!
ACERUM ANIMMUS-KAEDES!
WHAT? WHAT IS THI--
URK!
YOU SHOULD NEVER HAVE FOUGHT ME HERE, MALI...

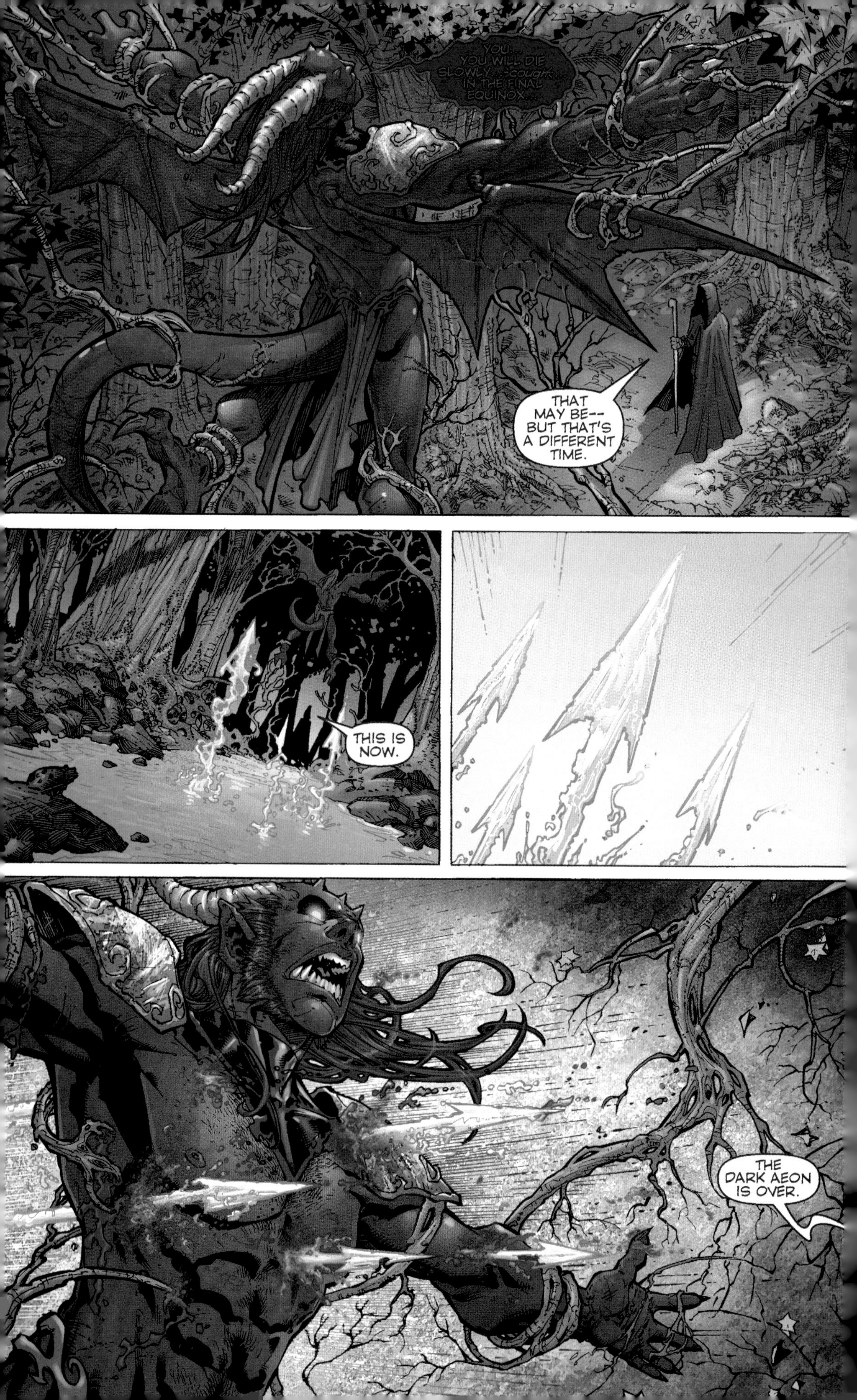
YOU... YOU WILL DIE SLOWLY... *cough*... IN THE FINAL EQUINOX...
THAT MAY BE-- BUT THAT'S A DIFFERENT TIME.
THIS IS NOW.
THE DARK AEON IS OVER.

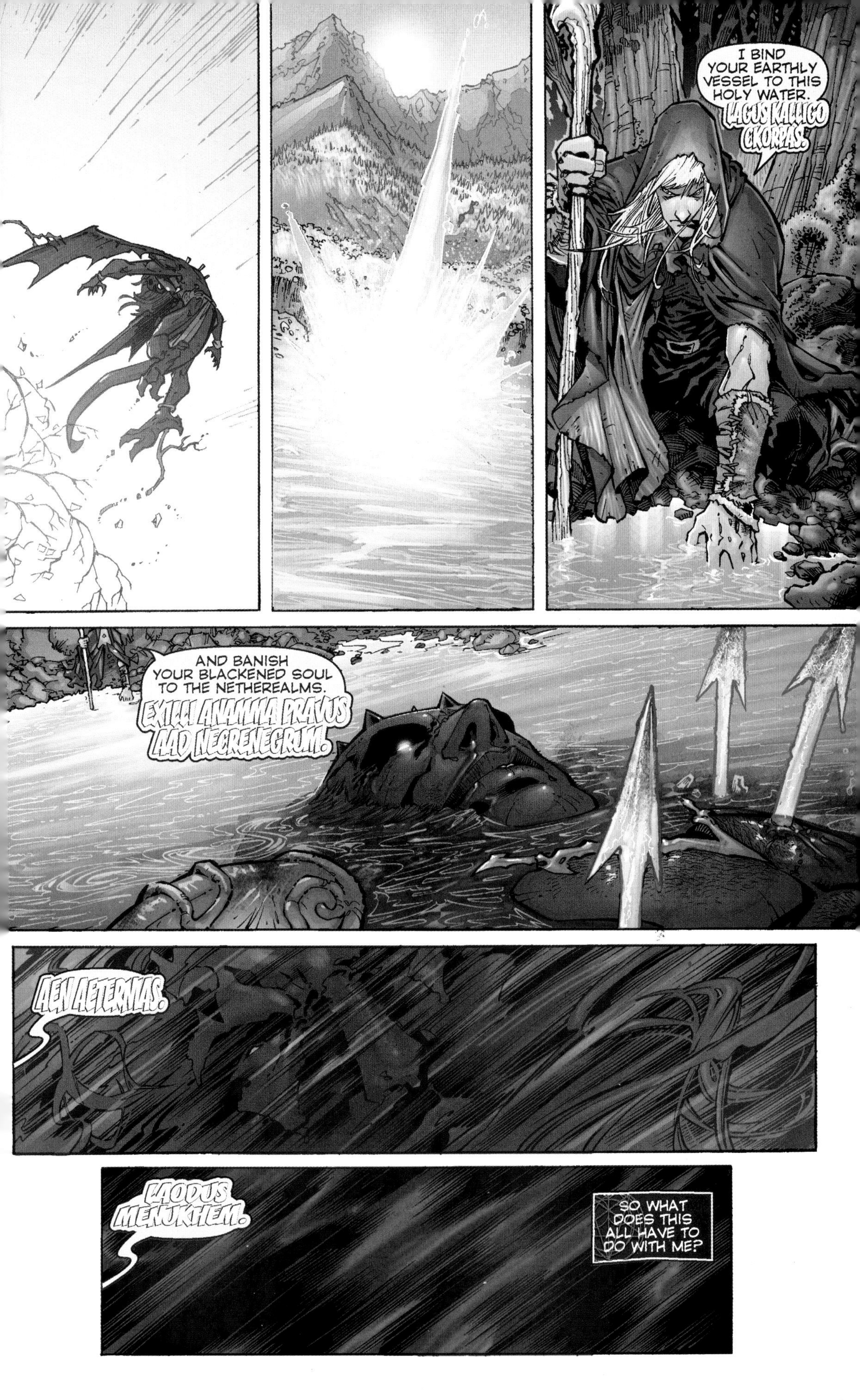
I BIND YOUR EARTHLY VESSEL TO THIS HOLY WATER. LAGUS KALLIGO CKORPAS.
AND BANISH YOUR BLACKENED SOUL TO THE NETHEREALMS. EXILLI ANAMMA PRAVUS AAD NECRENEGRUM.
AEN AETERMAS.
LAODUS MENUKHEM.
SO WHAT DOES THIS ALL HAVE TO DO WITH ME?

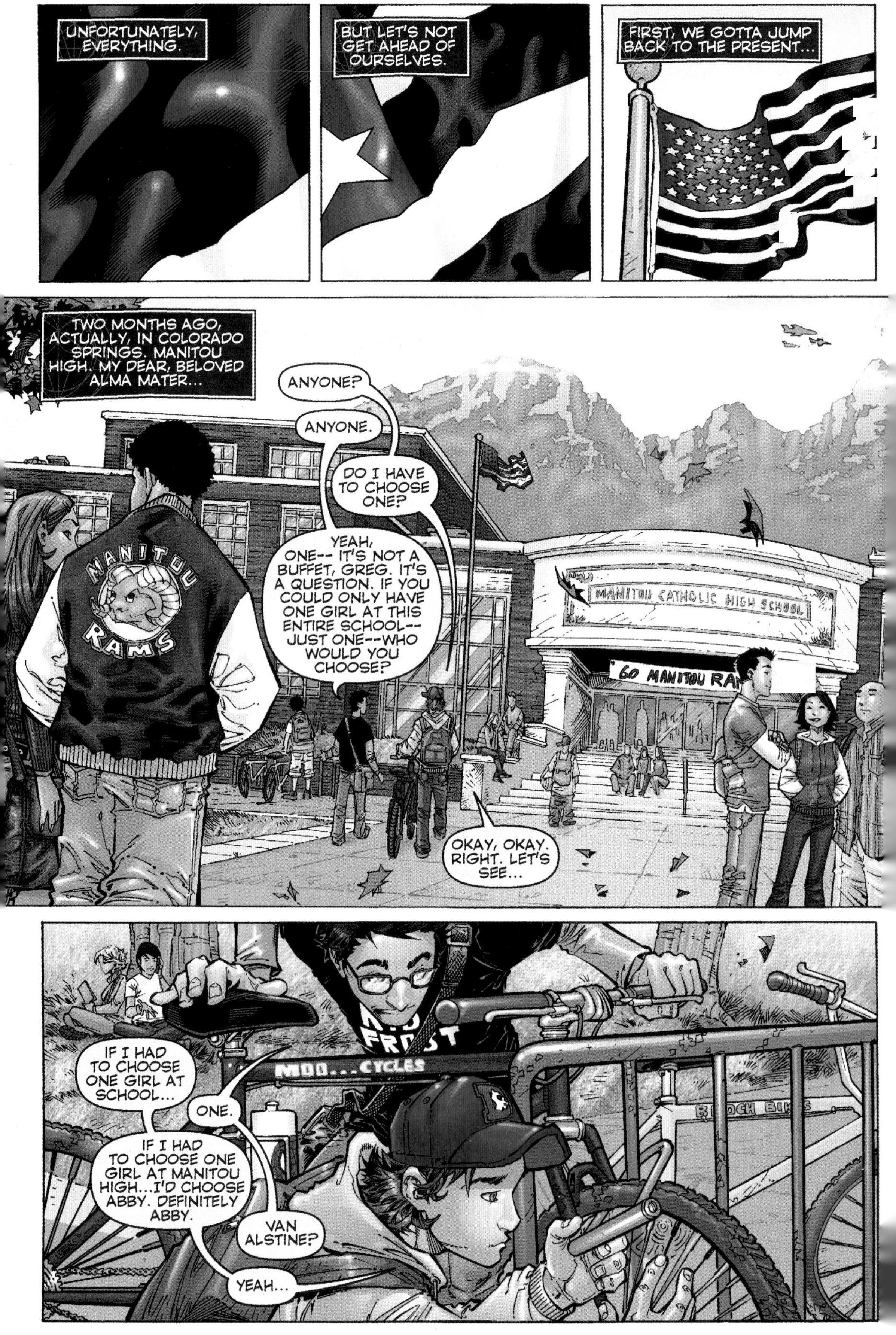
UNFORTUNATELY, EVERYTHING.
BUT LET'S NOT GET AHEAD OF OURSELVES.
FIRST, WE GOTTA JUMP BACK TO THE PRESENT...
TWO MONTHS AGO, ACTUALLY, IN COLORADO SPRINGS. MANITOU HIGH. MY DEAR, BELOVED ALMA MATER...
ANYONE?
ANYONE.
DO I HAVE TO CHOOSE ONE?
YEAH, ONE-- IT'S NOT A BUFFET, GREG. IT'S A QUESTION. IF YOU COULD ONLY HAVE ONE GIRL AT THIS ENTIRE SCHOOL-- JUST ONE--WHO WOULD YOU CHOOSE?
MANITOU RAMS
MANITOU CATHOLIC HIGH SCHOOL
GO MANITOU RA
OKAY, OKAY. RIGHT. LET'S SEE...
IF I HAD TO CHOOSE ONE GIRL AT SCHOOL...
ONE.
IF I HAD TO CHOOSE ONE GIRL AT MANITOU HIGH...I'D CHOOSE ABBY. DEFINITELY ABBY.
VAN ALSTINE?
YEAH...
MOO...CYCLES

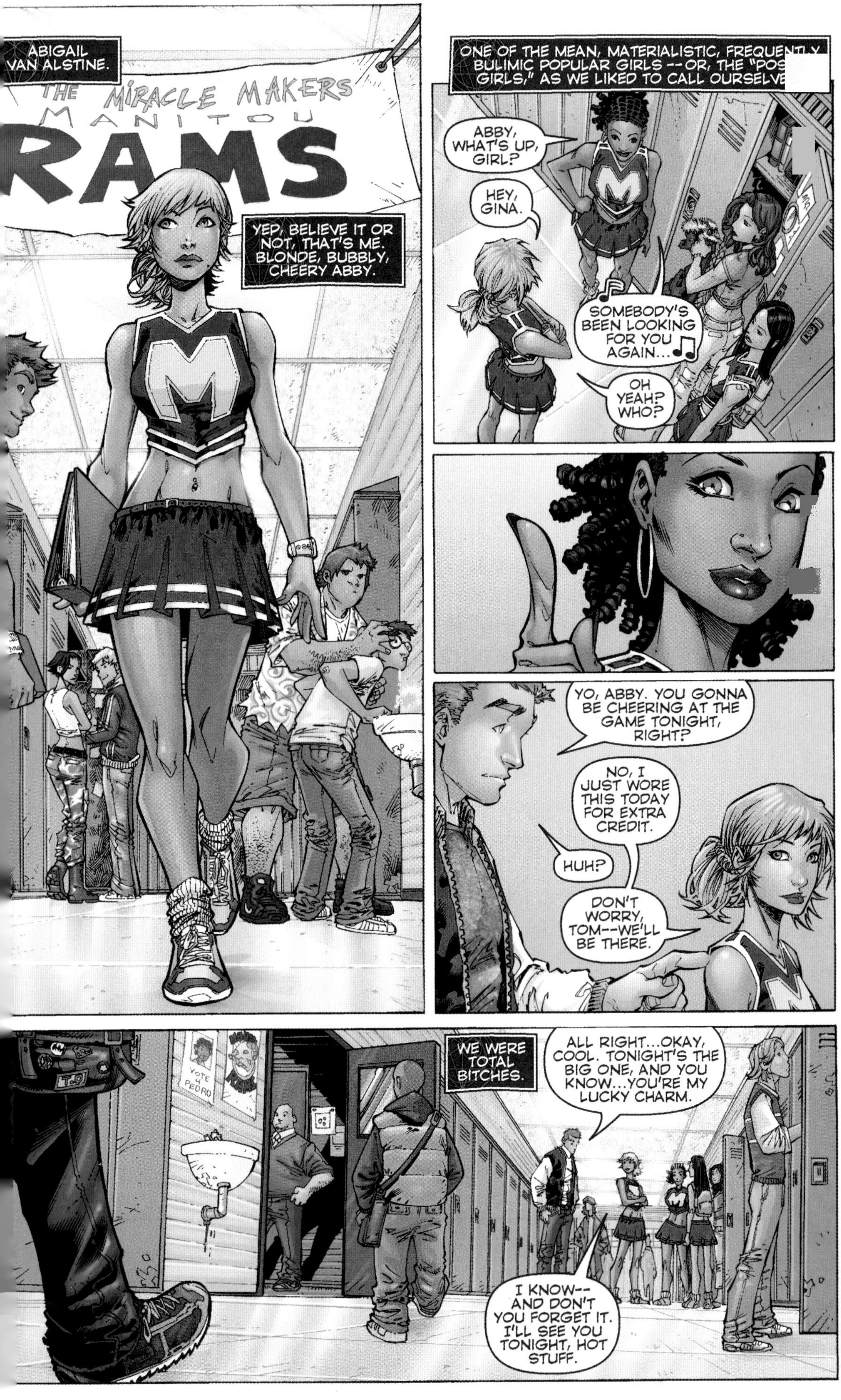
ABIGAIL VAN ALSTINE.
THE MIRACLE MAKERS
MANITOU RAMS
YEP, BELIEVE IT OR NOT, THAT'S ME. BLONDE, BUBBLY, CHEERY ABBY.
ONE OF THE MEAN, MATERIALISTIC, FREQUENTLY BULIMIC POPULAR GIRLS --OR, THE "POS GIRLS," AS WE LIKED TO CALL OURSELVE
ABBY, WHAT'S UP, GIRL?
HEY, GINA.
SOMEBODY'S BEEN LOOKING FOR YOU AGAIN...
OH YEAH? WHO?
YO, ABBY. YOU GONNA BE CHEERING AT THE GAME TONIGHT, RIGHT?
NO, I JUST WORE THIS TODAY FOR EXTRA CREDIT.
HUH?
DON'T WORRY, TOM--WE'LL BE THERE.
VOTE 4 PEDRO
WE WERE TOTAL BITCHES.
ALL RIGHT...OKAY, COOL. TONIGHT'S THE BIG ONE, AND YOU KNOW...YOU'RE MY LUCKY CHARM.
I KNOW-- AND DON'T YOU FORGET IT. I'LL SEE YOU TONIGHT, HOT STUFF.

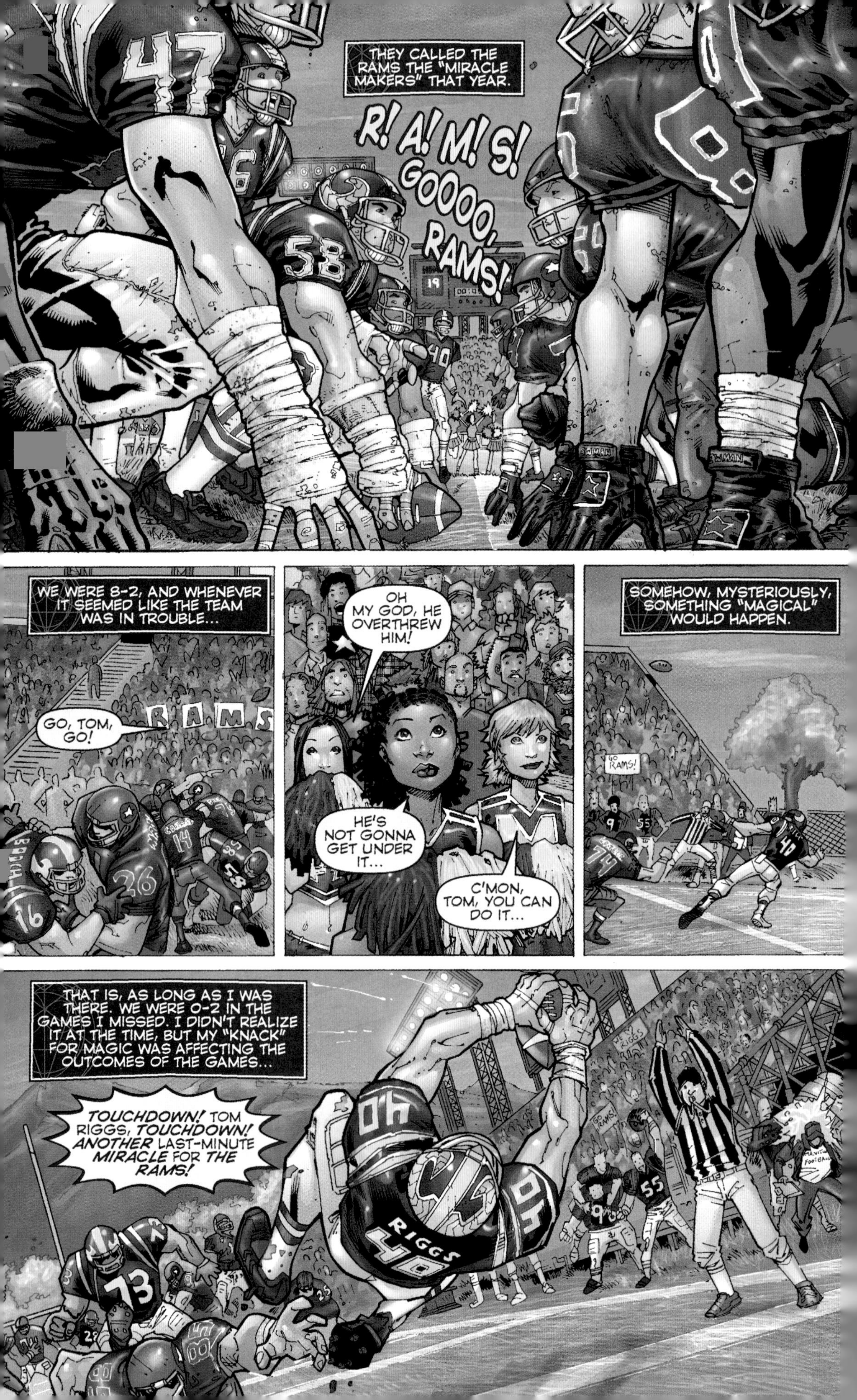
THEY CALLED THE RAMS THE "MIRACLE MAKERS" THAT YEAR.
R! A! M! S! GOOOO, RAMS!
WE WERE 8-2, AND WHENEVER IT SEEMED LIKE THE TEAM WAS IN TROUBLE...
RAMS
GO, TOM, GO!
OH MY GOD, HE OVERTHREW HIM!
HE'S NOT GONNA GET UNDER IT...
C'MON, TOM, YOU CAN DO IT...
SOMEHOW, MYSTERIOUSLY, SOMETHING "MAGICAL" WOULD HAPPEN.
GO RAMS!
THAT IS, AS LONG AS I WAS THERE. WE WERE 0-2 IN THE GAMES I MISSED. I DIDN'T REALIZE IT AT THE TIME, BUT MY "KNACK" FOR MAGIC WAS AFFECTING THE OUTCOMES OF THE GAMES...
TOUCHDOWN! TOM RIGGS, TOUCHDOWN! ANOTHER LAST-MINUTE MIRACLE FOR THE RAMS!
RIGGS
GO RAMS!

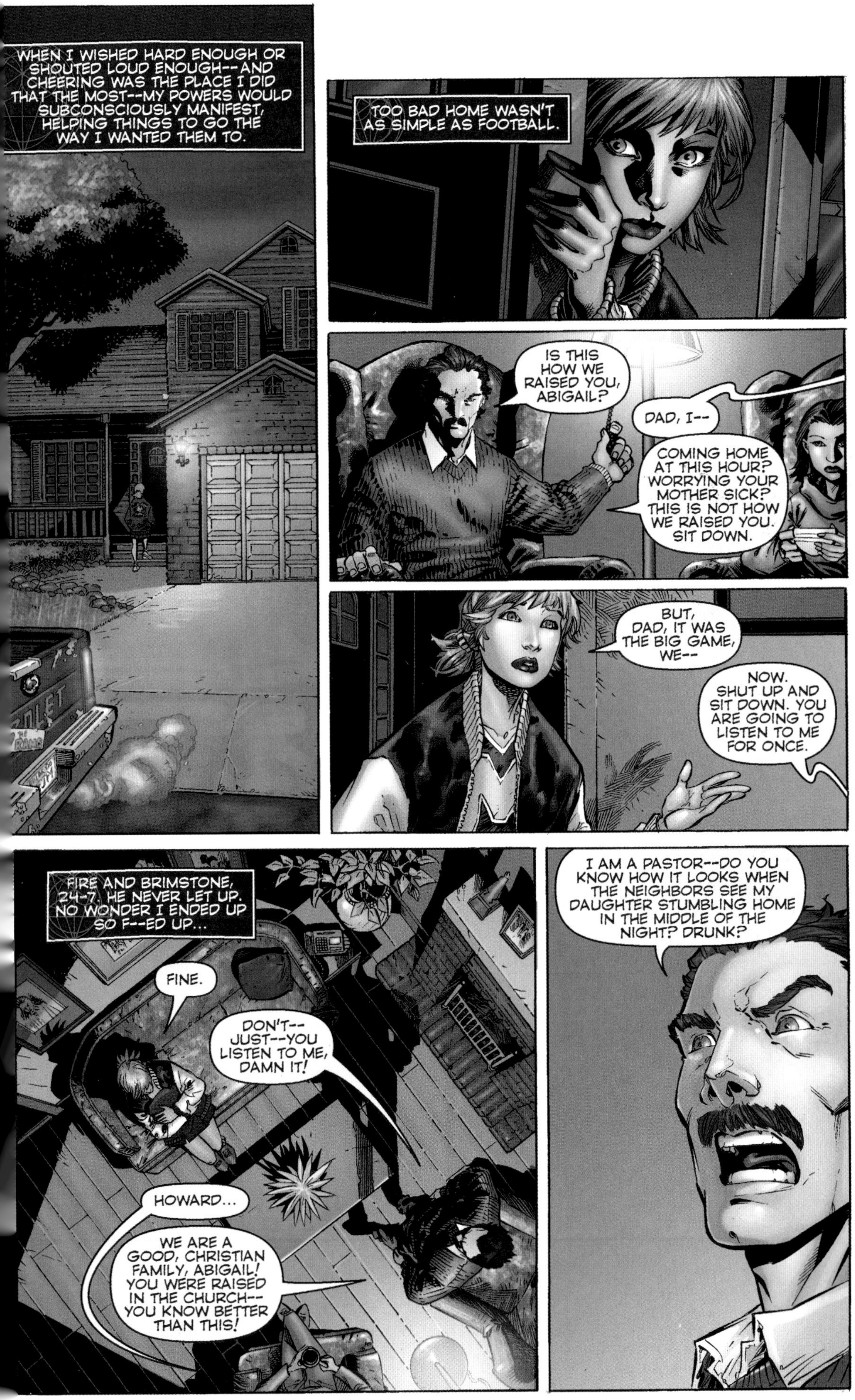
WHEN I WISHED HARD ENOUGH OR SHOUTED LOUD ENOUGH--AND CHEERING WAS THE PLACE I DID THAT THE MOST--MY POWERS WOULD SUBCONSCIOUSLY MANIFEST, HELPING THINGS TO GO THE WAY I WANTED THEM TO.
TOO BAD HOME WASN'T AS SIMPLE AS FOOTBALL.
IS THIS HOW WE RAISED YOU, ABIGAIL?
DAD, I--
COMING HOME AT THIS HOUR? WORRYING YOUR MOTHER SICK? THIS IS NOT HOW WE RAISED YOU. SIT DOWN.
BUT, DAD, IT WAS THE BIG GAME, WE--
NOW. SHUT UP AND SIT DOWN. YOU ARE GOING TO LISTEN TO ME FOR ONCE.
FIRE AND BRIMSTONE, 24-7. HE NEVER LET UP. NO WONDER I ENDED UP SO F--ED UP...
FINE.
DON'T-- JUST--YOU LISTEN TO ME, DAMN IT!
HOWARD...
WE ARE A GOOD, CHRISTIAN FAMILY, ABIGAIL! YOU WERE RAISED IN THE CHURCH-- YOU KNOW BETTER THAN THIS!
I AM A PASTOR--DO YOU KNOW HOW IT LOOKS WHEN THE NEIGHBORS SEE MY DAUGHTER STUMBLING HOME IN THE MIDDLE OF THE NIGHT? DRUNK?

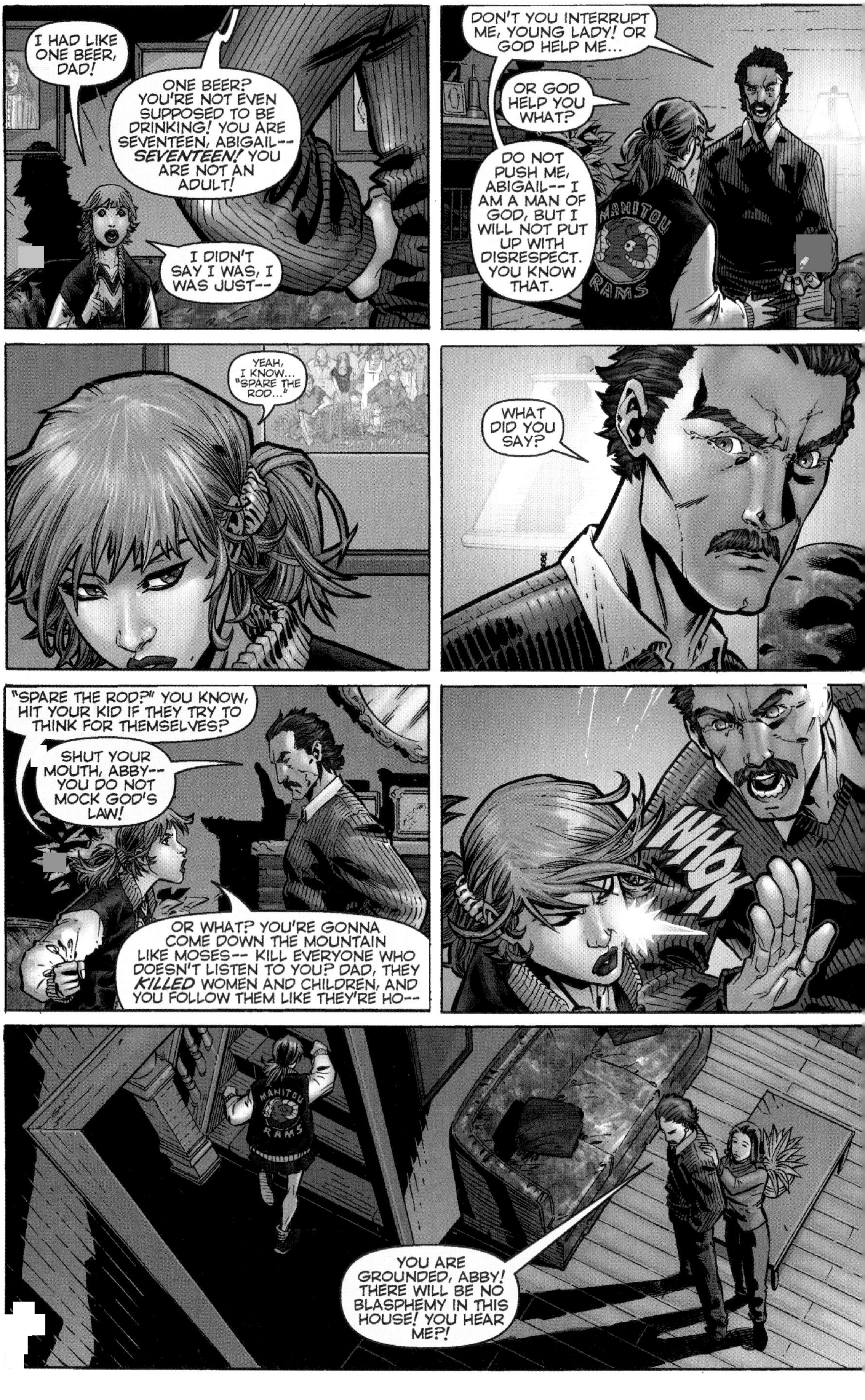

I HAD LIKE ONE BEER, DAD!
ONE BEER? YOU'RE NOT EVEN SUPPOSED TO BE DRINKING! YOU ARE SEVENTEEN, ABIGAIL-- *SEVENTEEN!* YOU ARE NOT AN ADULT!
I DIDN'T SAY I WAS, I WAS JUST--
DON'T YOU INTERRUPT ME, YOUNG LADY! OR GOD HELP ME...
OR GOD HELP YOU WHAT?
DO NOT PUSH ME, ABIGAIL-- I AM A MAN OF GOD, BUT I WILL NOT PUT UP WITH DISRESPECT. YOU KNOW THAT.
MANITOU RAMS
YEAH, I KNOW... "SPARE THE ROD..."
WHAT DID YOU SAY?
"SPARE THE ROD?" YOU KNOW, HIT YOUR KID IF THEY TRY TO THINK FOR THEMSELVES?
SHUT YOUR MOUTH, ABBY-- YOU DO NOT MOCK GOD'S LAW!
OR WHAT? YOU'RE GONNA COME DOWN THE MOUNTAIN LIKE MOSES-- KILL EVERYONE WHO DOESN'T LISTEN TO YOU? DAD, THEY *KILLED* WOMEN AND CHILDREN, AND YOU FOLLOW THEM LIKE THEY'RE HO--
WHOK
MANITOU RAMS
YOU ARE GROUNDED, ABBY! THERE WILL BE NO BLASPHEMY IN THIS HOUSE! YOU HEAR ME?!

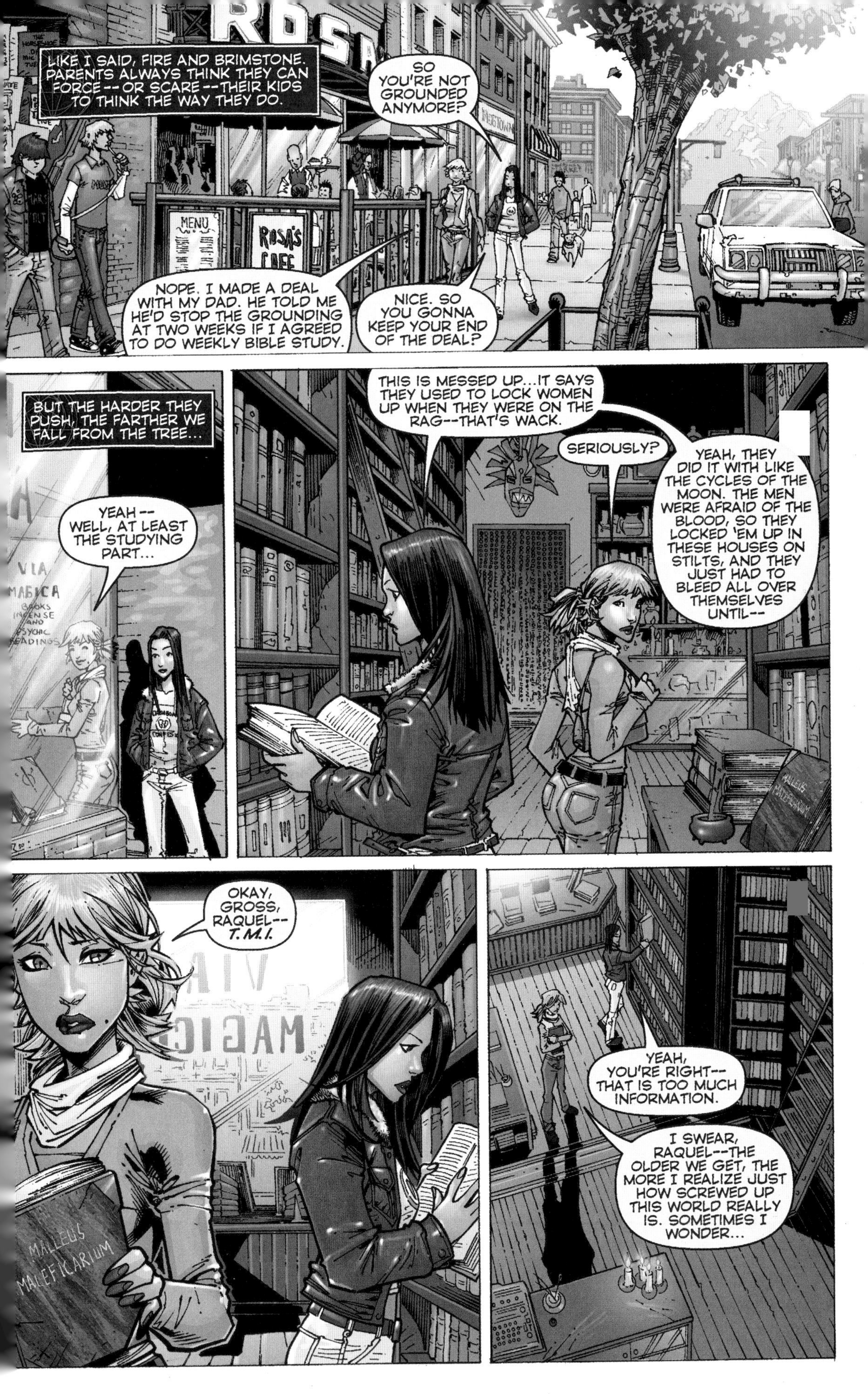

ROSA'S
LIKE I SAID, FIRE AND BRIMSTONE. PARENTS ALWAYS THINK THEY CAN FORCE--OR SCARE--THEIR KIDS TO THINK THE WAY THEY DO.
SO YOU'RE NOT GROUNDED ANYMORE?
MENU
ROSA'S CAFE
NOPE. I MADE A DEAL WITH MY DAD. HE TOLD ME HE'D STOP THE GROUNDING AT TWO WEEKS IF I AGREED TO DO WEEKLY BIBLE STUDY.
NICE. SO YOU GONNA KEEP YOUR END OF THE DEAL?
BUT THE HARDER THEY PUSH, THE FARTHER WE FALL FROM THE TREE...
YEAH--WELL, AT LEAST THE STUDYING PART...
VIA MAGICA
BOOKS INCENSE AND PSYCHIC READINGS
THIS IS MESSED UP...IT SAYS THEY USED TO LOCK WOMEN UP WHEN THEY WERE ON THE RAG--THAT'S WACK.
SERIOUSLY?
YEAH, THEY DID IT WITH LIKE THE CYCLES OF THE MOON. THE MEN WERE AFRAID OF THE BLOOD, SO THEY LOCKED 'EM UP IN THESE HOUSES ON STILTS, AND THEY JUST HAD TO BLEED ALL OVER THEMSELVES UNTIL--
MALLEUS MALEFICARUM
OKAY, GROSS, RAQUEL--*T.M.I.*
MALLEUS MALEFICARUM
YEAH, YOU'RE RIGHT--THAT IS TOO MUCH INFORMATION.
I SWEAR, RAQUEL--THE OLDER WE GET, THE MORE I REALIZE JUST HOW SCREWED UP THIS WORLD REALLY IS. SOMETIMES I WONDER...

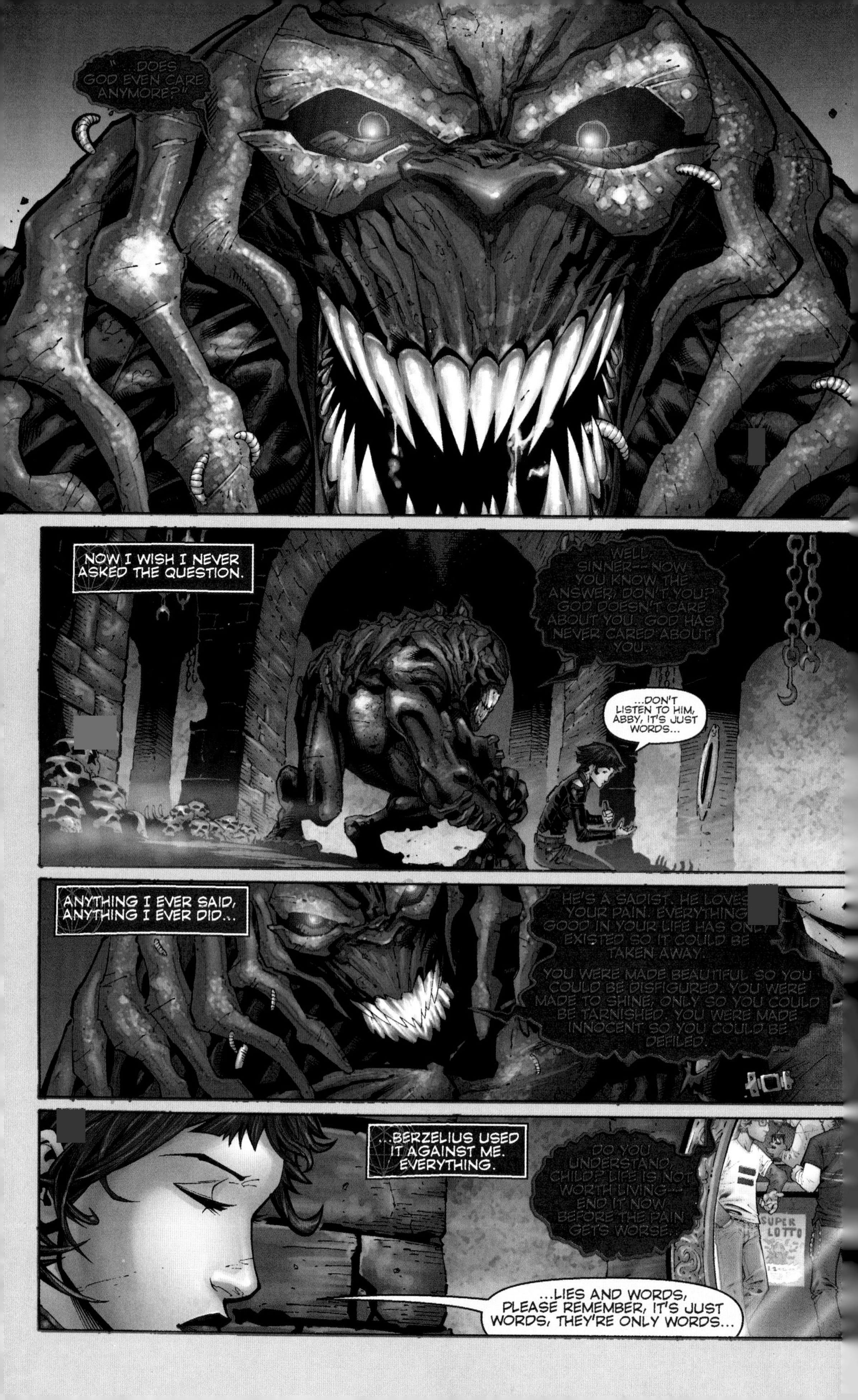
"...DOES GOD EVEN CARE ANYMORE?"
NOW I WISH I NEVER ASKED THE QUESTION.
WELL, SINNER-- NOW YOU KNOW THE ANSWER, DON'T YOU? GOD DOESN'T CARE ABOUT YOU. GOD HAS NEVER CARED ABOUT YOU.
...DON'T LISTEN TO HIM, ABBY, IT'S JUST WORDS...
ANYTHING I EVER SAID, ANYTHING I EVER DID...
HE'S A SADIST. HE LOVES YOUR PAIN. EVERYTHING GOOD IN YOUR LIFE HAS ONLY EXISTED SO IT COULD BE TAKEN AWAY.
YOU WERE MADE BEAUTIFUL SO YOU COULD BE DISFIGURED. YOU WERE MADE TO SHINE, ONLY SO YOU COULD BE TARNISHED. YOU WERE MADE INNOCENT SO YOU COULD BE DEFILED.
...BERZELIUS USED IT AGAINST ME. EVERYTHING.
DO YOU UNDERSTAND, CHILD? LIFE IS NOT WORTH LIVING-- END IT NOW BEFORE THE PAIN GETS WORSE.
...LIES AND WORDS, PLEASE REMEMBER, IT'S JUST WORDS, THEY'RE ONLY WORDS...
SUPER LOTTO

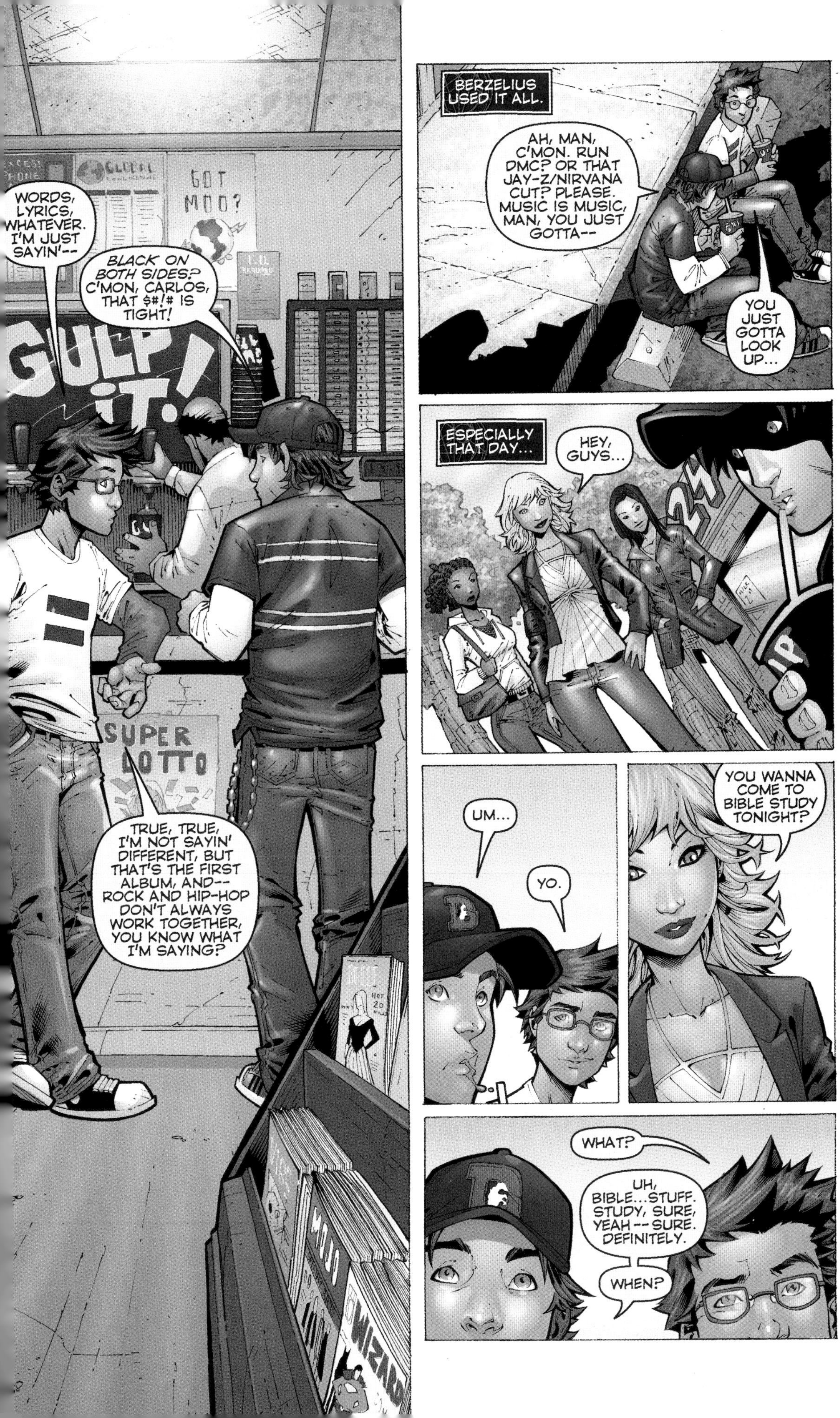
WORDS, LYRICS, WHATEVER. I'M JUST SAYIN'--
BLACK ON BOTH SIDES? C'MON, CARLOS, THAT $#!# IS TIGHT!
TRUE, TRUE, I'M NOT SAYIN' DIFFERENT, BUT THAT'S THE FIRST ALBUM, AND-- ROCK AND HIP-HOP DON'T ALWAYS WORK TOGETHER, YOU KNOW WHAT I'M SAYING?
GULP IT!
GOT MOO?
SUPER LOTTO
BERZELIUS USED IT ALL.
AH, MAN, C'MON. RUN DMC? OR THAT JAY-Z/NIRVANA CUT? PLEASE. MUSIC IS MUSIC, MAN, YOU JUST GOTTA--
YOU JUST GOTTA LOOK UP...
ESPECIALLY THAT DAY...
HEY, GUYS...
UM...
YO.
YOU WANNA COME TO BIBLE STUDY TONIGHT?
WHAT?
UH, BIBLE... STUFF. STUDY, SURE, YEAH -- SURE. DEFINITELY.
WHEN?

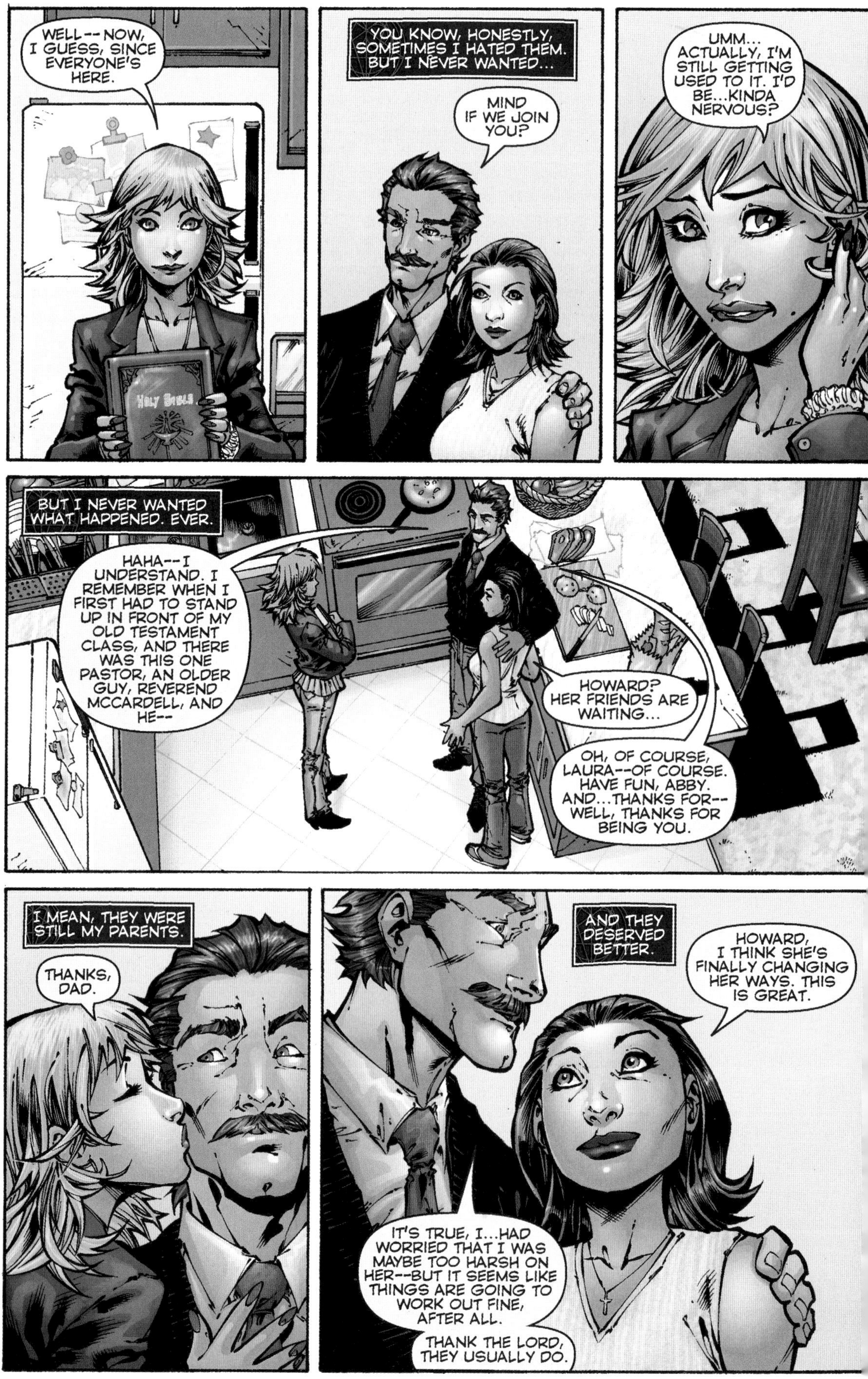
WELL--NOW, I GUESS, SINCE EVERYONE'S HERE.
YOU KNOW, HONESTLY, SOMETIMES I HATED THEM. BUT I NEVER WANTED...
MIND IF WE JOIN YOU?
UMM... ACTUALLY, I'M STILL GETTING USED TO IT. I'D BE...KINDA NERVOUS?
BUT I NEVER WANTED WHAT HAPPENED. EVER.
HAHA--I UNDERSTAND. I REMEMBER WHEN I FIRST HAD TO STAND UP IN FRONT OF MY OLD TESTAMENT CLASS, AND THERE WAS THIS ONE PASTOR, AN OLDER GUY, REVEREND MCCARDELL, AND HE--
HOWARD? HER FRIENDS ARE WAITING...
OH, OF COURSE, LAURA--OF COURSE. HAVE FUN, ABBY. AND...THANKS FOR--WELL, THANKS FOR BEING YOU.
I MEAN, THEY WERE STILL MY PARENTS.
THANKS, DAD.
AND THEY DESERVED BETTER.
HOWARD, I THINK SHE'S FINALLY CHANGING HER WAYS. THIS IS GREAT.
IT'S TRUE, I...HAD WORRIED THAT I WAS MAYBE TOO HARSH ON HER--BUT IT SEEMS LIKE THINGS ARE GOING TO WORK OUT FINE, AFTER ALL.
THANK THE LORD, THEY USUALLY DO.

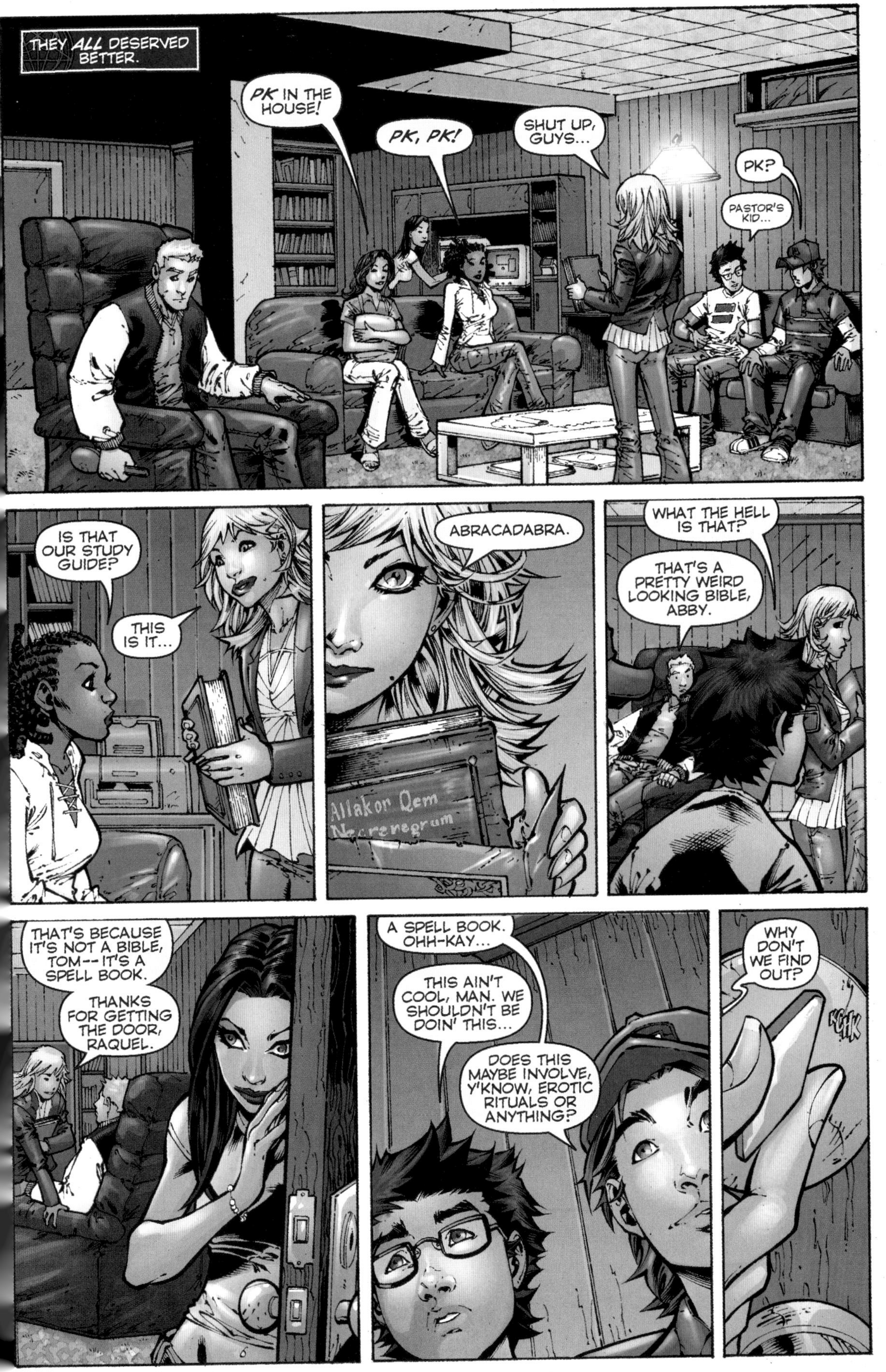
THEY ALL DESERVED BETTER.
PK IN THE HOUSE!
PK, PK!
SHUT UP, GUYS...
PK?
PASTOR'S KID...
IS THAT OUR STUDY GUIDE?
THIS IS IT...
ABRACADABRA.
WHAT THE HELL IS THAT?
THAT'S A PRETTY WEIRD LOOKING BIBLE, ABBY.
THAT'S BECAUSE IT'S NOT A BIBLE, TOM--IT'S A SPELL BOOK.
THANKS FOR GETTING THE DOOR, RAQUEL.
A SPELL BOOK. OHH-KAY...
THIS AIN'T COOL, MAN. WE SHOULDN'T BE DOIN' THIS...
DOES THIS MAYBE INVOLVE, Y'KNOW, EROTIC RITUALS OR ANYTHING?
WHY DON'T WE FIND OUT?

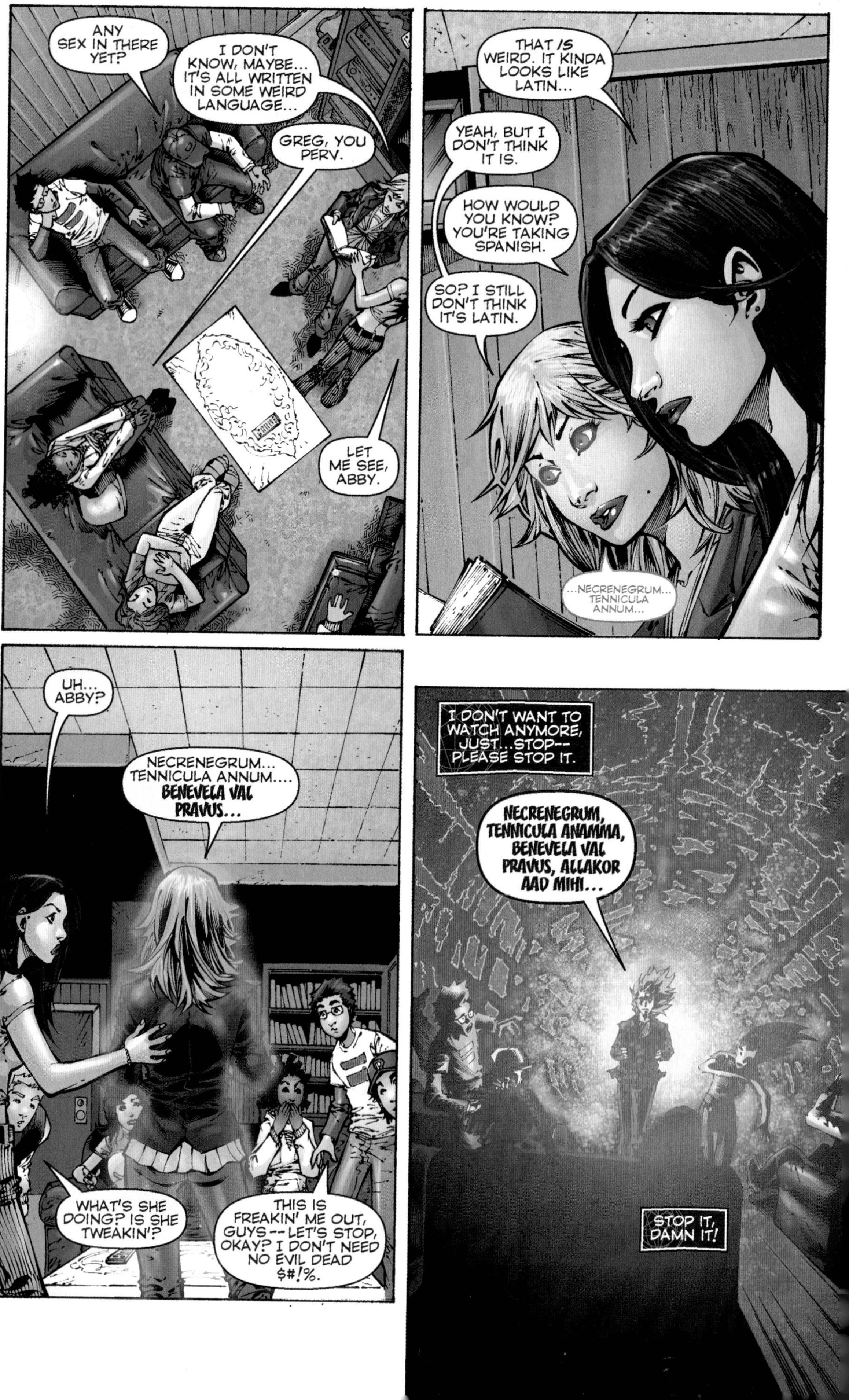
ANY SEX IN THERE YET?
I DON'T KNOW, MAYBE... IT'S ALL WRITTEN IN SOME WEIRD LANGUAGE...
GREG, YOU PERV.
LET ME SEE, ABBY.
THAT IS WEIRD. IT KINDA LOOKS LIKE LATIN...
YEAH, BUT I DON'T THINK IT IS.
HOW WOULD YOU KNOW? YOU'RE TAKING SPANISH.
SO? I STILL DON'T THINK IT'S LATIN.
...NECRENEGRUM... TENNICULA ANNUM...
UH... ABBY?
NECRENEGRUM... TENNICULA ANNUM.... BENEVELA VAL PRAVUS...
WHAT'S SHE DOING? IS SHE TWEAKIN'?
THIS IS FREAKIN' ME OUT, GUYS--LET'S STOP, OKAY? I DON'T NEED NO EVIL DEAD $#!%.
I DON'T WANT TO WATCH ANYMORE, JUST...STOP-- PLEASE STOP IT.
NECRENEGRUM, TENNICULA ANAMMA, BENEVELA VAL PRAVUS, ALLAKOR AAD MIHI...
STOP IT, DAMN IT!

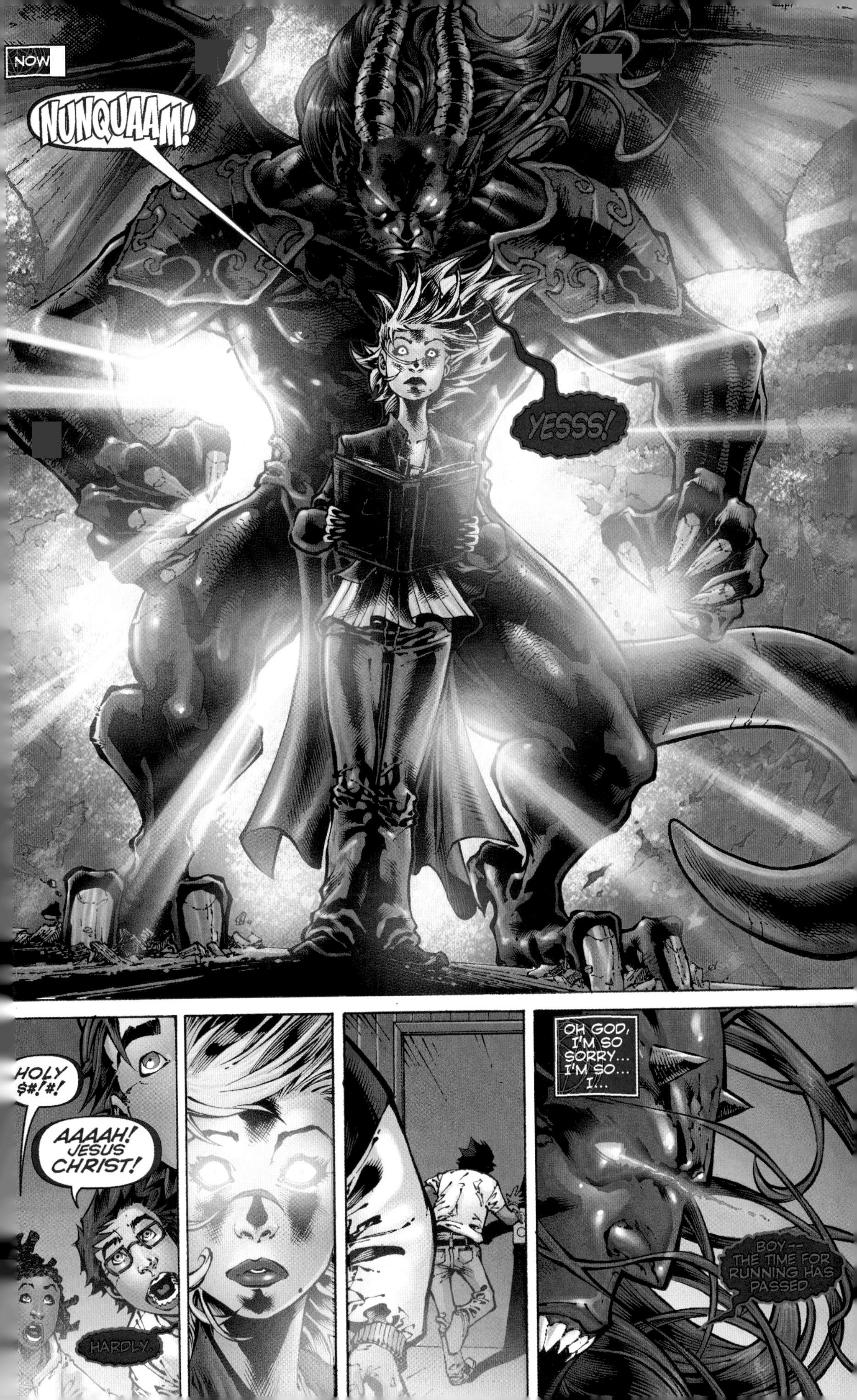
NOW
NUNQUAAM!
YESSS!
HOLY $#!#!
AAAAH! JESUS CHRIST!
HARDLY.
OH GOD, I'M SO SORRY... I'M SO... I...
BOY -- THE TIME FOR RUNNING HAS PASSED.

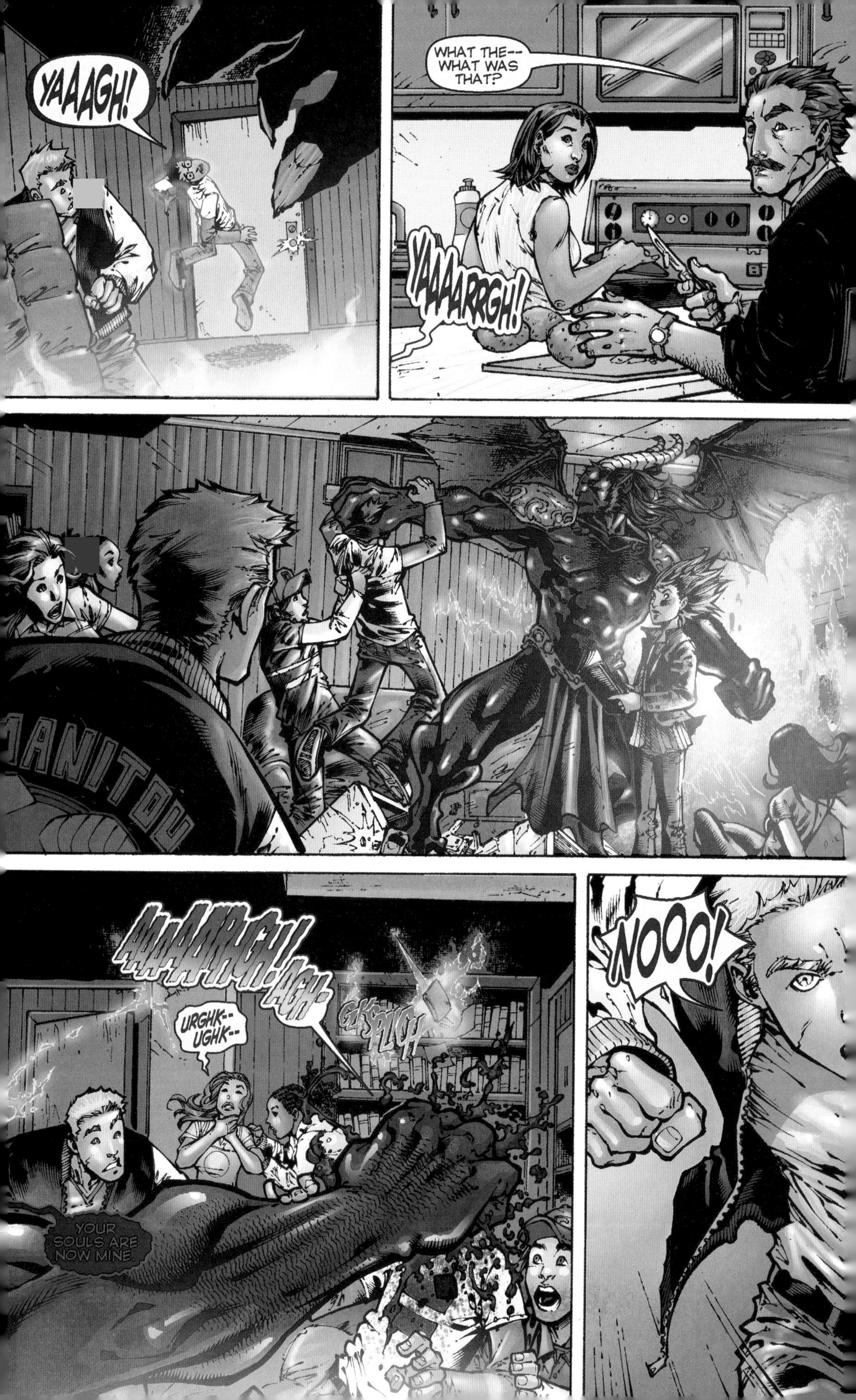
YAAAGH!
WHAT THE-- WHAT WAS THAT?
YAAAARRGH!
AAAAARRGH!
AGH-
URGHK-- UGHK--
GKSPLCH
YOUR SOULS ARE NOW MINE.
NOOO!

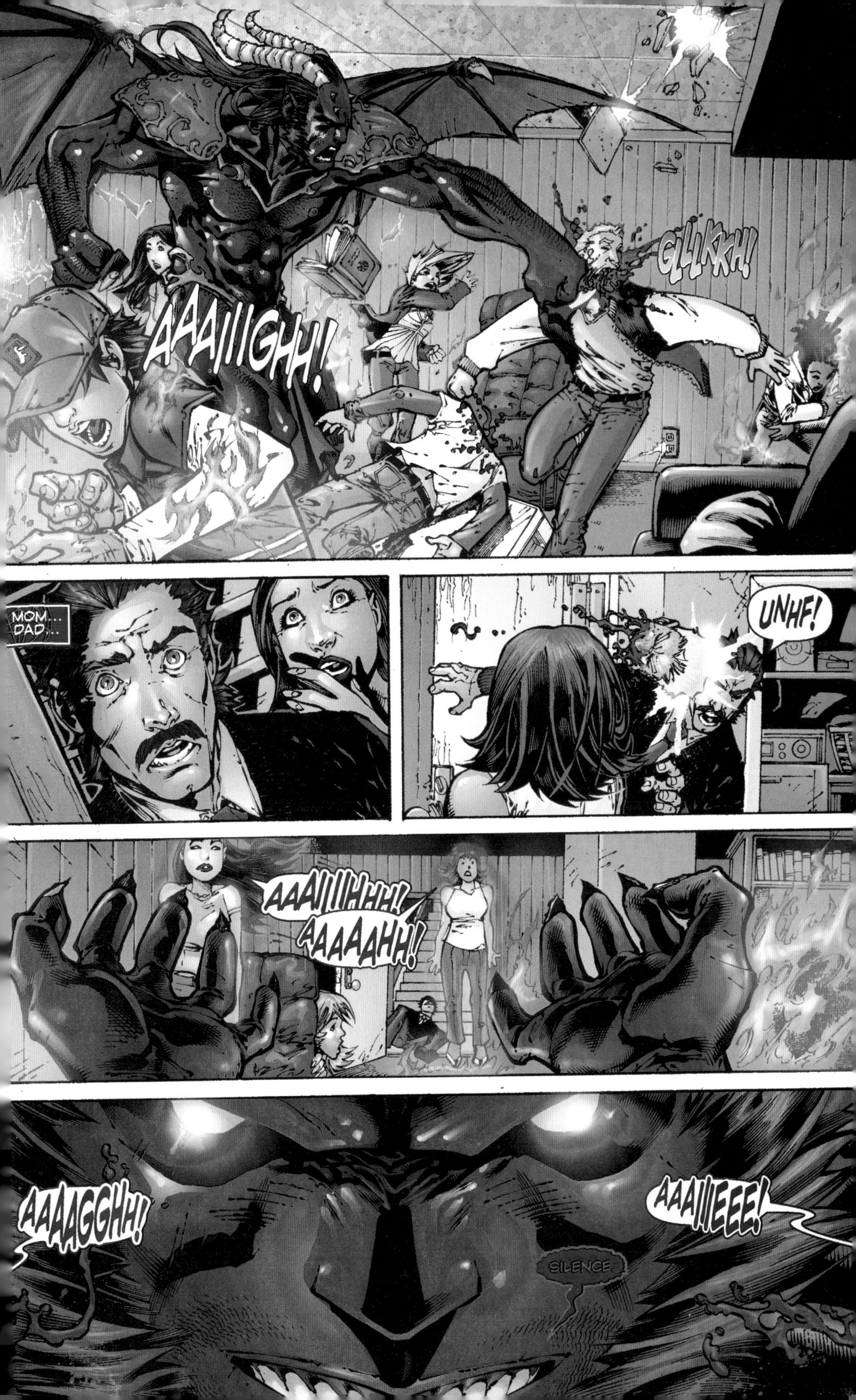
AAAIIIGHH!
GLLLKKH!
MOM... DAD...
?...
UNHF!
AAAIIIHHH!
AAAAAHH!
AAAAGGHH!
AAAIIIEEE!
SILENCE.

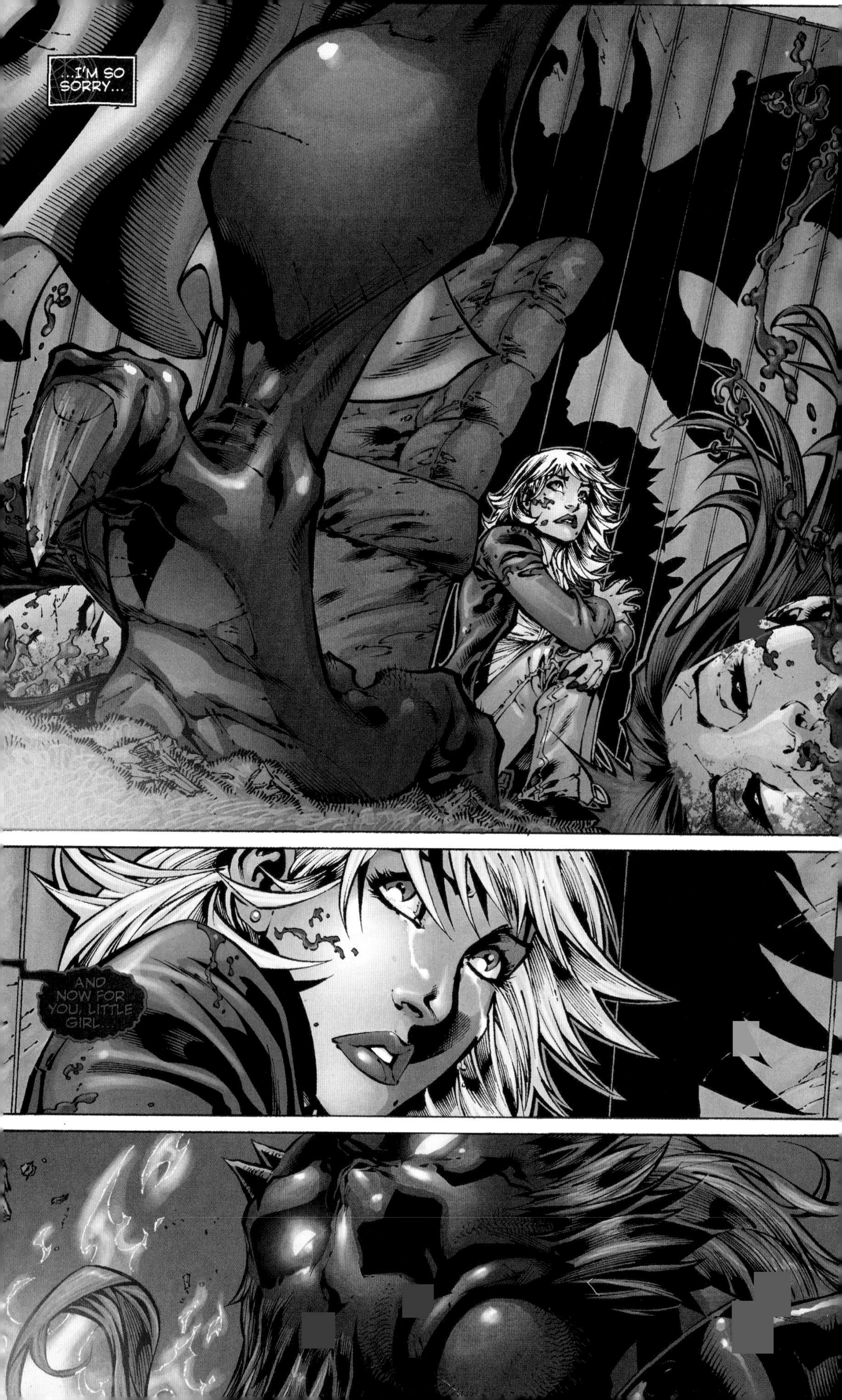
...I'M SO SORRY...
AND NOW FOR YOU, LITTLE GIRL...

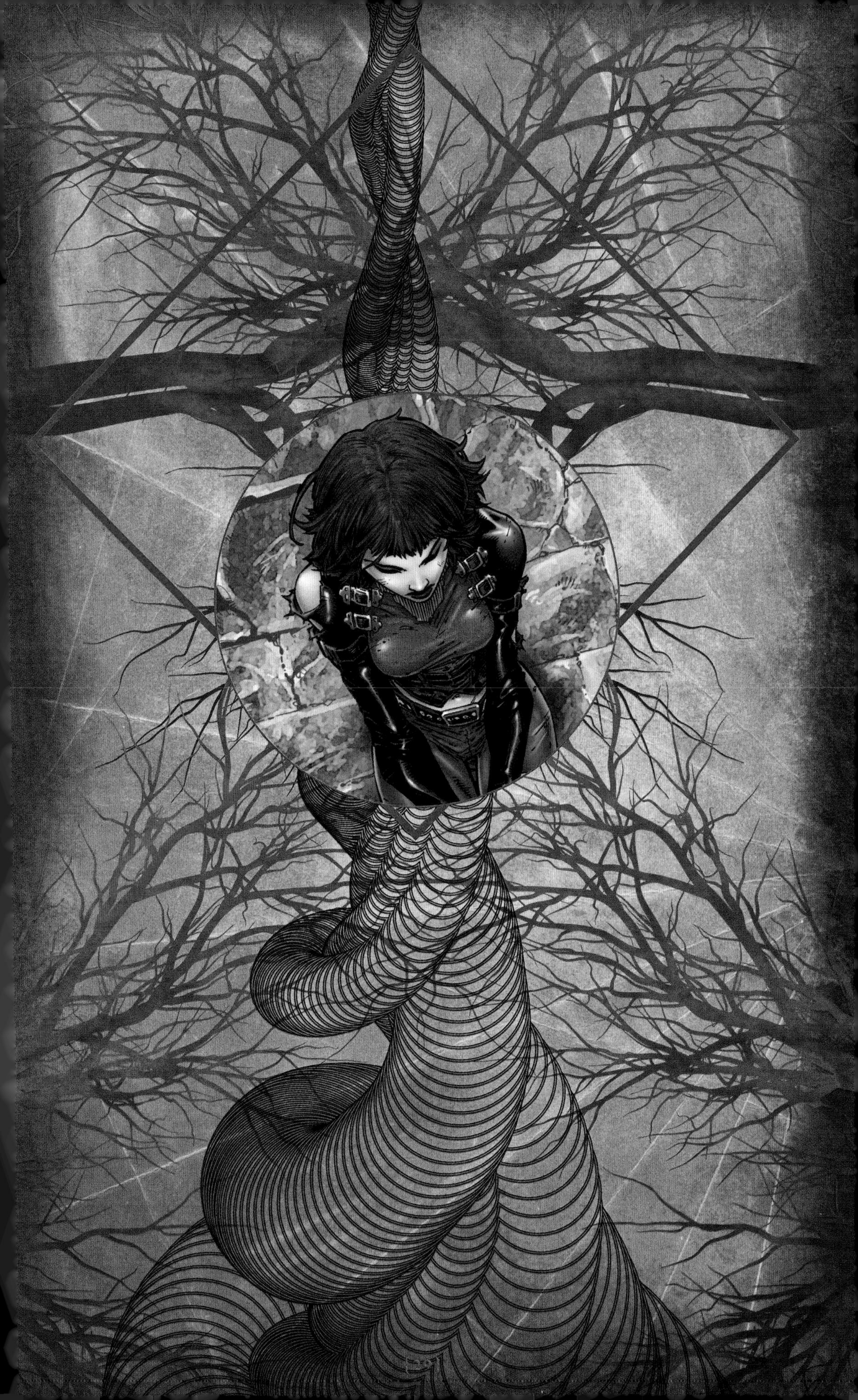

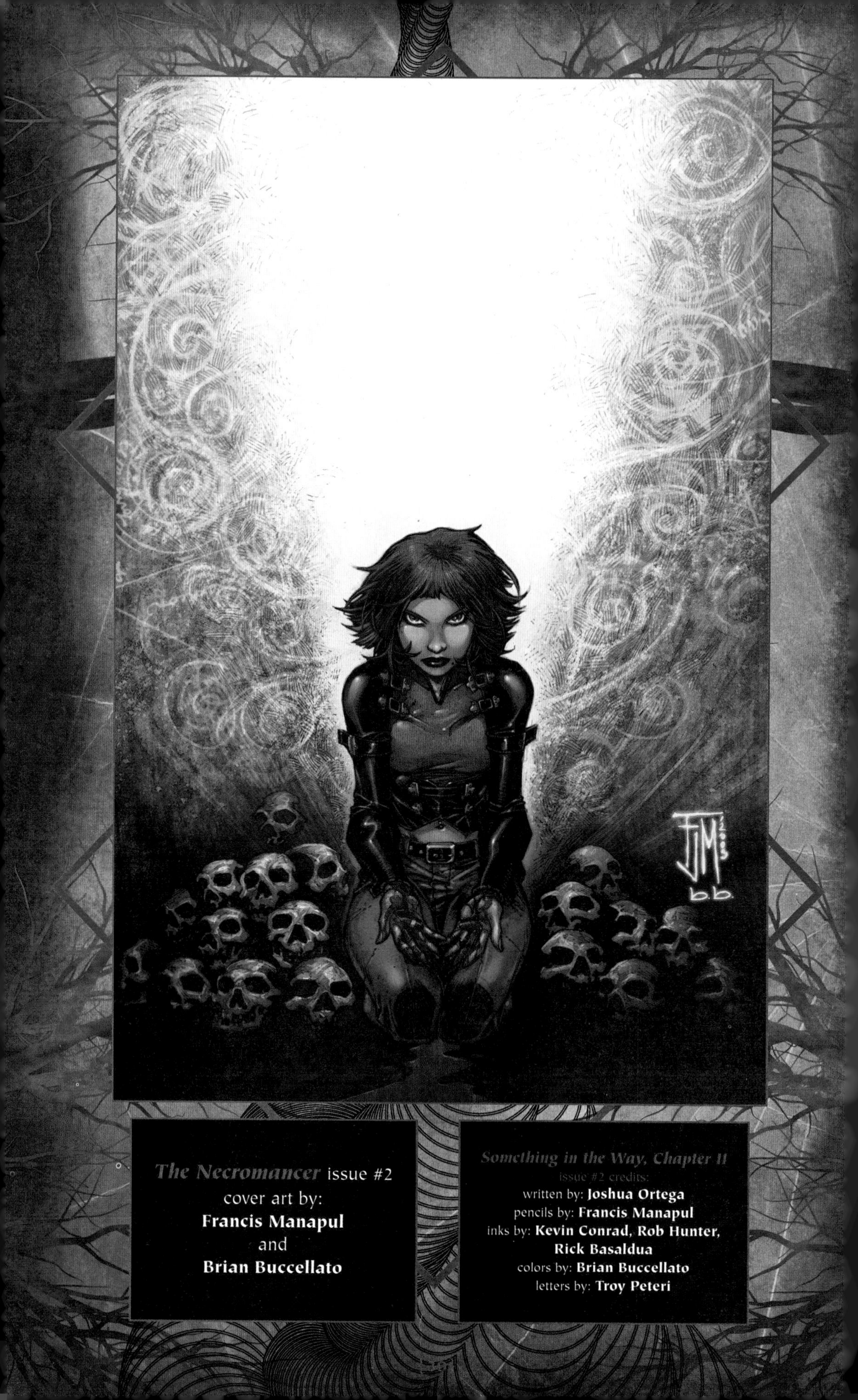

The Necromancer issue #2
cover art by:
Francis Manapul
and
Brian Buccellato

Something in the Way, Chapter II
issue #2 credits:
written by: **Joshua Ortega**
pencils by: **Francis Manapul**
inks by: **Kevin Conrad, Rob Hunter, Rick Basaldua**
colors by: **Brian Buccellato**
letters by: **Troy Peteri**

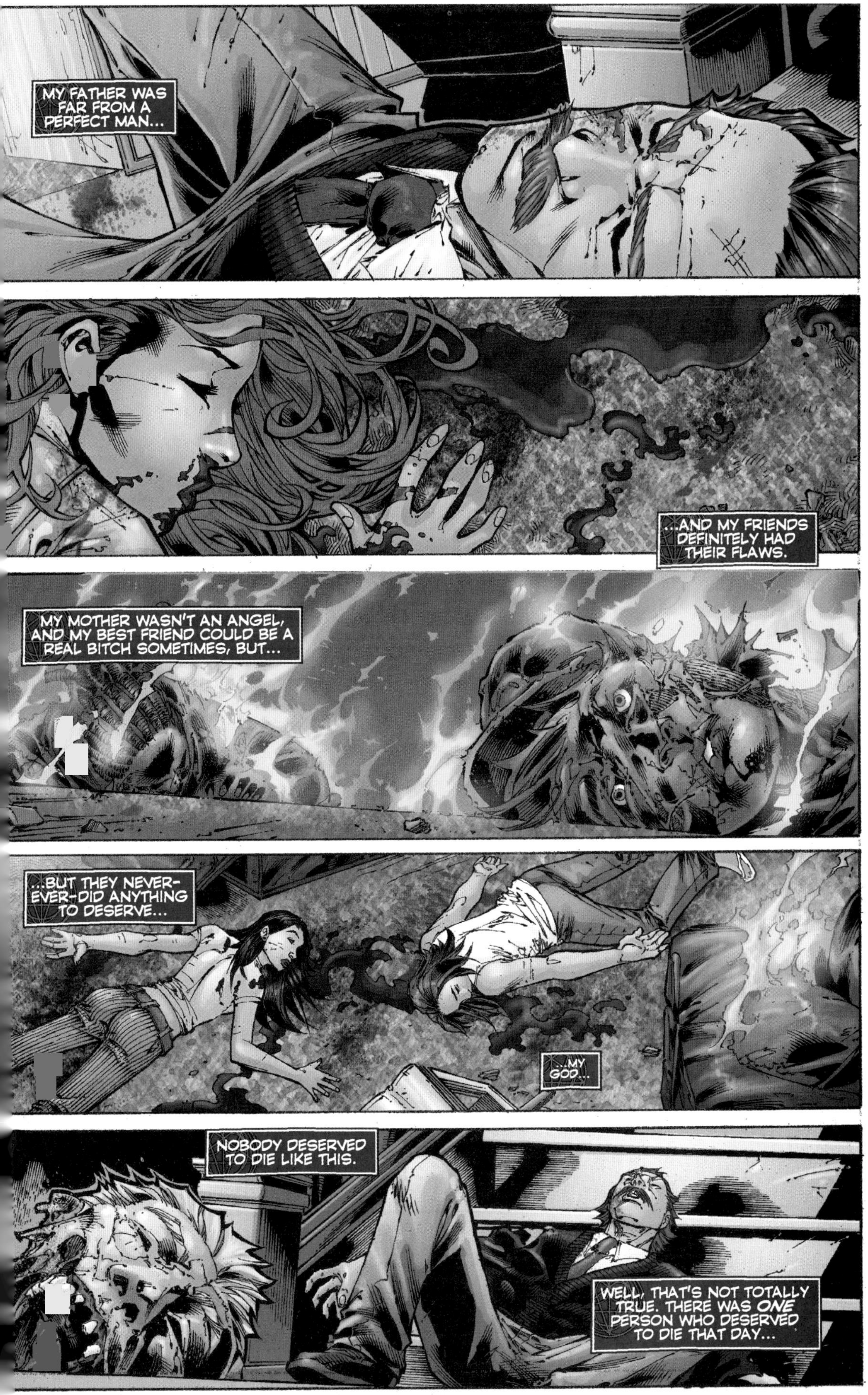
MY FATHER WAS FAR FROM A PERFECT MAN...
...AND MY FRIENDS DEFINITELY HAD THEIR FLAWS.
MY MOTHER WASN'T AN ANGEL, AND MY BEST FRIEND COULD BE A REAL BITCH SOMETIMES, BUT...
...BUT THEY NEVER--EVER--DID ANYTHING TO DESERVE...
...MY GOD...
NOBODY DESERVED TO DIE LIKE THIS.
WELL, THAT'S NOT TOTALLY TRUE. THERE WAS *ONE* PERSON WHO DESERVED TO DIE THAT DAY...

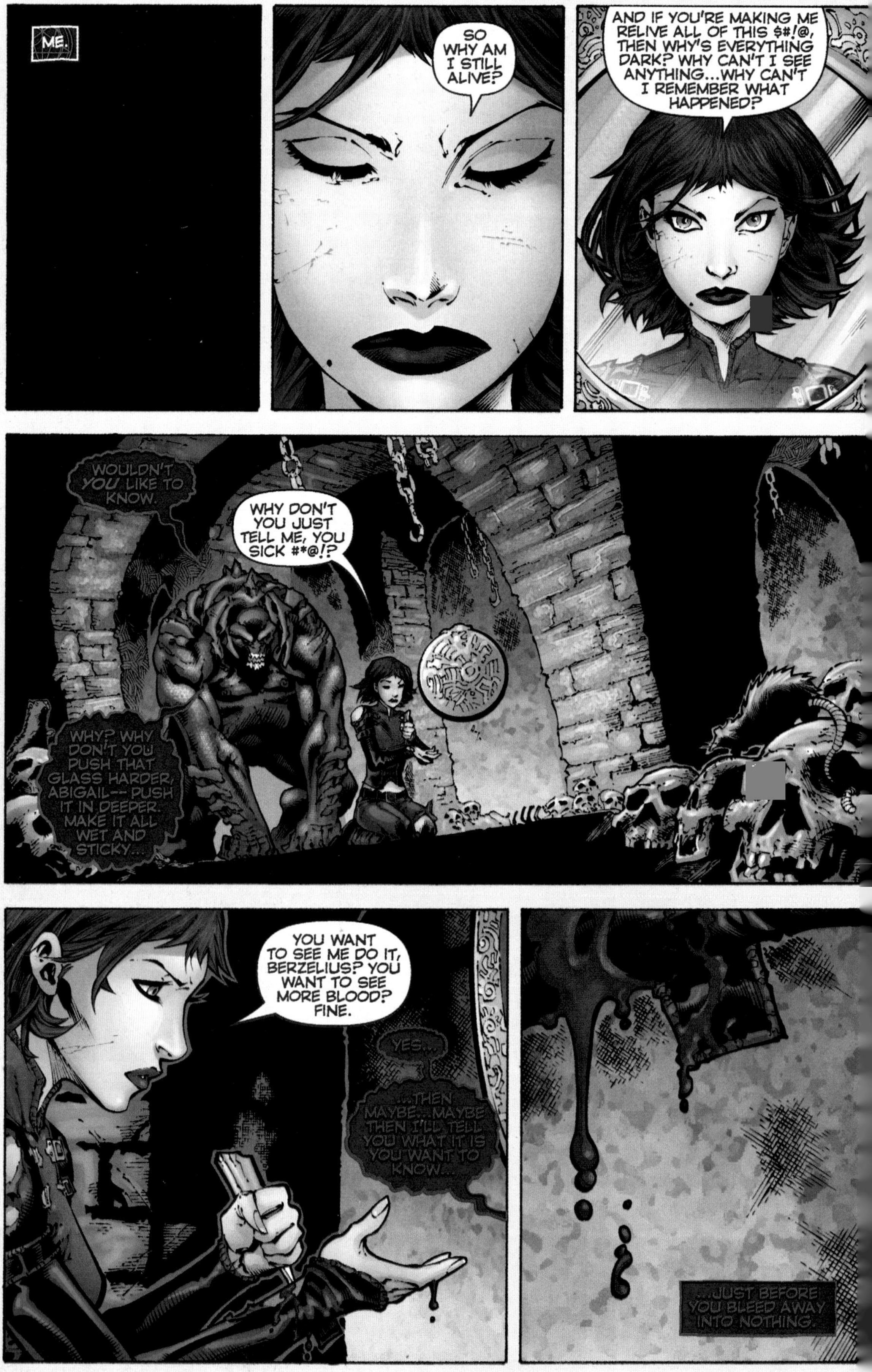
ME.
SO WHY AM I STILL ALIVE?
AND IF YOU'RE MAKING ME RELIVE ALL OF THIS $#!@, THEN WHY'S EVERYTHING DARK? WHY CAN'T I SEE ANYTHING...WHY CAN'T I REMEMBER WHAT HAPPENED?
WOULDN'T YOU LIKE TO KNOW.
WHY DON'T YOU JUST TELL ME, YOU SICK #*@!?
WHY? WHY DON'T YOU PUSH THAT GLASS HARDER, ABIGAIL-- PUSH IT IN DEEPER. MAKE IT ALL WET AND STICKY...
YOU WANT TO SEE ME DO IT, BERZELIUS? YOU WANT TO SEE MORE BLOOD? FINE.
YES...
...THEN MAYBE... MAYBE THEN I'LL TELL YOU WHAT IT IS YOU WANT TO KNOW...
...JUST BEFORE YOU BLEED AWAY INTO NOTHING.

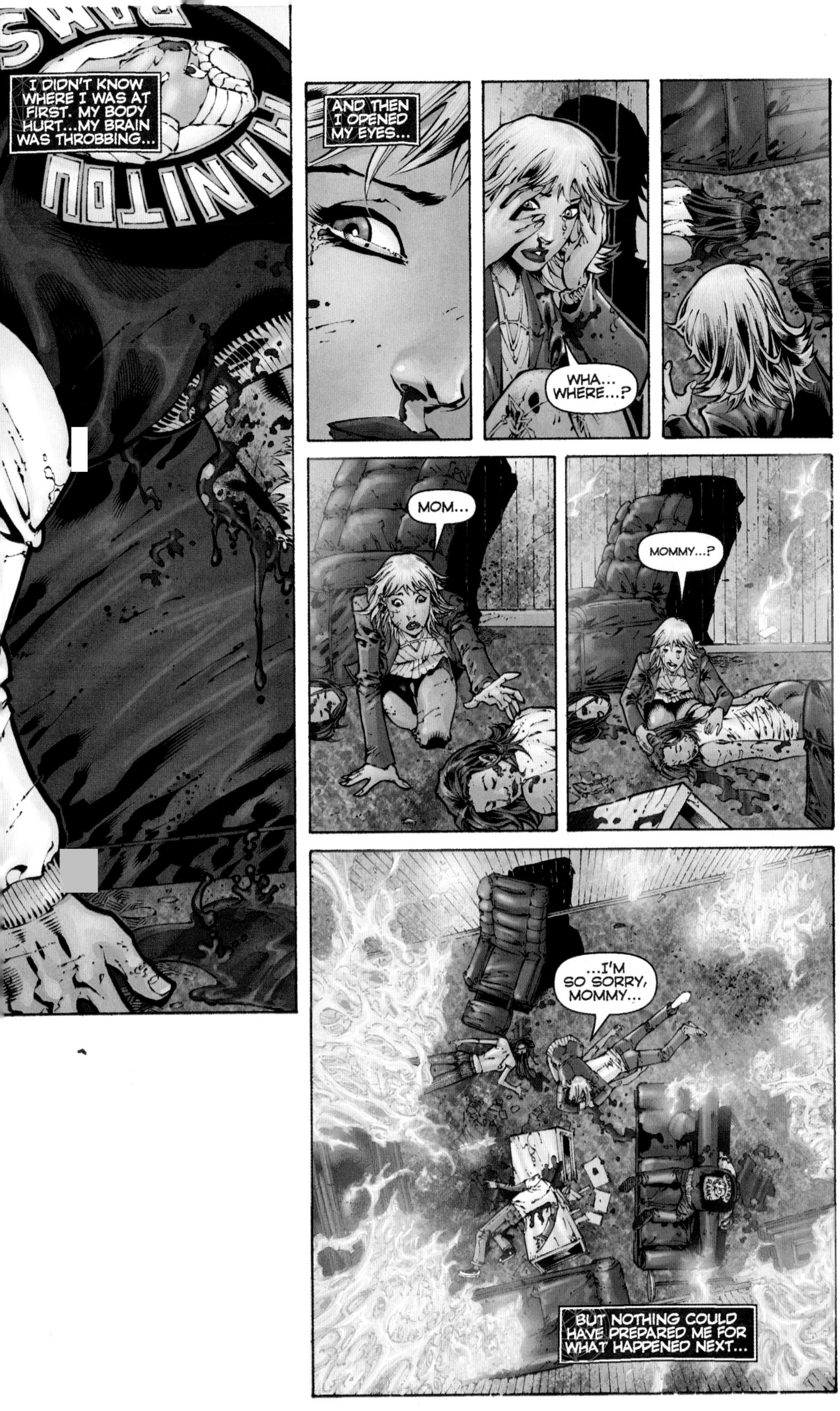
I DIDN'T KNOW WHERE I WAS AT FIRST. MY BODY HURT...MY BRAIN WAS THROBBING...
AND THEN I OPENED MY EYES...
WHA... WHERE...?
MOM...
MOMMY...?
...I'M SO SORRY, MOMMY...
BUT NOTHING COULD HAVE PREPARED ME FOR WHAT HAPPENED NEXT...

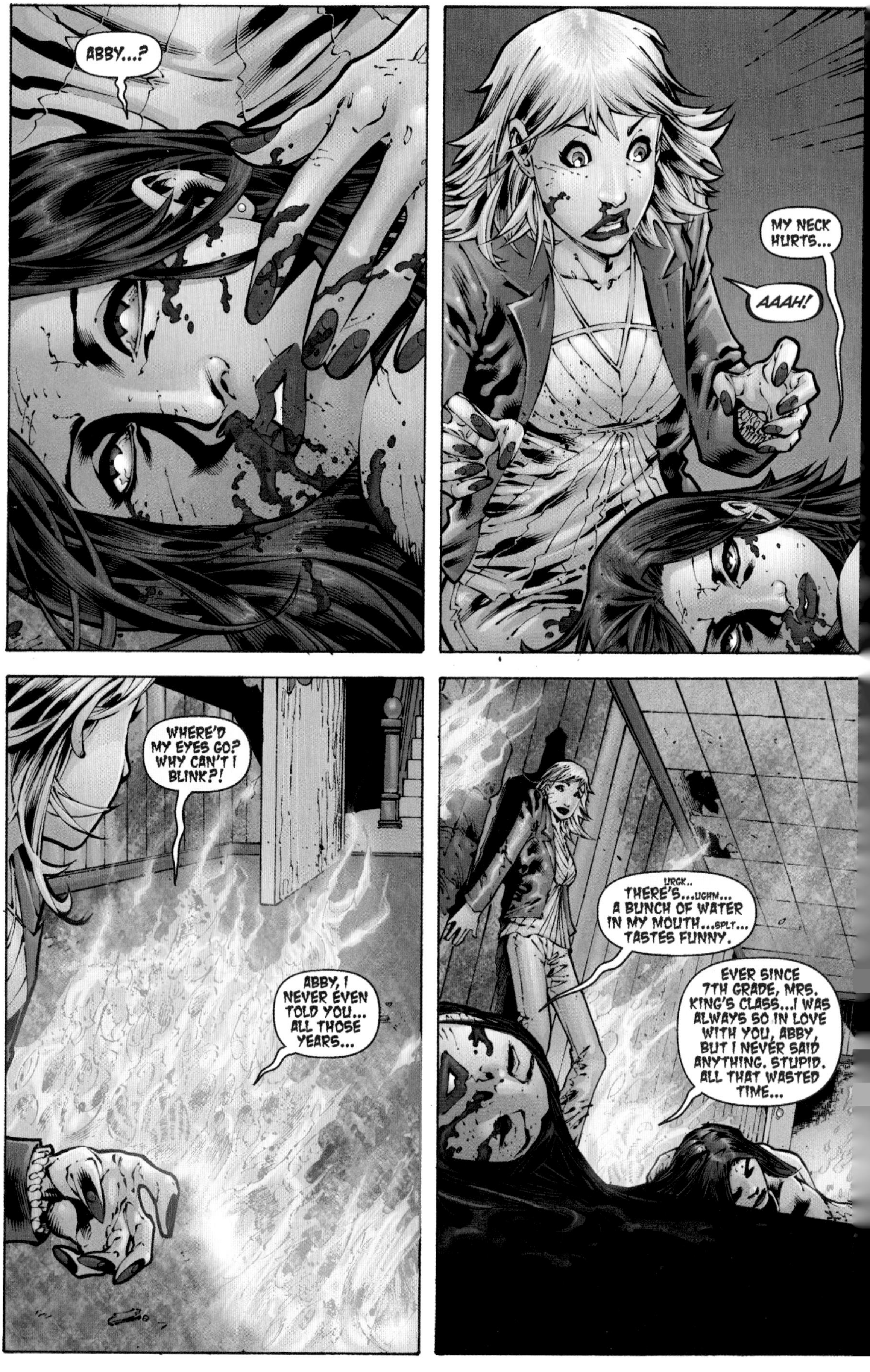
ABBY...?
MY NECK HURTS...
AAAH!
WHERE'D MY EYES GO? WHY CAN'T I BLINK?!
ABBY, I NEVER EVEN TOLD YOU... ALL THOSE YEARS...
URGK.. THERE'S...UGHM... A BUNCH OF WATER IN MY MOUTH...SPLT... TASTES FUNNY.
EVER SINCE 7TH GRADE, MRS. KING'S CLASS...I WAS ALWAYS SO IN LOVE WITH YOU, ABBY, BUT I NEVER SAID ANYTHING. STUPID. ALL THAT WASTED TIME...

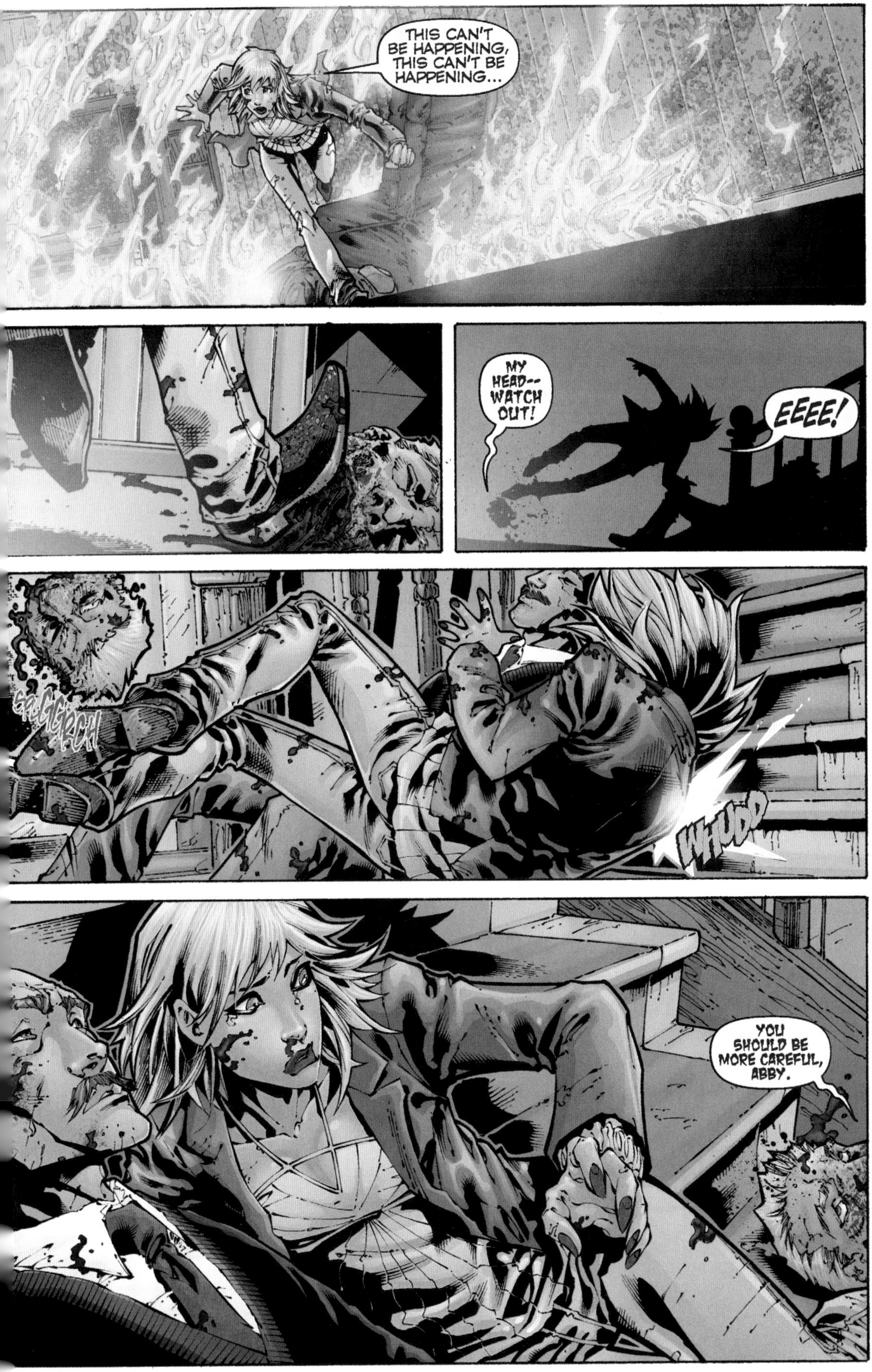
THIS CAN'T BE HAPPENING, THIS CAN'T BE HAPPENING...
MY HEAD-- WATCH OUT!
EEEE!
WHUDD
YOU SHOULD BE MORE CAREFUL, ABBY.

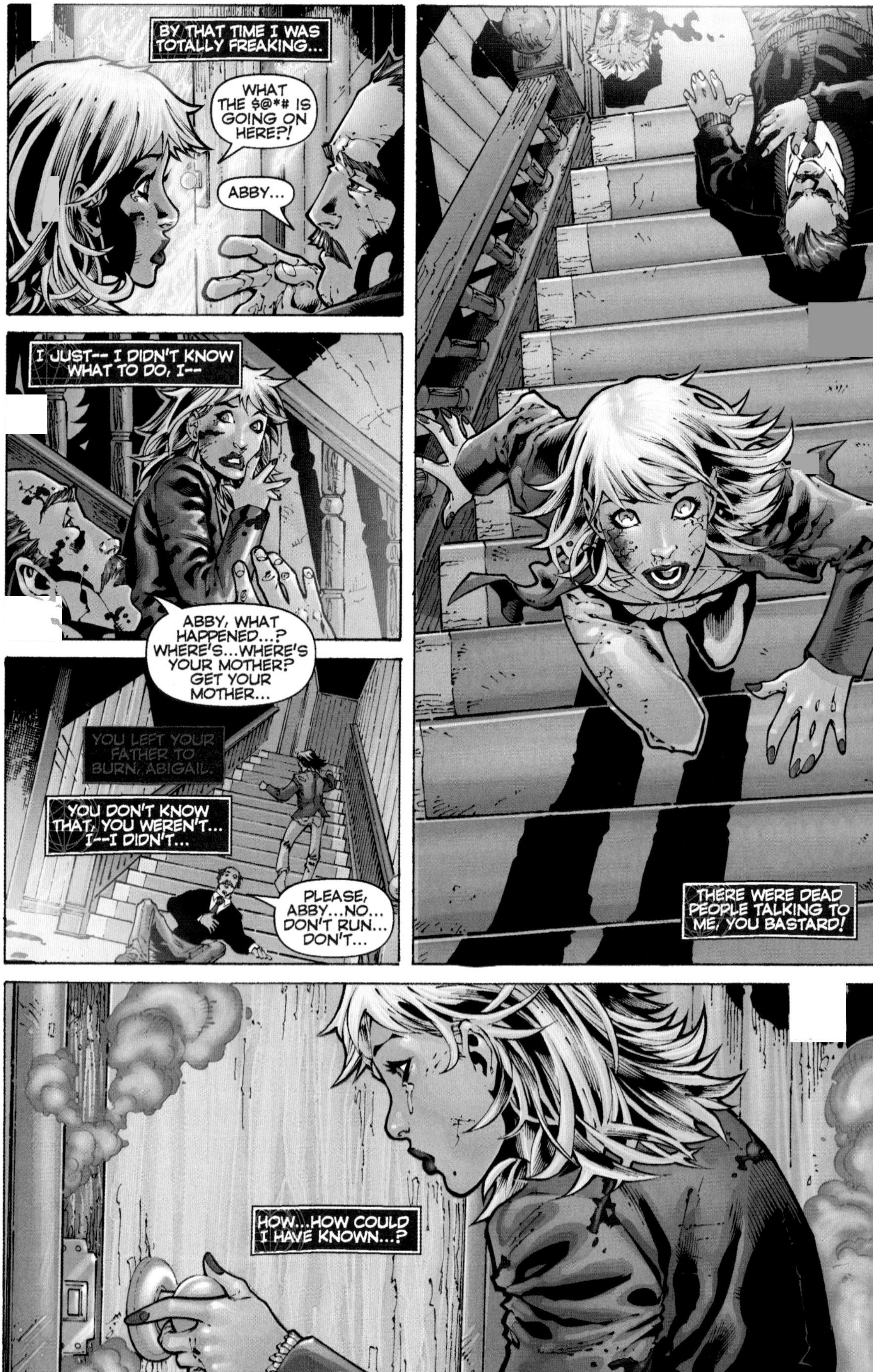
BY THAT TIME I WAS TOTALLY FREAKING...
WHAT THE $@*# IS GOING ON HERE?!
ABBY...
I JUST-- I DIDN'T KNOW WHAT TO DO, I--
ABBY, WHAT HAPPENED...? WHERE'S...WHERE'S YOUR MOTHER? GET YOUR MOTHER...
YOU LEFT YOUR FATHER TO BURN, ABIGAIL.
YOU DON'T KNOW THAT, YOU WEREN'T... I--I DIDN'T...
PLEASE, ABBY...NO... DON'T RUN... DON'T...
THERE WERE DEAD PEOPLE TALKING TO ME, YOU BASTARD!
HOW...HOW COULD I HAVE KNOWN...?

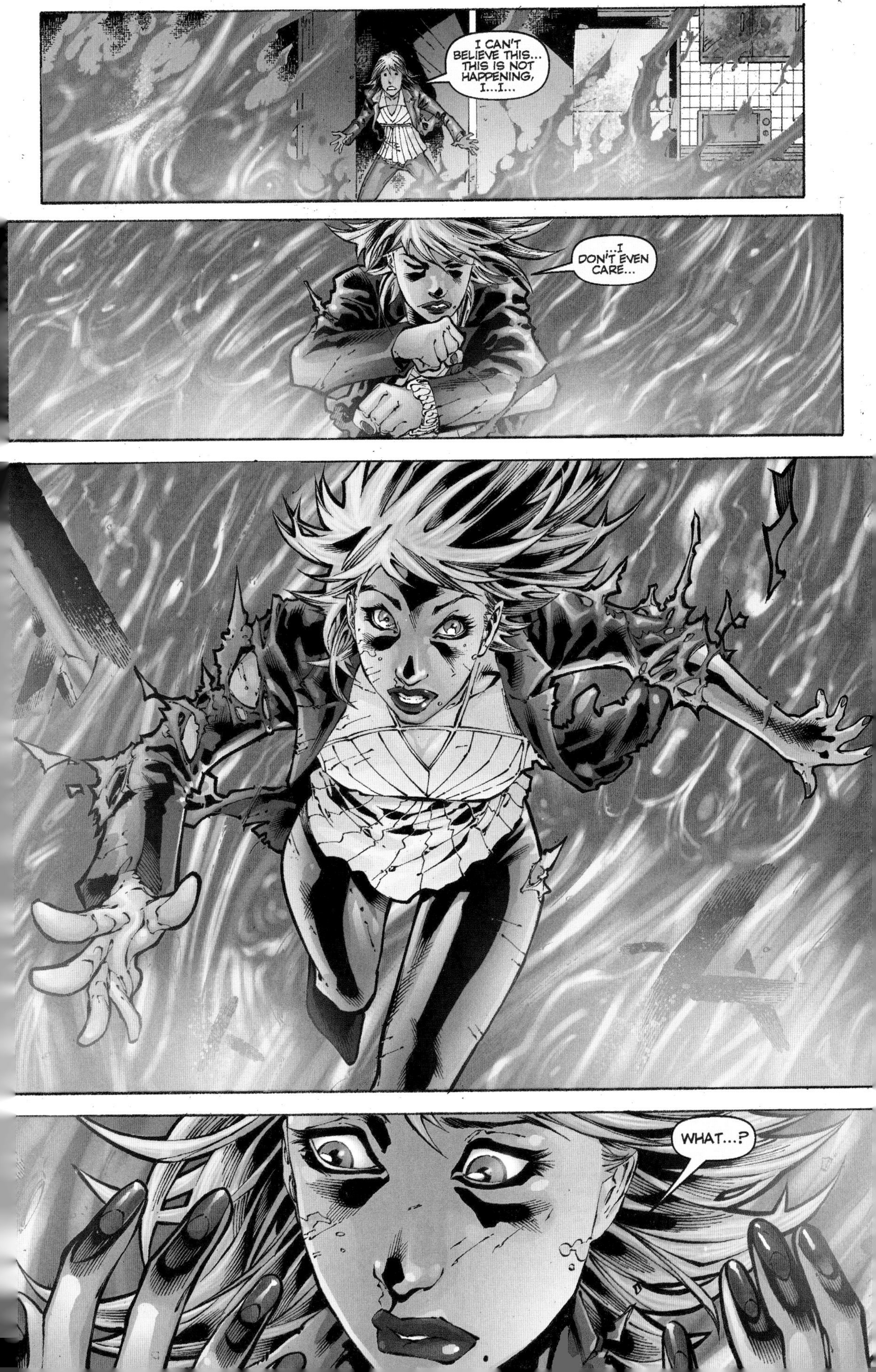
I CAN'T BELIEVE THIS... THIS IS NOT HAPPENING, I...I...
...I DON'T EVEN CARE...
WHAT...?

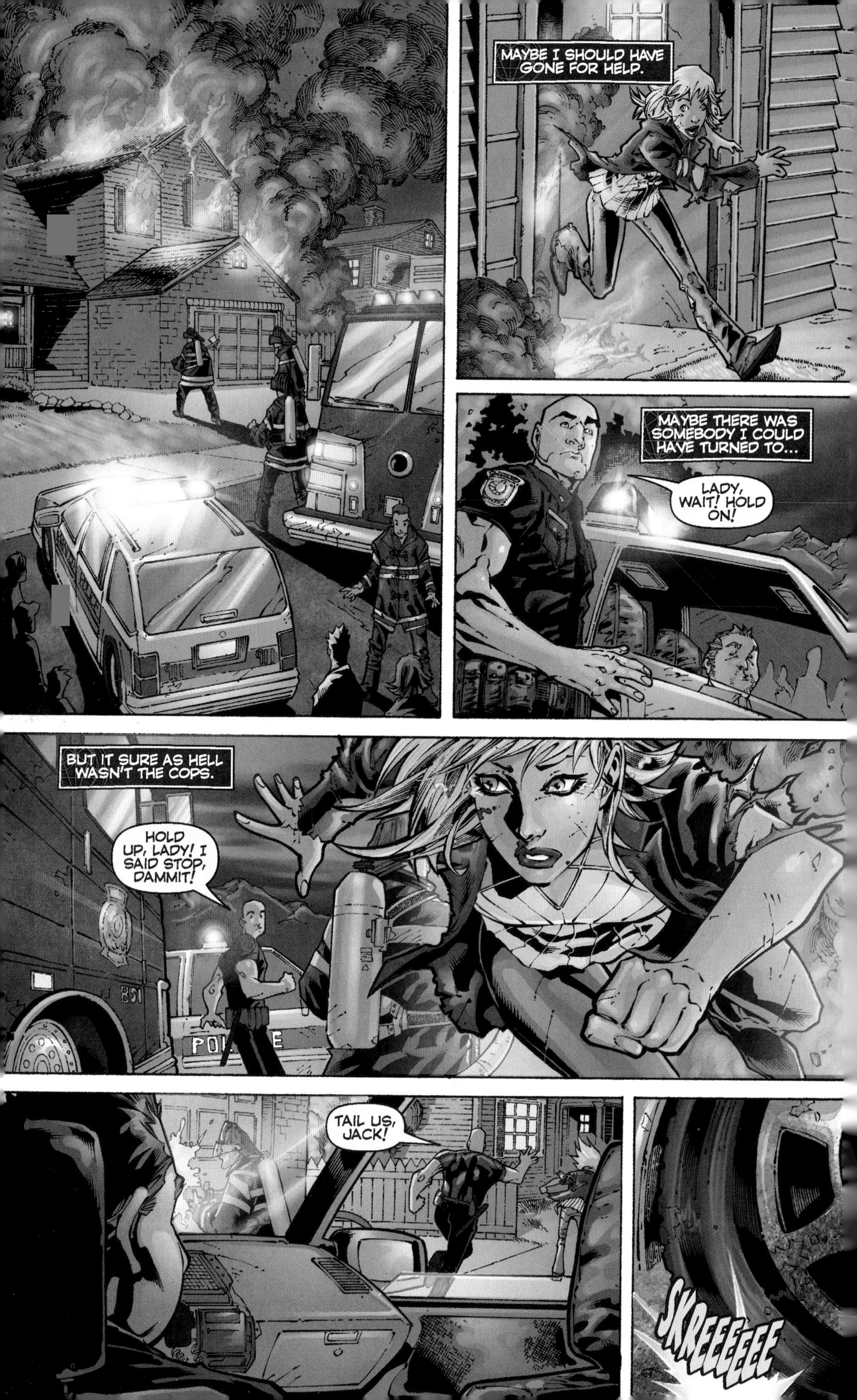
MAYBE I SHOULD HAVE GONE FOR HELP.
MAYBE THERE WAS SOMEBODY I COULD HAVE TURNED TO...
LADY, WAIT! HOLD ON!
BUT IT SURE AS HELL WASN'T THE COPS.
HOLD UP, LADY! I SAID STOP, DAMMIT!
TAIL US, JACK!
SKREEEEEEE

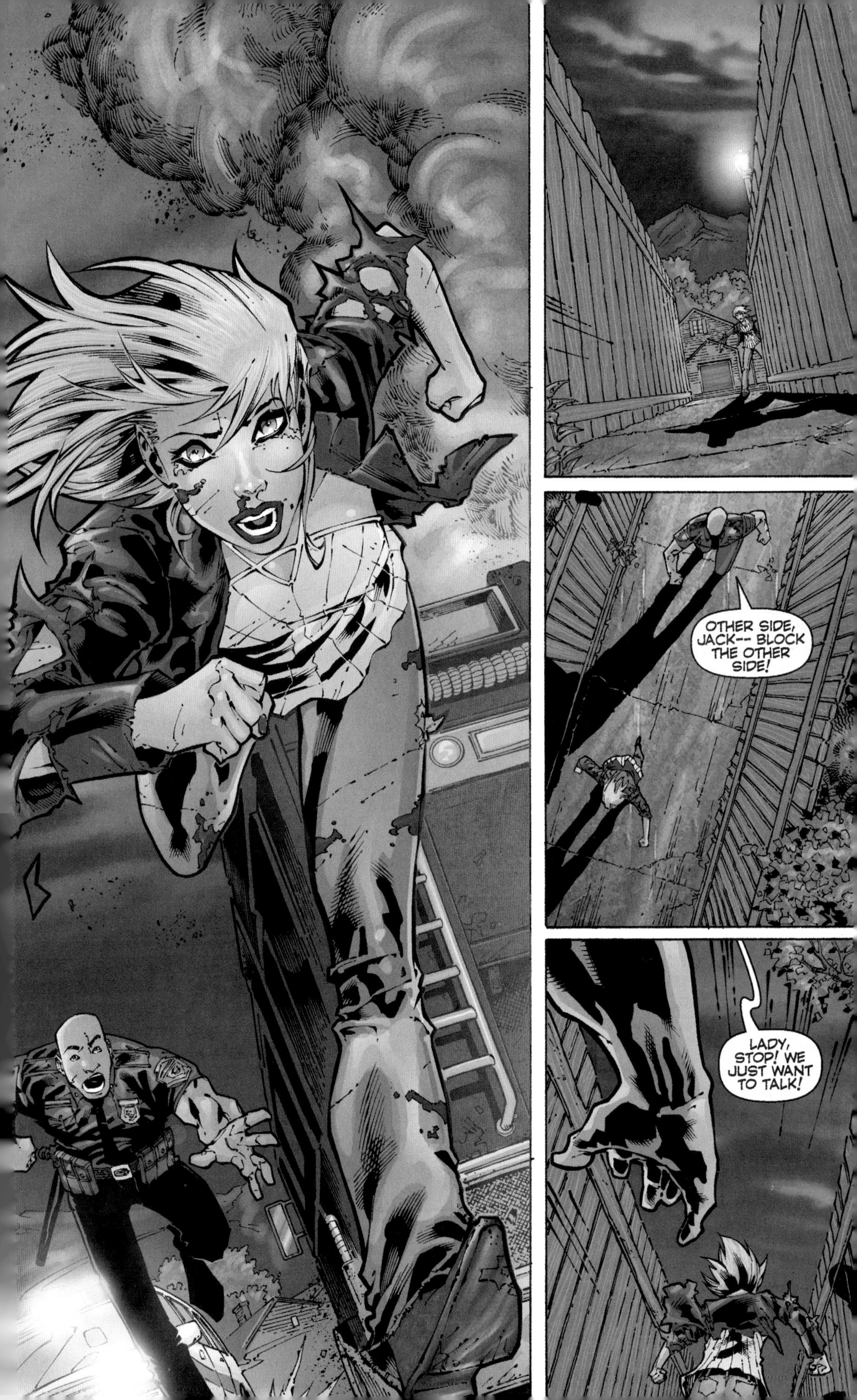
OTHER SIDE, JACK-- BLOCK THE OTHER SIDE!
LADY, STOP! WE JUST WANT TO TALK!

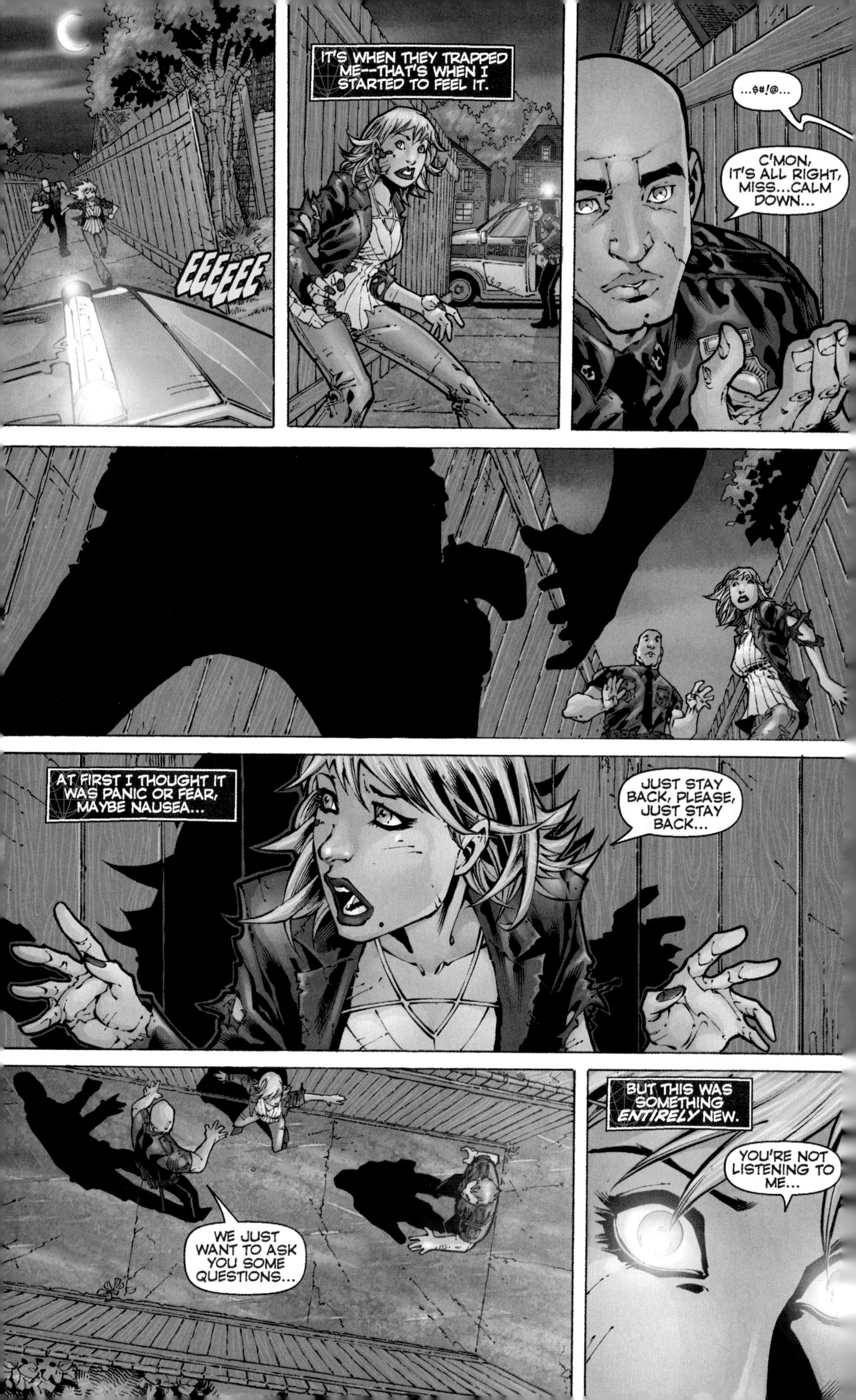
EEEEEE
IT'S WHEN THEY TRAPPED ME--THAT'S WHEN I STARTED TO FEEL IT.
...$#!@...
C'MON, IT'S ALL RIGHT, MISS...CALM DOWN...
AT FIRST I THOUGHT IT WAS PANIC OR FEAR, MAYBE NAUSEA...
JUST STAY BACK, PLEASE, JUST STAY BACK...
WE JUST WANT TO ASK YOU SOME QUESTIONS...
BUT THIS WAS SOMETHING *ENTIRELY* NEW.
YOU'RE NOT LISTENING TO ME...

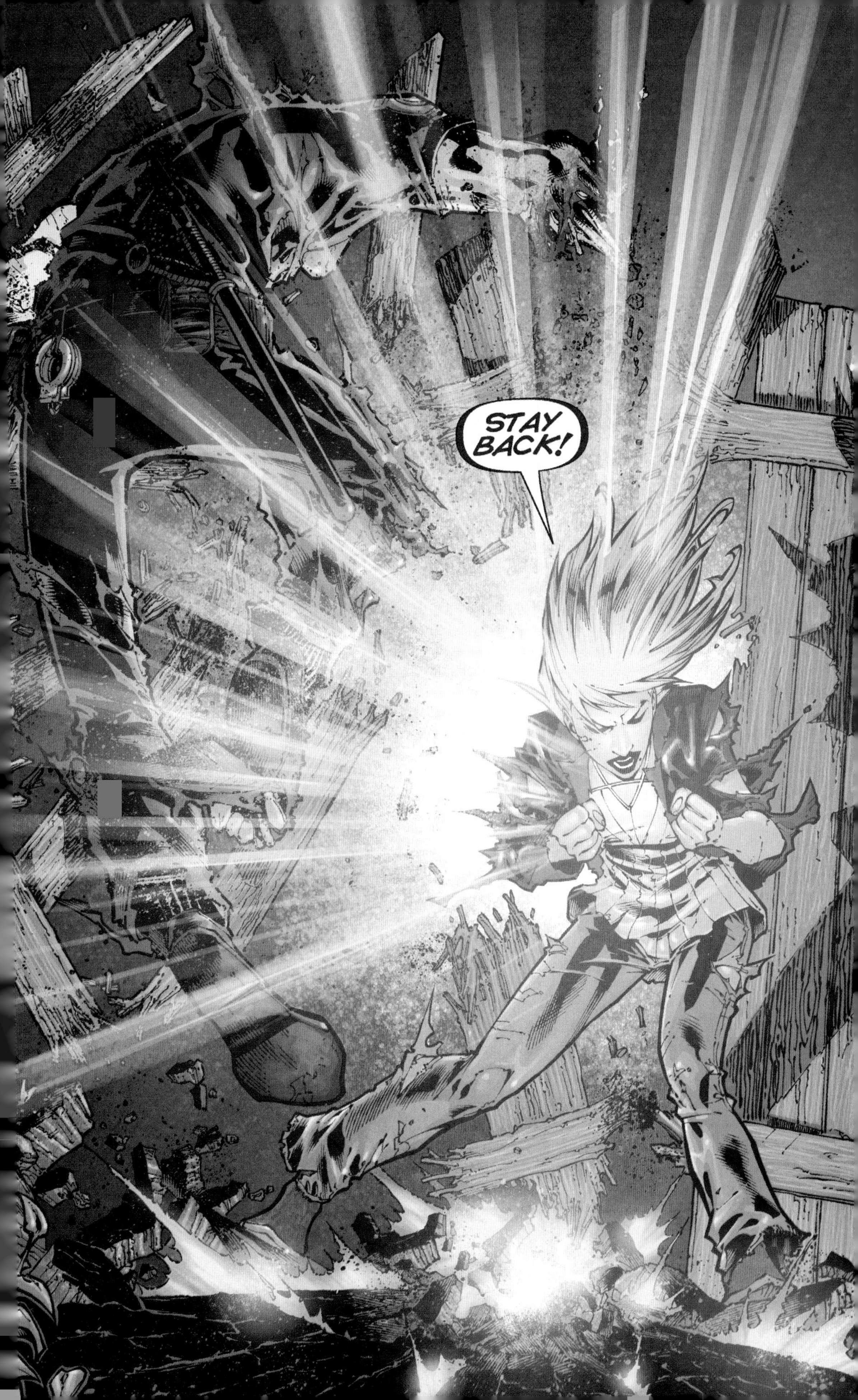
STAY BACK!

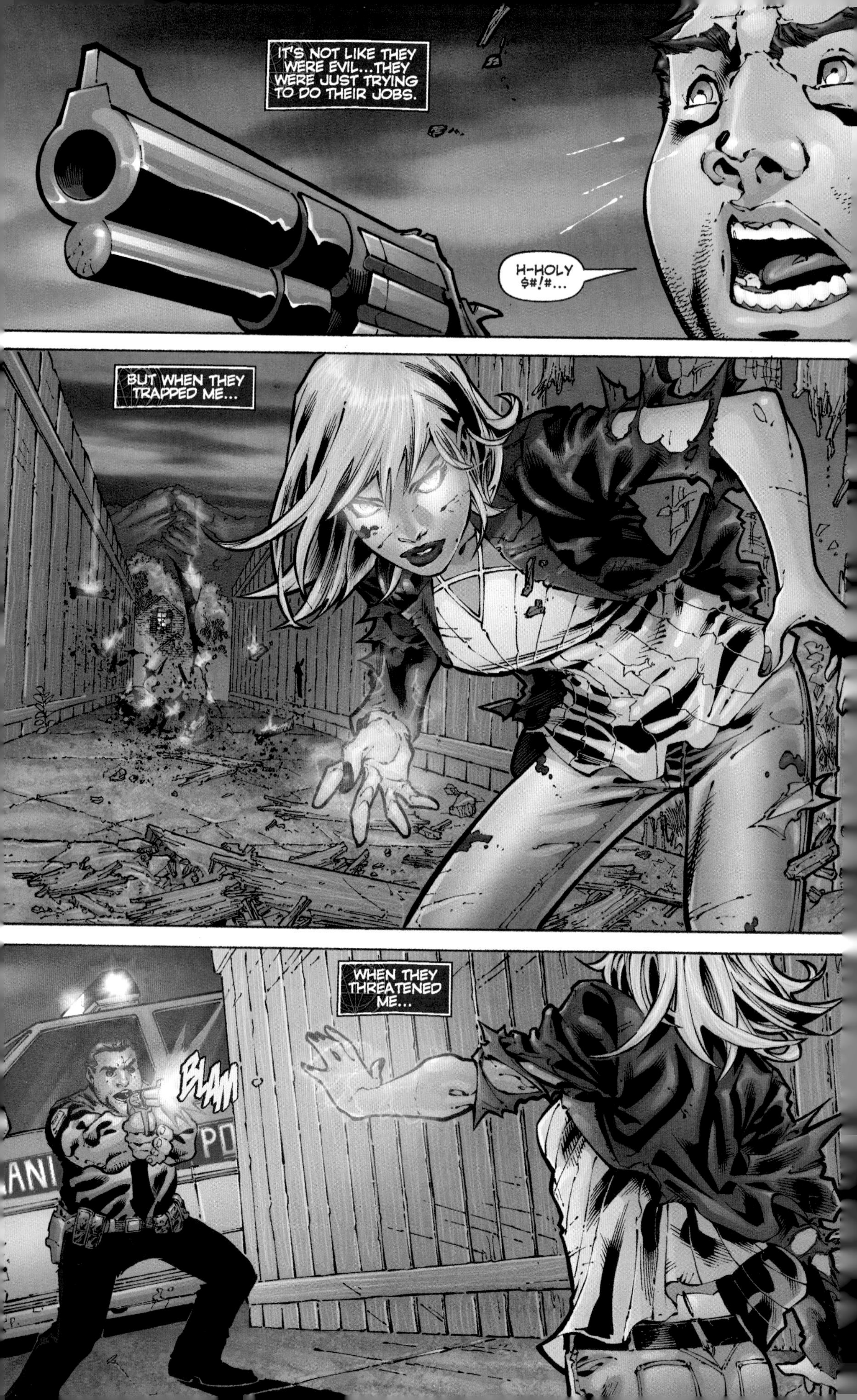
IT'S NOT LIKE THEY WERE EVIL...THEY WERE JUST TRYING TO DO THEIR JOBS.
H-HOLY $#!#...
BUT WHEN THEY TRAPPED ME...
WHEN THEY THREATENED ME...
BLAM
PD

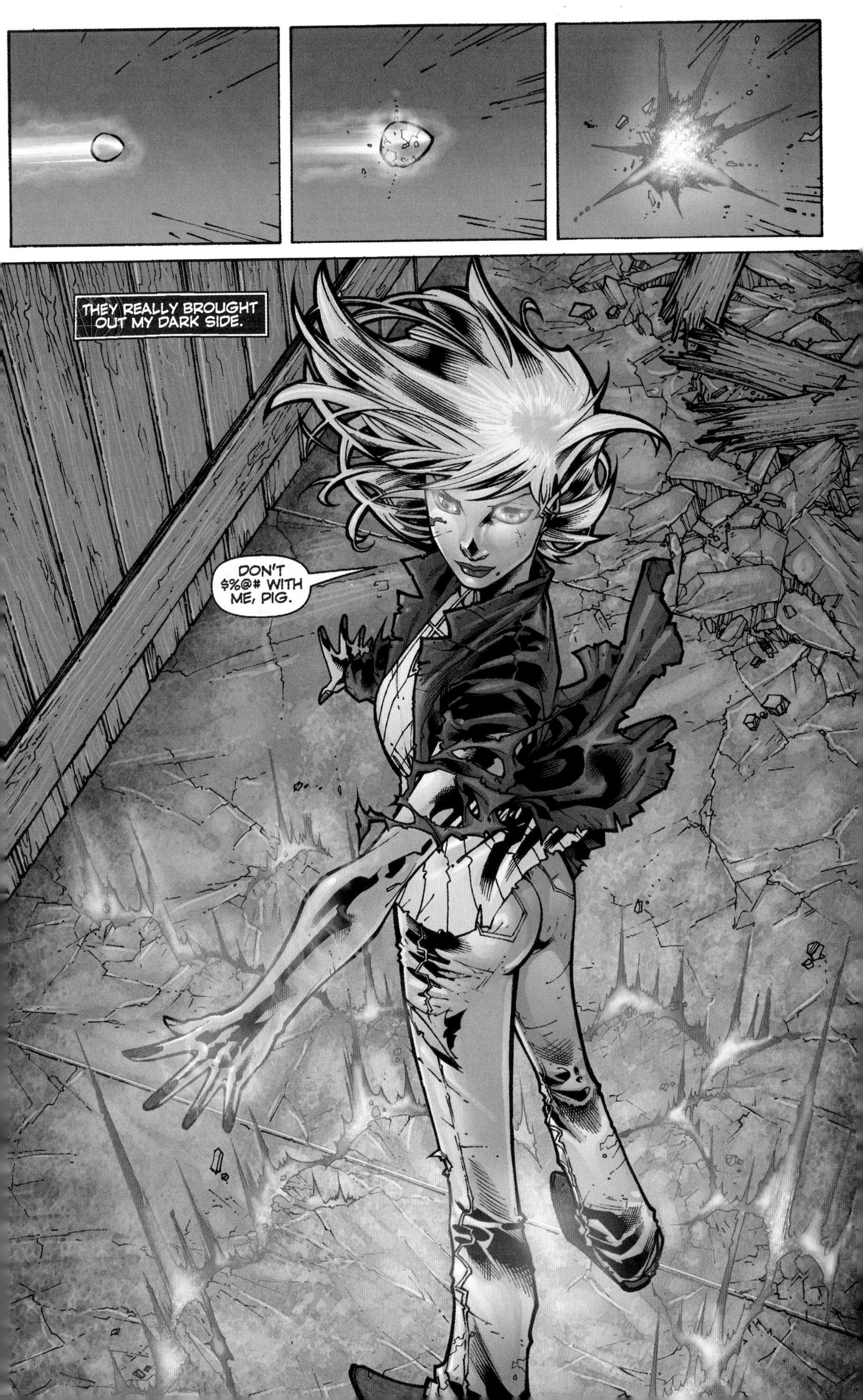
THEY REALLY BROUGHT OUT MY DARK SIDE.
DON'T $%@# WITH ME, PIG.

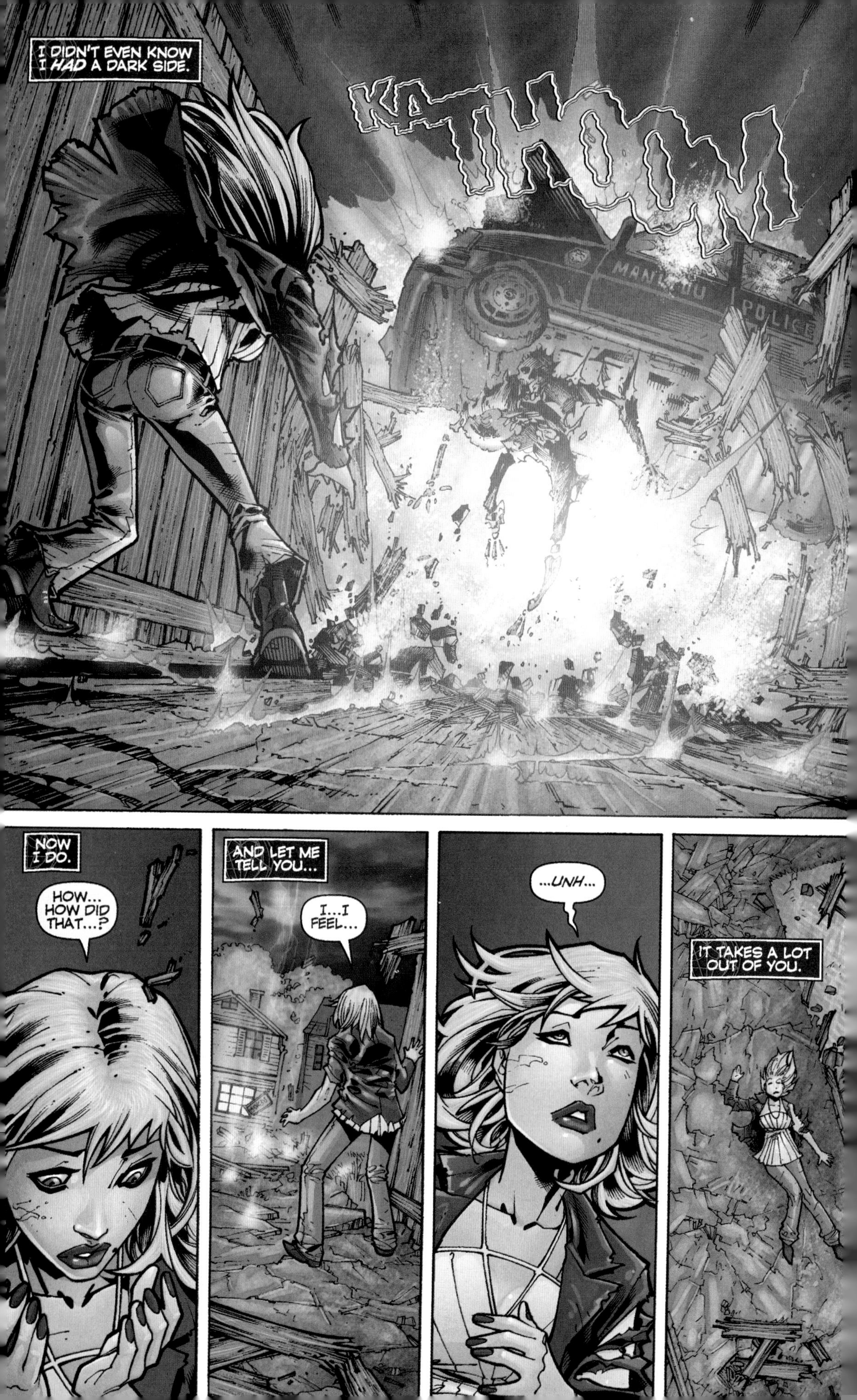
I DIDN'T EVEN KNOW I *HAD* A DARK SIDE.
KATHOOM
POLICE
NOW I DO.
HOW... HOW DID THAT...?
AND LET ME TELL YOU...
I...I FEEL...
...UNH...
IT TAKES A LOT OUT OF YOU.

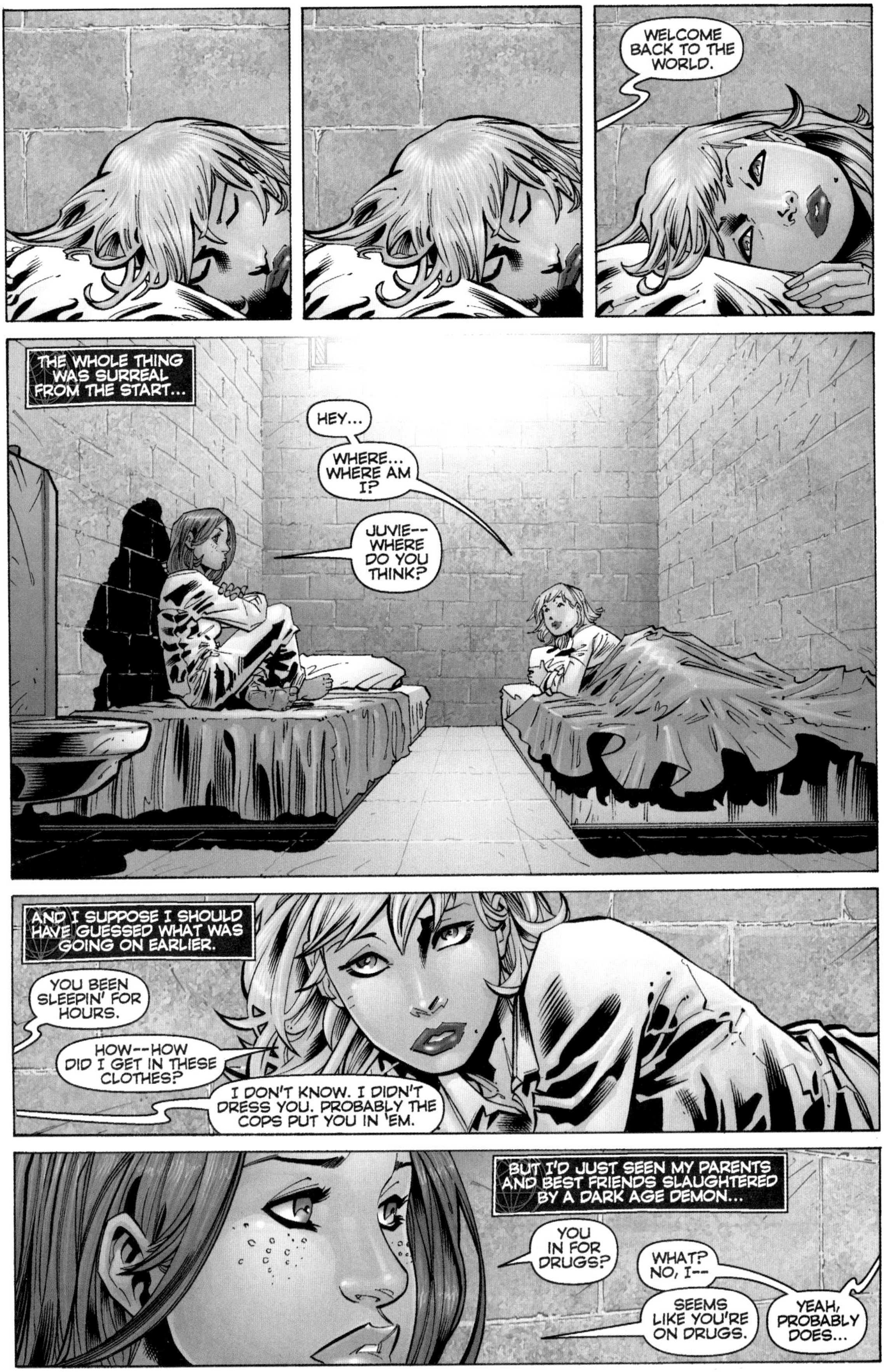
WELCOME BACK TO THE WORLD.
THE WHOLE THING WAS SURREAL FROM THE START...
HEY...
WHERE... WHERE AM I?
JUVIE-- WHERE DO YOU THINK?
AND I SUPPOSE I SHOULD HAVE GUESSED WHAT WAS GOING ON EARLIER.
YOU BEEN SLEEPIN' FOR HOURS.
HOW--HOW DID I GET IN THESE CLOTHES?
I DON'T KNOW. I DIDN'T DRESS YOU. PROBABLY THE COPS PUT YOU IN 'EM.
BUT I'D JUST SEEN MY PARENTS AND BEST FRIENDS SLAUGHTERED BY A DARK AGE DEMON...
YOU IN FOR DRUGS?
WHAT? NO, I--
SEEMS LIKE YOU'RE ON DRUGS.
YEAH, PROBABLY DOES...

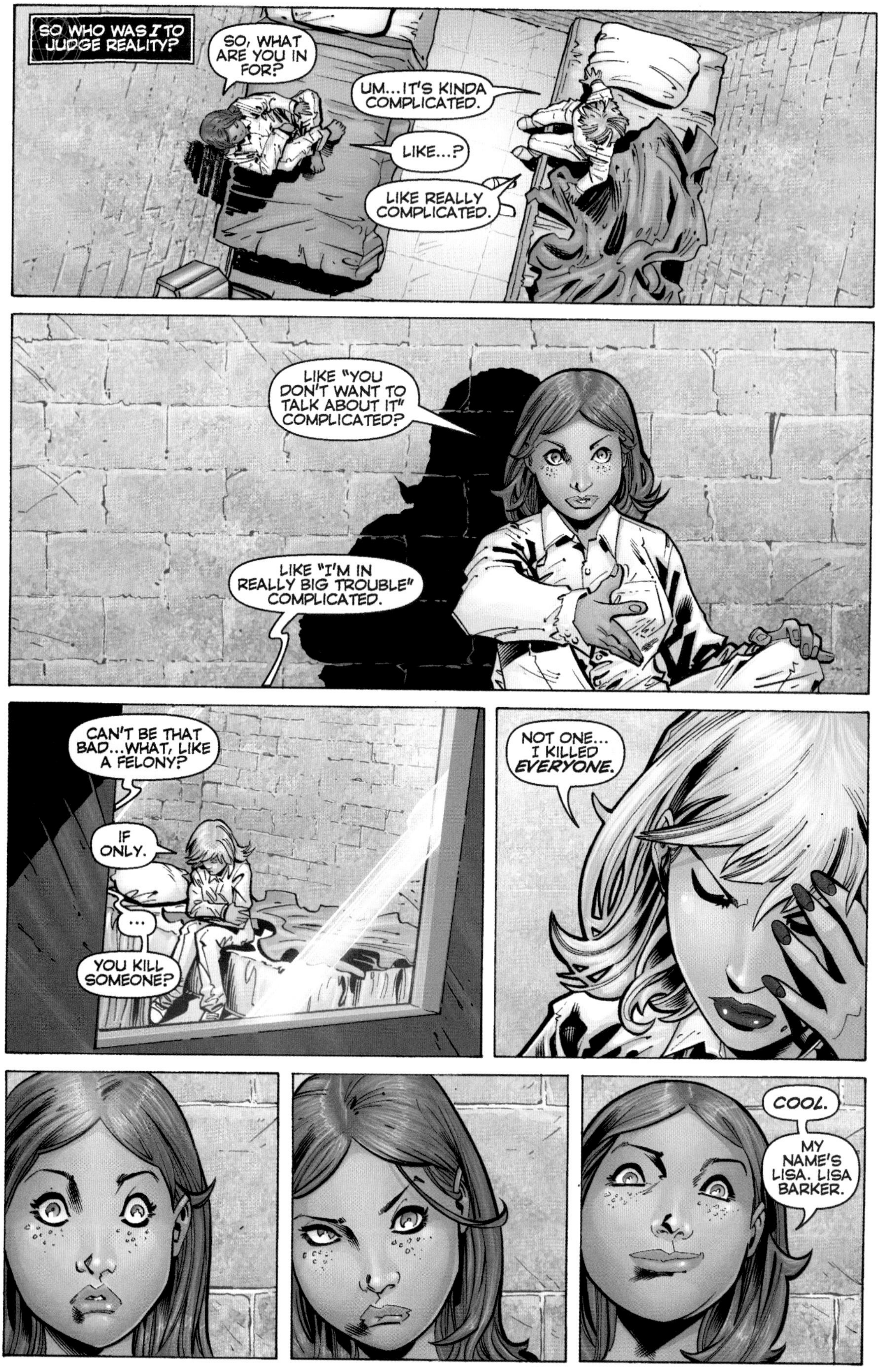

SO WHO WAS *I* TO JUDGE REALITY?
SO, WHAT ARE YOU IN FOR?
UM...IT'S KINDA COMPLICATED.
LIKE...?
LIKE REALLY COMPLICATED.
LIKE "YOU DON'T WANT TO TALK ABOUT IT" COMPLICATED?
LIKE "I'M IN REALLY BIG TROUBLE" COMPLICATED.
CAN'T BE THAT BAD...WHAT, LIKE A FELONY?
IF ONLY.
...
YOU KILL SOMEONE?
NOT ONE... I KILLED *EVERYONE*.
COOL.
MY NAME'S LISA. LISA BARKER.

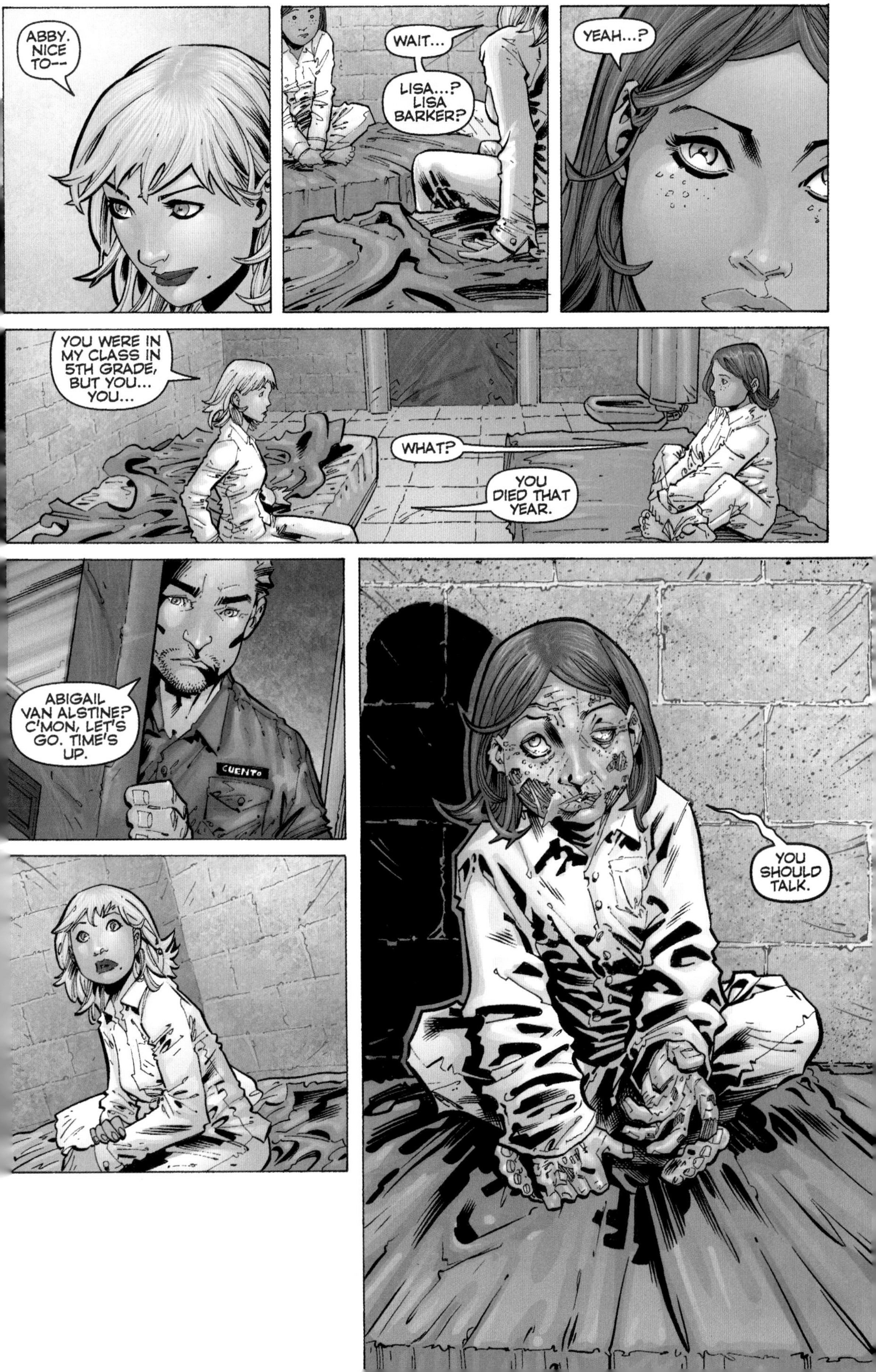
ABBY. NICE TO--
WAIT...
LISA...? LISA BARKER?
YEAH...?
YOU WERE IN MY CLASS IN 5TH GRADE, BUT YOU... YOU...
WHAT?
YOU DIED THAT YEAR.
ABIGAIL VAN ALSTINE? C'MON, LET'S GO. TIME'S UP.
CUENTO
YOU SHOULD TALK.

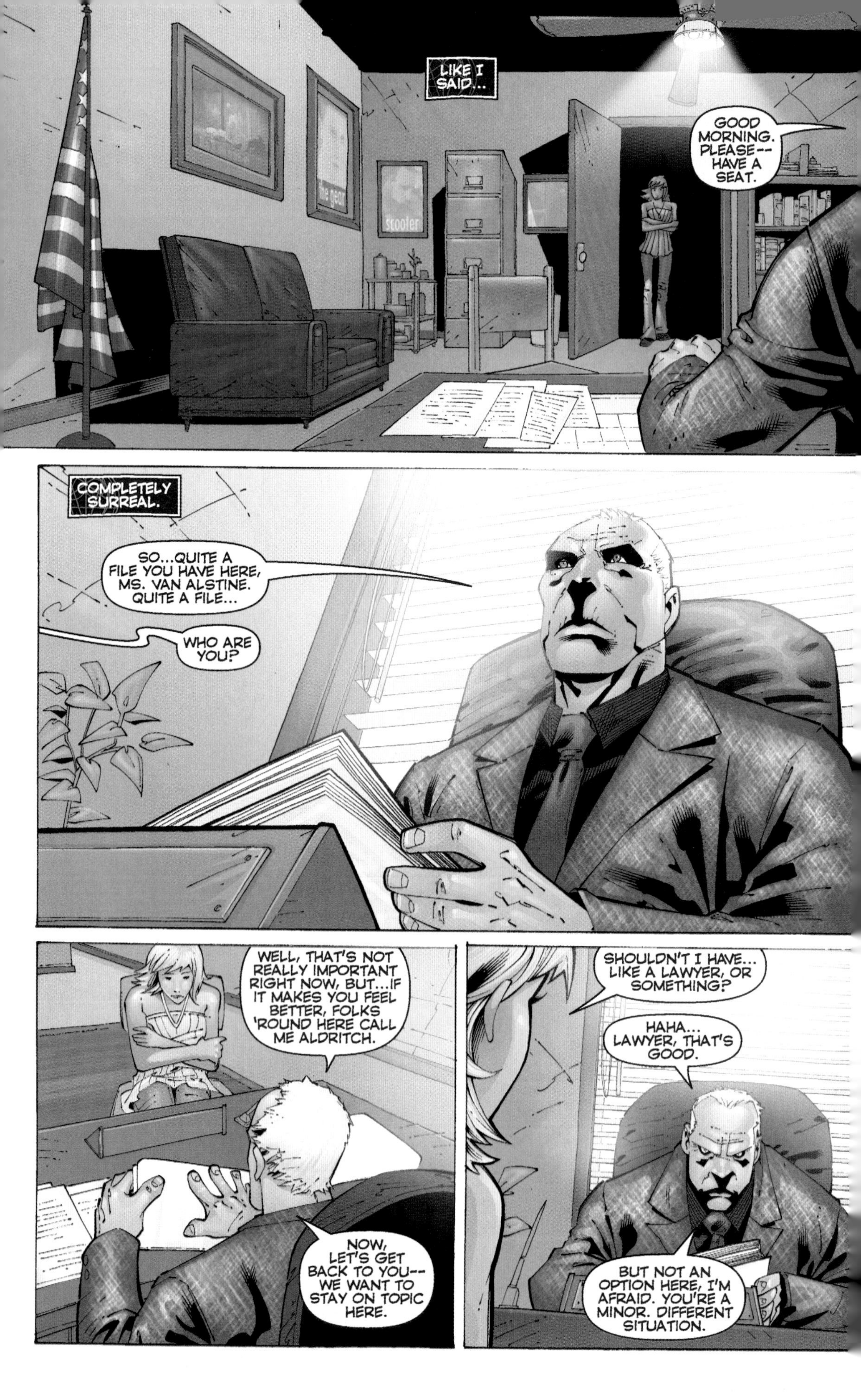

LIKE I SAID...
GOOD MORNING. PLEASE-- HAVE A SEAT.
the gear
scooter
COMPLETELY SURREAL.
SO...QUITE A FILE YOU HAVE HERE, MS. VAN ALSTINE. QUITE A FILE...
WHO ARE YOU?
WELL, THAT'S NOT REALLY IMPORTANT RIGHT NOW, BUT...IF IT MAKES YOU FEEL BETTER, FOLKS 'ROUND HERE CALL ME ALDRITCH.
NOW, LET'S GET BACK TO YOU-- WE WANT TO STAY ON TOPIC HERE.
SHOULDN'T I HAVE... LIKE A LAWYER, OR SOMETHING?
HAHA... LAWYER, THAT'S GOOD.
BUT NOT AN OPTION HERE, I'M AFRAID. YOU'RE A MINOR. DIFFERENT SITUATION.

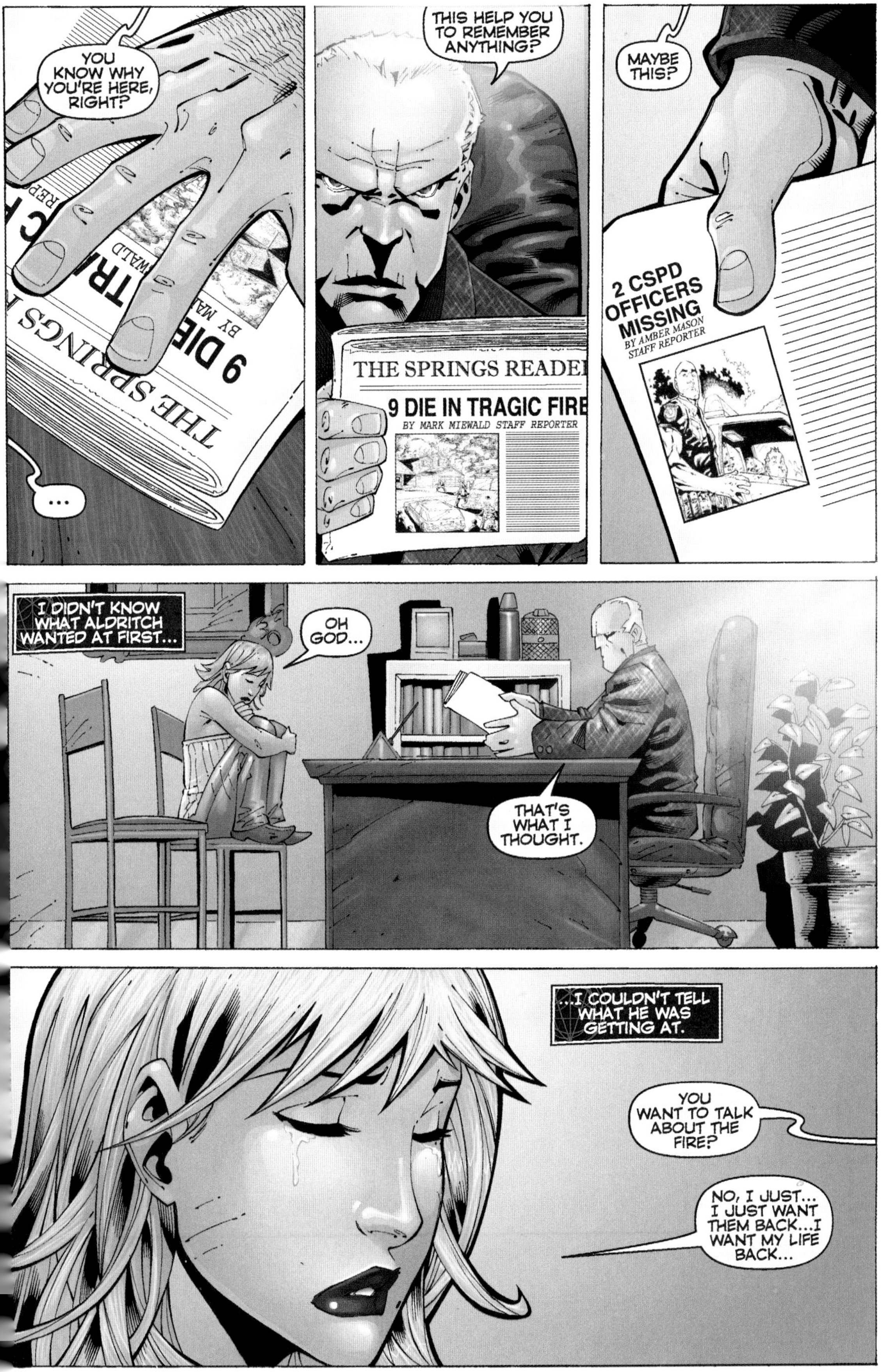

YOU KNOW WHY YOU'RE HERE, RIGHT?
...
THIS HELP YOU TO REMEMBER ANYTHING?
THE SPRINGS READE
9 DIE IN TRAGIC FIRE
BY MARK MIEWALD STAFF REPORTER
MAYBE THIS?
2 CSPD OFFICERS MISSING
BY AMBER MASON STAFF REPORTER
I DIDN'T KNOW WHAT ALDRITCH WANTED AT FIRST...
OH GOD...
THAT'S WHAT I THOUGHT.
...I COULDN'T TELL WHAT HE WAS GETTING AT.
YOU WANT TO TALK ABOUT THE FIRE?
NO, I JUST... I JUST WANT THEM BACK...I WANT MY LIFE BACK...

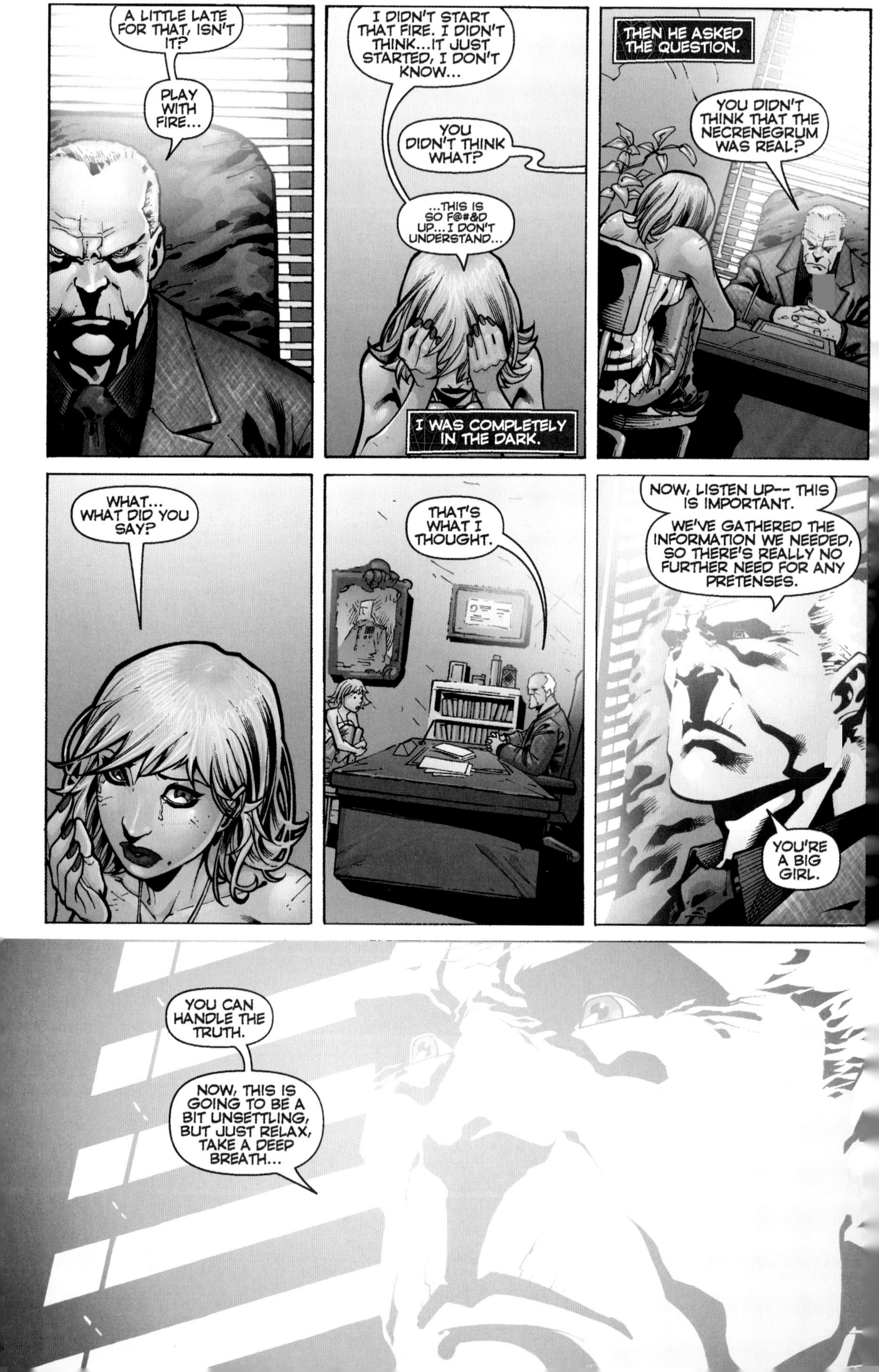
A LITTLE LATE FOR THAT, ISN'T IT?
PLAY WITH FIRE...
I DIDN'T START THAT FIRE. I DIDN'T THINK...IT JUST STARTED, I DON'T KNOW...
YOU DIDN'T THINK WHAT?
...THIS IS SO F@#&D UP...I DON'T UNDERSTAND...
I WAS COMPLETELY IN THE DARK.
THEN HE ASKED THE QUESTION.
YOU DIDN'T THINK THAT THE NECRENEGRUM WAS REAL?
WHAT... WHAT DID YOU SAY?
THAT'S WHAT I THOUGHT.
NOW, LISTEN UP-- THIS IS IMPORTANT.
WE'VE GATHERED THE INFORMATION WE NEEDED, SO THERE'S REALLY NO FURTHER NEED FOR ANY PRETENSES.
YOU'RE A BIG GIRL.
YOU CAN HANDLE THE TRUTH.
NOW, THIS IS GOING TO BE A BIT UNSETTLING, BUT JUST RELAX, TAKE A DEEP BREATH...

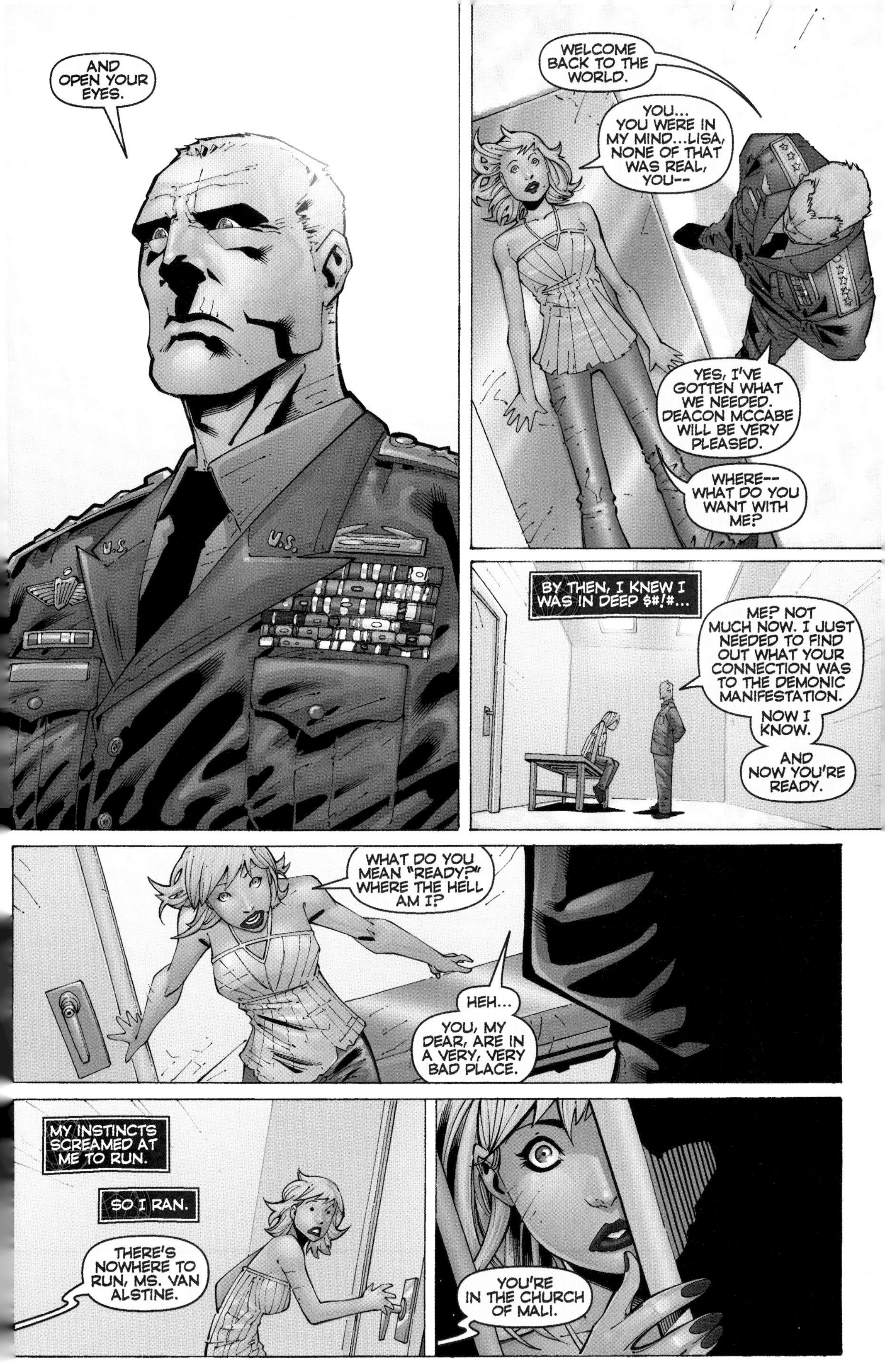
AND OPEN YOUR EYES.
WELCOME BACK TO THE WORLD.
YOU... YOU WERE IN MY MIND...LISA, NONE OF THAT WAS REAL, YOU--
YES, I'VE GOTTEN WHAT WE NEEDED. DEACON MCCABE WILL BE VERY PLEASED.
WHERE-- WHAT DO YOU WANT WITH ME?
BY THEN, I KNEW I WAS IN DEEP $#!#...
ME? NOT MUCH NOW. I JUST NEEDED TO FIND OUT WHAT YOUR CONNECTION WAS TO THE DEMONIC MANIFESTATION.
NOW I KNOW.
AND NOW YOU'RE READY.
WHAT DO YOU MEAN "READY?" WHERE THE HELL AM I?
HEH...
YOU, MY DEAR, ARE IN A VERY, VERY BAD PLACE.
MY INSTINCTS SCREAMED AT ME TO RUN.
SO I RAN.
THERE'S NOWHERE TO RUN, MS. VAN ALSTINE.
YOU'RE IN THE CHURCH OF MALI.

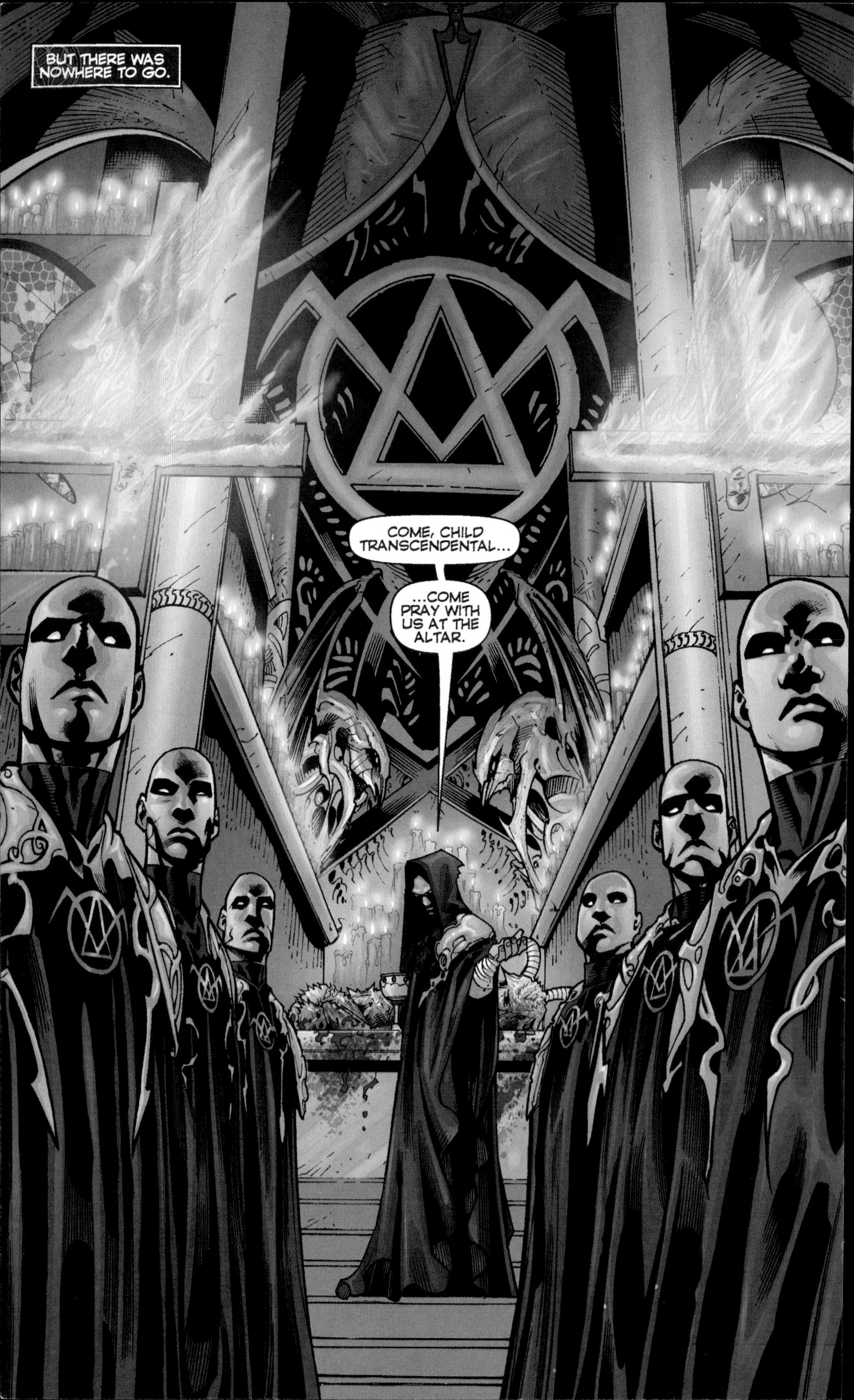
BUT THERE WAS NOWHERE TO GO.
COME, CHILD TRANSCENDENTAL...
...COME PRAY WITH US AT THE ALTAR.

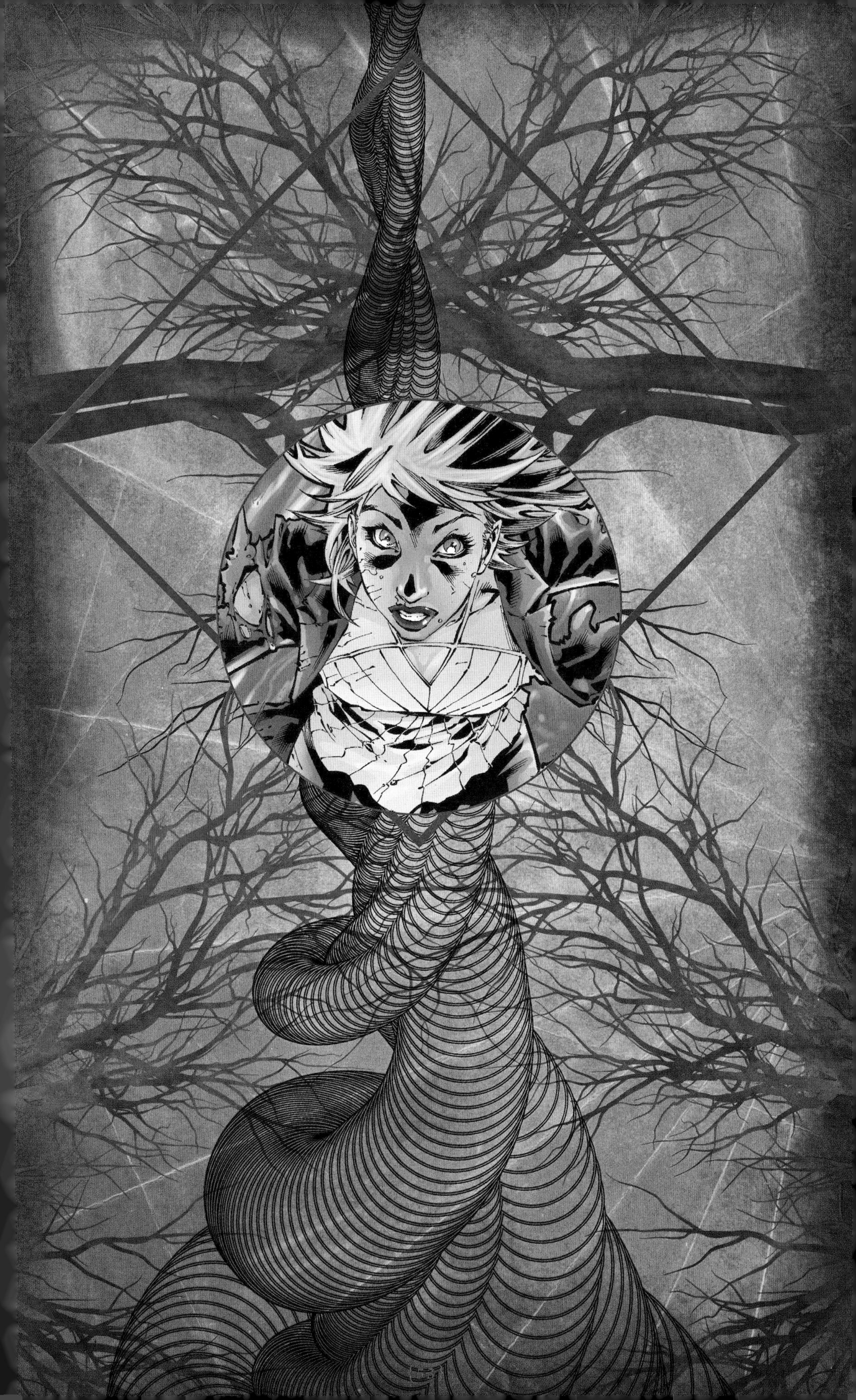

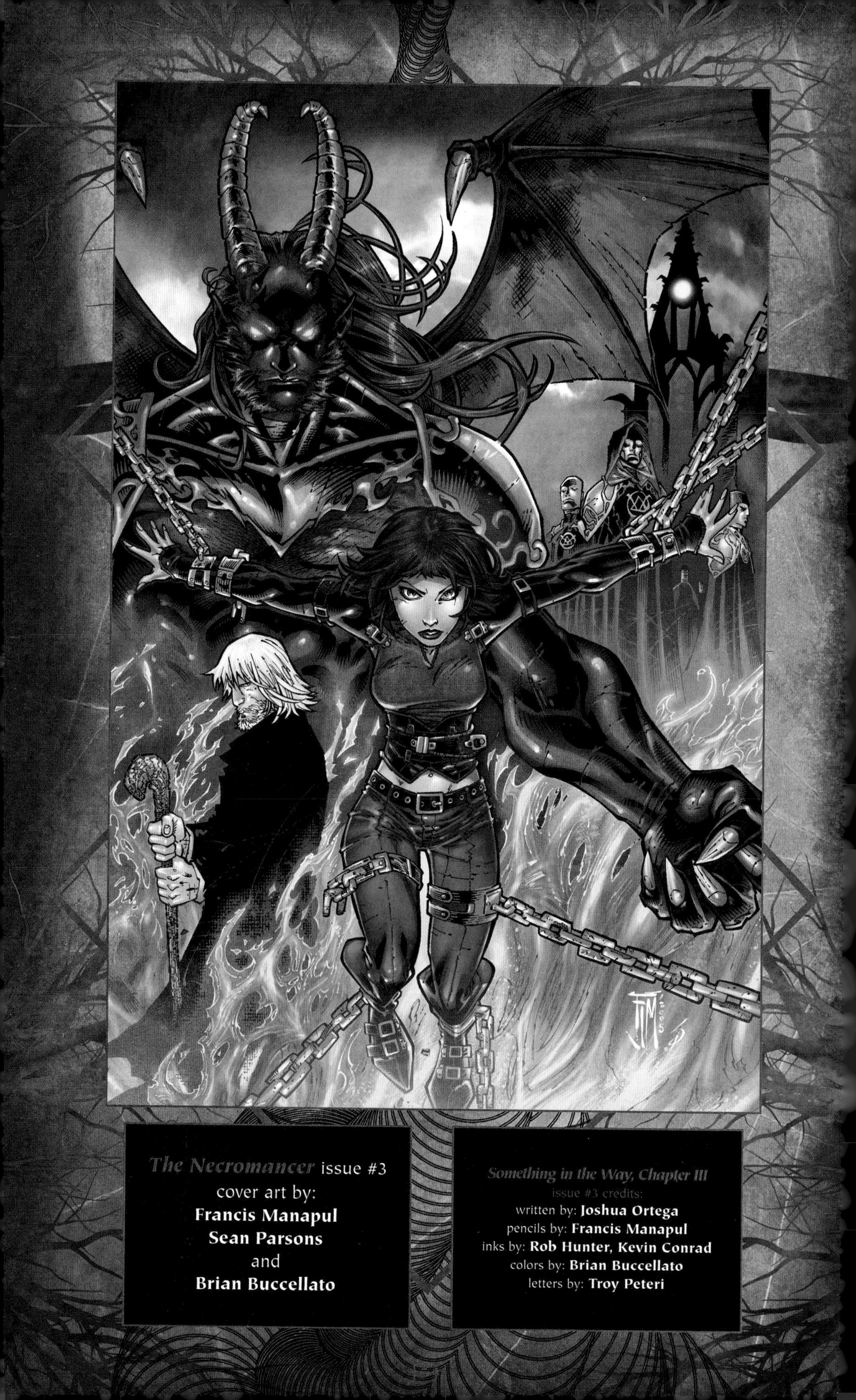

The Necromancer issue #3
cover art by:
Francis Manapul
Sean Parsons
and
Brian Buccellato

Something in the Way, Chapter III
issue #3 credits:
written by: **Joshua Ortega**
pencils by: **Francis Manapul**
inks by: **Rob Hunter, Kevin Conrad**
colors by: **Brian Buccellato**
letters by: **Troy Peteri**

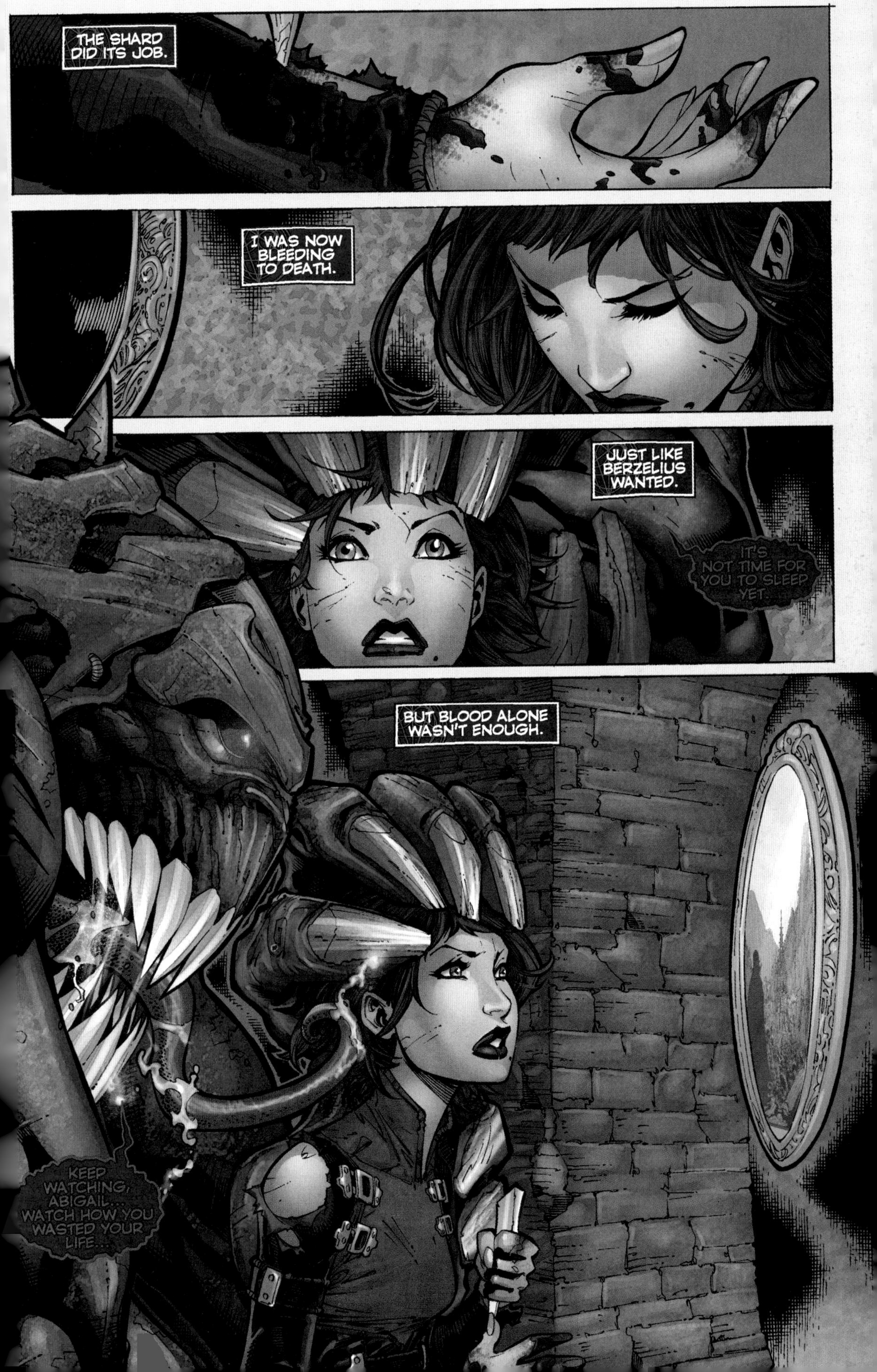
THE SHARD DID ITS JOB.
I WAS NOW BLEEDING TO DEATH.
JUST LIKE BERZELIUS WANTED.
IT'S NOT TIME FOR YOU TO SLEEP YET.
BUT BLOOD ALONE WASN'T ENOUGH.
KEEP WATCHING, ABIGAIL... WATCH HOW YOU WASTED YOUR LIFE...

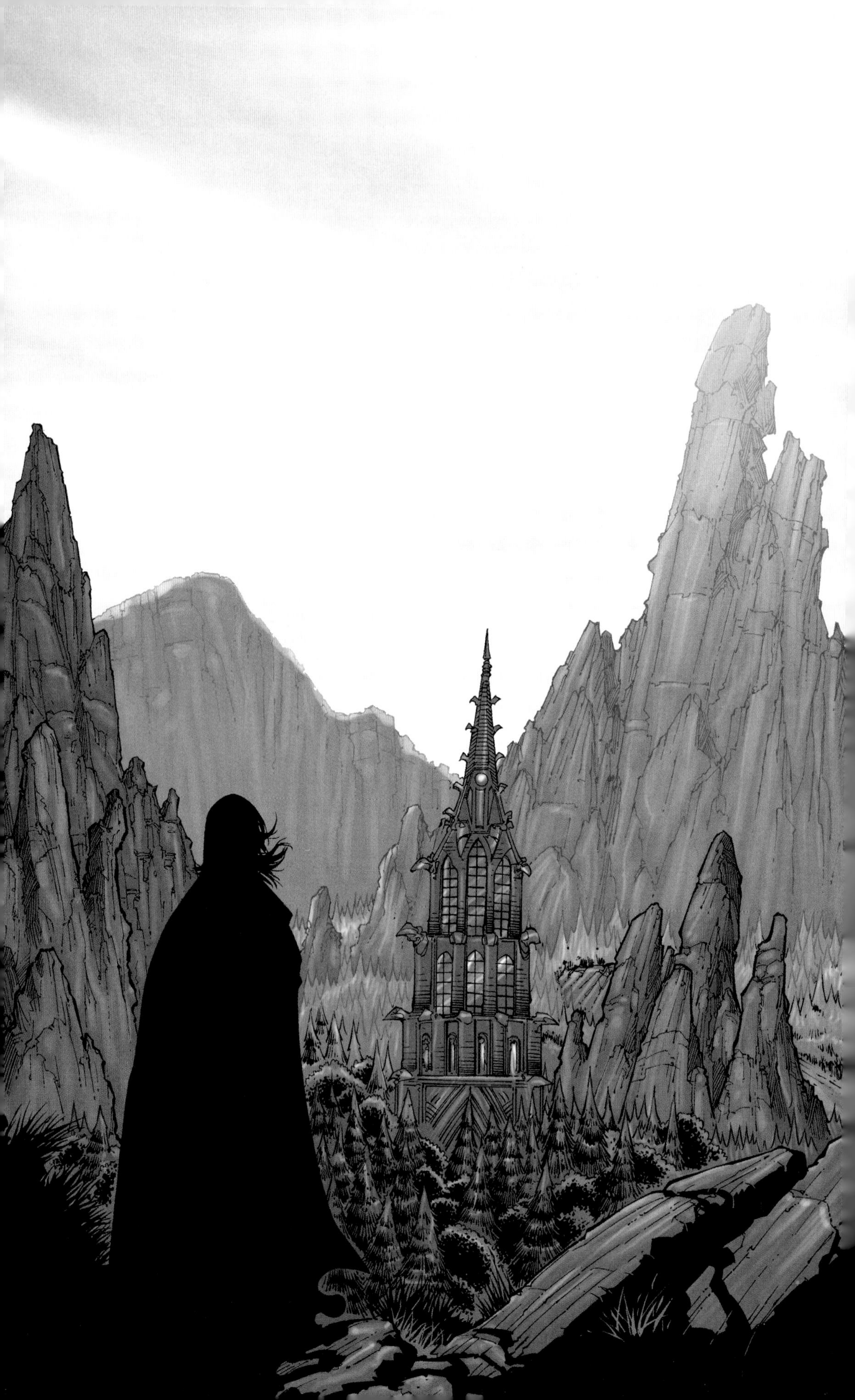

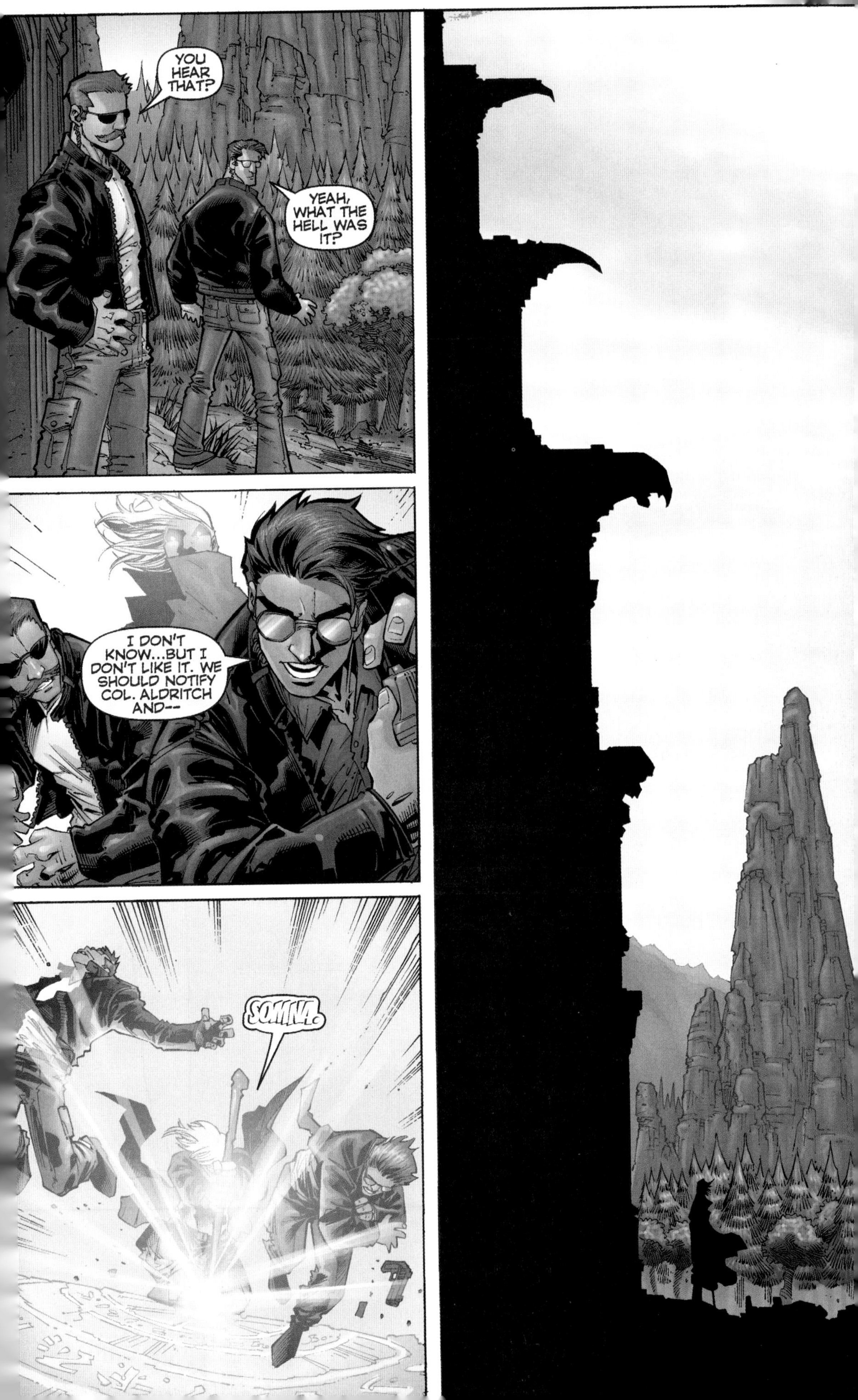
YOU HEAR THAT?
YEAH, WHAT THE HELL WAS IT?
I DON'T KNOW...BUT I DON'T LIKE IT. WE SHOULD NOTIFY COL. ALDRITCH AND--
SOMNA.

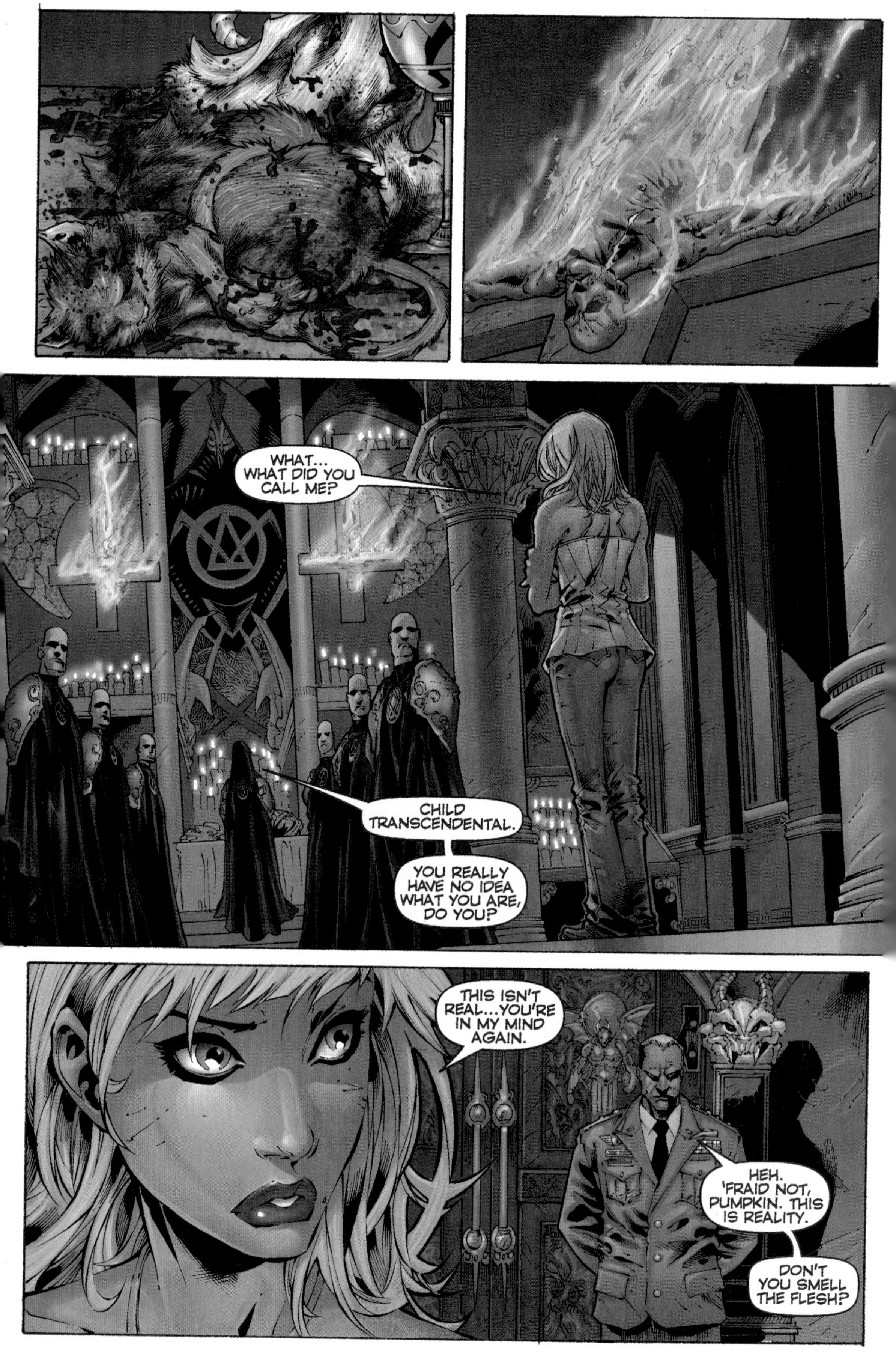
WHAT... WHAT DID YOU CALL ME?
CHILD TRANSCENDENTAL.
YOU REALLY HAVE NO IDEA WHAT YOU ARE, DO YOU?
THIS ISN'T REAL...YOU'RE IN MY MIND AGAIN.
HEH. 'FRAID NOT, PUMPKIN. THIS IS REALITY.
DON'T YOU SMELL THE FLESH?

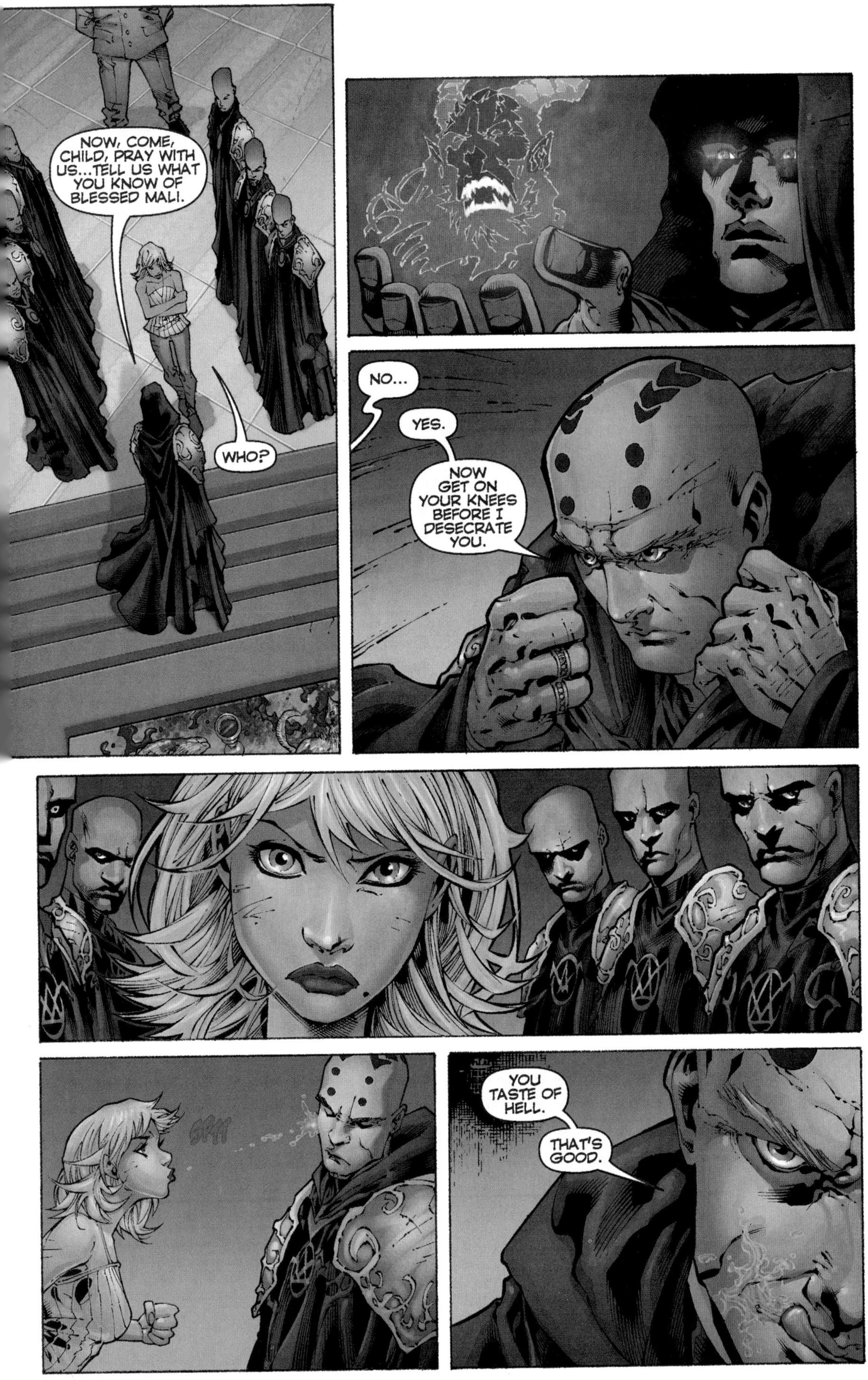
NOW, COME, CHILD, PRAY WITH US...TELL US WHAT YOU KNOW OF BLESSED MALI.
WHO?
NO...
YES.
NOW GET ON YOUR KNEES BEFORE I DESECRATE YOU.
YOU TASTE OF HELL.
THAT'S GOOD.

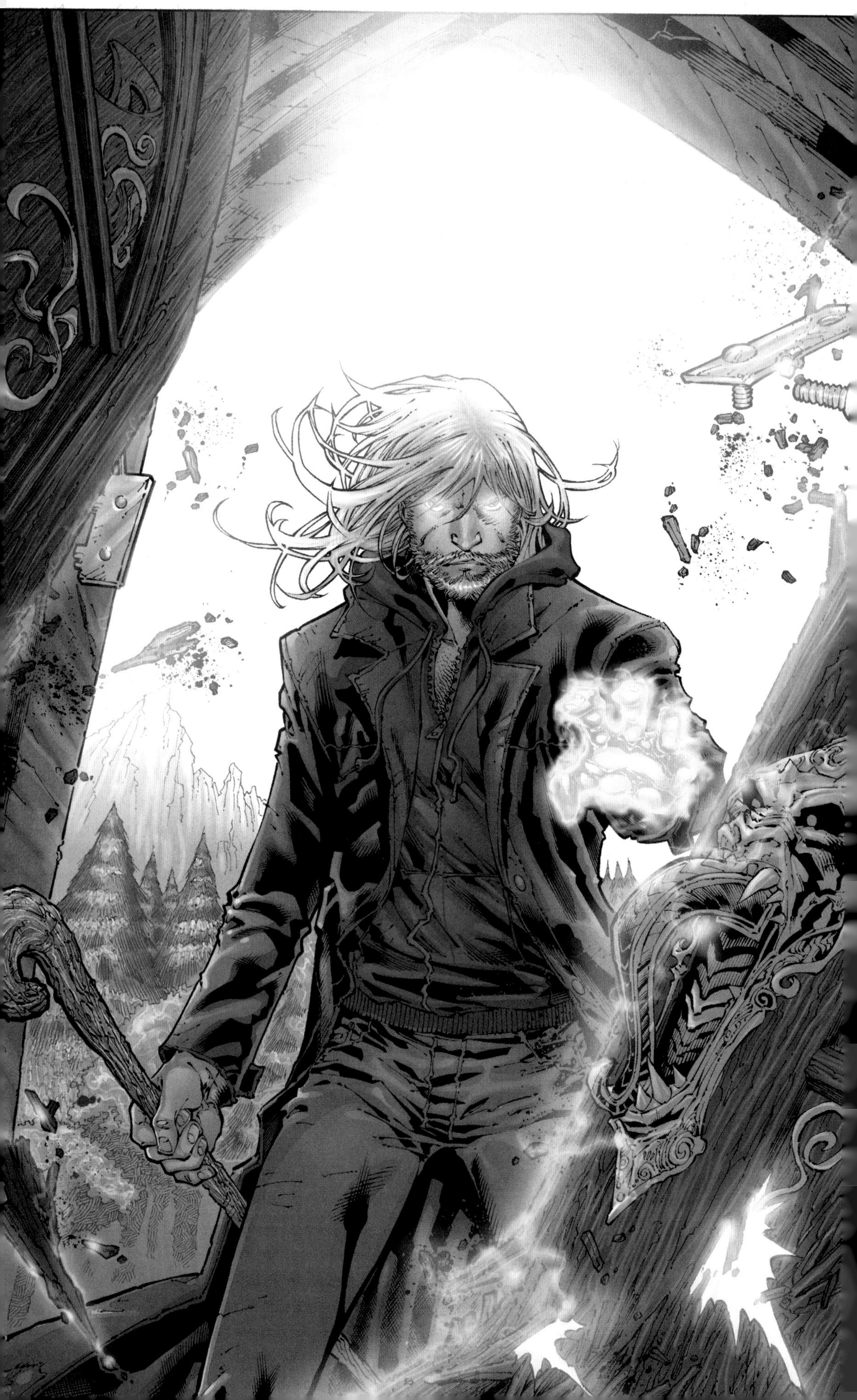

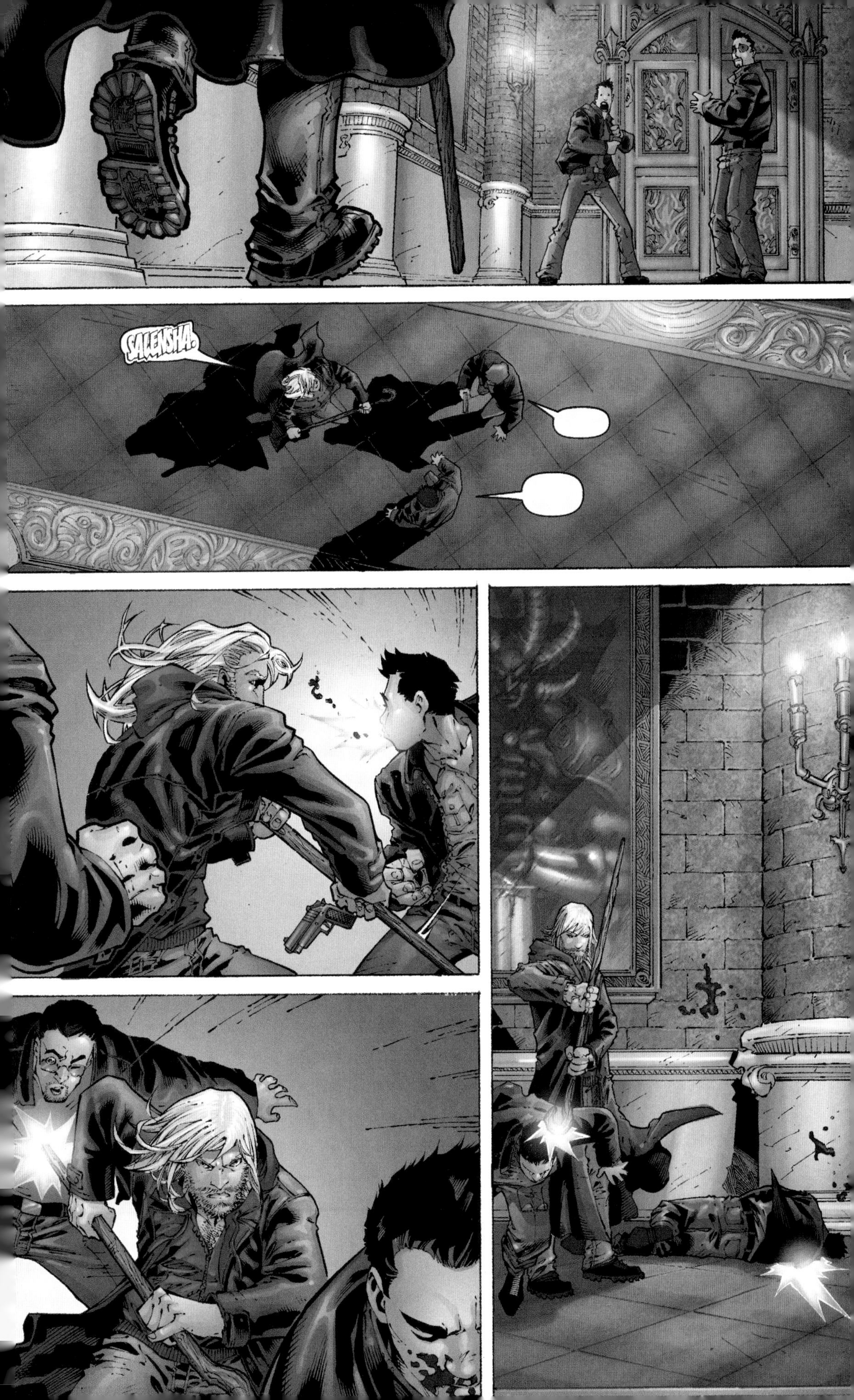
SALENSHA.

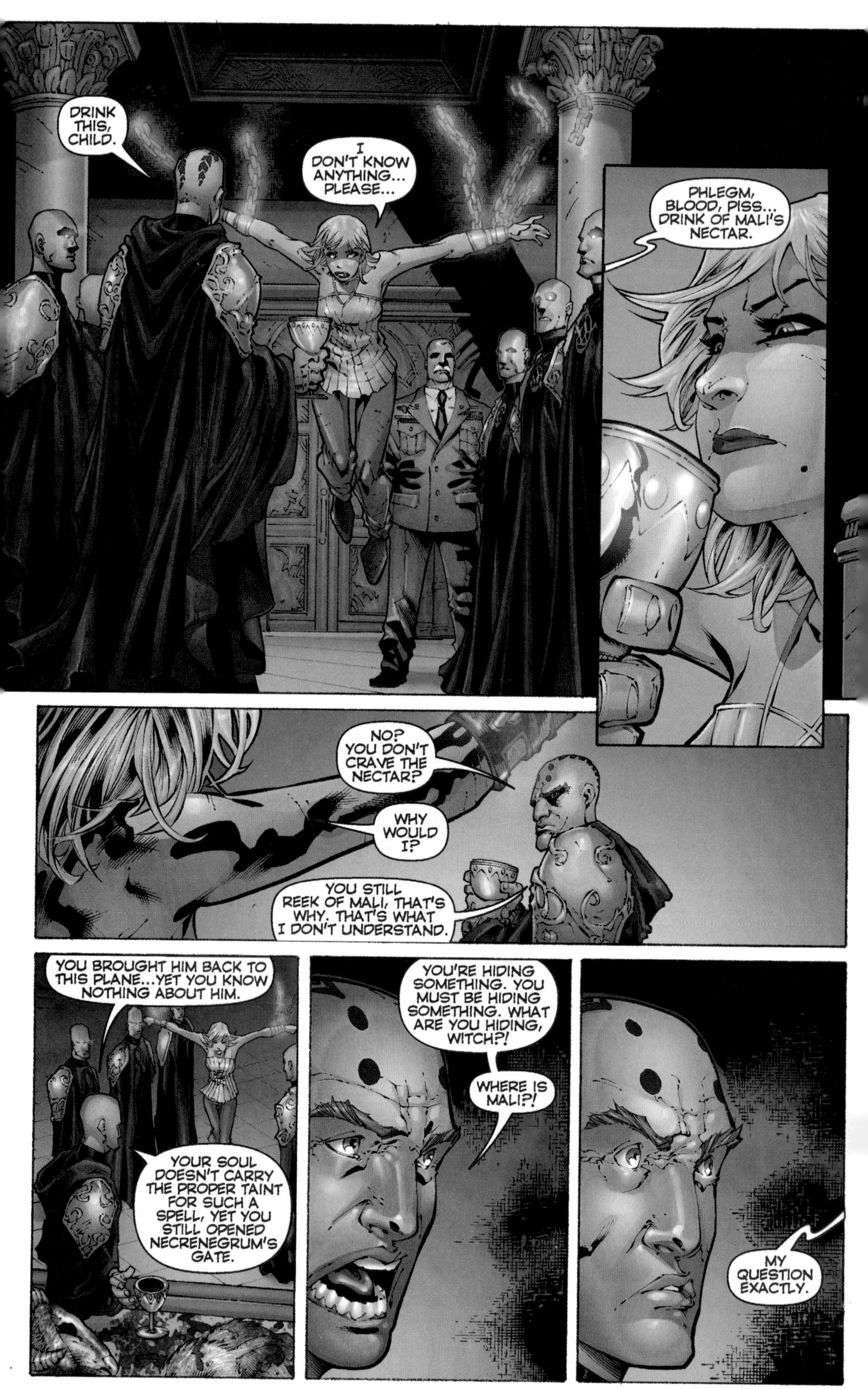
DRINK THIS, CHILD.
I DON'T KNOW ANYTHING... PLEASE...
PHLEGM, BLOOD, PISS... DRINK OF MALI'S NECTAR.
NO? YOU DON'T CRAVE THE NECTAR?
WHY WOULD I?
YOU STILL REEK OF MALI, THAT'S WHY. THAT'S WHAT I DON'T UNDERSTAND.
YOU BROUGHT HIM BACK TO THIS PLANE...YET YOU KNOW NOTHING ABOUT HIM.
YOUR SOUL DOESN'T CARRY THE PROPER TAINT FOR SUCH A SPELL, YET YOU STILL OPENED NECRENEGRUM'S GATE.
YOU'RE HIDING SOMETHING. YOU MUST BE HIDING SOMETHING. WHAT ARE YOU HIDING, WITCH?!
WHERE IS MALI?!
MY QUESTION EXACTLY.

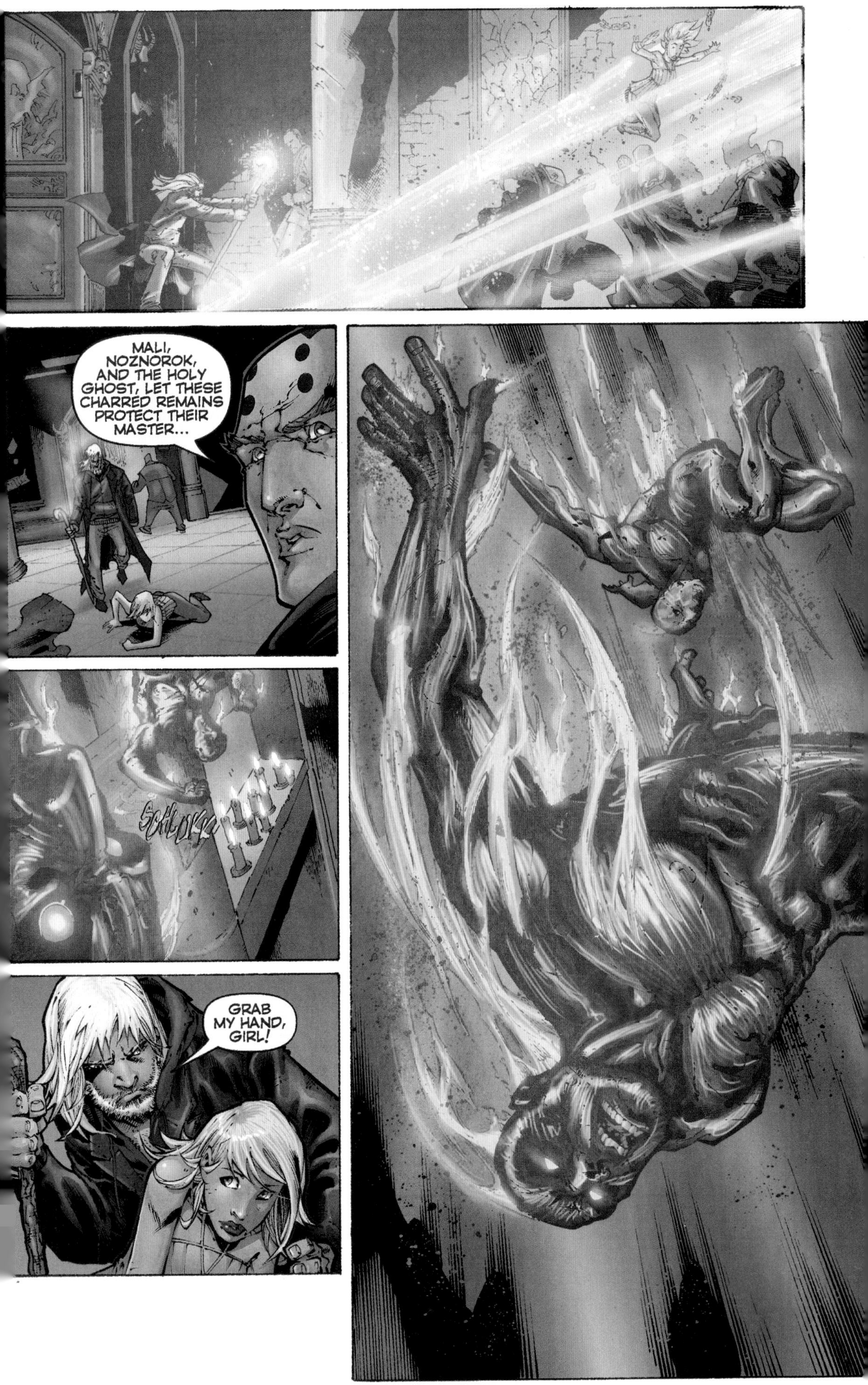
MALI, NOZNOROK, AND THE HOLY GHOST, LET THESE CHARRED REMAINS PROTECT THEIR MASTER...
SCHLOKK
GRAB MY HAND, GIRL!

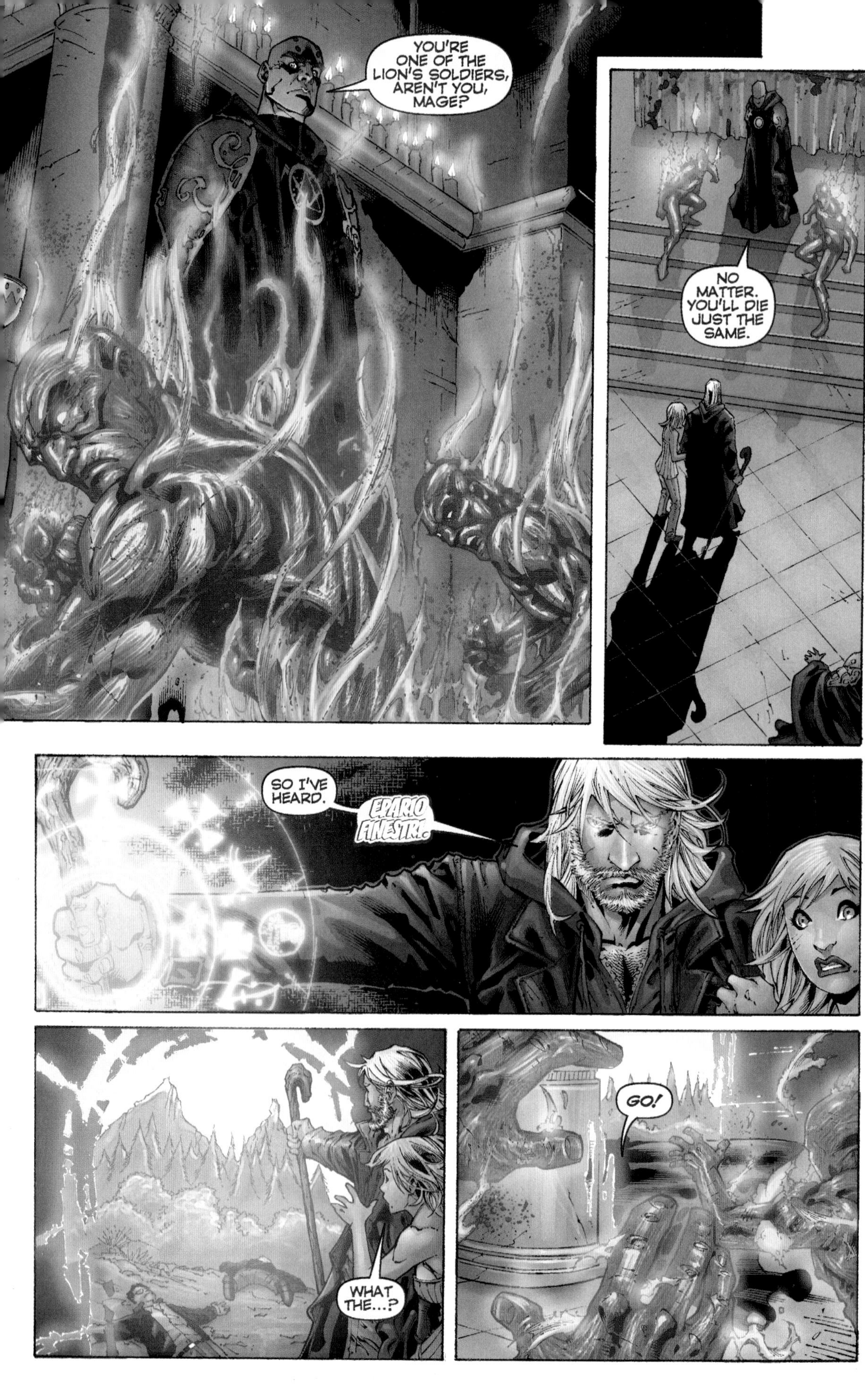
YOU'RE ONE OF THE LION'S SOLDIERS, AREN'T YOU, MAGE?
NO MATTER. YOU'LL DIE JUST THE SAME.
SO I'VE HEARD.
EPARIO FINESTRI.
WHAT THE...?
GO!

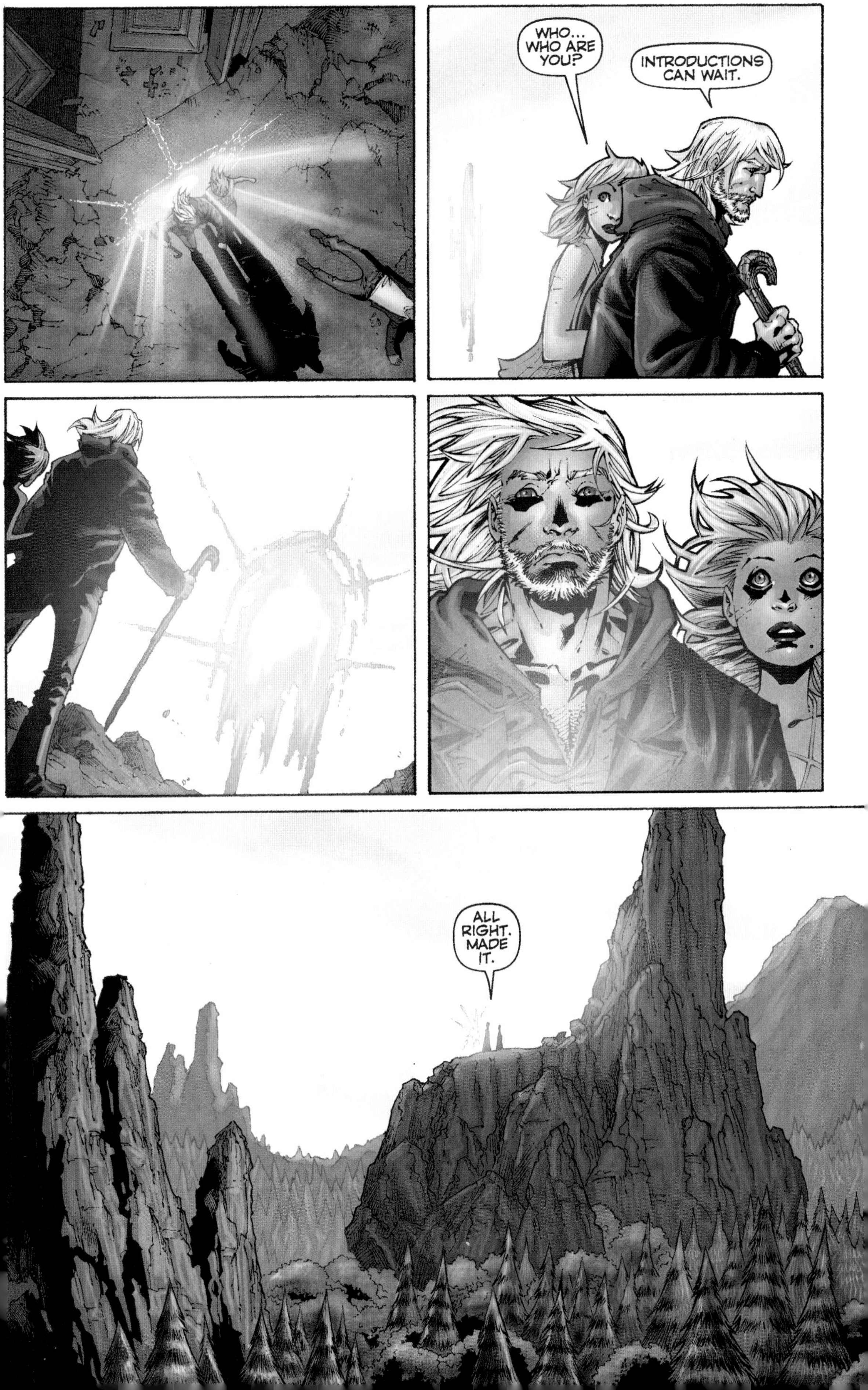
WHO... WHO ARE YOU?
INTRODUCTIONS CAN WAIT.
ALL RIGHT. MADE IT.

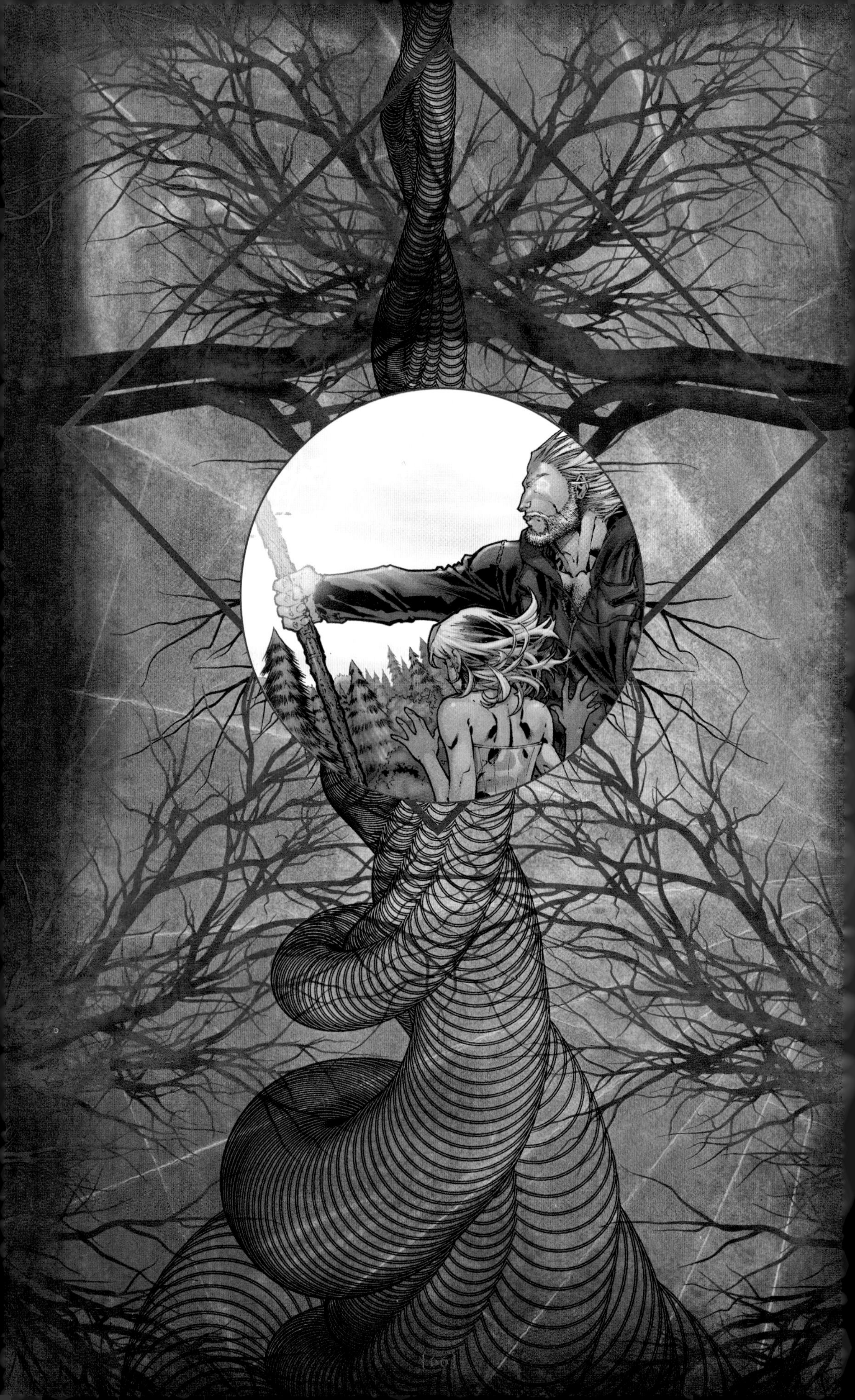

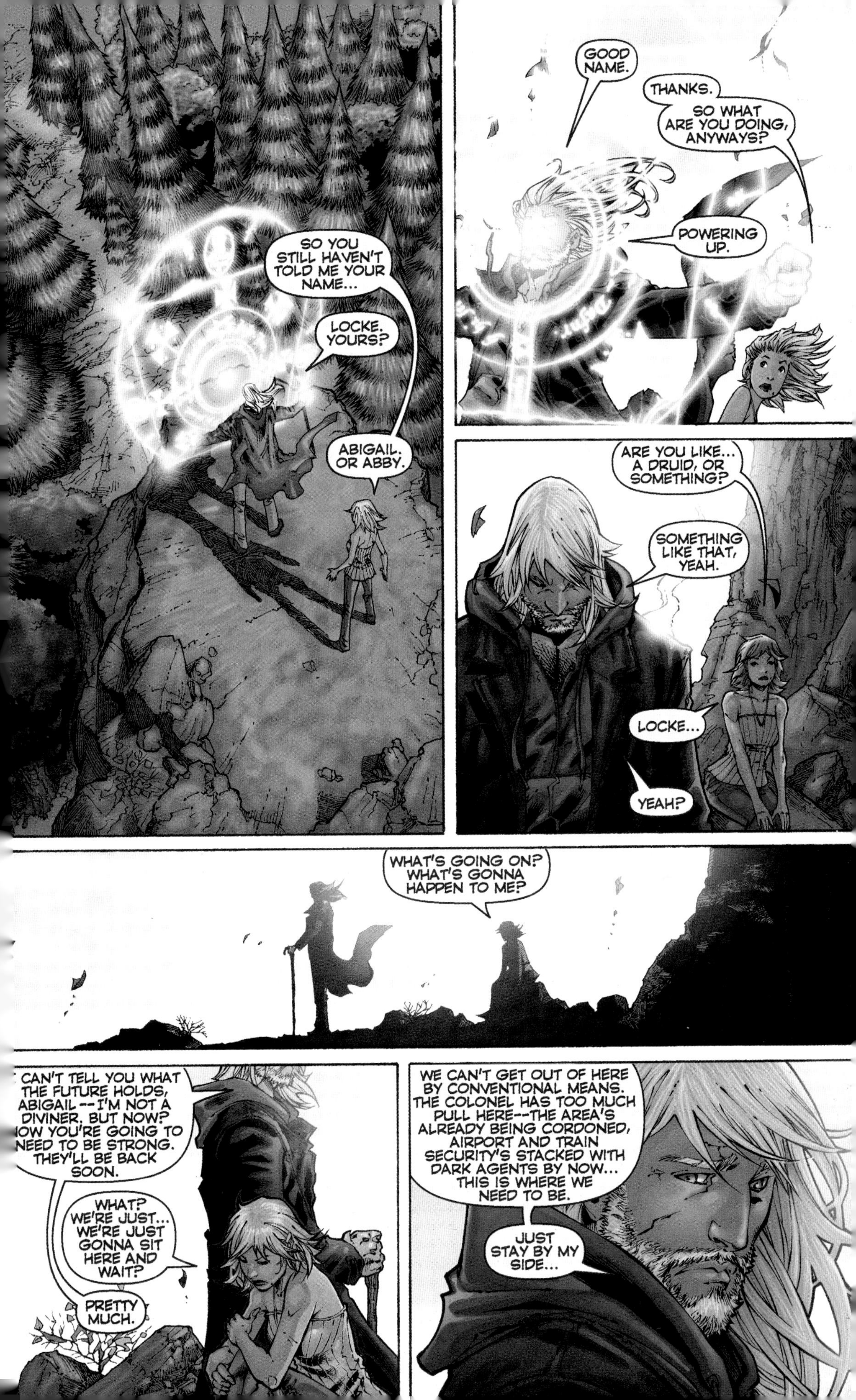
SO YOU STILL HAVEN'T TOLD ME YOUR NAME...
LOCKE. YOURS?
ABIGAIL. OR ABBY.
GOOD NAME.
THANKS.
SO WHAT ARE YOU DOING, ANYWAYS?
POWERING UP.
ARE YOU LIKE... A DRUID, OR SOMETHING?
SOMETHING LIKE THAT, YEAH.
LOCKE...
YEAH?
WHAT'S GOING ON? WHAT'S GONNA HAPPEN TO ME?
CAN'T TELL YOU WHAT THE FUTURE HOLDS, ABIGAIL -- I'M NOT A DIVINER. BUT NOW? NOW YOU'RE GOING TO NEED TO BE STRONG. THEY'LL BE BACK SOON.
WHAT? WE'RE JUST... WE'RE JUST GONNA SIT HERE AND WAIT?
PRETTY MUCH.
WE CAN'T GET OUT OF HERE BY CONVENTIONAL MEANS. THE COLONEL HAS TOO MUCH PULL HERE--THE AREA'S ALREADY BEING CORDONED, AIRPORT AND TRAIN SECURITY'S STACKED WITH DARK AGENTS BY NOW... THIS IS WHERE WE NEED TO BE.
JUST STAY BY MY SIDE...

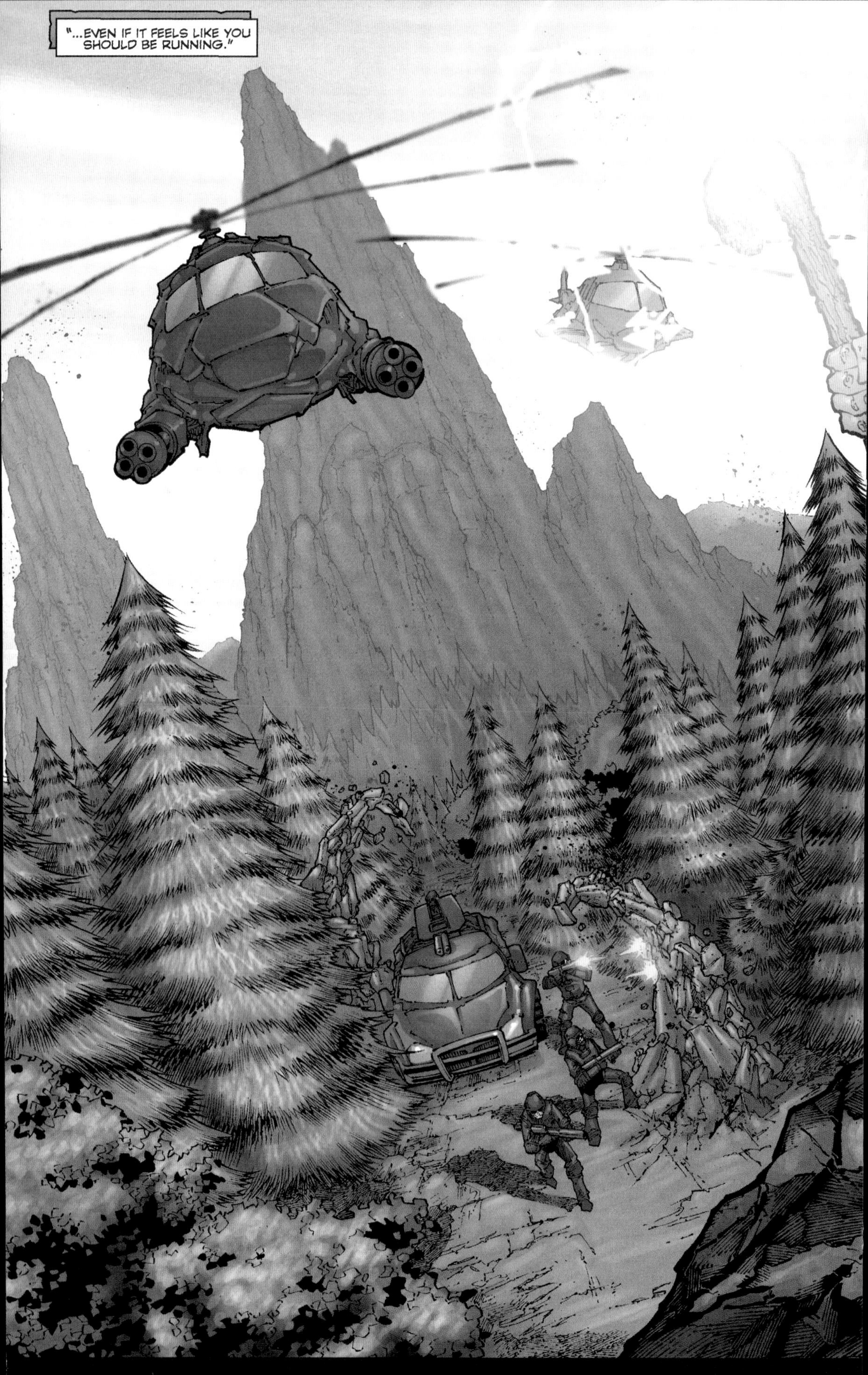
"...EVEN IF IT FEELS LIKE YOU SHOULD BE RUNNING."

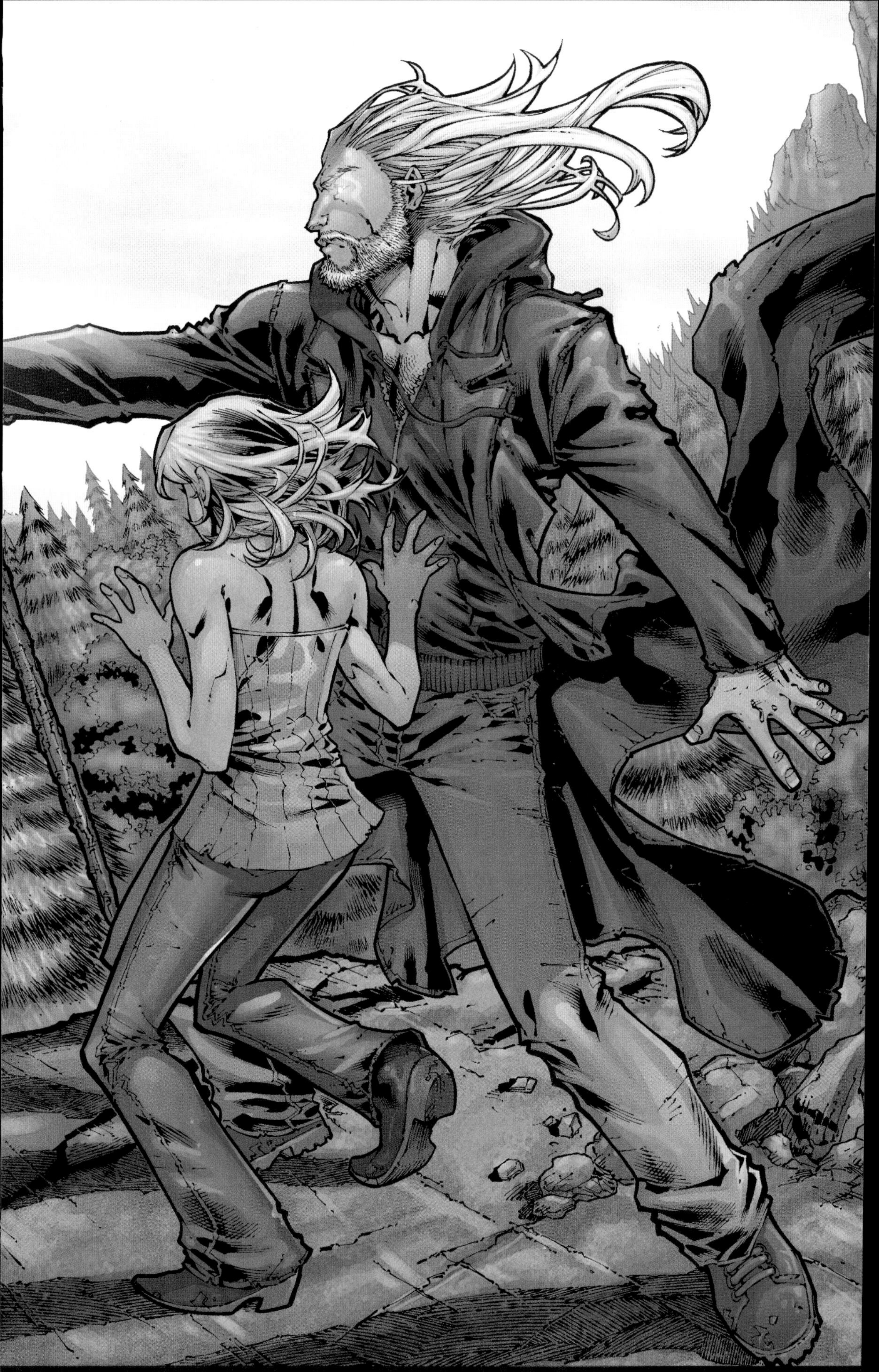

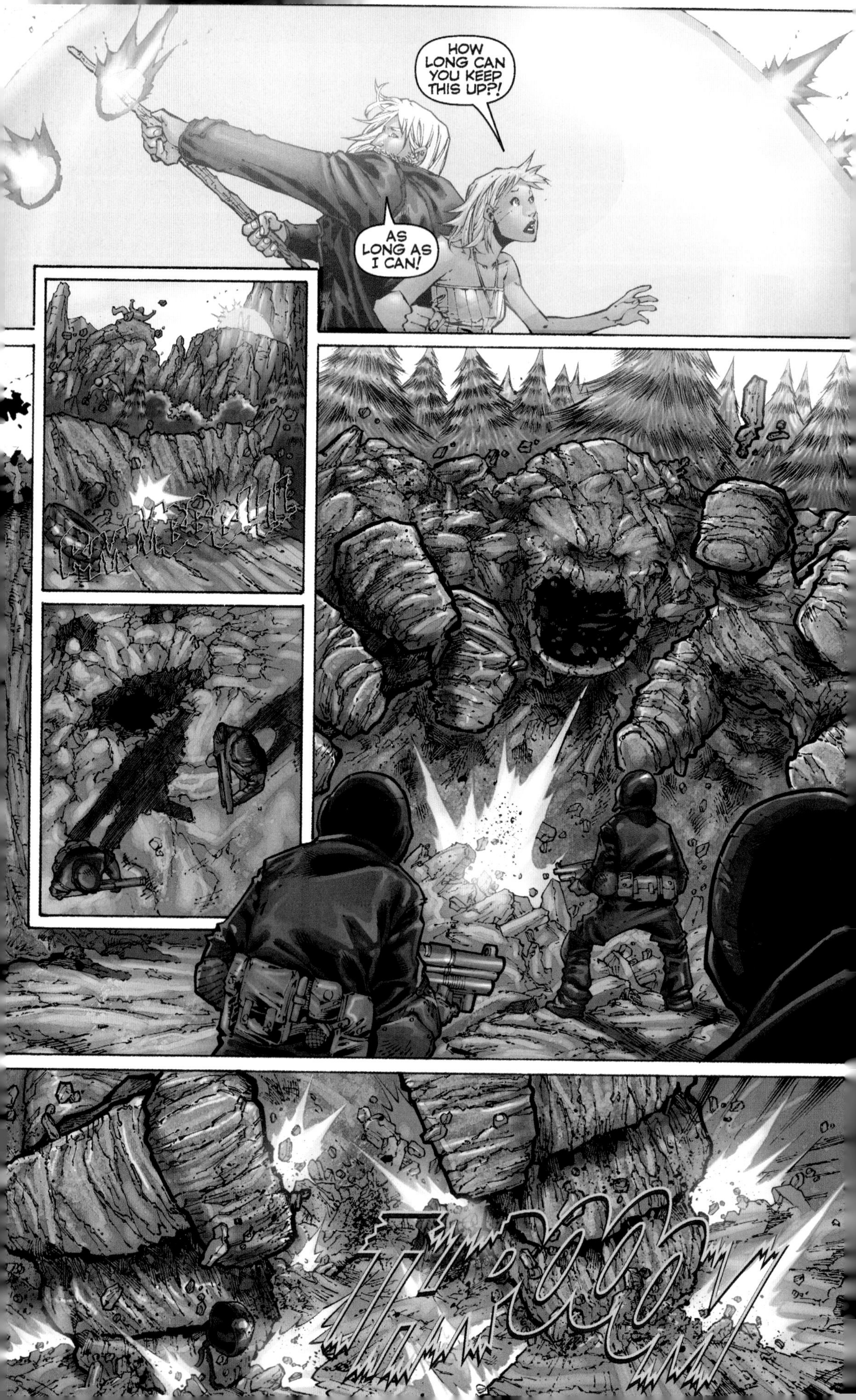
HOW LONG CAN YOU KEEP THIS UP?!
AS LONG AS I CAN!

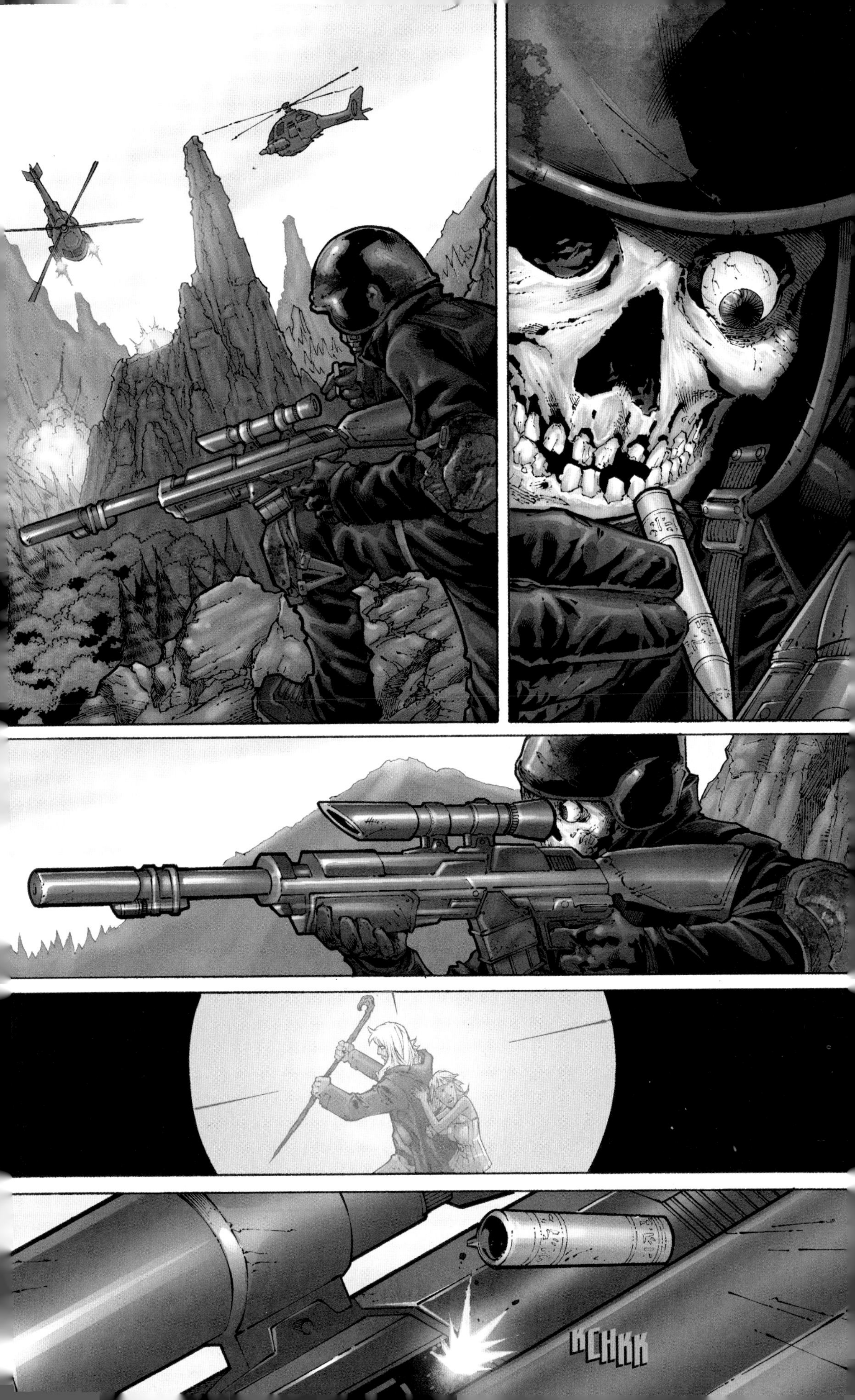
KCHKK

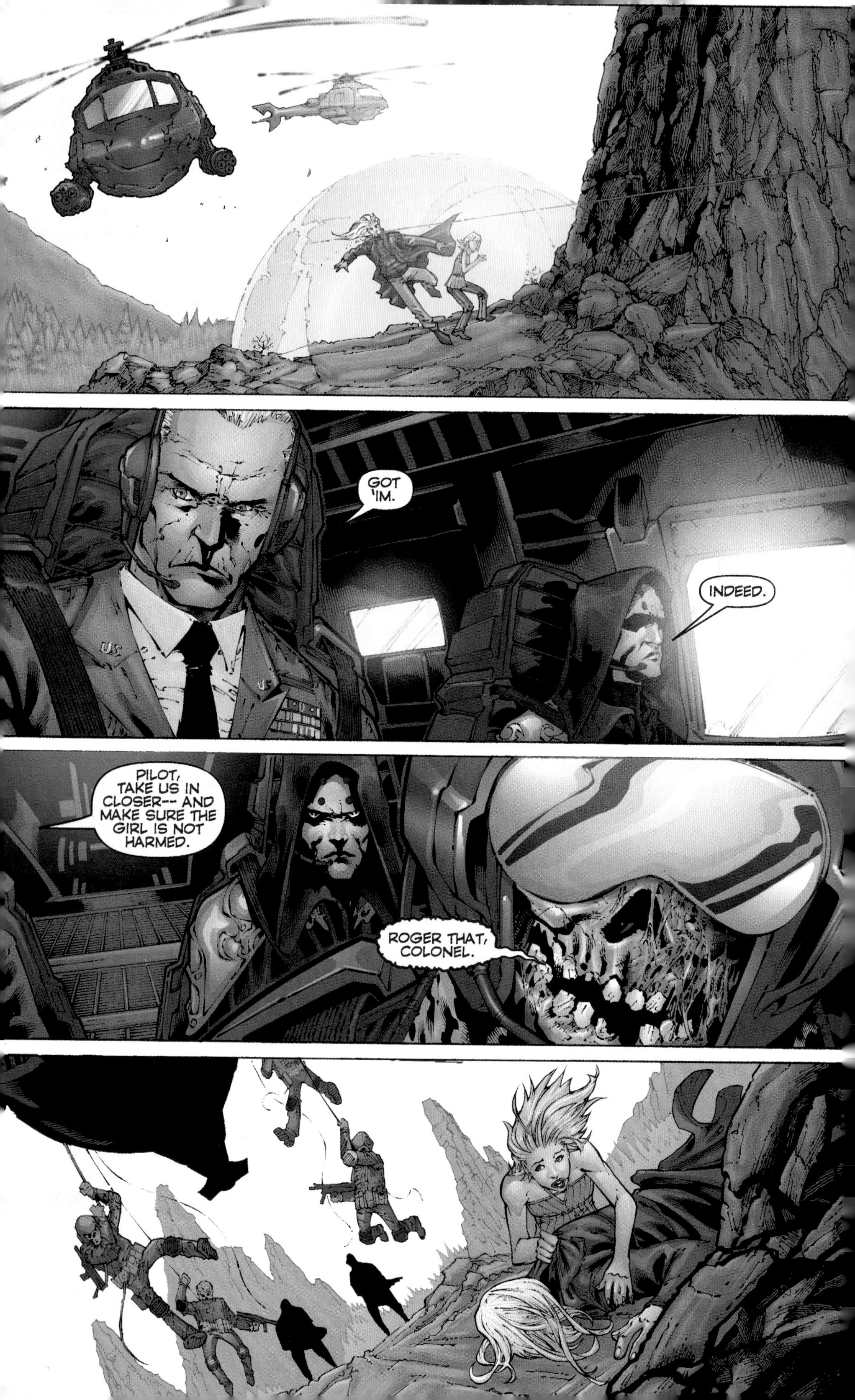
GOT 'IM.
INDEED.
PILOT, TAKE US IN CLOSER-- AND MAKE SURE THE GIRL IS NOT HARMED.
ROGER THAT, COLONEL.

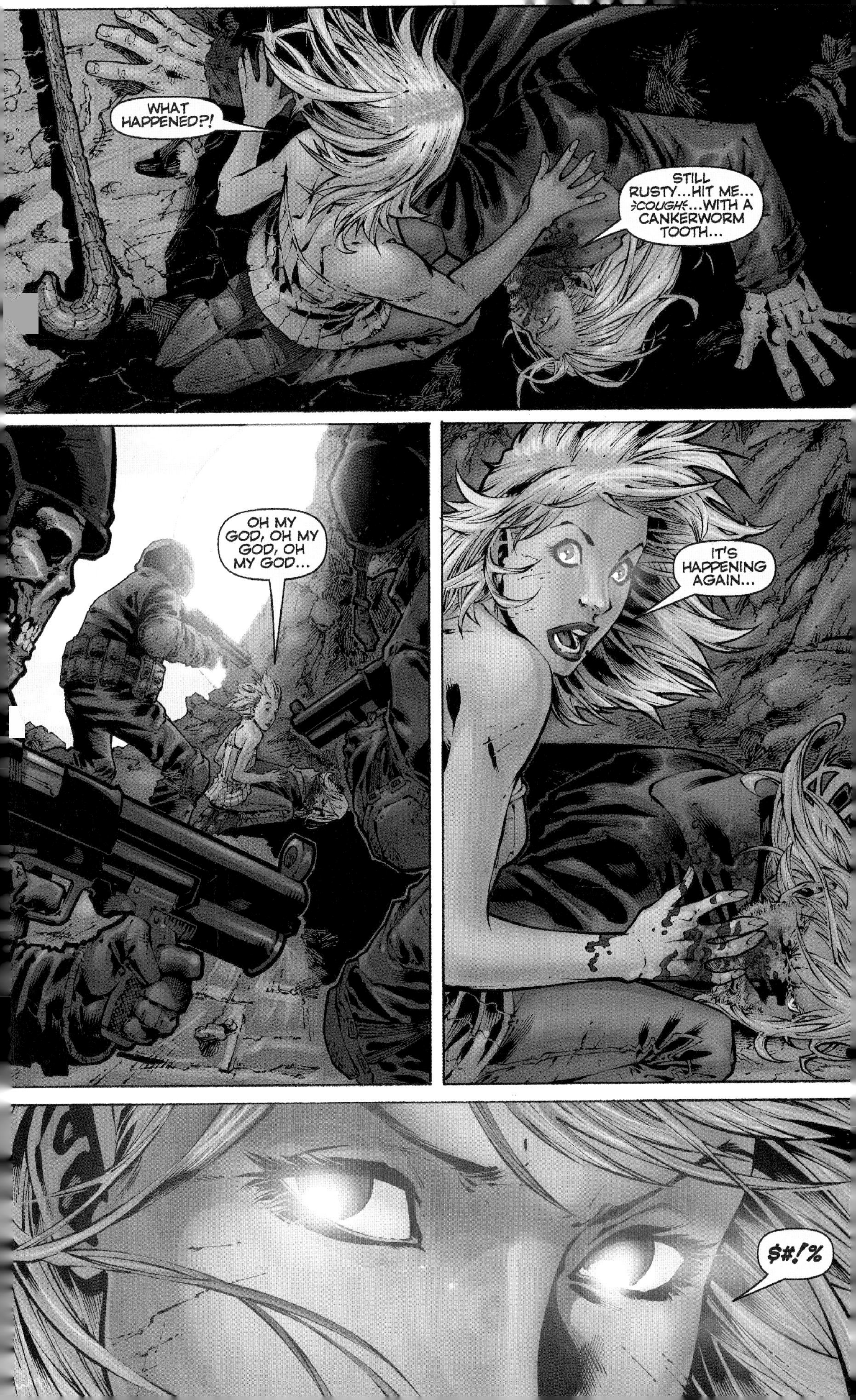
WHAT HAPPENED?!
STILL RUSTY...HIT ME... *COUGH*...WITH A CANKERWORM TOOTH...
OH MY GOD, OH MY GOD, OH MY GOD...
IT'S HAPPENING AGAIN...
$#!%

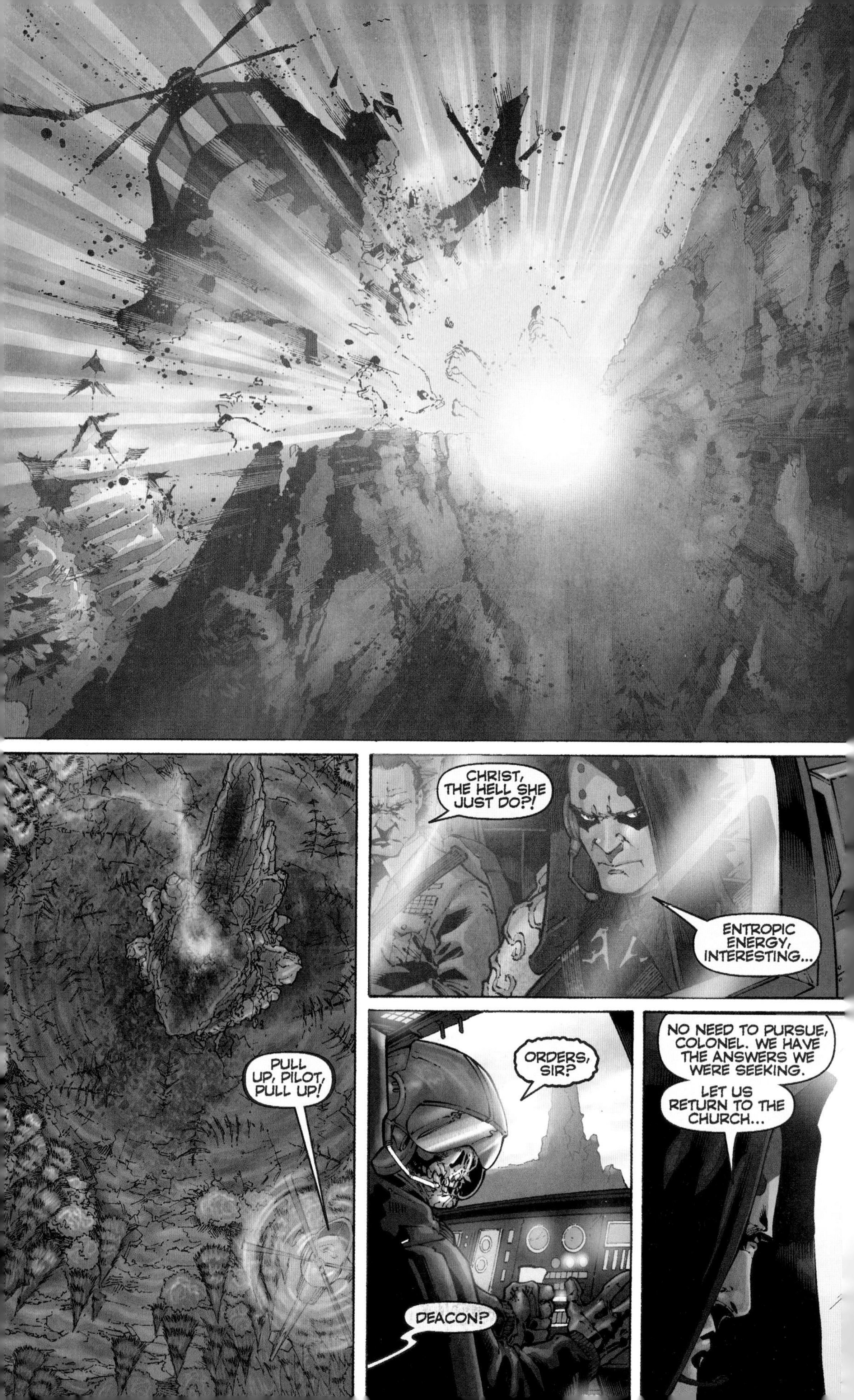

PULL UP, PILOT, PULL UP!
CHRIST, THE HELL SHE JUST DO?!
ENTROPIC ENERGY, INTERESTING...
ORDERS, SIR?
DEACON?
NO NEED TO PURSUE, COLONEL. WE HAVE THE ANSWERS WE WERE SEEKING.
LET US RETURN TO THE CHURCH...

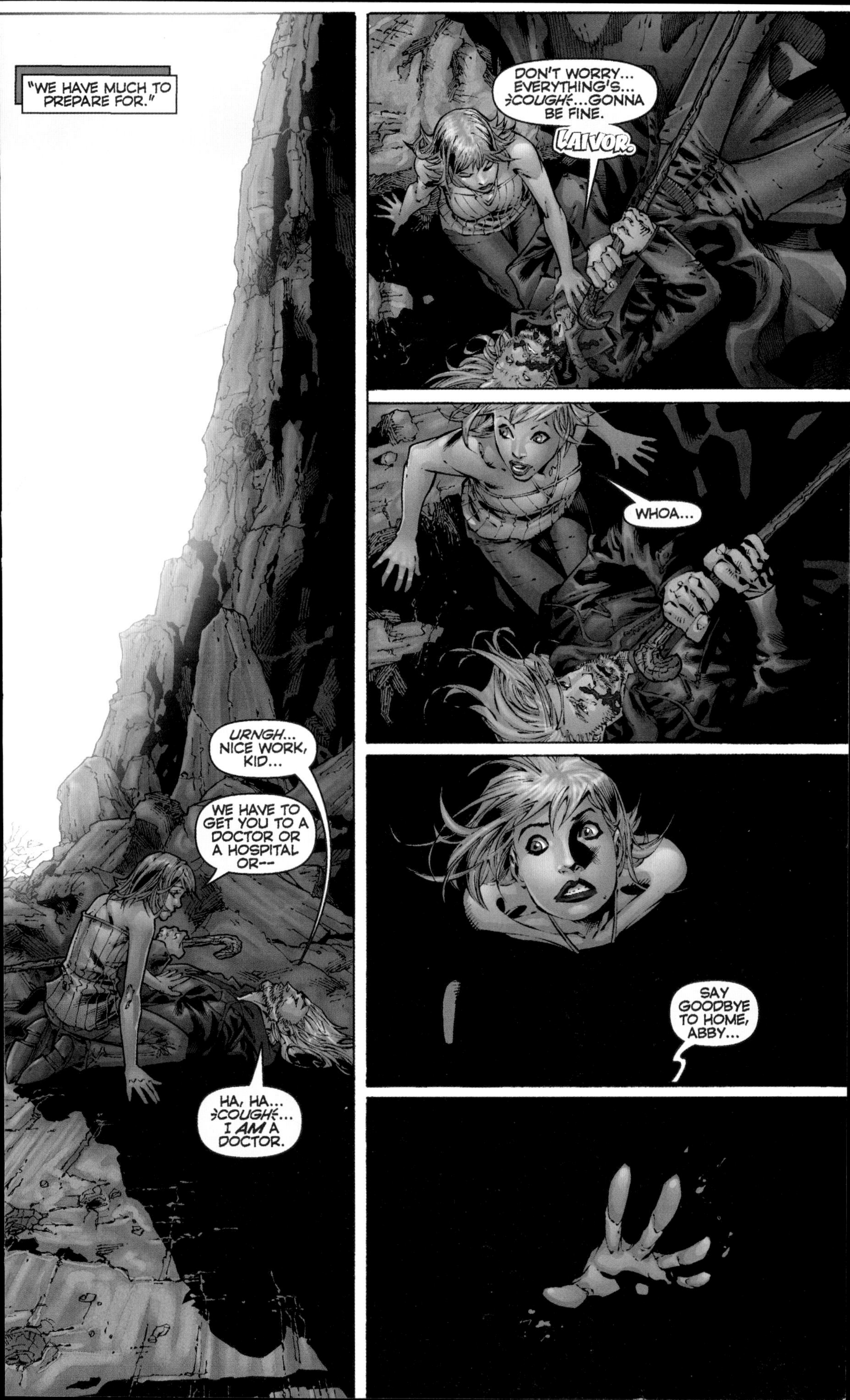

"WE HAVE MUCH TO PREPARE FOR."
URNGH... NICE WORK, KID...
WE HAVE TO GET YOU TO A DOCTOR OR A HOSPITAL OR--
HA, HA... COUGH... I AM A DOCTOR.
DON'T WORRY... EVERYTHING'S... COUGH...GONNA BE FINE.
WHOA...
SAY GOODBYE TO HOME, ABBY...

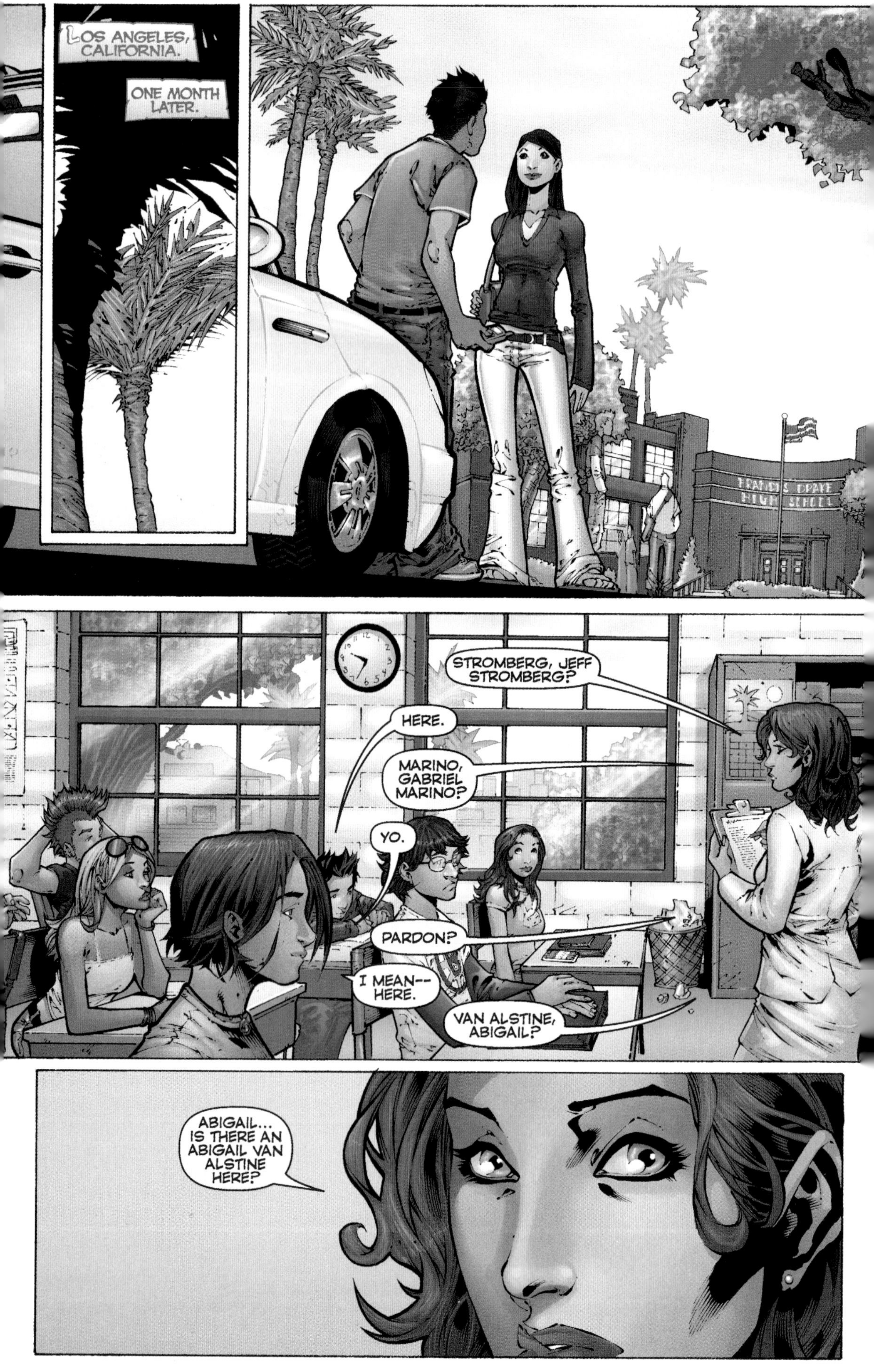
LOS ANGELES, CALIFORNIA.
ONE MONTH LATER.
FRANCIS DRAKE HIGH SCHOOL
STROMBERG, JEFF STROMBERG?
HERE.
MARINO, GABRIEL MARINO?
YO.
PARDON?
I MEAN-- HERE.
VAN ALSTINE, ABIGAIL?
ABIGAIL... IS THERE AN ABIGAIL VAN ALSTINE HERE?

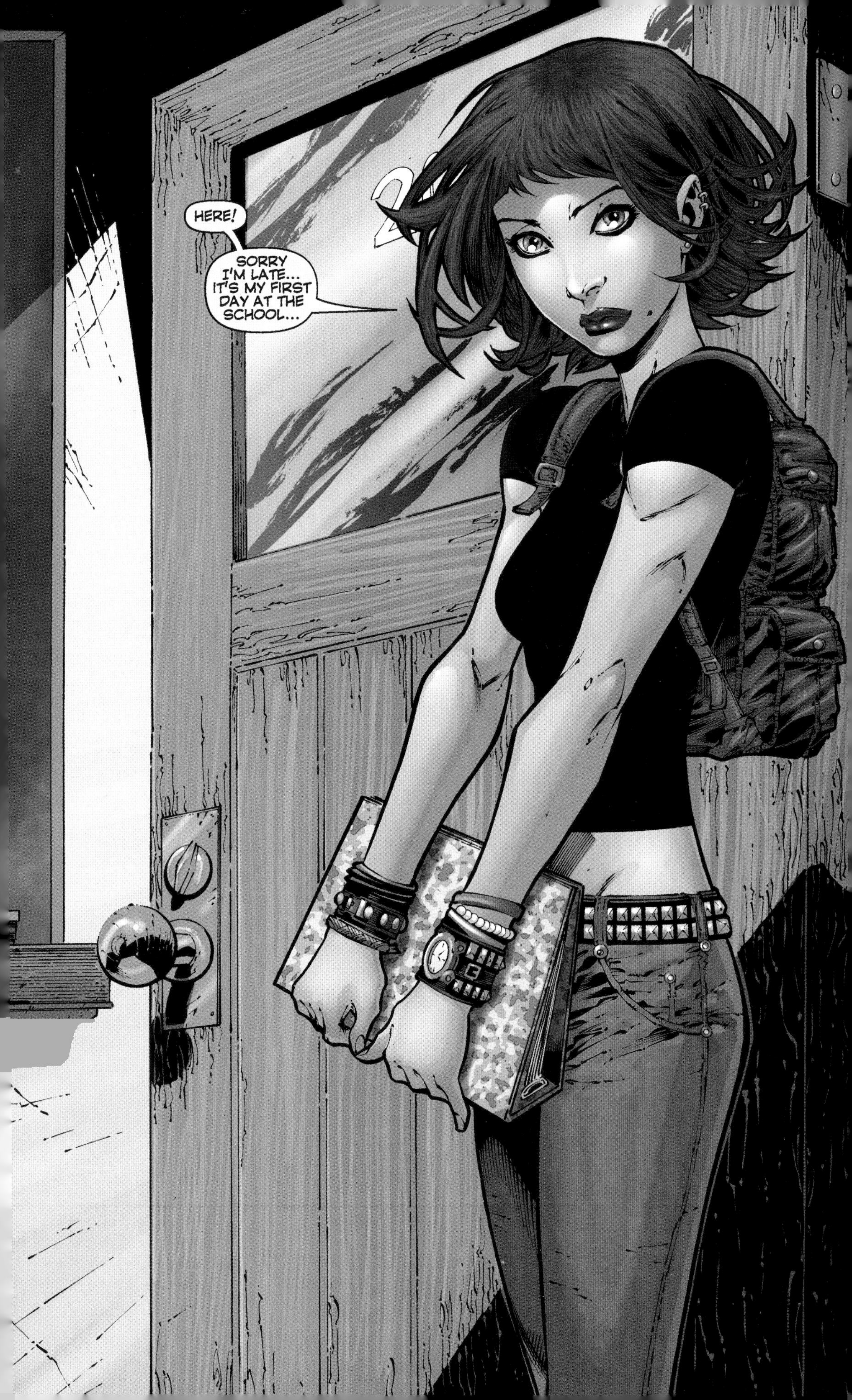
HERE!
SORRY I'M LATE... IT'S MY FIRST DAY AT THE SCHOOL...

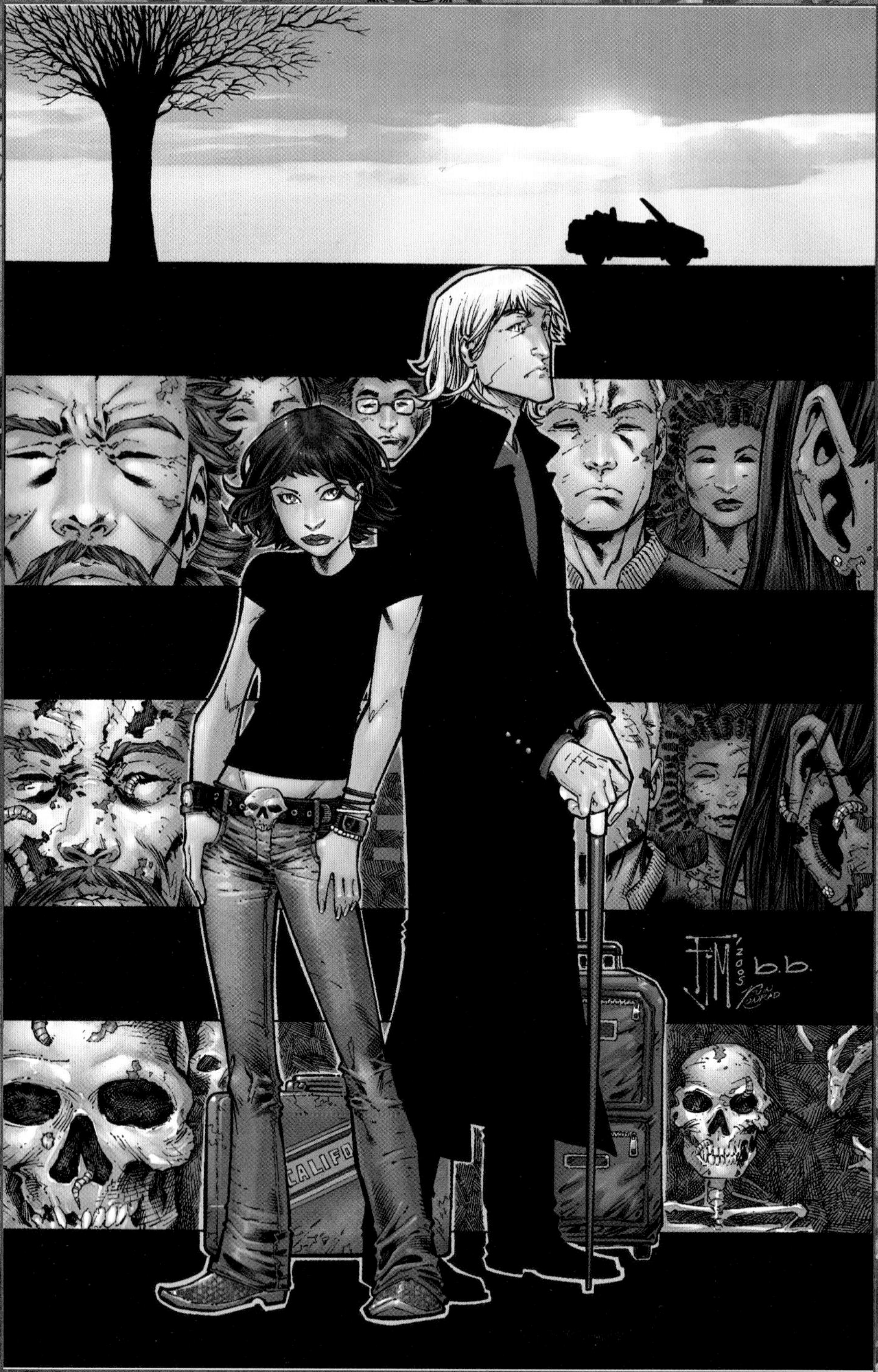

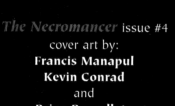

The Necromancer issue #4
cover art by:
Francis Manapul
Kevin Conrad
and
Brian Buccellato

Lithium, Chapter I
issue #4 credits:
written by: **Joshua Ortega**
pencils by: **Francis Manapul**
inks by: **Rob Hunter, Mark Prudeaux**
colors by: **Brian Buccellato, Blond**
letters by: **Troy Peteri**

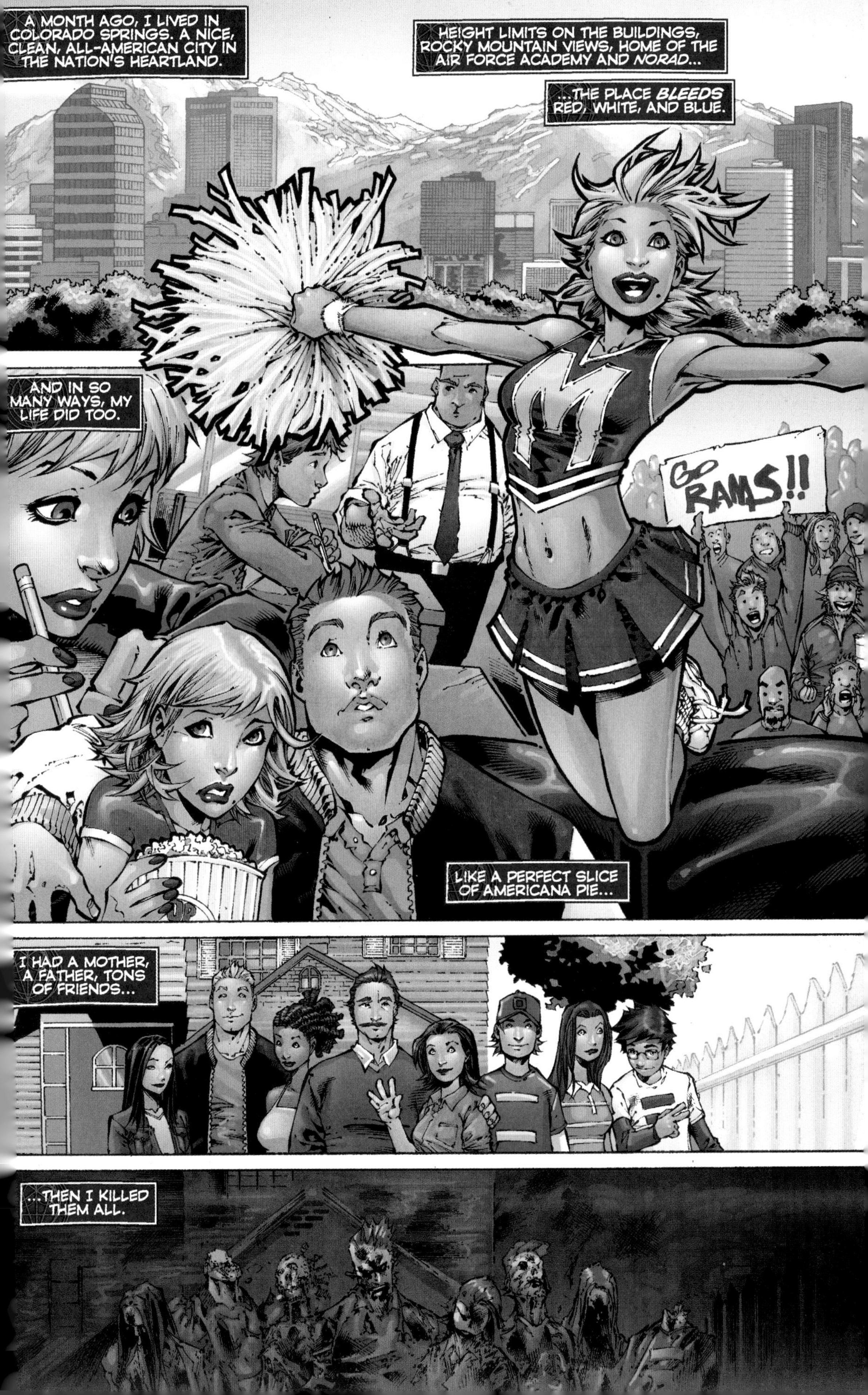
A MONTH AGO, I LIVED IN COLORADO SPRINGS. A NICE, CLEAN, ALL-AMERICAN CITY IN THE NATION'S HEARTLAND.
HEIGHT LIMITS ON THE BUILDINGS, ROCKY MOUNTAIN VIEWS, HOME OF THE AIR FORCE ACADEMY AND NORAD...
...THE PLACE BLEEDS RED, WHITE, AND BLUE.
AND IN SO MANY WAYS, MY LIFE DID TOO.
GO RAMS!!
LIKE A PERFECT SLICE OF AMERICANA PIE...
I HAD A MOTHER, A FATHER, TONS OF FRIENDS...
...THEN I KILLED THEM ALL.

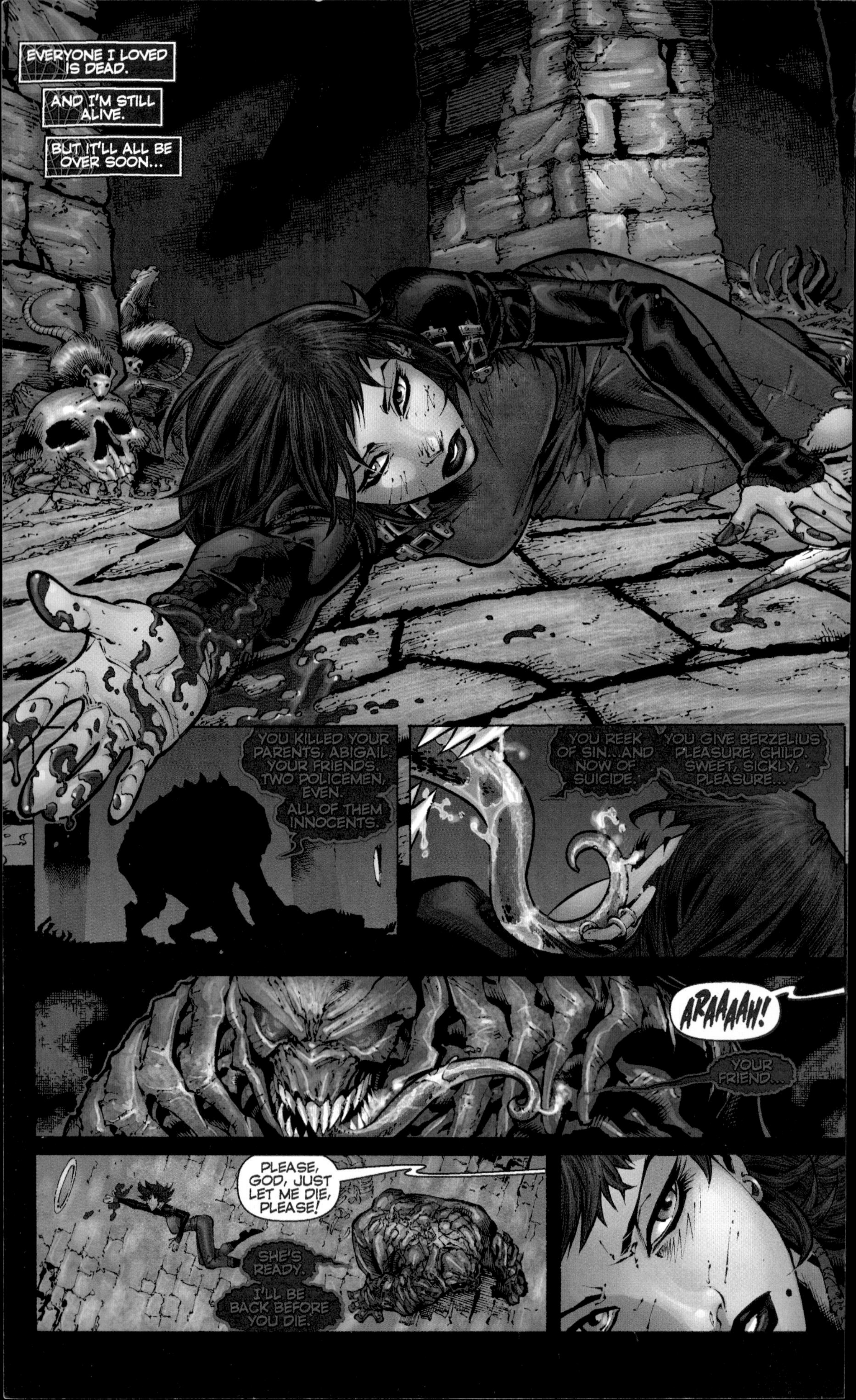
EVERYONE I LOVED IS DEAD.
AND I'M STILL ALIVE.
BUT IT'LL ALL BE OVER SOON...
YOU KILLED YOUR PARENTS, ABIGAIL. YOUR FRIENDS. TWO POLICEMEN, EVEN.
ALL OF THEM INNOCENTS.
YOU REEK OF SIN...AND NOW OF SUICIDE.
YOU GIVE BERZELIUS PLEASURE, CHILD. SWEET, SICKLY, PLEASURE...
ARAAAAH!
YOUR FRIEND...
PLEASE, GOD, JUST LET ME DIE, PLEASE!
SHE'S READY.
I'LL BE BACK BEFORE YOU DIE.

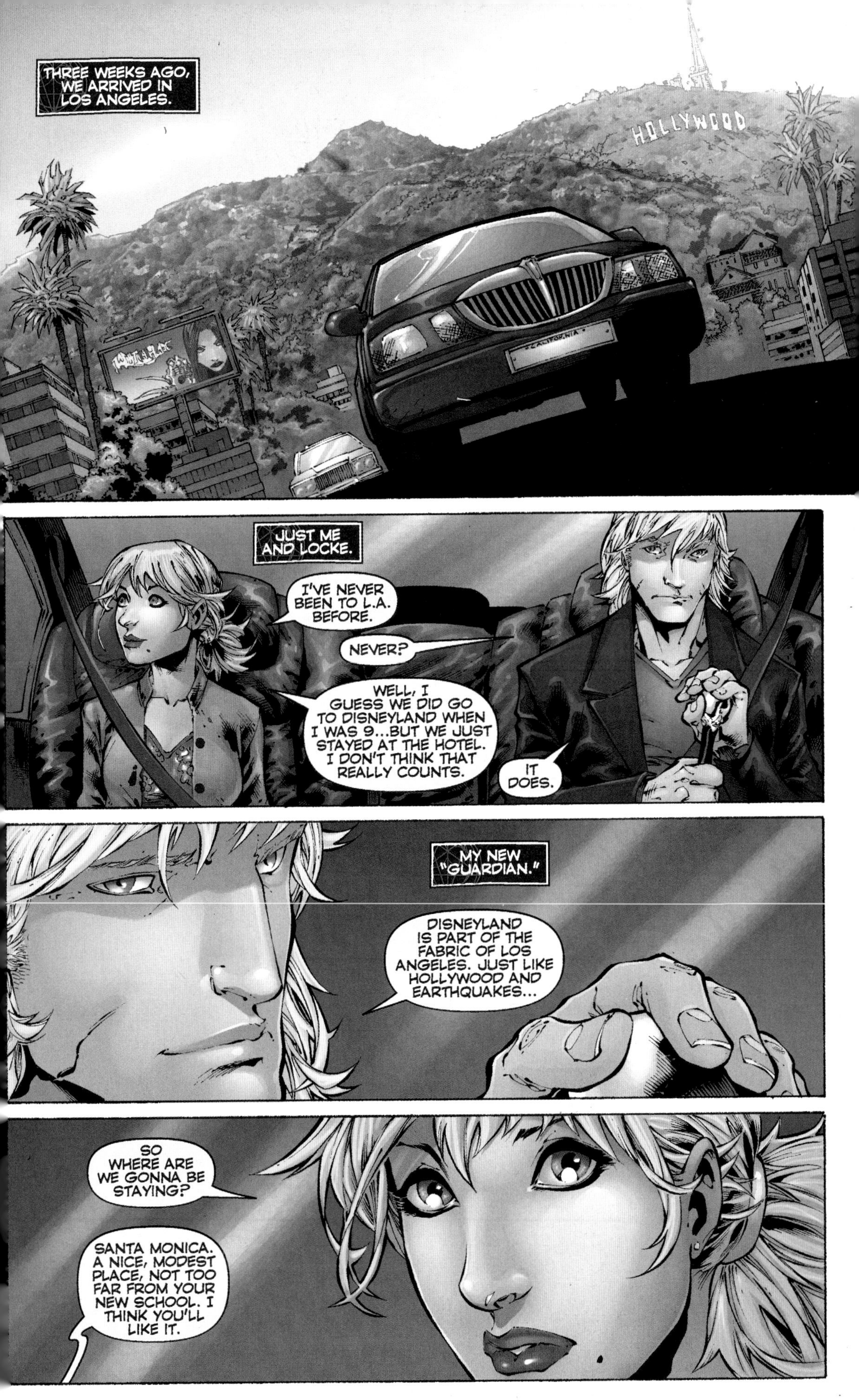
THREE WEEKS AGO, WE ARRIVED IN LOS ANGELES.
HOLLYWOOD
JUST ME AND LOCKE.
I'VE NEVER BEEN TO L.A. BEFORE.
NEVER?
WELL, I GUESS WE DID GO TO DISNEYLAND WHEN I WAS 9...BUT WE JUST STAYED AT THE HOTEL. I DON'T THINK THAT REALLY COUNTS.
IT DOES.
MY NEW "GUARDIAN."
DISNEYLAND IS PART OF THE FABRIC OF LOS ANGELES. JUST LIKE HOLLYWOOD AND EARTHQUAKES...
SO WHERE ARE WE GONNA BE STAYING?
SANTA MONICA. A NICE, MODEST PLACE, NOT TOO FAR FROM YOUR NEW SCHOOL. I THINK YOU'LL LIKE IT.

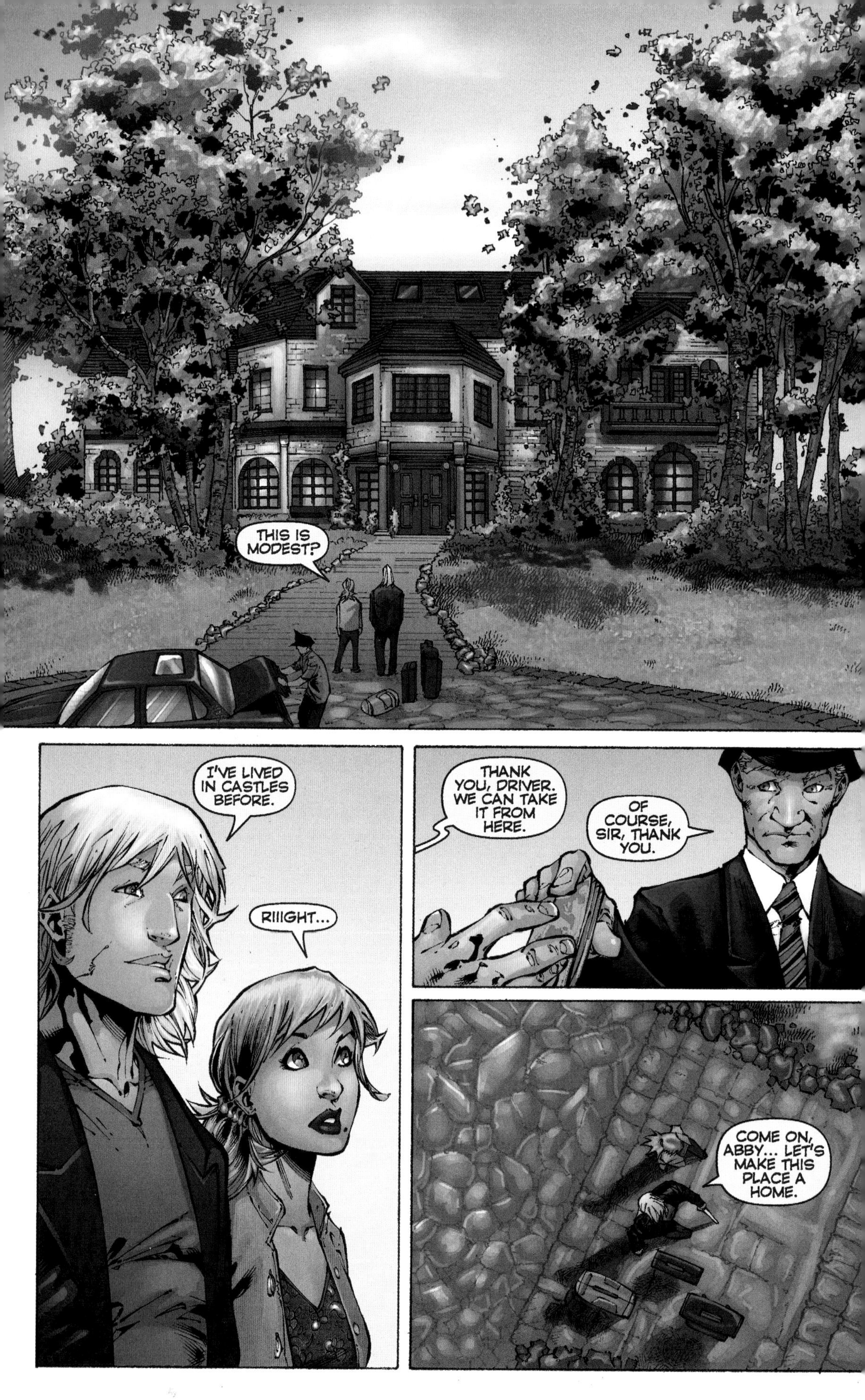
THIS IS MODEST?
I'VE LIVED IN CASTLES BEFORE.
RIIIGHT...
THANK YOU, DRIVER. WE CAN TAKE IT FROM HERE.
OF COURSE, SIR, THANK YOU.
COME ON, ABBY... LET'S MAKE THIS PLACE A HOME.

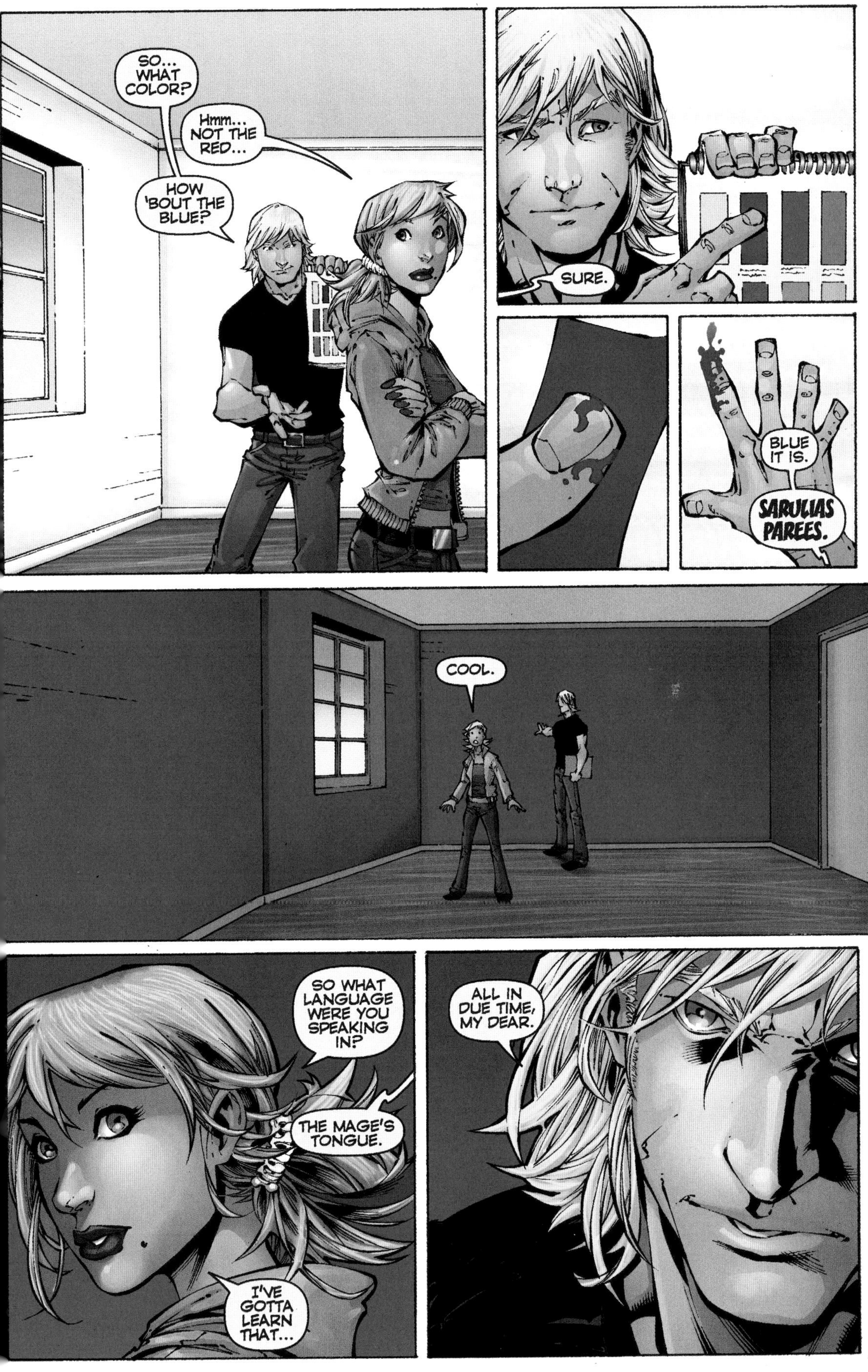
SO... WHAT COLOR?
Hmm... NOT THE RED...
HOW 'BOUT THE BLUE?
SURE.
BLUE IT IS.
SARULIAS PAREES.
COOL.
SO WHAT LANGUAGE WERE YOU SPEAKING IN?
THE MAGE'S TONGUE.
I'VE GOTTA LEARN THAT...
ALL IN DUE TIME, MY DEAR.

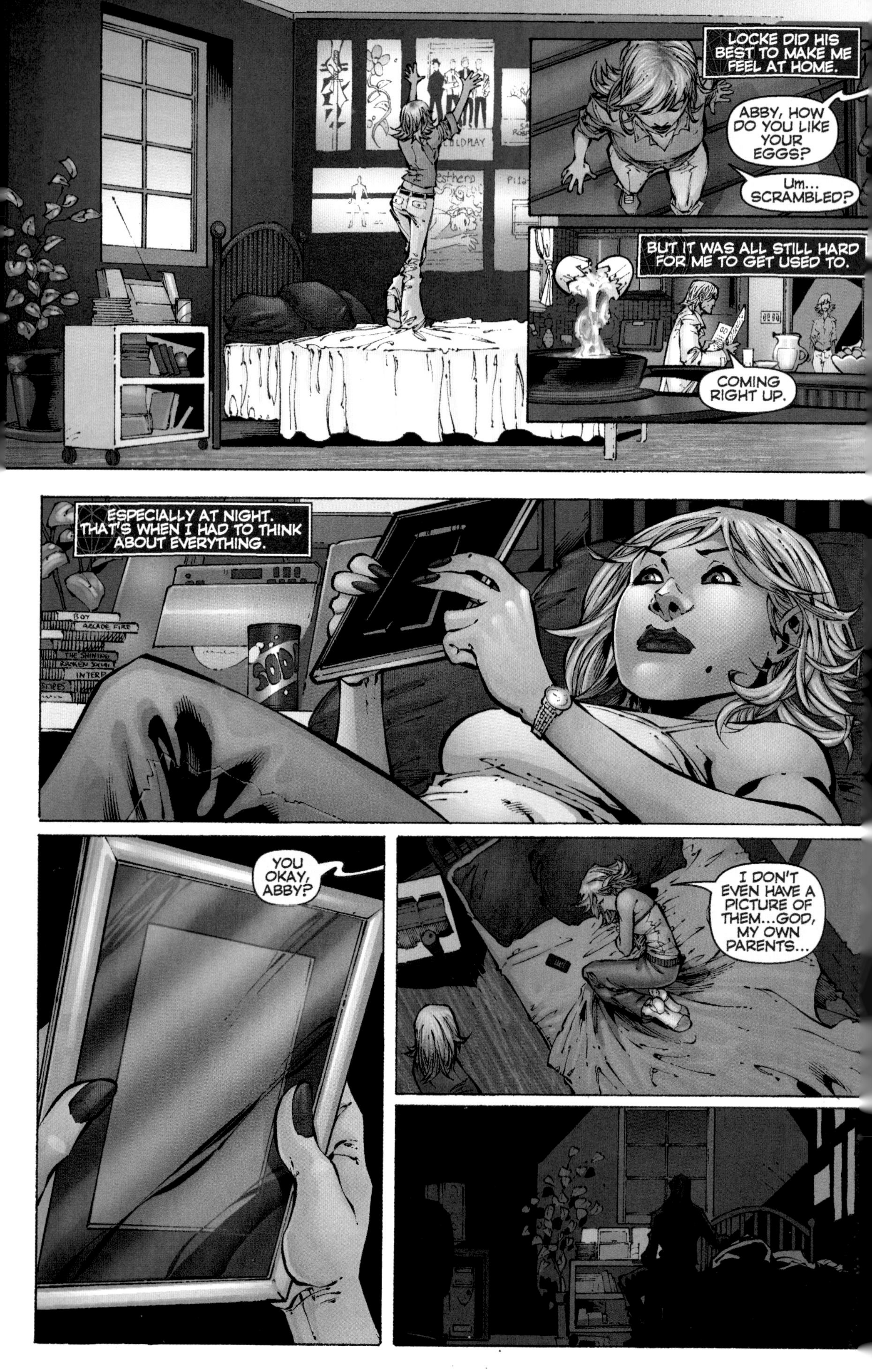
LOCKE DID HIS BEST TO MAKE ME FEEL AT HOME.
ABBY, HOW DO YOU LIKE YOUR EGGS?
Um... SCRAMBLED?
BUT IT WAS ALL STILL HARD FOR ME TO GET USED TO.
COMING RIGHT UP.
ESPECIALLY AT NIGHT. THAT'S WHEN I HAD TO THINK ABOUT EVERYTHING.
YOU OKAY, ABBY?
I DON'T EVEN HAVE A PICTURE OF THEM...GOD, MY OWN PARENTS...

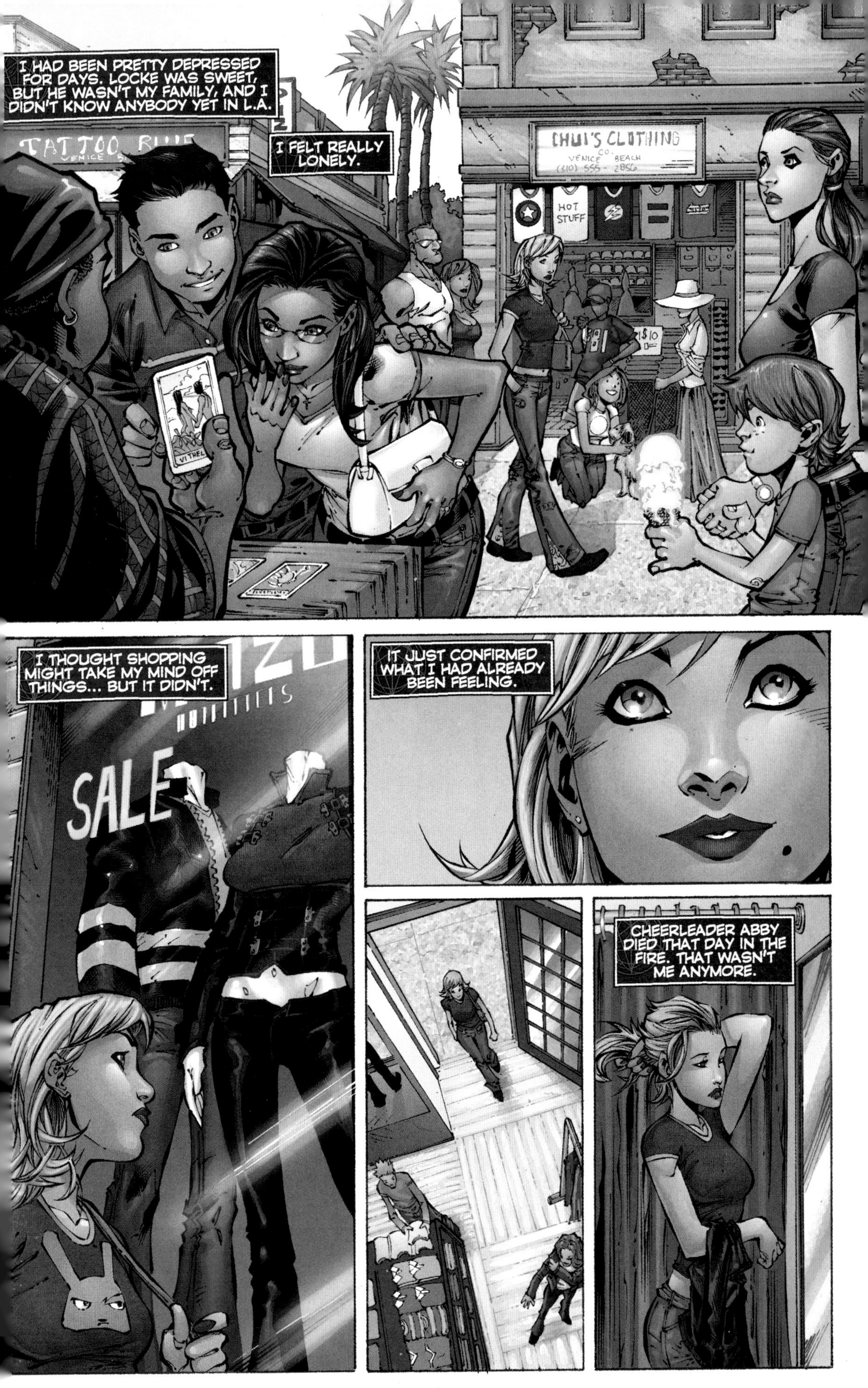
I HAD BEEN PRETTY DEPRESSED FOR DAYS. LOCKE WAS SWEET, BUT HE WASN'T MY FAMILY, AND I DIDN'T KNOW ANYBODY YET IN L.A.
I FELT REALLY LONELY.
TATTOO
CHUI'S CLOTHING CO. VENICE BEACH (310) 555 - 2856
HOT STUFF
$10
I THOUGHT SHOPPING MIGHT TAKE MY MIND OFF THINGS... BUT IT DIDN'T.
SALE
IT JUST CONFIRMED WHAT I HAD ALREADY BEEN FEELING.
CHEERLEADER ABBY DIED THAT DAY IN THE FIRE. THAT WASN'T ME ANYMORE.

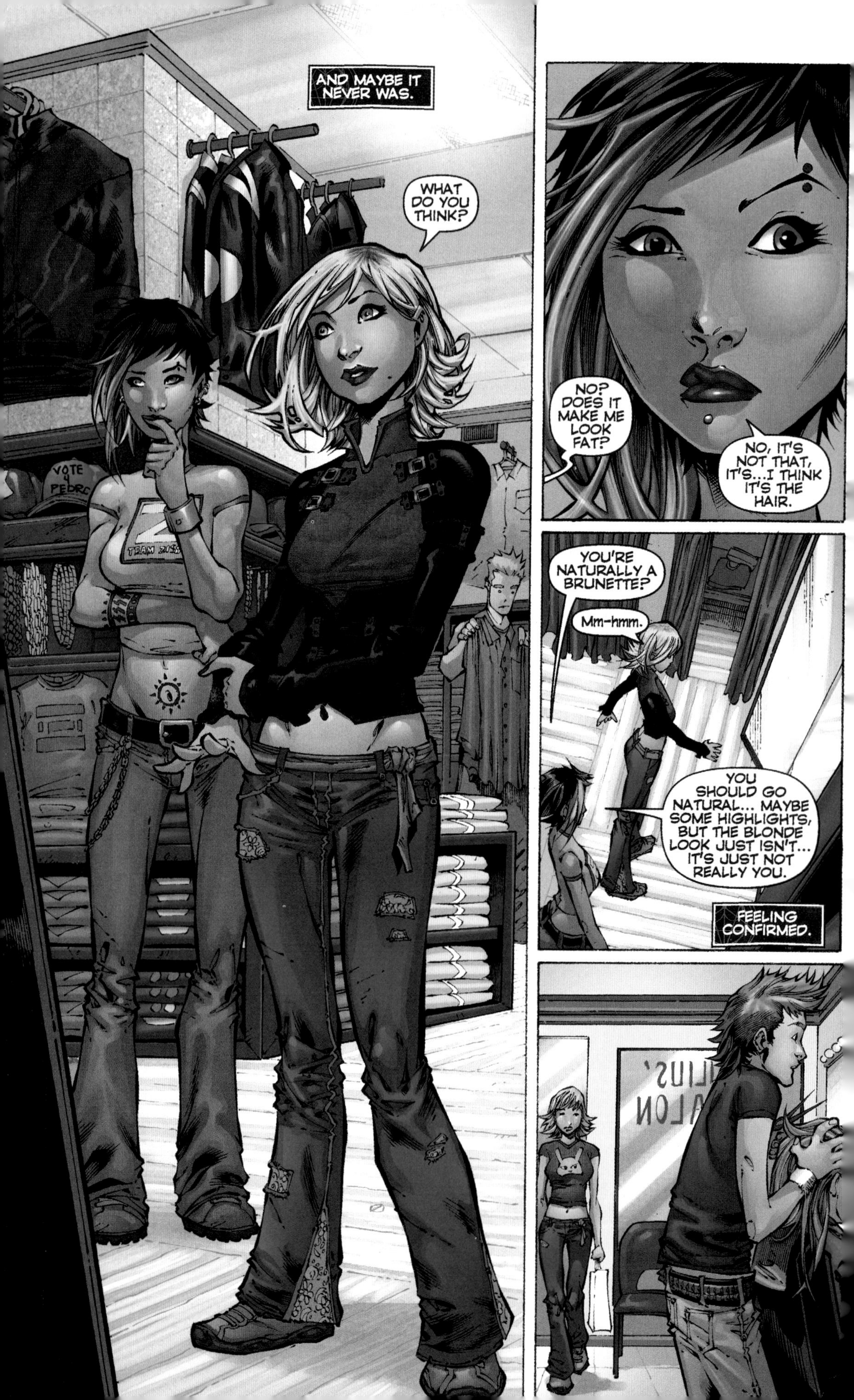
AND MAYBE IT NEVER WAS.
WHAT DO YOU THINK?
VOTE 4 PEDRO
NO? DOES IT MAKE ME LOOK FAT?
NO, IT'S NOT THAT, IT'S...I THINK IT'S THE HAIR.
YOU'RE NATURALLY A BRUNETTE?
Mm-hmm.
YOU SHOULD GO NATURAL... MAYBE SOME HIGHLIGHTS, BUT THE BLONDE LOOK JUST ISN'T... IT'S JUST NOT REALLY YOU.
FEELING CONFIRMED.

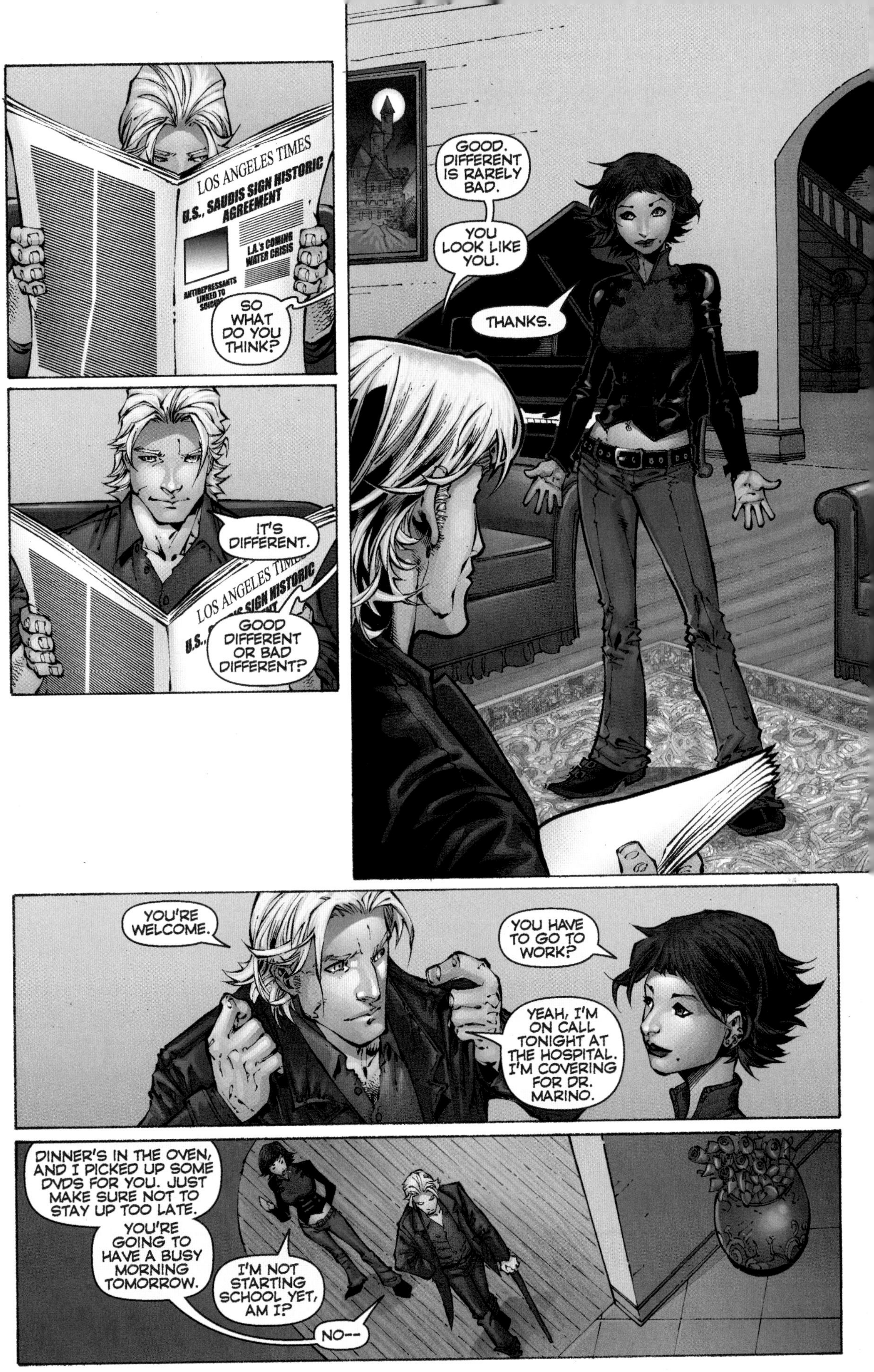
LOS ANGELES TIMES
U.S., SAUDIS SIGN HISTORIC AGREEMENT
L.A.'s COMING WATER CRISIS
ANTIDEPRESSANTS LINKED TO
SO WHAT DO YOU THINK?
IT'S DIFFERENT.
LOS ANGELES TIMES
GOOD DIFFERENT OR BAD DIFFERENT?
GOOD. DIFFERENT IS RARELY BAD.
YOU LOOK LIKE YOU.
THANKS.
YOU'RE WELCOME.
YOU HAVE TO GO TO WORK?
YEAH, I'M ON CALL TONIGHT AT THE HOSPITAL. I'M COVERING FOR DR. MARINO.
DINNER'S IN THE OVEN, AND I PICKED UP SOME DVDS FOR YOU. JUST MAKE SURE NOT TO STAY UP TOO LATE.
YOU'RE GOING TO HAVE A BUSY MORNING TOMORROW.
I'M NOT STARTING SCHOOL YET, AM I?
NO--

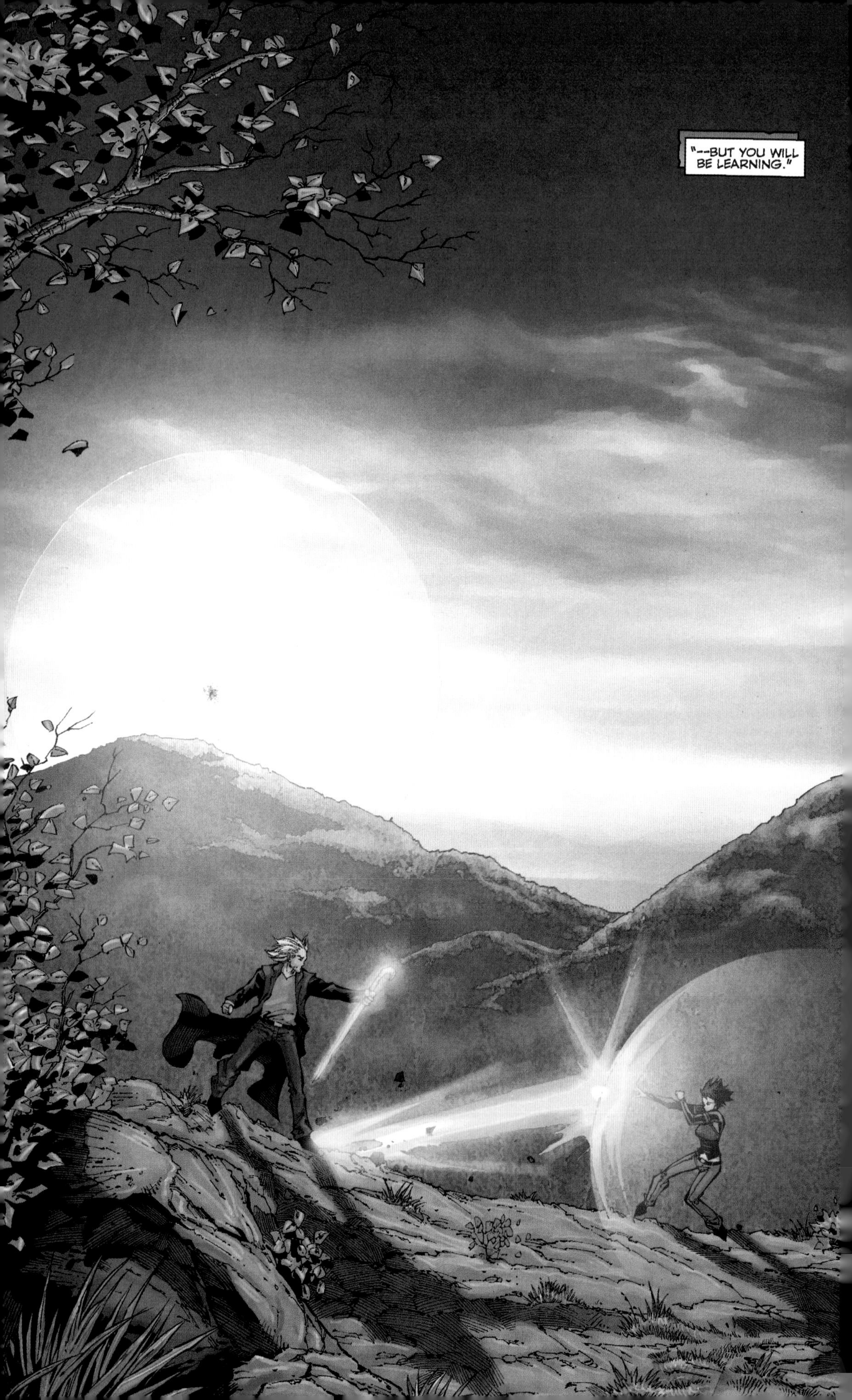
"--BUT YOU WILL BE LEARNING."

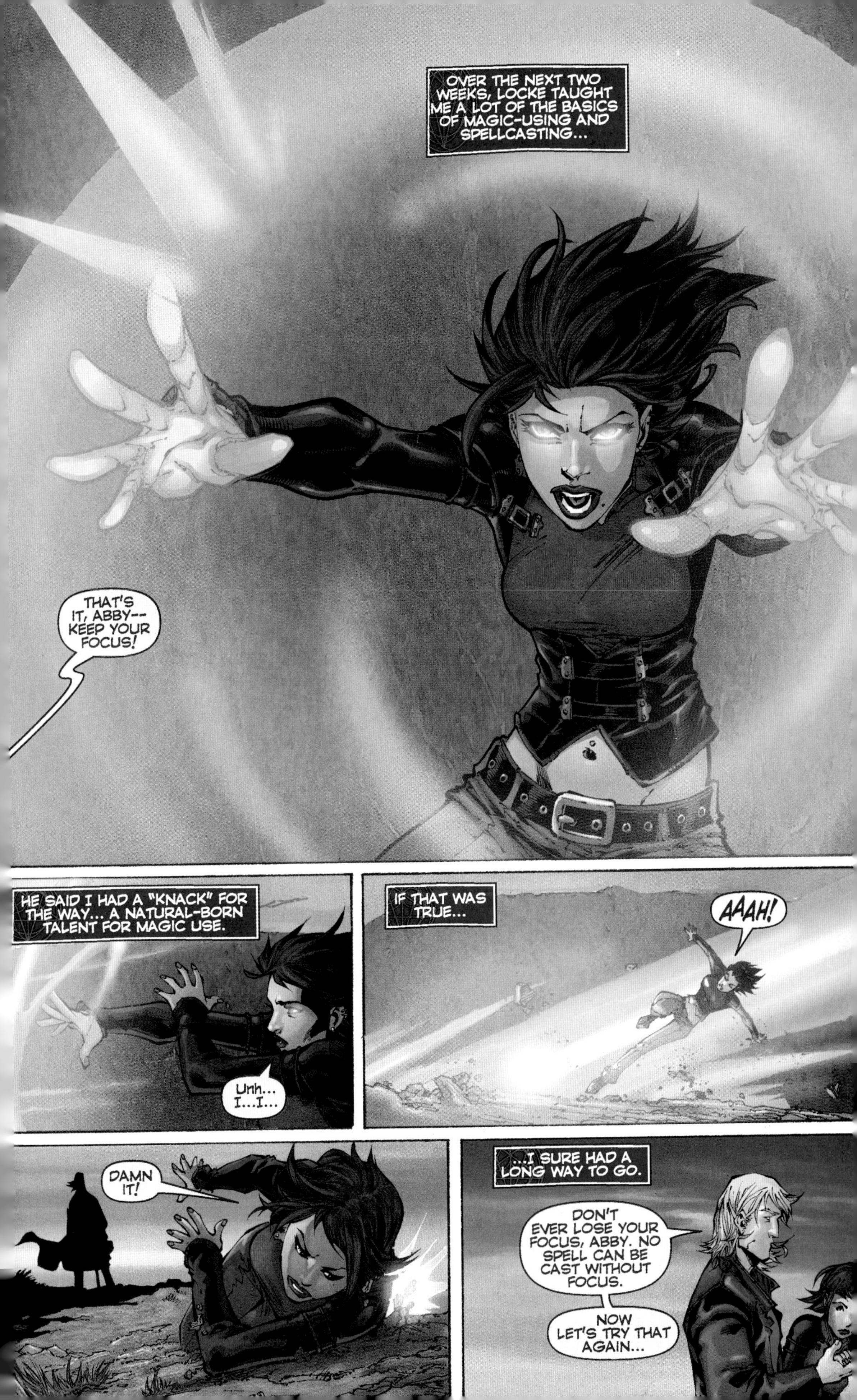
OVER THE NEXT TWO WEEKS, LOCKE TAUGHT ME A LOT OF THE BASICS OF MAGIC-USING AND SPELLCASTING...
THAT'S IT, ABBY-- KEEP YOUR FOCUS!
HE SAID I HAD A "KNACK" FOR THE WAY... A NATURAL-BORN TALENT FOR MAGIC USE.
Unh... I...I...
IF THAT WAS TRUE...
AAAH!
DAMN IT!
...I SURE HAD A LONG WAY TO GO.
DON'T EVER LOSE YOUR FOCUS, ABBY. NO SPELL CAN BE CAST WITHOUT FOCUS.
NOW LET'S TRY THAT AGAIN...

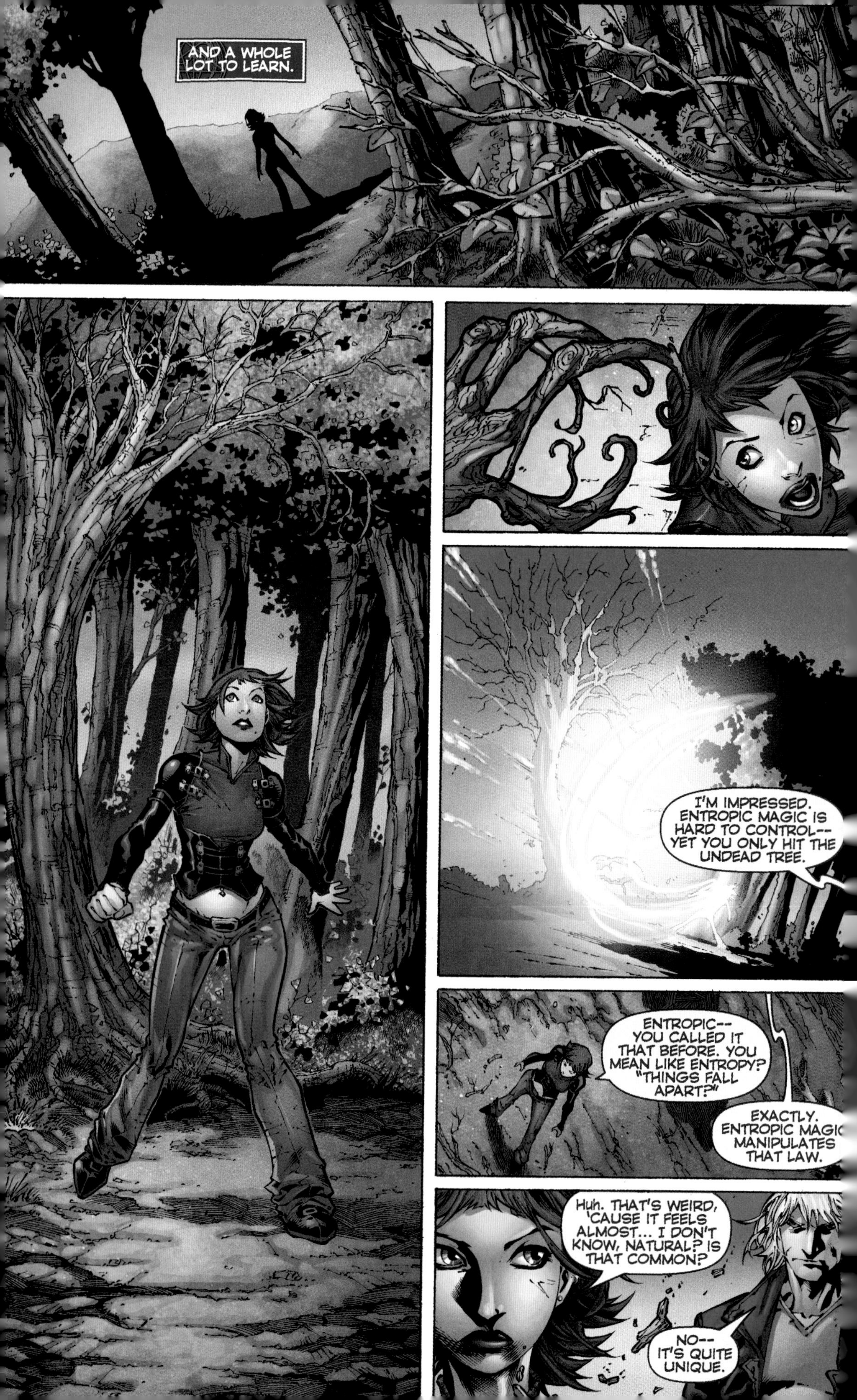
AND A WHOLE LOT TO LEARN.
I'M IMPRESSED. ENTROPIC MAGIC IS HARD TO CONTROL-- YET YOU ONLY HIT THE UNDEAD TREE.
ENTROPIC-- YOU CALLED IT THAT BEFORE. YOU MEAN LIKE ENTROPY? "THINGS FALL APART?"
EXACTLY. ENTROPIC MAGIC MANIPULATES THAT LAW.
Huh. THAT'S WEIRD, 'CAUSE IT FEELS ALMOST... I DON'T KNOW, NATURAL? IS THAT COMMON?
NO-- IT'S QUITE UNIQUE.

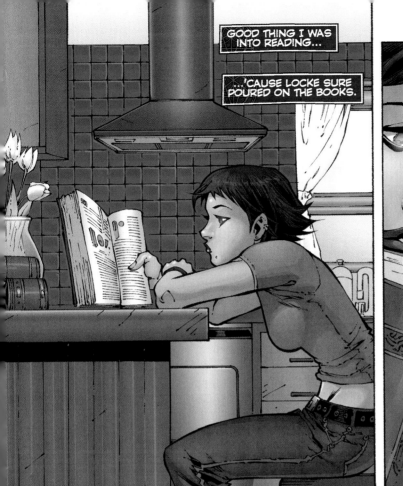

GOOD THING I WAS INTO READING...

...'CAUSE LOCKE SURE POURED ON THE BOOKS.

NICE WORK.

BUT DON'T STAY UP TOO LATE TONIGHT.

‡SIGH‡... MORE MAGIC TRAINING?

NO...

YOU START SCHOOL TOMORROW.

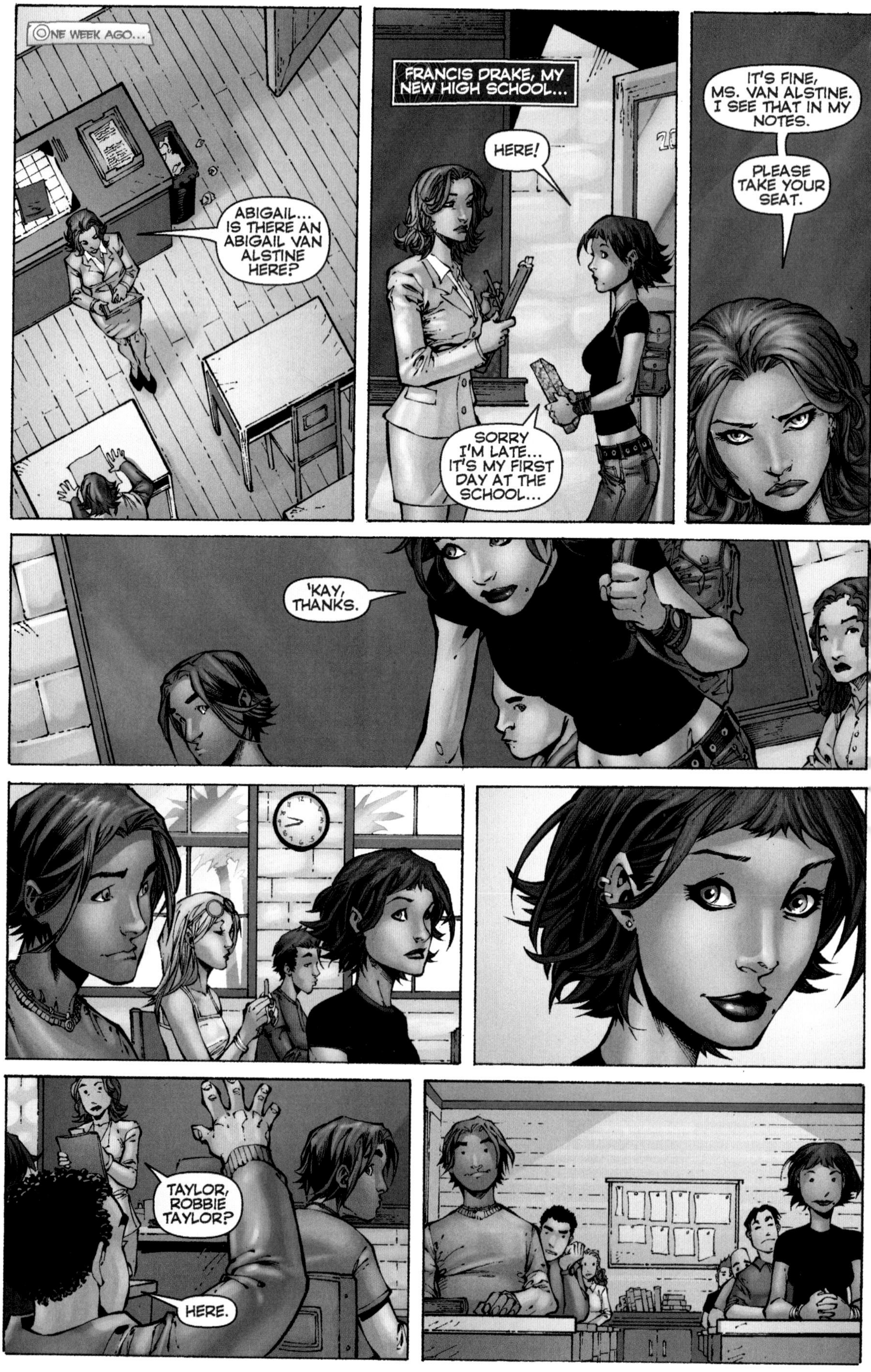
ONE WEEK AGO...
ABIGAIL... IS THERE AN ABIGAIL VAN ALSTINE HERE?
FRANCIS DRAKE, MY NEW HIGH SCHOOL...
HERE!
SORRY I'M LATE... IT'S MY FIRST DAY AT THE SCHOOL...
IT'S FINE, MS. VAN ALSTINE. I SEE THAT IN MY NOTES.
PLEASE TAKE YOUR SEAT.
'KAY, THANKS.
TAYLOR, ROBBIE TAYLOR?
HERE.

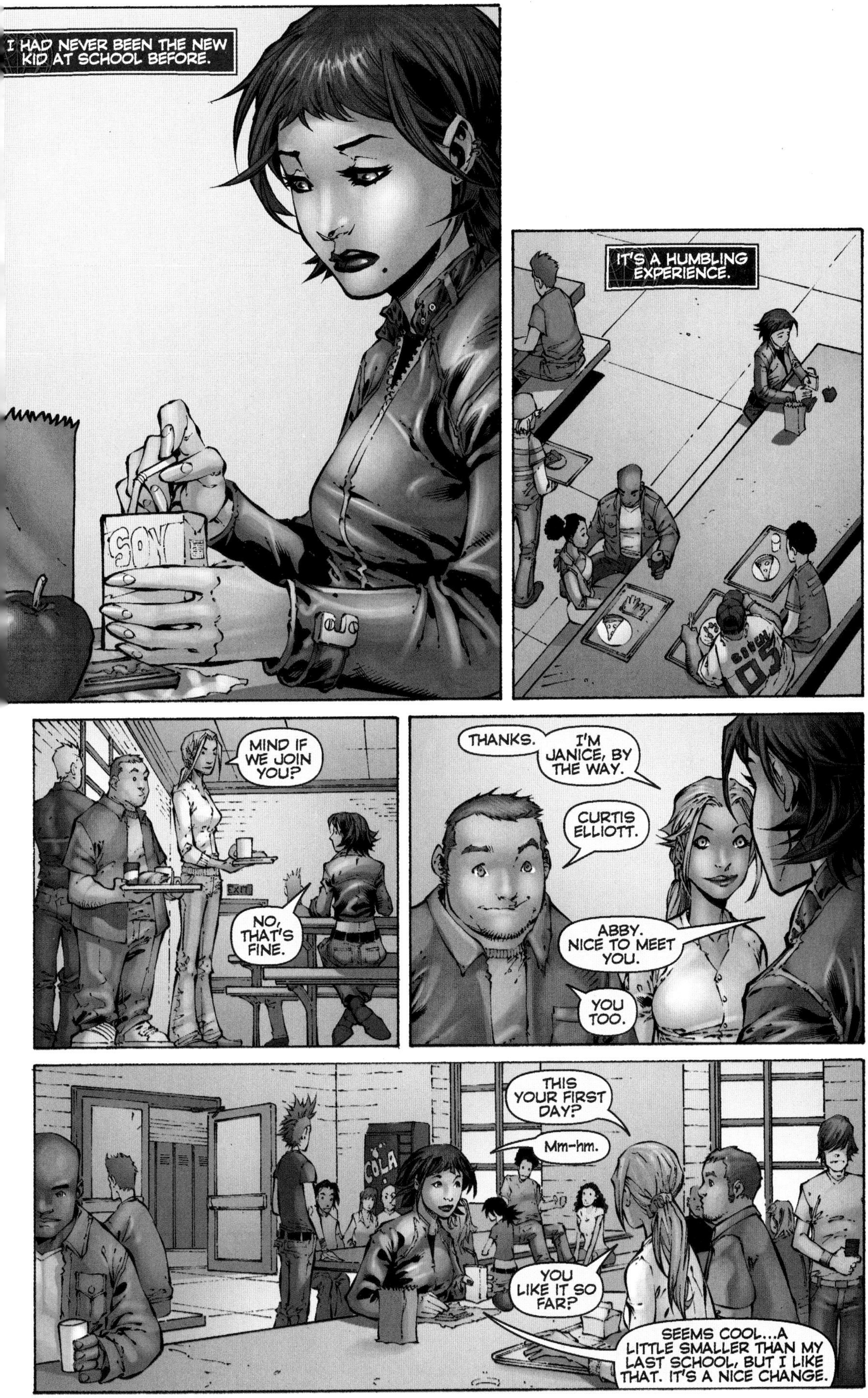
I HAD NEVER BEEN THE NEW KID AT SCHOOL BEFORE.
IT'S A HUMBLING EXPERIENCE.
MIND IF WE JOIN YOU?
NO, THAT'S FINE.
EXIT
THANKS.
I'M JANICE, BY THE WAY.
CURTIS ELLIOTT.
ABBY. NICE TO MEET YOU.
YOU TOO.
THIS YOUR FIRST DAY?
Mm-hm.
COLA
YOU LIKE IT SO FAR?
SEEMS COOL...A LITTLE SMALLER THAN MY LAST SCHOOL, BUT I LIKE THAT. IT'S A NICE CHANGE.

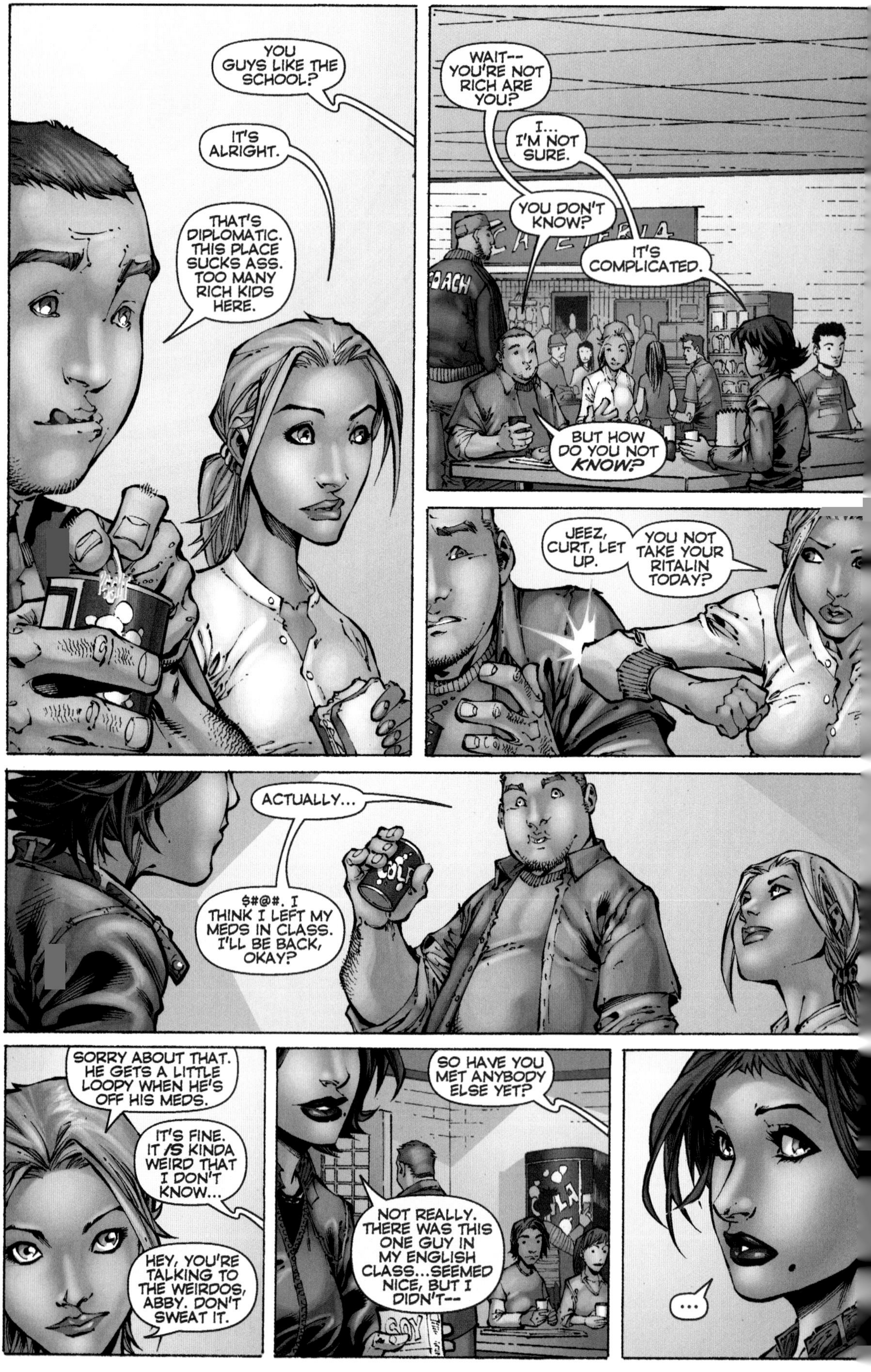
YOU GUYS LIKE THE SCHOOL?
IT'S ALRIGHT.
THAT'S DIPLOMATIC. THIS PLACE SUCKS ASS. TOO MANY RICH KIDS HERE.
WAIT-- YOU'RE NOT RICH ARE YOU?
I... I'M NOT SURE.
YOU DON'T KNOW?
IT'S COMPLICATED.
BUT HOW DO YOU NOT *KNOW?*
COACH
JEEZ, CURT, LET UP.
YOU NOT TAKE YOUR RITALIN TODAY?
ACTUALLY...
$#@#. I THINK I LEFT MY MEDS IN CLASS. I'LL BE BACK, OKAY?
SORRY ABOUT THAT. HE GETS A LITTLE LOOPY WHEN HE'S OFF HIS MEDS.
IT'S FINE. IT *IS* KINDA WEIRD THAT I DON'T KNOW...
HEY, YOU'RE TALKING TO THE WEIRDOS, ABBY. DON'T SWEAT IT.
SO HAVE YOU MET ANYBODY ELSE YET?
NOT REALLY. THERE WAS THIS ONE GUY IN MY ENGLISH CLASS...SEEMED NICE, BUT I DIDN'T--
...

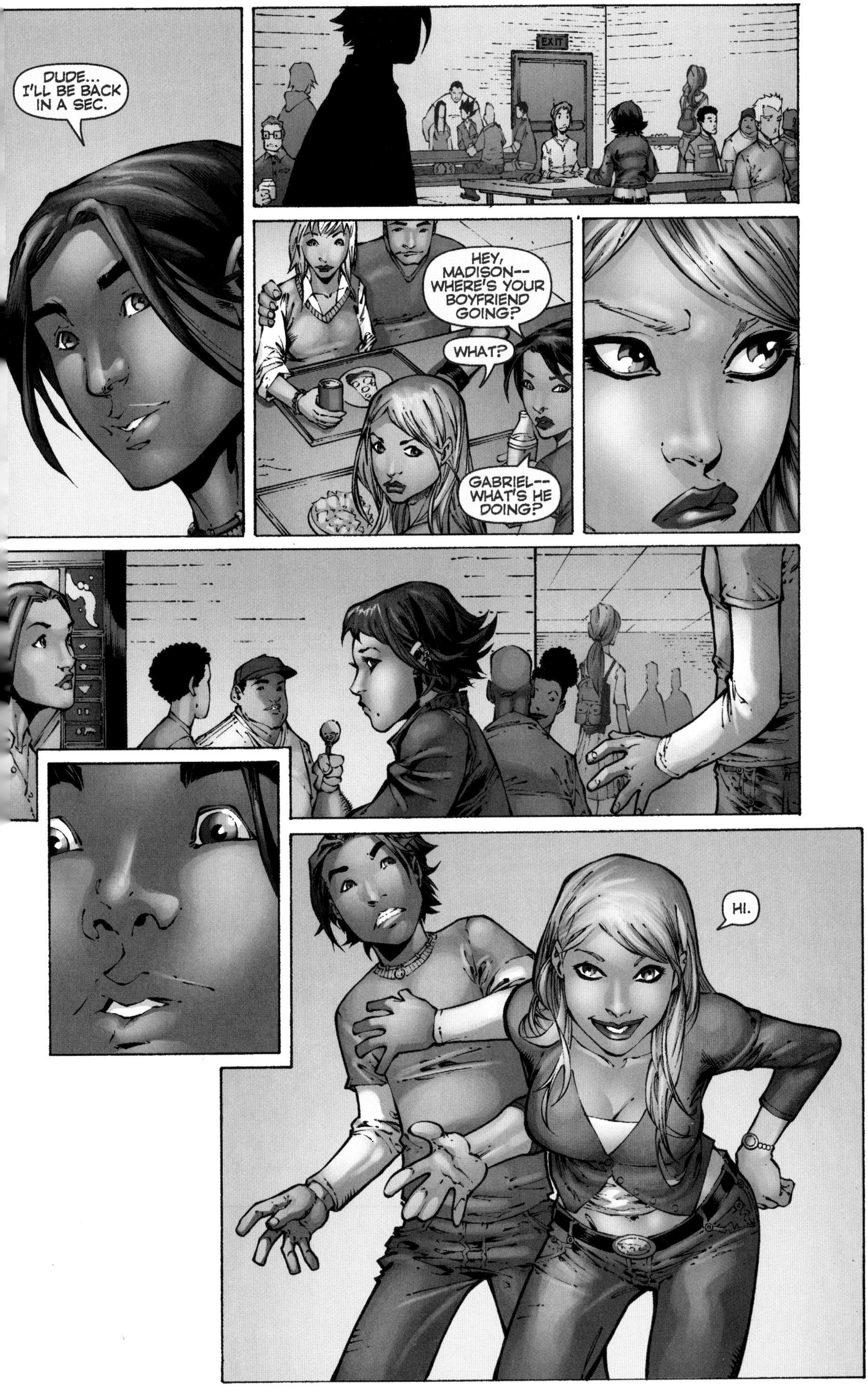
DUDE... I'LL BE BACK IN A SEC.
EXIT
HEY, MADISON-- WHERE'S YOUR BOYFRIEND GOING?
WHAT?
GABRIEL-- WHAT'S HE DOING?
HI.

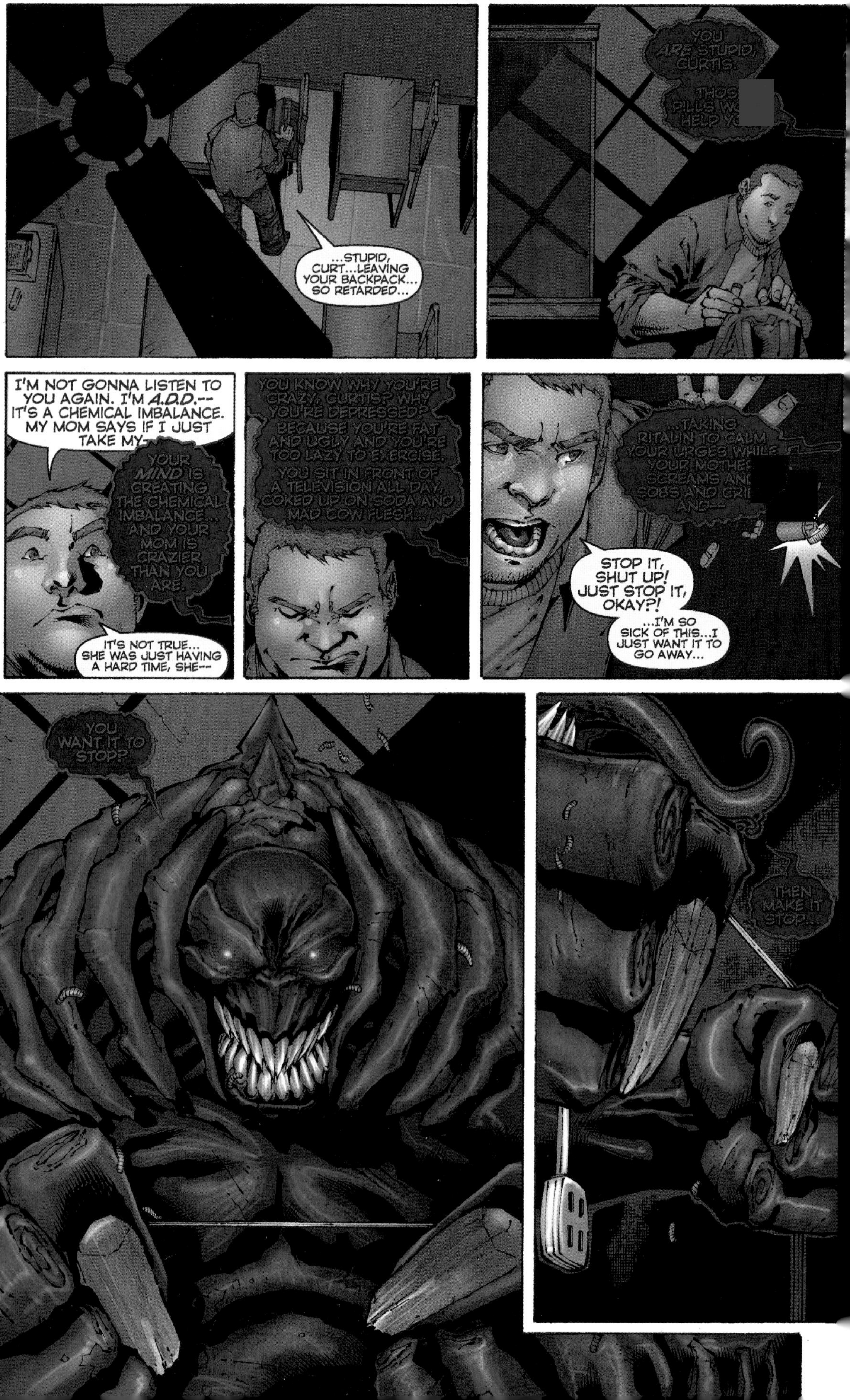
...STUPID, CURT...LEAVING YOUR BACKPACK... SO RETARDED...
YOU ARE STUPID, CURTIS.
THOS[redacted] PILLS W[redacted] HELP Y[redacted]
I'M NOT GONNA LISTEN TO YOU AGAIN. I'M A.D.D.-- IT'S A CHEMICAL IMBALANCE. MY MOM SAYS IF I JUST TAKE MY--
YOUR MIND IS CREATING THE CHEMICAL IMBALANCE... AND YOUR MOM IS CRAZIER THAN YOU ARE.
IT'S NOT TRUE... SHE WAS JUST HAVING A HARD TIME, SHE--
YOU KNOW WHY YOU'RE CRAZY, CURTIS? WHY YOU'RE DEPRESSED? BECAUSE YOU'RE FAT AND UGLY AND YOU'RE TOO LAZY TO EXERCISE.
YOU SIT IN FRONT OF A TELEVISION ALL DAY, COKED UP ON SODA AND MAD COW FLESH...
...TAKING RITALIN TO CALM YOUR URGES WHILE YOUR MOTHE[redacted] SCREAMS AN[redacted] SOBS AND CRI[redacted] AND--
STOP IT, SHUT UP! JUST STOP IT, OKAY?!
...I'M SO SICK OF THIS...I JUST WANT IT TO GO AWAY...
YOU WANT IT TO STOP?
THEN MAKE IT STOP...

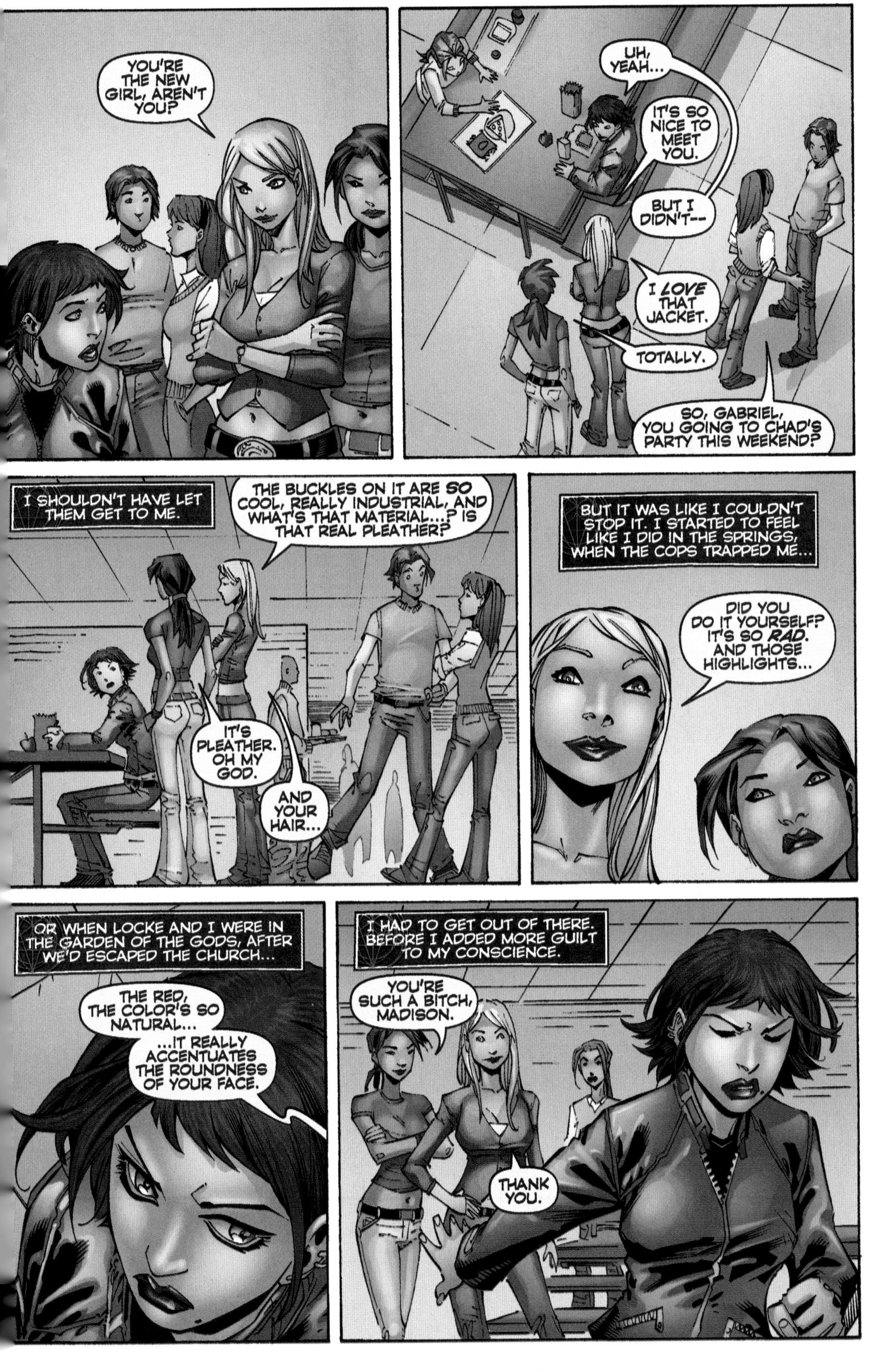
YOU'RE THE NEW GIRL, AREN'T YOU?
UH, YEAH...
IT'S SO NICE TO MEET YOU.
BUT I DIDN'T--
I LOVE THAT JACKET.
TOTALLY.
SO, GABRIEL, YOU GOING TO CHAD'S PARTY THIS WEEKEND?
I SHOULDN'T HAVE LET THEM GET TO ME.
THE BUCKLES ON IT ARE SO COOL, REALLY INDUSTRIAL, AND WHAT'S THAT MATERIAL...? IS THAT REAL PLEATHER?
IT'S PLEATHER. OH MY GOD.
AND YOUR HAIR...
BUT IT WAS LIKE I COULDN'T STOP IT. I STARTED TO FEEL LIKE I DID IN THE SPRINGS, WHEN THE COPS TRAPPED ME...
DID YOU DO IT YOURSELF? IT'S SO RAD. AND THOSE HIGHLIGHTS...
OR WHEN LOCKE AND I WERE IN THE GARDEN OF THE GODS, AFTER WE'D ESCAPED THE CHURCH...
THE RED, THE COLOR'S SO NATURAL...
...IT REALLY ACCENTUATES THE ROUNDNESS OF YOUR FACE.
I HAD TO GET OUT OF THERE. BEFORE I ADDED MORE GUILT TO MY CONSCIENCE.
YOU'RE SUCH A BITCH, MADISON.
THANK YOU.

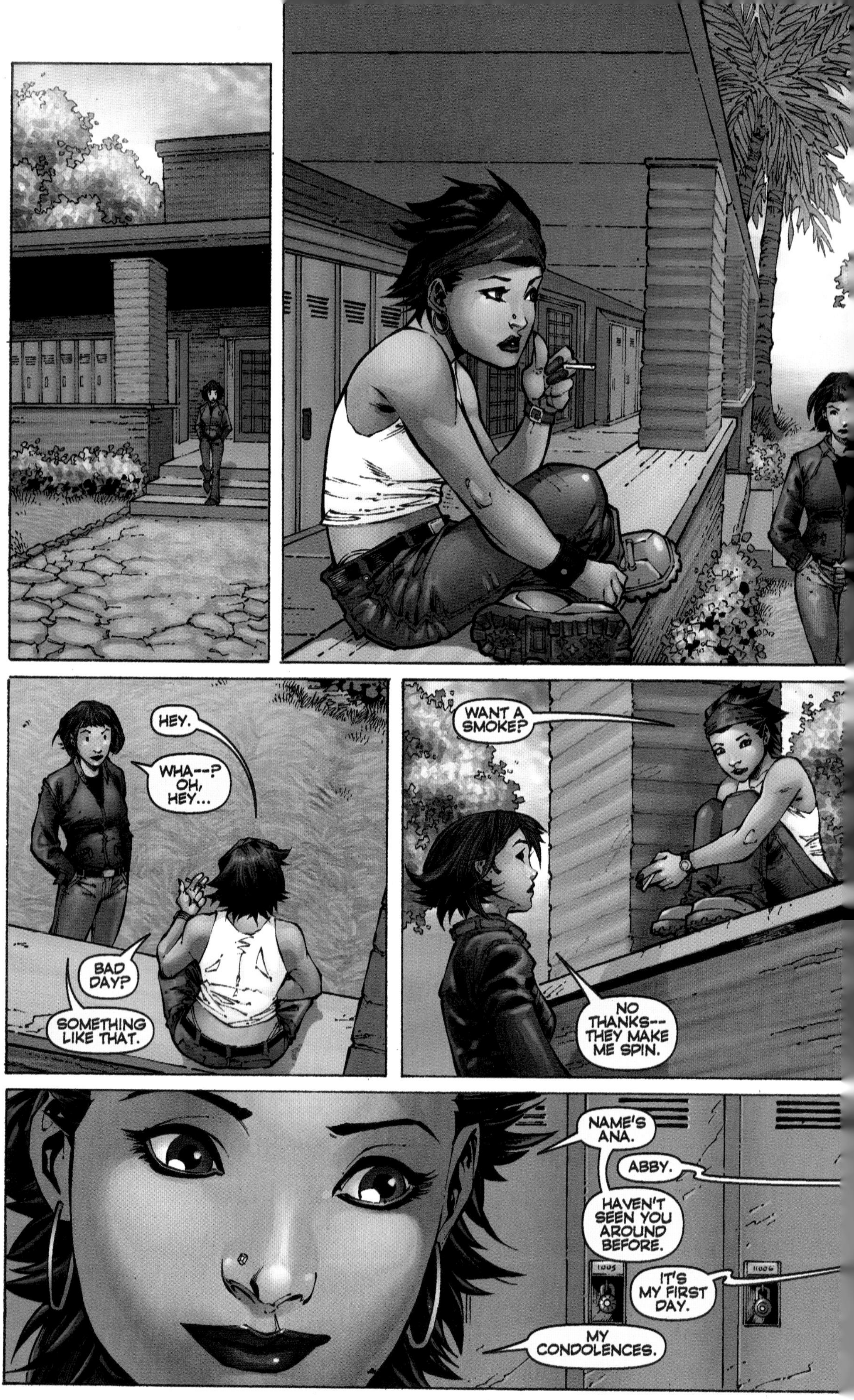
HEY.
WHA--? OH, HEY...
BAD DAY?
SOMETHING LIKE THAT.
WANT A SMOKE?
NO THANKS-- THEY MAKE ME SPIN.
NAME'S ANA.
ABBY.
HAVEN'T SEEN YOU AROUND BEFORE.
IT'S MY FIRST DAY.
MY CONDOLENCES.

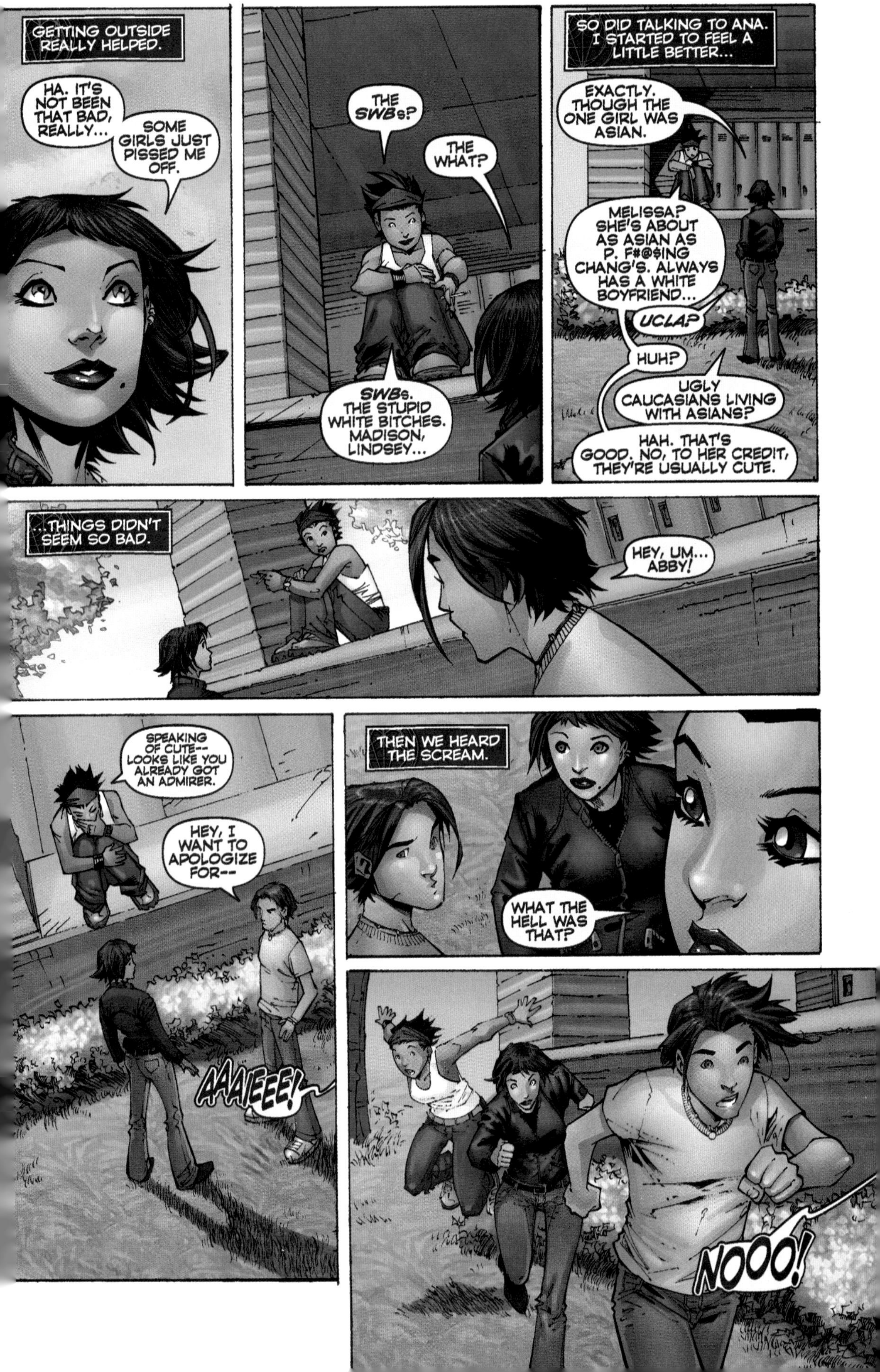
GETTING OUTSIDE REALLY HELPED.
HA. IT'S NOT BEEN THAT BAD, REALLY...
SOME GIRLS JUST PISSED ME OFF.
THE SWBs?
THE WHAT?
SWBs. THE STUPID WHITE BITCHES. MADISON, LINDSEY...
SO DID TALKING TO ANA. I STARTED TO FEEL A LITTLE BETTER...
EXACTLY. THOUGH THE ONE GIRL WAS ASIAN.
MELISSA? SHE'S ABOUT AS ASIAN AS P. F#@$ING CHANG'S. ALWAYS HAS A WHITE BOYFRIEND...
UCLA?
HUH?
UGLY CAUCASIANS LIVING WITH ASIANS?
HAH. THAT'S GOOD. NO, TO HER CREDIT, THEY'RE USUALLY CUTE.
...THINGS DIDN'T SEEM SO BAD.
HEY, UM... ABBY!
SPEAKING OF CUTE-- LOOKS LIKE YOU ALREADY GOT AN ADMIRER.
HEY, I WANT TO APOLOGIZE FOR--
AAAIEEE!
THEN WE HEARD THE SCREAM.
WHAT THE HELL WAS THAT?
NOOO!

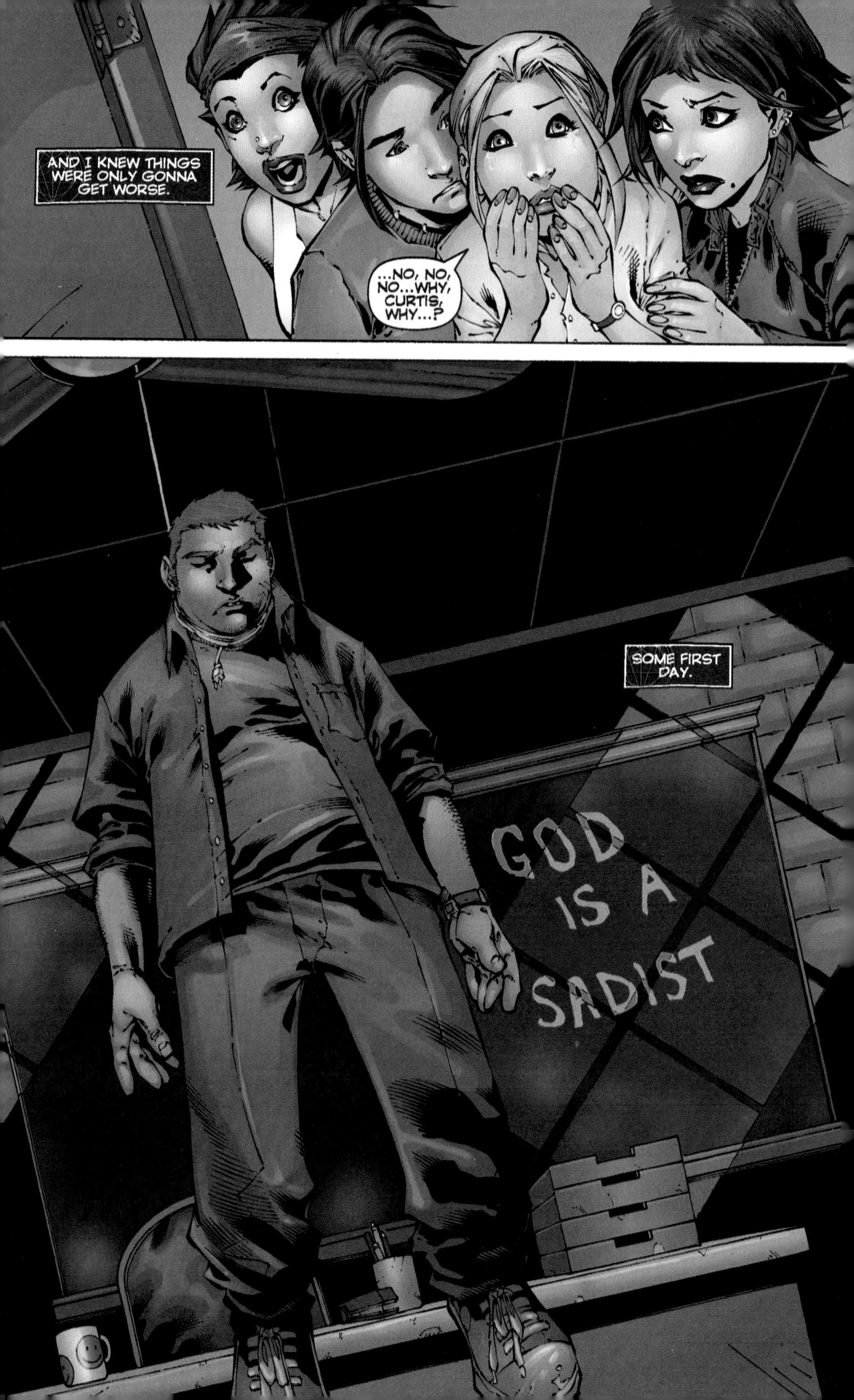
AND I KNEW THINGS WERE ONLY GONNA GET WORSE.
...NO, NO, NO...WHY, CURTIS, WHY...?
SOME FIRST DAY.
GOD IS A SADIST

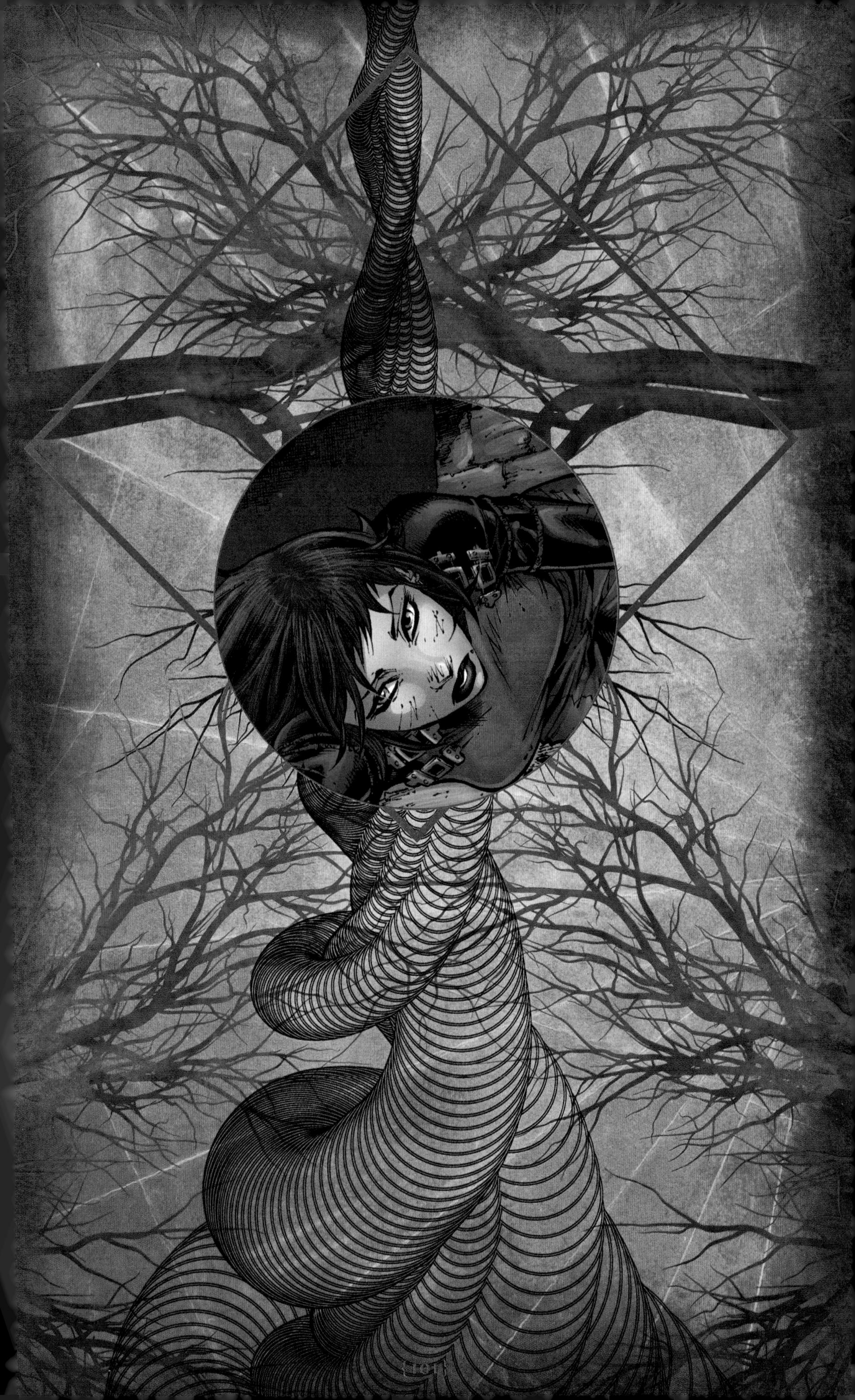

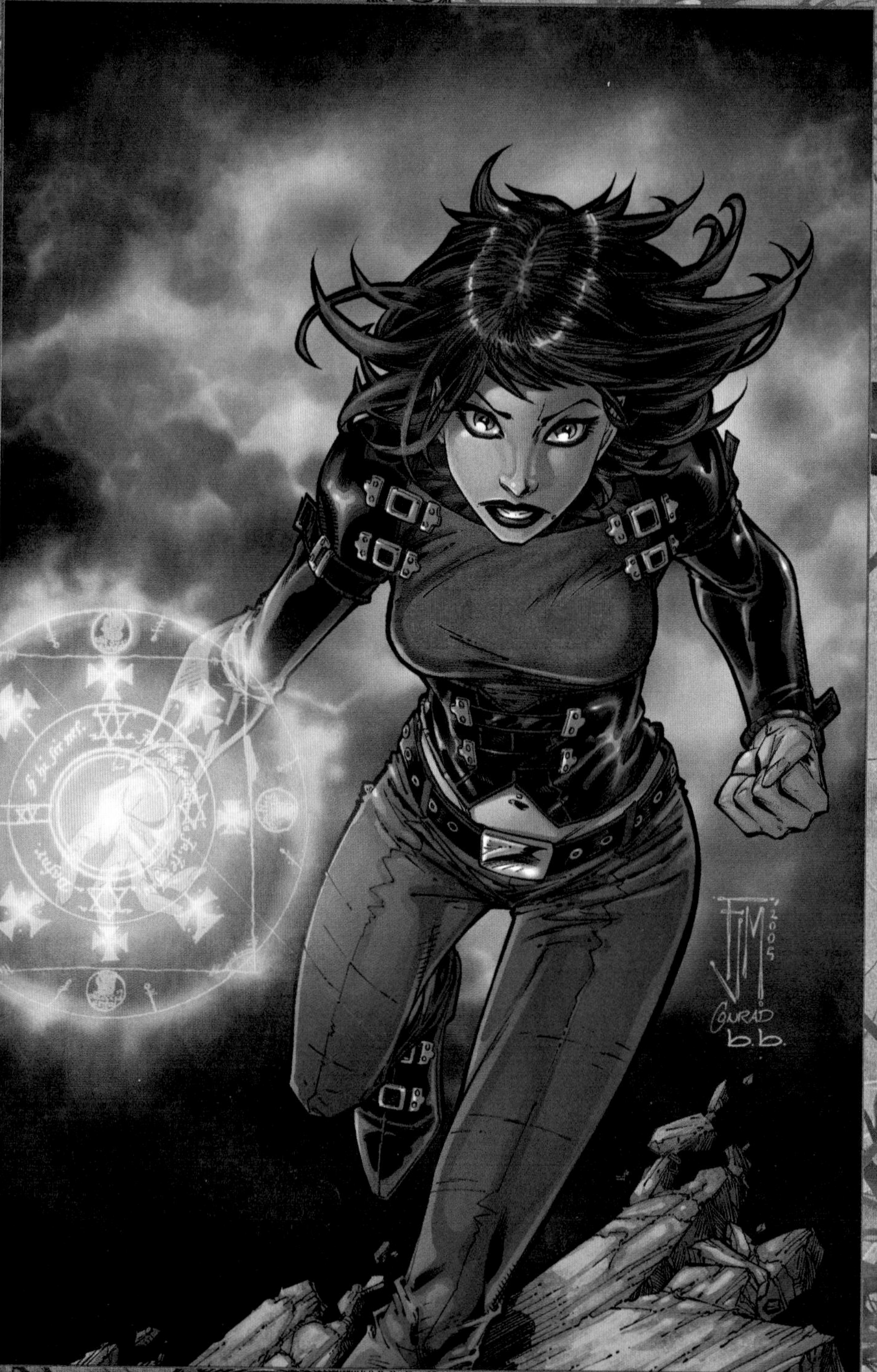

The Necromancer issue #5
cover art by:
Francis Manapul
Kevin Conrad
and
Brian Buccellato

Lithium, Chapter II
issue #5 credits:
written by: **Joshua Ortega**
pencils by: **Francis Manapul**
inks by: **Rob Hunter**
colors by: **Brian Buccellato, Arsia Rozegar**
letters by: **Troy Peteri**

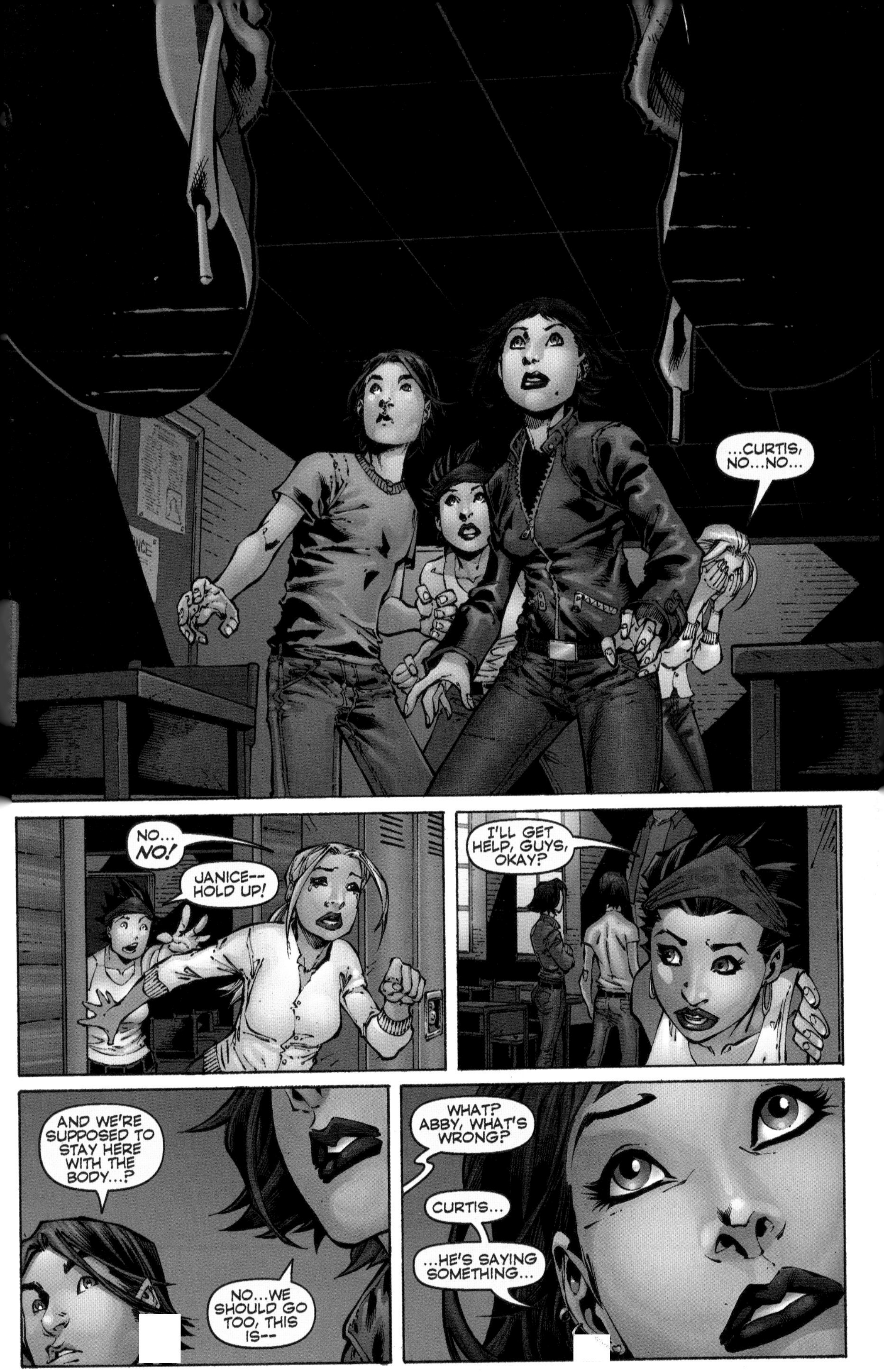
...CURTIS, NO...NO...
NO... NO!
JANICE-- HOLD UP!
I'LL GET HELP, GUYS, OKAY?
AND WE'RE SUPPOSED TO STAY HERE WITH THE BODY...?
NO...WE SHOULD GO TOO, THIS IS--
WHAT? ABBY, WHAT'S WRONG?
CURTIS...
...HE'S SAYING SOMETHING...

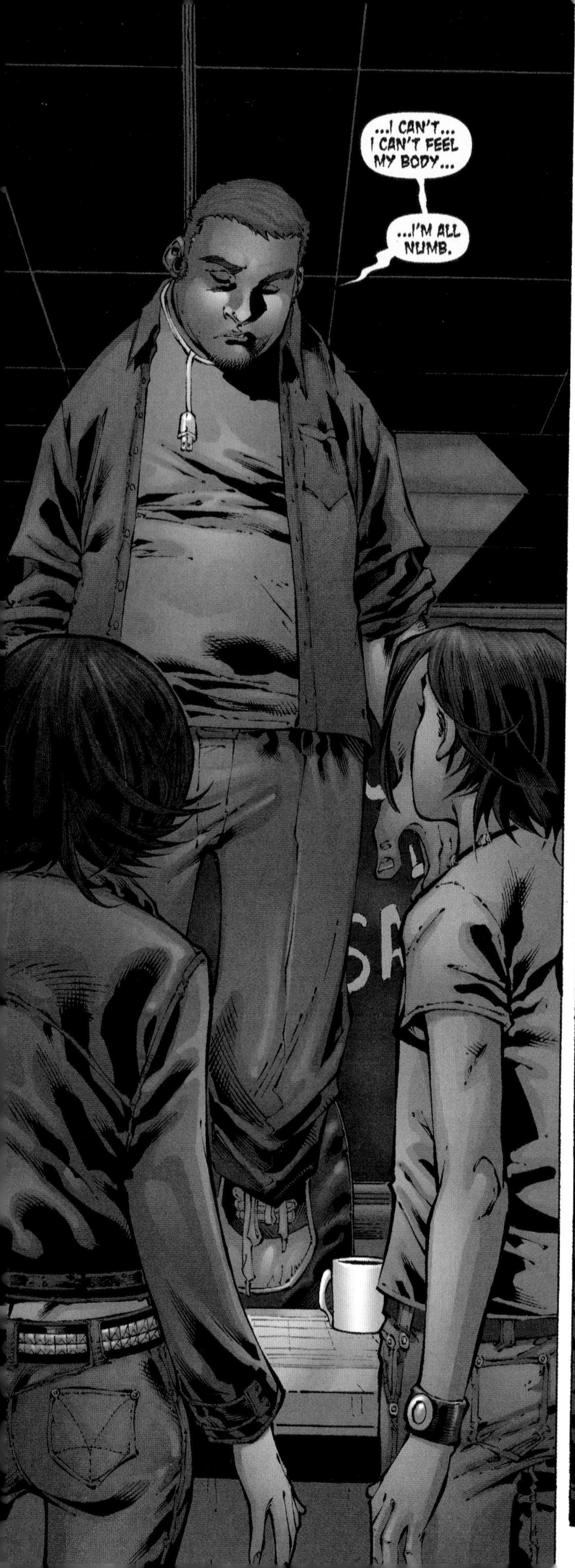
...I CAN'T...
I CAN'T FEEL
MY BODY...
...I'M ALL
NUMB.

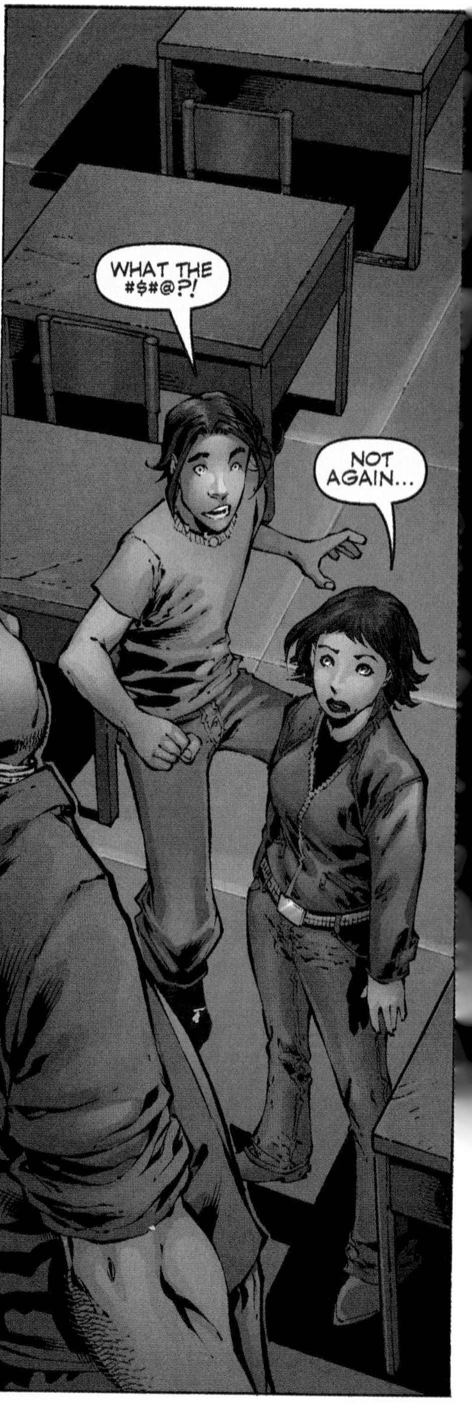
WHAT THE
#$#@?!
NOT
AGAIN...

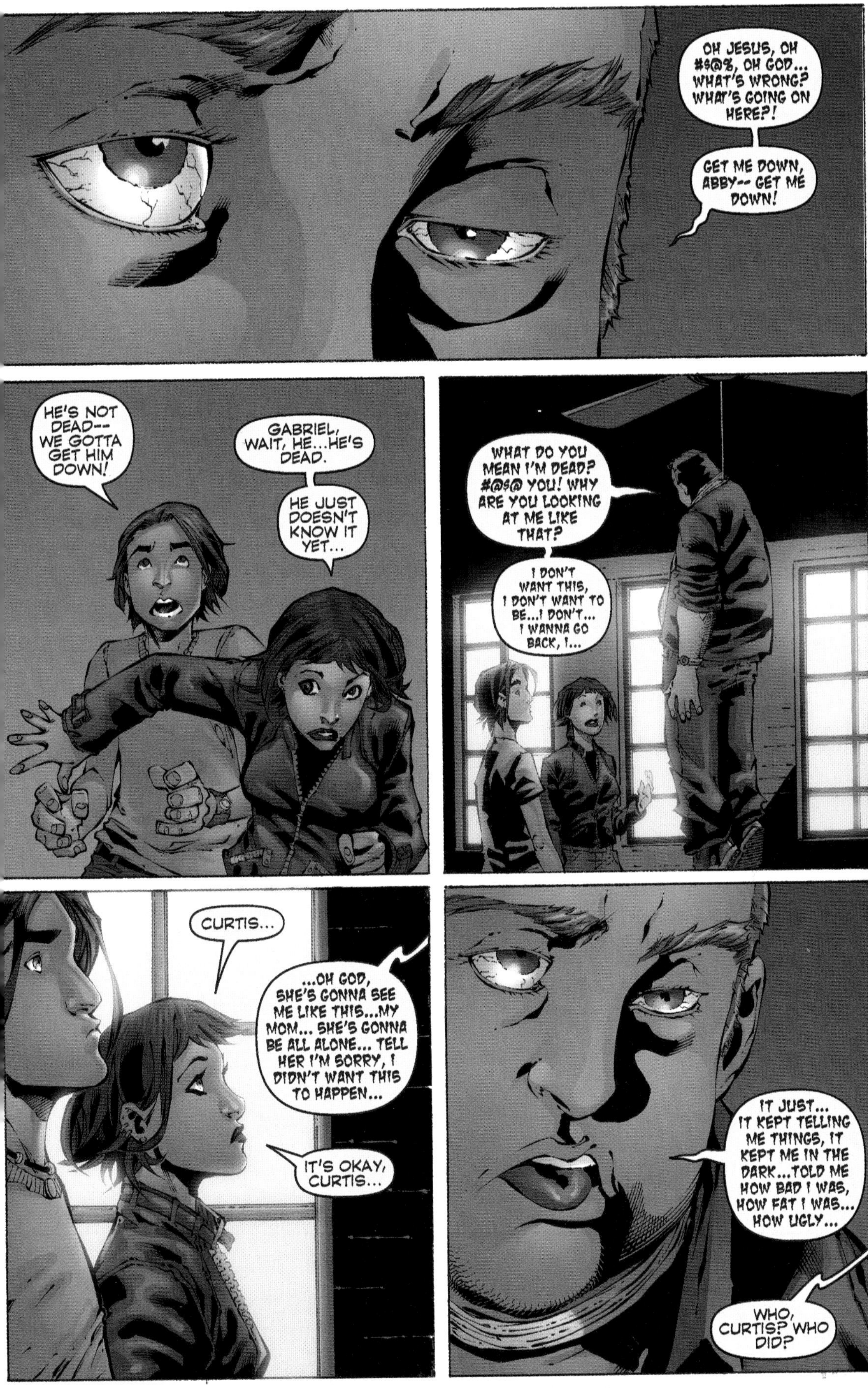
OH JESUS, OH #$@%, OH GOD... WHAT'S WRONG? WHAT'S GOING ON HERE?!
GET ME DOWN, ABBY-- GET ME DOWN!
HE'S NOT DEAD-- WE GOTTA GET HIM DOWN!
GABRIEL, WAIT, HE...HE'S DEAD.
HE JUST DOESN'T KNOW IT YET...
WHAT DO YOU MEAN I'M DEAD? #@$@ YOU! WHY ARE YOU LOOKING AT ME LIKE THAT?
I DON'T WANT THIS, I DON'T WANT TO BE...I DON'T... I WANNA GO BACK, I...
CURTIS...
...OH GOD, SHE'S GONNA SEE ME LIKE THIS...MY MOM... SHE'S GONNA BE ALL ALONE... TELL HER I'M SORRY, I DIDN'T WANT THIS TO HAPPEN...
IT'S OKAY, CURTIS...
IT JUST... IT KEPT TELLING ME THINGS, IT KEPT ME IN THE DARK...TOLD ME HOW BAD I WAS, HOW FAT I WAS... HOW UGLY...
WHO, CURTIS? WHO DID?

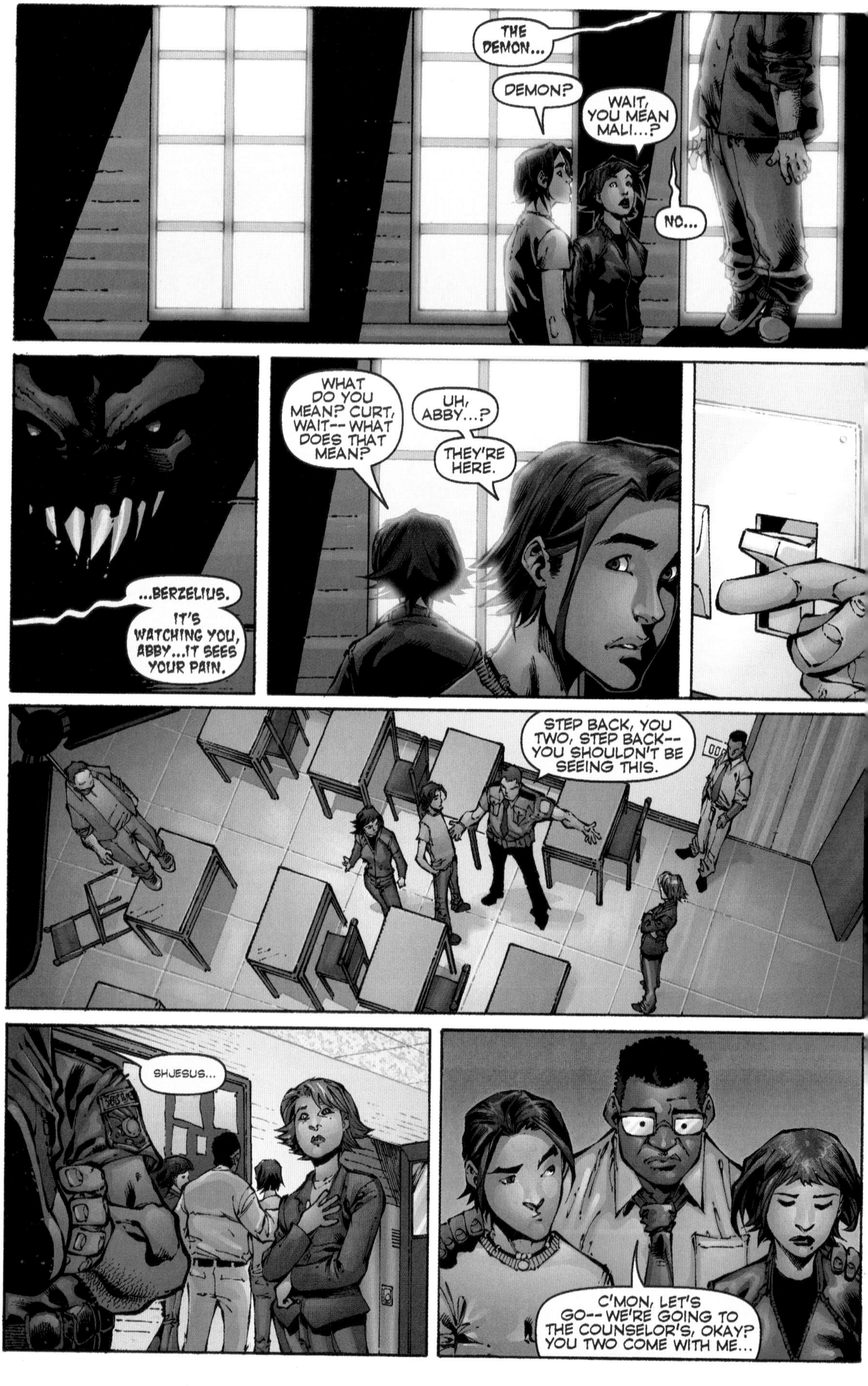
THE DEMON...
DEMON?
WAIT, YOU MEAN MALI...?
NO...
...BERZELIUS. IT'S WATCHING YOU, ABBY...IT SEES YOUR PAIN.
WHAT DO YOU MEAN? CURT, WAIT-- WHAT DOES THAT MEAN?
UH, ABBY...?
THEY'RE HERE.
STEP BACK, YOU TWO, STEP BACK-- YOU SHOULDN'T BE SEEING THIS.
SHJESUS...
C'MON, LET'S GO-- WE'RE GOING TO THE COUNSELOR'S, OKAY? YOU TWO COME WITH ME...

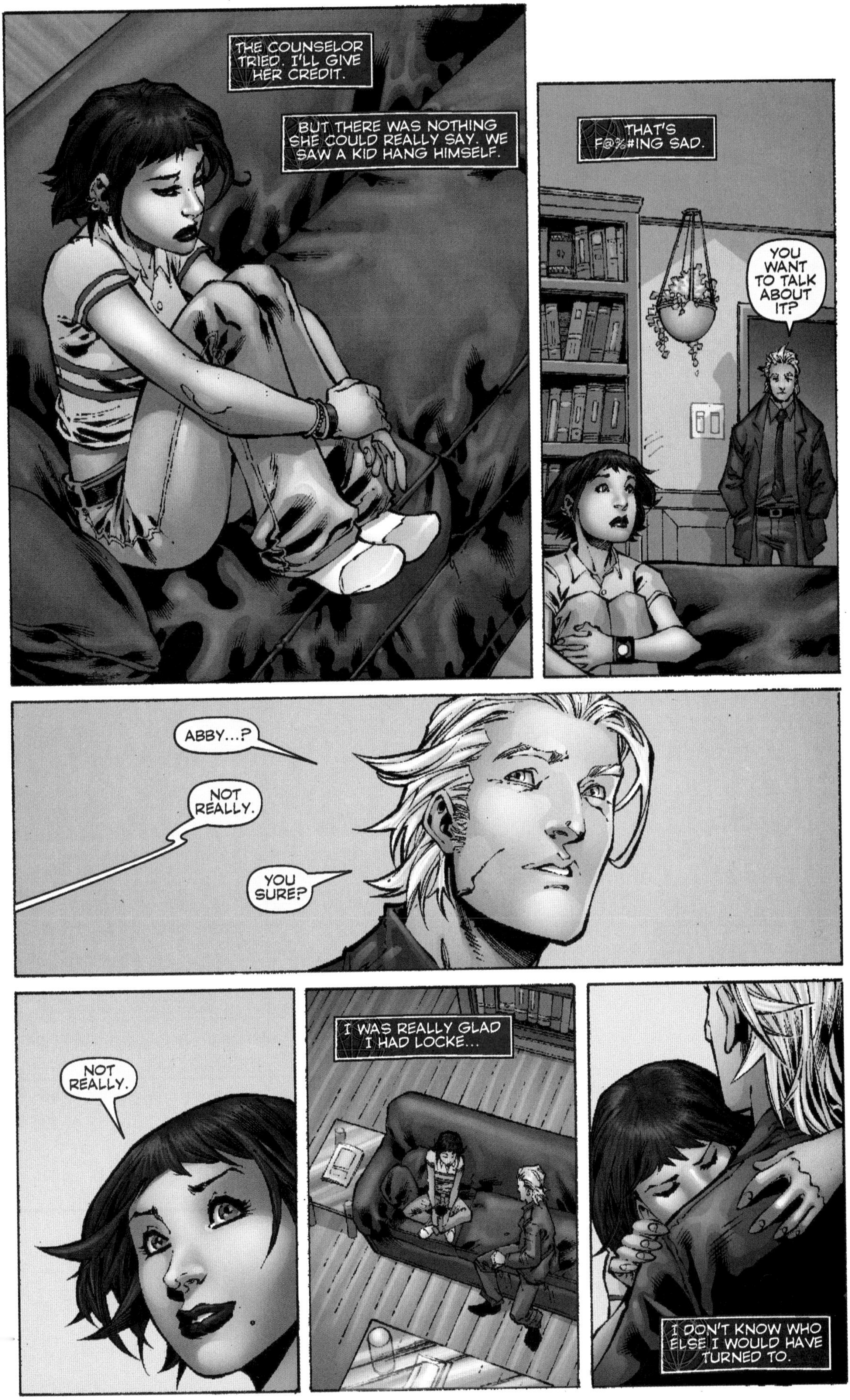
THE COUNSELOR TRIED. I'LL GIVE HER CREDIT.
BUT THERE WAS NOTHING SHE COULD REALLY SAY. WE SAW A KID HANG HIMSELF.
THAT'S F@%#ING SAD.
YOU WANT TO TALK ABOUT IT?
ABBY...?
NOT REALLY.
YOU SURE?
NOT REALLY.
I WAS REALLY GLAD I HAD LOCKE...
I DON'T KNOW WHO ELSE I WOULD HAVE TURNED TO.

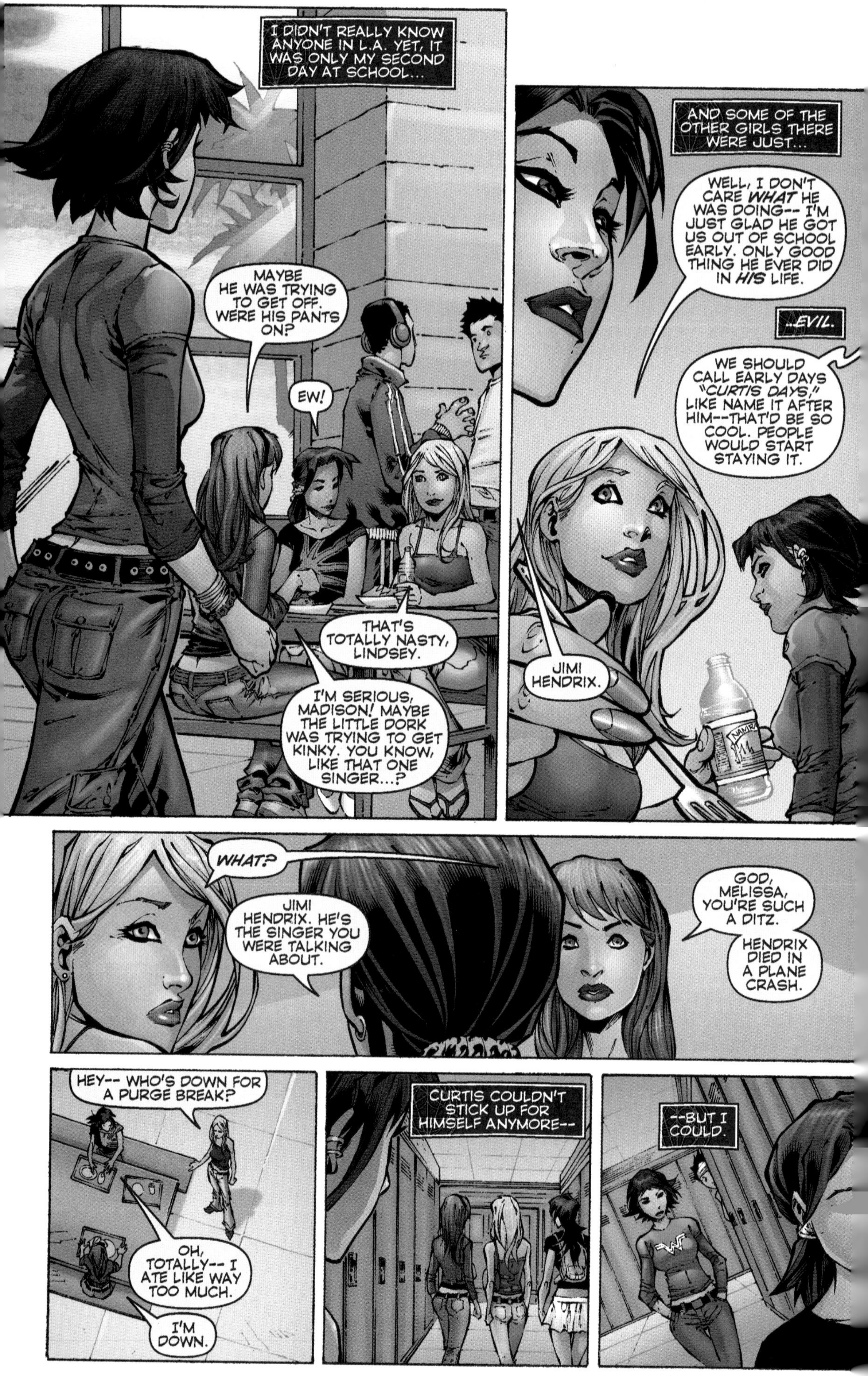
I DIDN'T REALLY KNOW ANYONE IN L.A. YET, IT WAS ONLY MY SECOND DAY AT SCHOOL...
MAYBE HE WAS TRYING TO GET OFF. WERE HIS PANTS ON?
EW!
THAT'S TOTALLY NASTY, LINDSEY.
I'M SERIOUS, MADISON! MAYBE THE LITTLE DORK WAS TRYING TO GET KINKY. YOU KNOW, LIKE THAT ONE SINGER...?
AND SOME OF THE OTHER GIRLS THERE WERE JUST...
WELL, I DON'T CARE WHAT HE WAS DOING-- I'M JUST GLAD HE GOT US OUT OF SCHOOL EARLY. ONLY GOOD THING HE EVER DID IN HIS LIFE.
...EVIL.
WE SHOULD CALL EARLY DAYS "CURTIS DAYS," LIKE NAME IT AFTER HIM--THAT'D BE SO COOL. PEOPLE WOULD START STAYING IT.
JIMI HENDRIX.
WHAT?
JIMI HENDRIX. HE'S THE SINGER YOU WERE TALKING ABOUT.
GOD, MELISSA, YOU'RE SUCH A DITZ.
HENDRIX DIED IN A PLANE CRASH.
HEY-- WHO'S DOWN FOR A PURGE BREAK?
OH, TOTALLY-- I ATE LIKE WAY TOO MUCH.
I'M DOWN.
CURTIS COULDN'T STICK UP FOR HIMSELF ANYMORE--
--BUT I COULD.

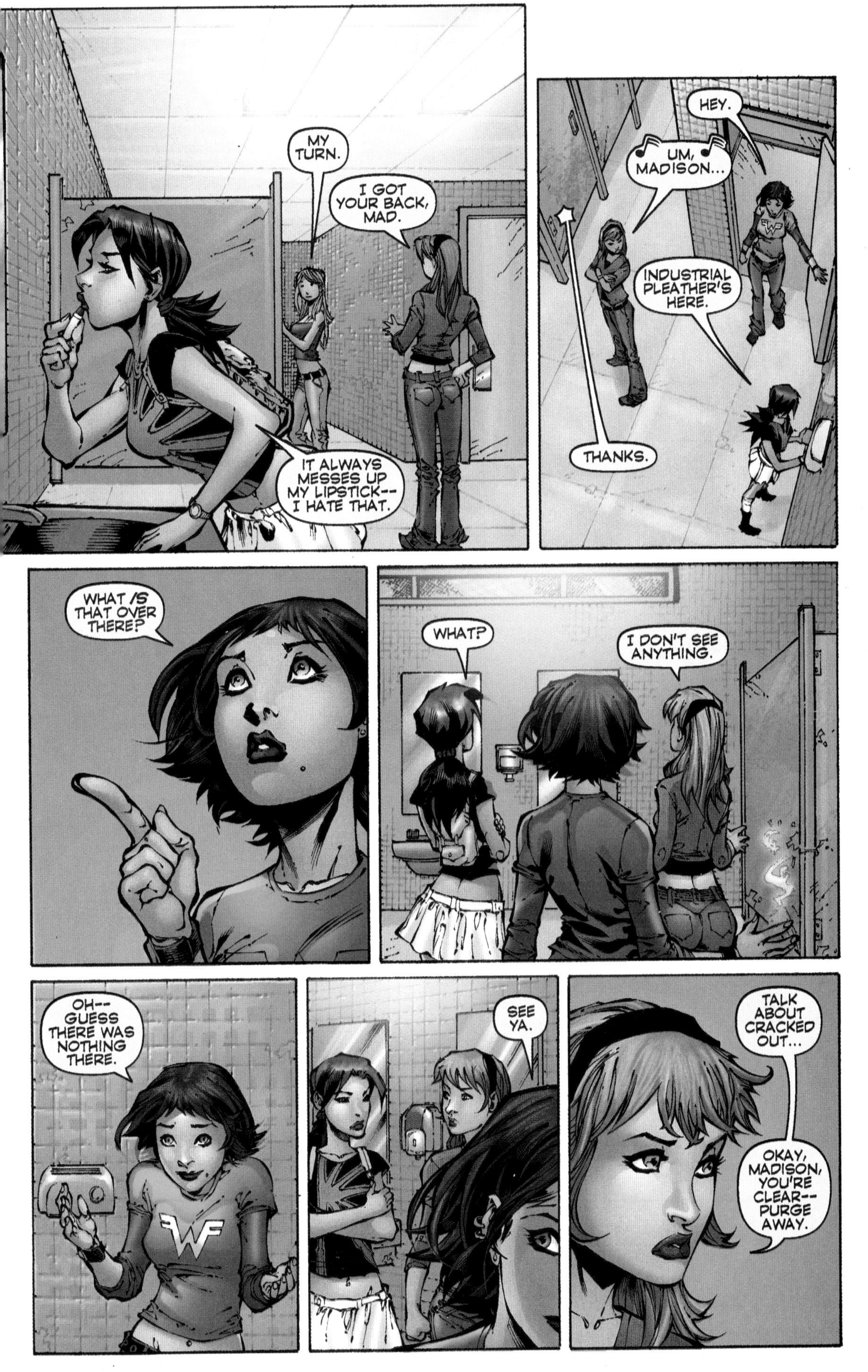
MY TURN.
I GOT YOUR BACK, MAD.
IT ALWAYS MESSES UP MY LIPSTICK-- I HATE THAT.
HEY.
UM, MADISON...
INDUSTRIAL PLEATHER'S HERE.
THANKS.
WHAT IS THAT OVER THERE?
WHAT?
I DON'T SEE ANYTHING.
OH-- GUESS THERE WAS NOTHING THERE.
SEE YA.
TALK ABOUT CRACKED OUT...
OKAY, MADISON, YOU'RE CLEAR-- PURGE AWAY.

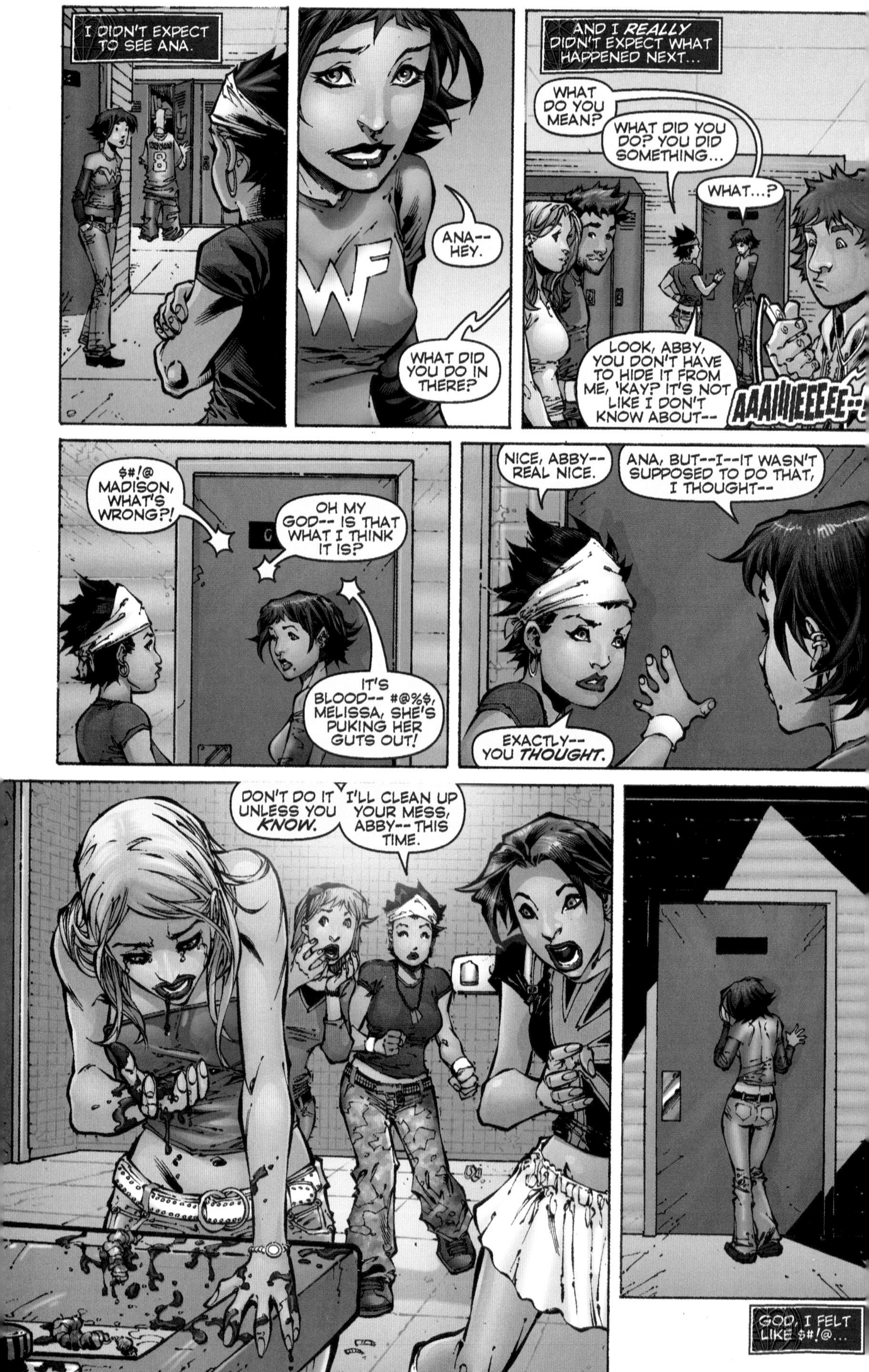

I DIDN'T EXPECT TO SEE ANA.
ANA-- HEY.
WHAT DID YOU DO IN THERE?
AND I *REALLY* DIDN'T EXPECT WHAT HAPPENED NEXT...
WHAT DO YOU MEAN?
WHAT DID YOU DO? YOU DID SOMETHING...
WHAT...?
LOOK, ABBY, YOU DON'T HAVE TO HIDE IT FROM ME, 'KAY? IT'S NOT LIKE I DON'T KNOW ABOUT--
AAAIIIEEEEE--!
$#!@ MADISON, WHAT'S WRONG?!
OH MY GOD-- IS THAT WHAT I THINK IT IS?
IT'S BLOOD-- #@%$, MELISSA, SHE'S PUKING HER GUTS OUT!
NICE, ABBY-- REAL NICE.
ANA, BUT--I--IT WASN'T SUPPOSED TO DO THAT, I THOUGHT--
EXACTLY-- YOU *THOUGHT*.
DON'T DO IT UNLESS YOU *KNOW*.
I'LL CLEAN UP YOUR MESS, ABBY-- THIS TIME.
GOD, I FELT LIKE $#!@...

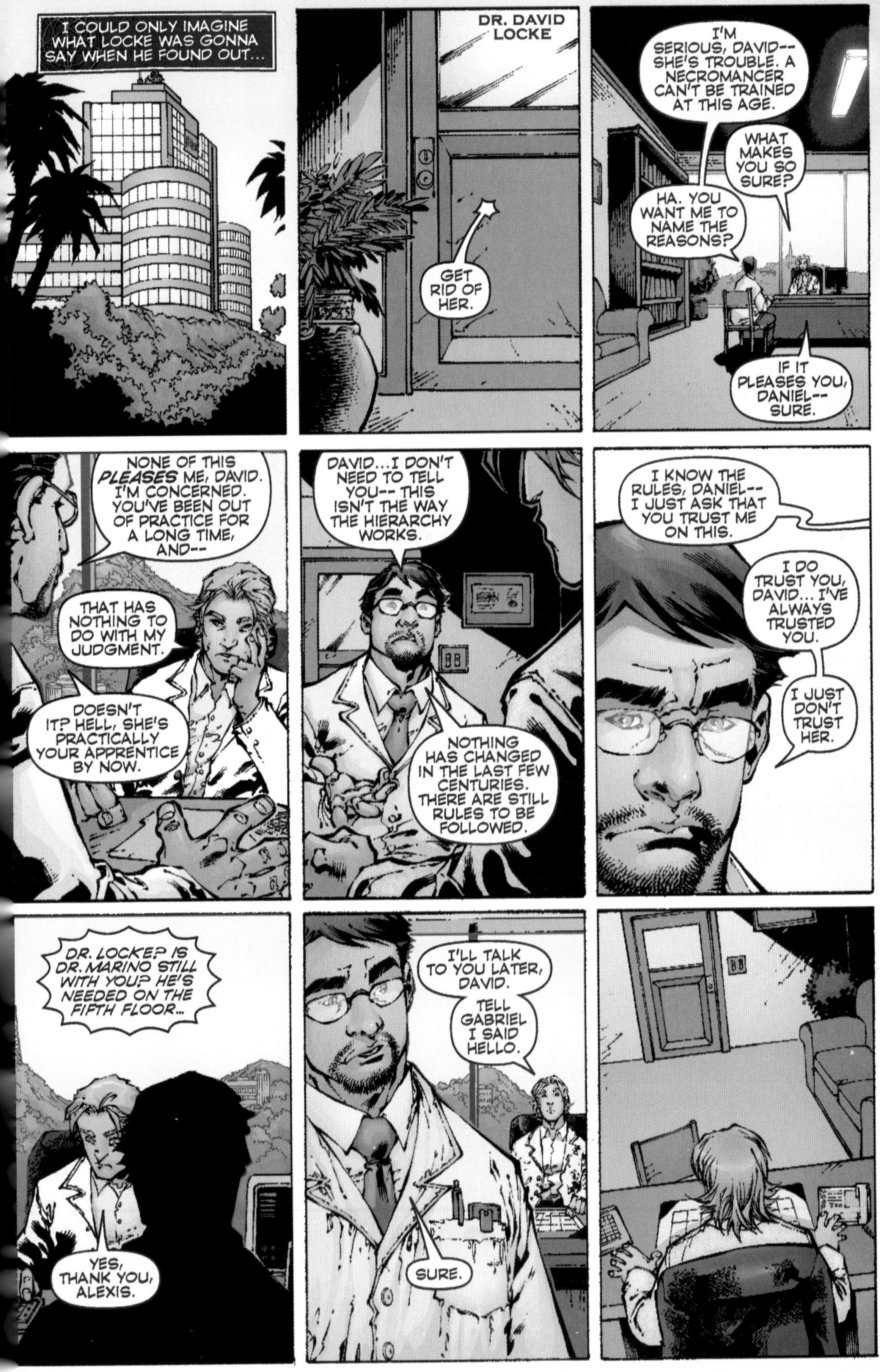
I COULD ONLY IMAGINE WHAT LOCKE WAS GONNA SAY WHEN HE FOUND OUT...
DR. DAVID LOCKE
GET RID OF HER.
I'M SERIOUS, DAVID-- SHE'S TROUBLE. A NECROMANCER CAN'T BE TRAINED AT THIS AGE.
WHAT MAKES YOU SO SURE?
HA. YOU WANT ME TO NAME THE REASONS?
IF IT PLEASES YOU, DANIEL-- SURE.
NONE OF THIS PLEASES ME, DAVID. I'M CONCERNED. YOU'VE BEEN OUT OF PRACTICE FOR A LONG TIME, AND--
THAT HAS NOTHING TO DO WITH MY JUDGMENT.
DOESN'T IT? HELL, SHE'S PRACTICALLY YOUR APPRENTICE BY NOW.
DAVID...I DON'T NEED TO TELL YOU-- THIS ISN'T THE WAY THE HIERARCHY WORKS.
NOTHING HAS CHANGED IN THE LAST FEW CENTURIES. THERE ARE STILL RULES TO BE FOLLOWED.
I KNOW THE RULES, DANIEL-- I JUST ASK THAT YOU TRUST ME ON THIS.
I DO TRUST YOU, DAVID... I'VE ALWAYS TRUSTED YOU.
I JUST DON'T TRUST HER.
DR. LOCKE? IS DR. MARINO STILL WITH YOU? HE'S NEEDED ON THE FIFTH FLOOR...
YES, THANK YOU, ALEXIS.
I'LL TALK TO YOU LATER, DAVID.
TELL GABRIEL I SAID HELLO.
SURE.

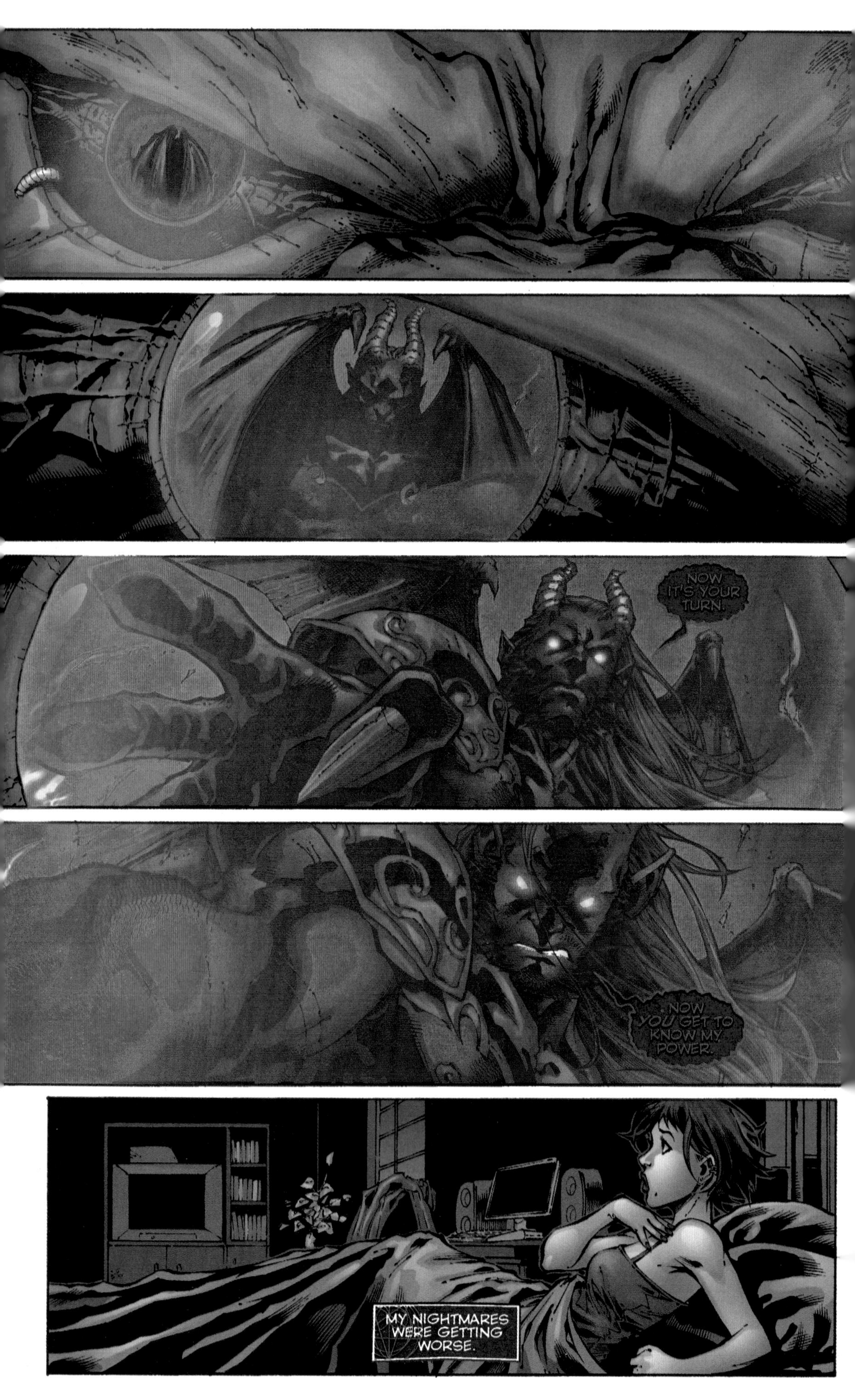
NOW IT'S YOUR TURN.
NOW YOU GET TO KNOW MY POWER.
MY NIGHTMARES WERE GETTING WORSE.

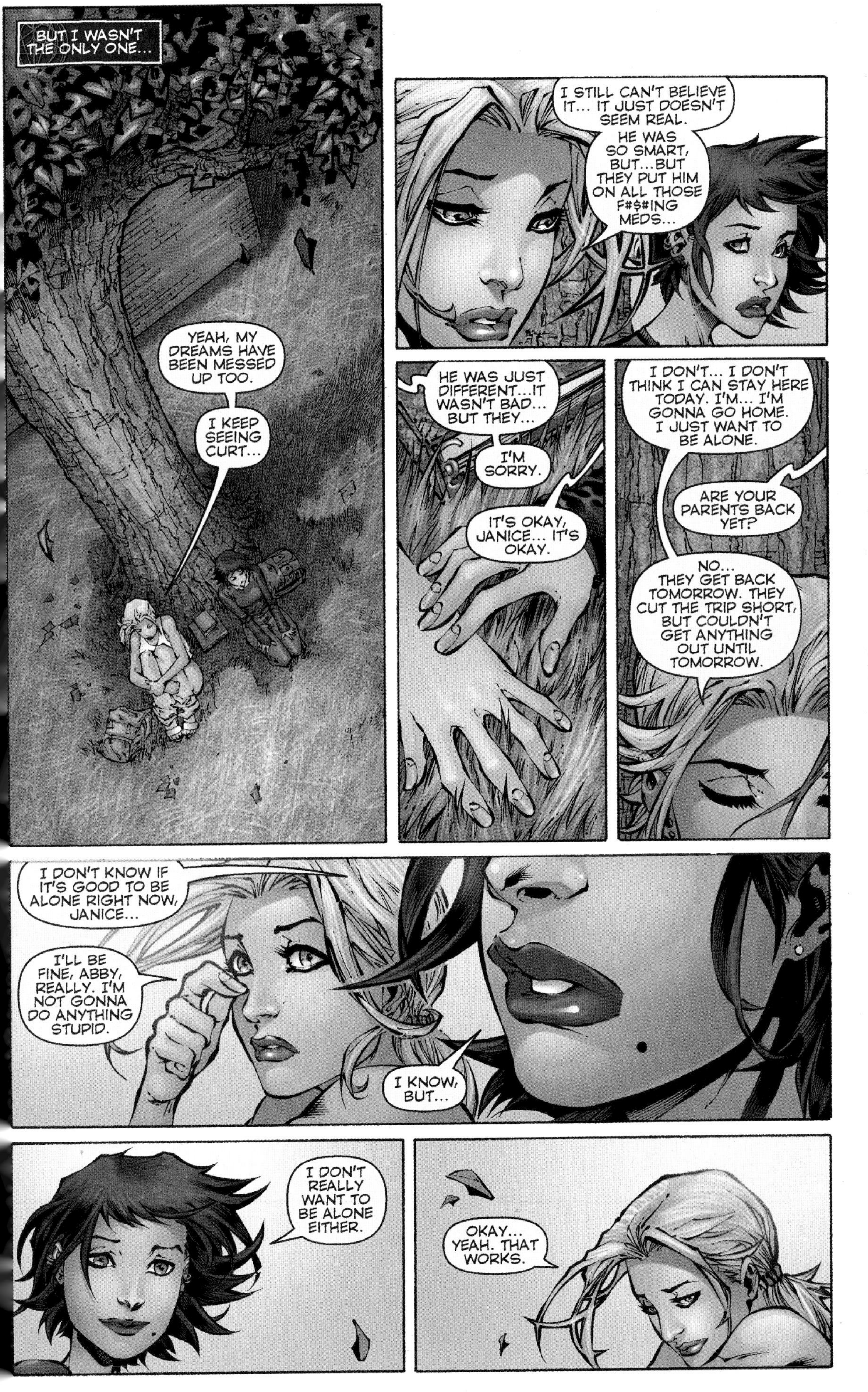
BUT I WASN'T THE ONLY ONE...
I STILL CAN'T BELIEVE IT... IT JUST DOESN'T SEEM REAL.
HE WAS SO SMART, BUT...BUT THEY PUT HIM ON ALL THOSE F#$#ING MEDS...
YEAH, MY DREAMS HAVE BEEN MESSED UP TOO.
I KEEP SEEING CURT...
HE WAS JUST DIFFERENT...IT WASN'T BAD... BUT THEY...
I'M SORRY.
IT'S OKAY, JANICE... IT'S OKAY.
I DON'T... I DON'T THINK I CAN STAY HERE TODAY. I'M... I'M GONNA GO HOME. I JUST WANT TO BE ALONE.
ARE YOUR PARENTS BACK YET?
NO... THEY GET BACK TOMORROW. THEY CUT THE TRIP SHORT, BUT COULDN'T GET ANYTHING OUT UNTIL TOMORROW.
I DON'T KNOW IF IT'S GOOD TO BE ALONE RIGHT NOW, JANICE...
I'LL BE FINE, ABBY, REALLY. I'M NOT GONNA DO ANYTHING STUPID.
I KNOW, BUT...
I DON'T REALLY WANT TO BE ALONE EITHER.
OKAY... YEAH. THAT WORKS.

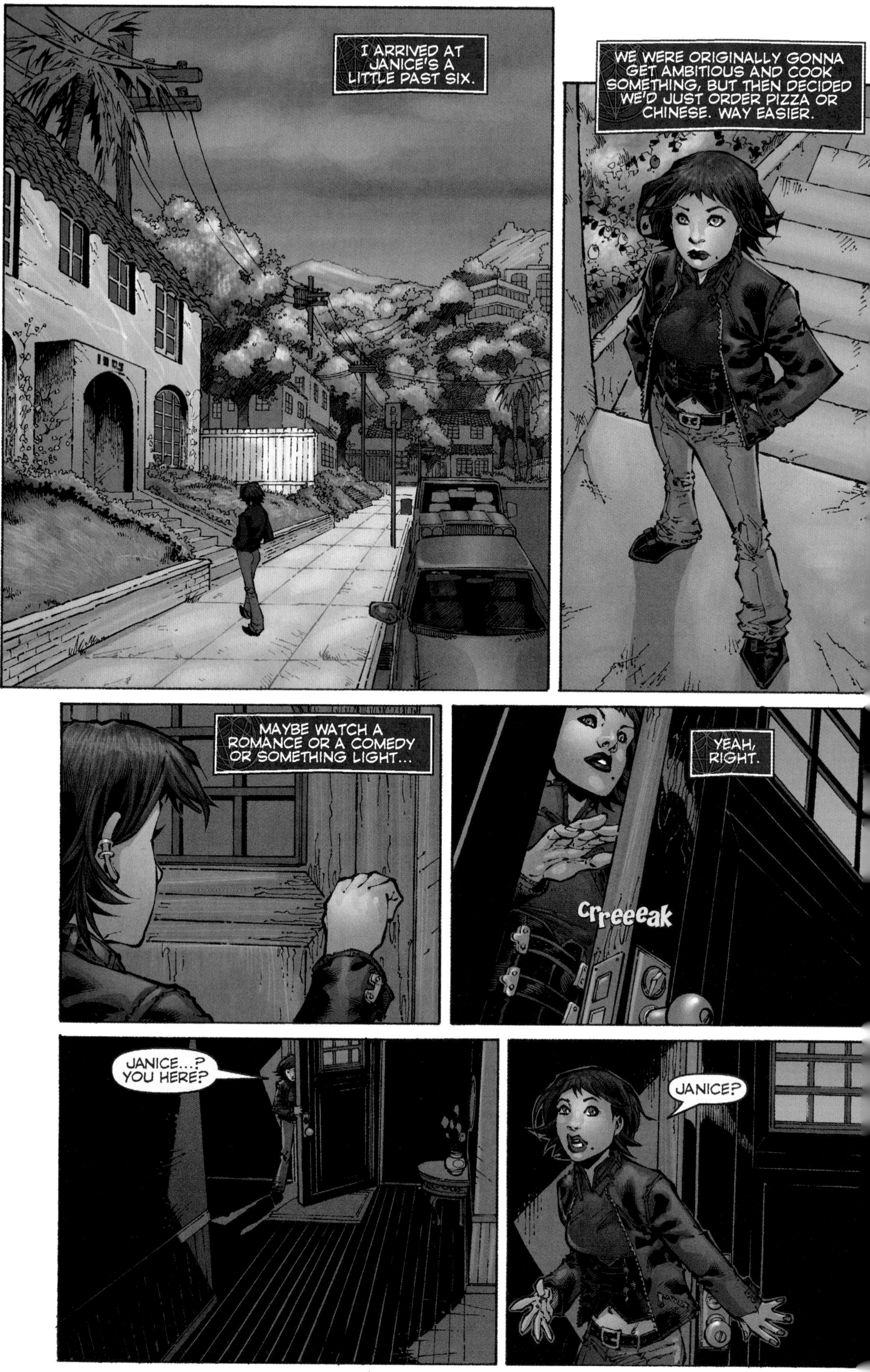
I ARRIVED AT JANICE'S A LITTLE PAST SIX.
WE WERE ORIGINALLY GONNA GET AMBITIOUS AND COOK SOMETHING, BUT THEN DECIDED WE'D JUST ORDER PIZZA OR CHINESE. WAY EASIER.
MAYBE WATCH A ROMANCE OR A COMEDY OR SOMETHING LIGHT...
YEAH, RIGHT.
crreeeak
JANICE...? YOU HERE?
JANICE?

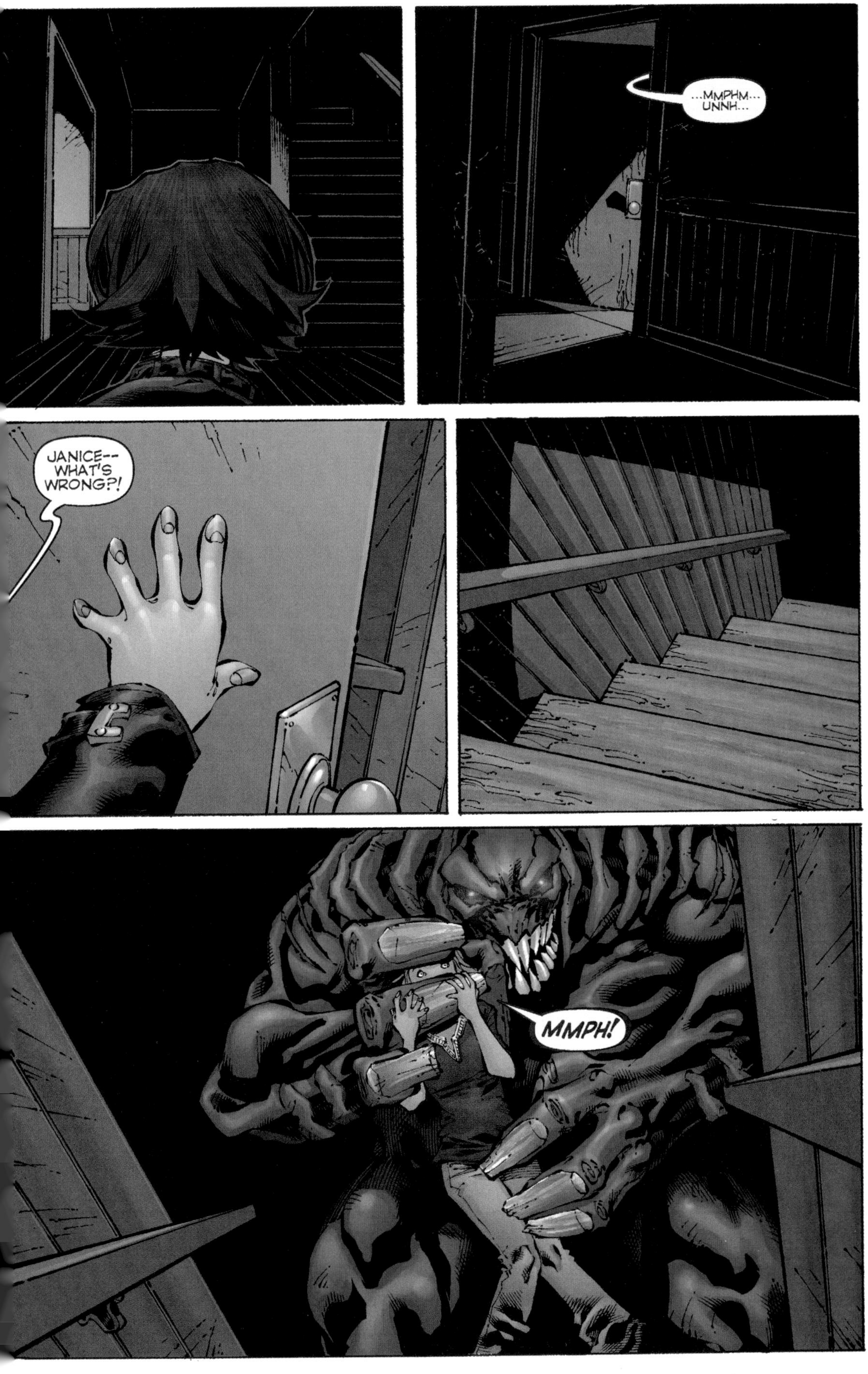
...MMPHM... UNNH...
JANICE-- WHAT'S WRONG?!
MMPH!

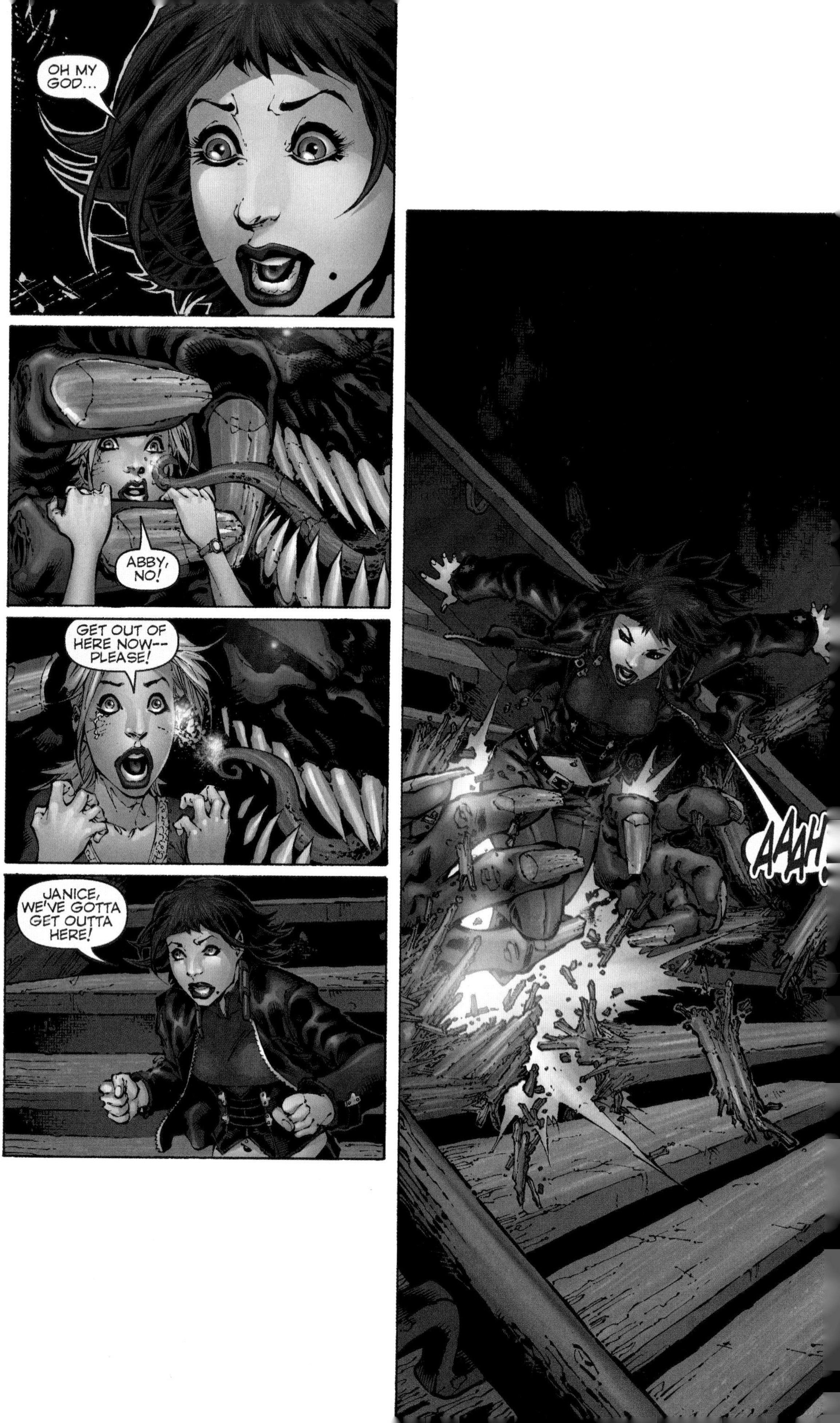
OH MY GOD...
ABBY, NO!
GET OUT OF HERE NOW-- PLEASE!
JANICE, WE'VE GOTTA GET OUTTA HERE!
AAAH!

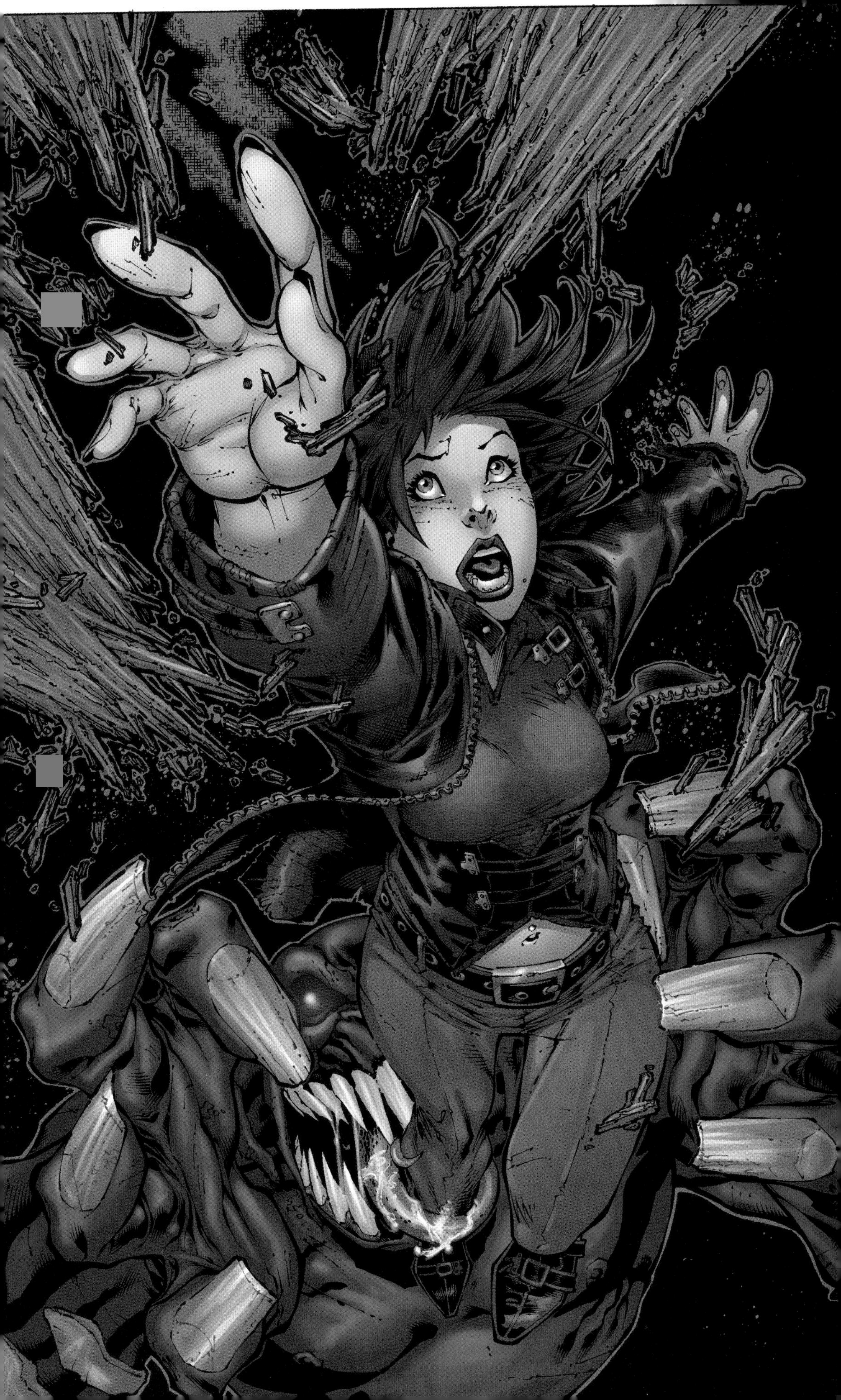

UNH!

I DIDN'T KNOW WHERE I WAS--

--I STILL DON'T, REALLY.

BUT I KNEW ENOUGH TO FIGHT BACK.

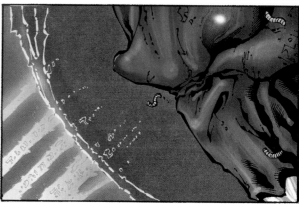

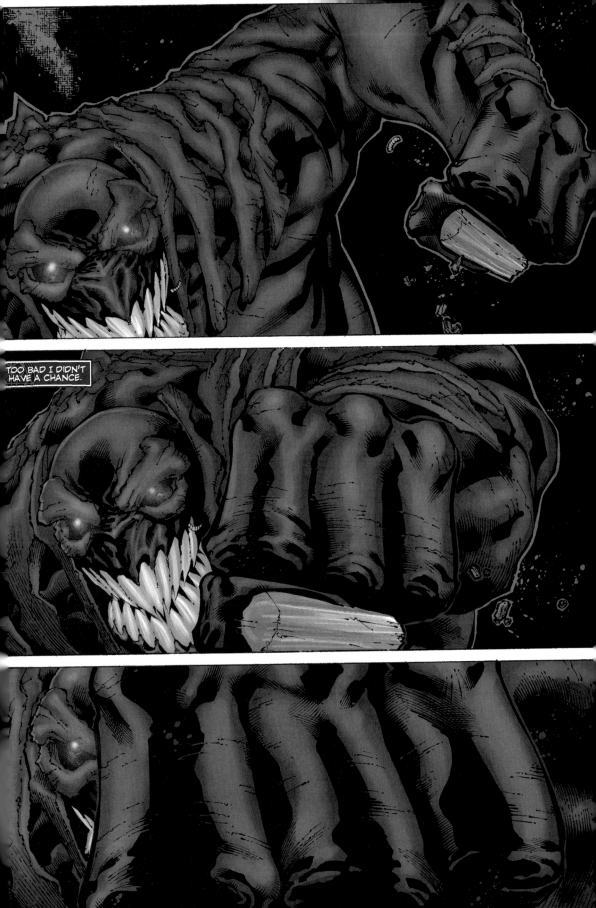

TOO BAD I DIDN'T
HAVE A CHANCE.

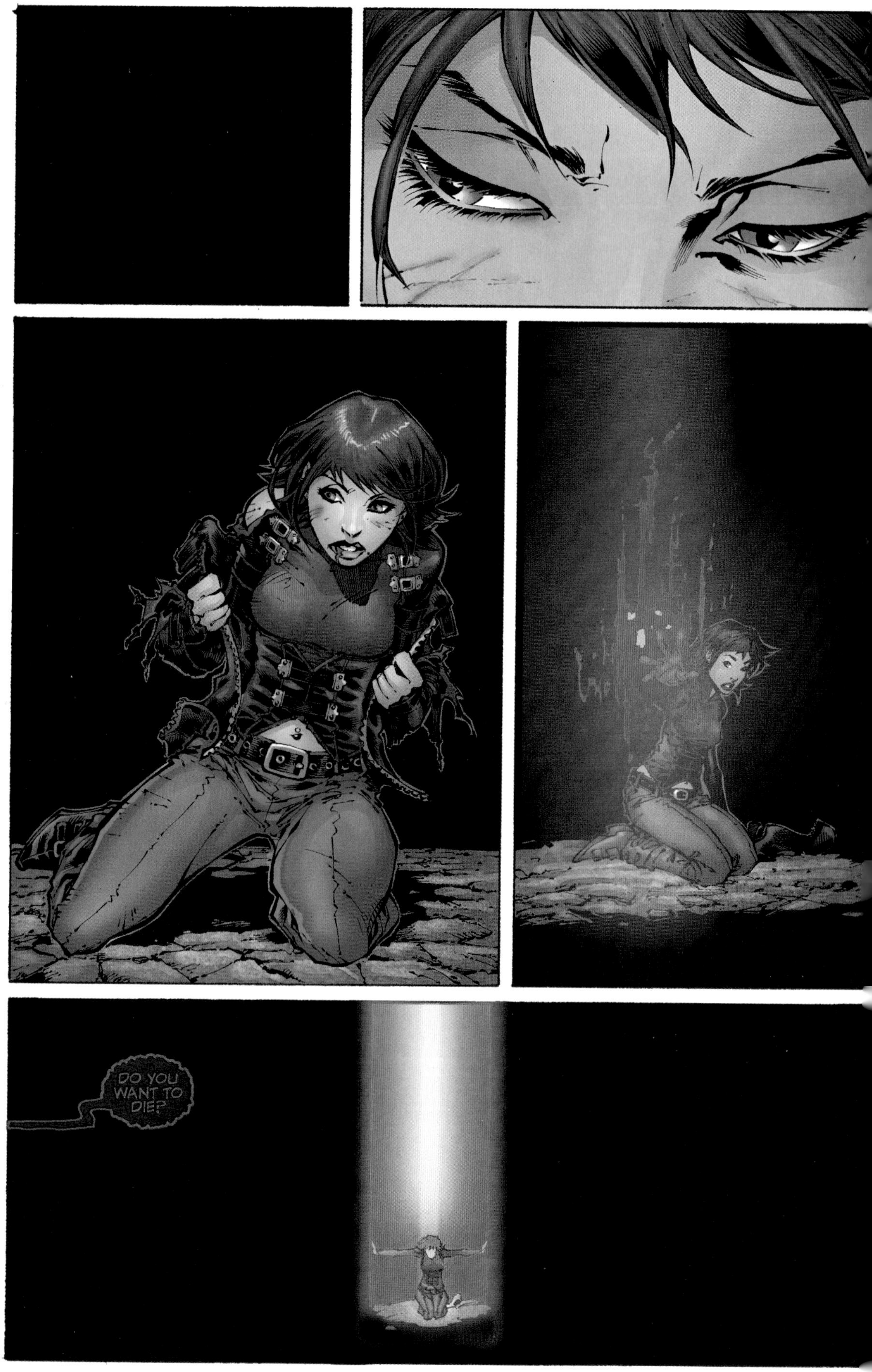
DO YOU WANT TO DIE?

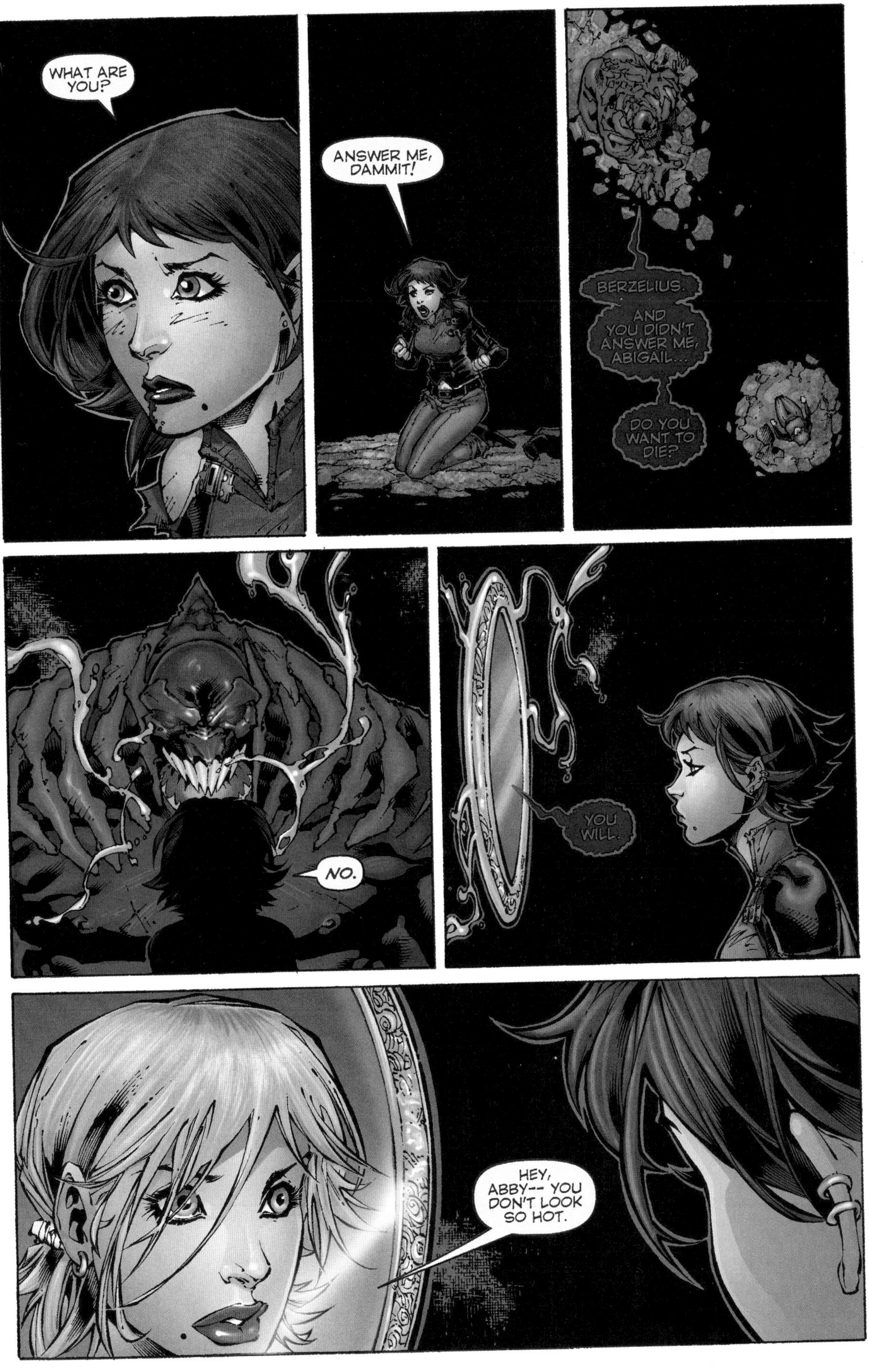
WHAT ARE YOU?
ANSWER ME, DAMMIT!
BERZELIUS.
AND YOU DIDN'T ANSWER ME, ABIGAIL...
DO YOU WANT TO DIE?
NO.
YOU WILL.
HEY, ABBY-- YOU DON'T LOOK SO HOT.

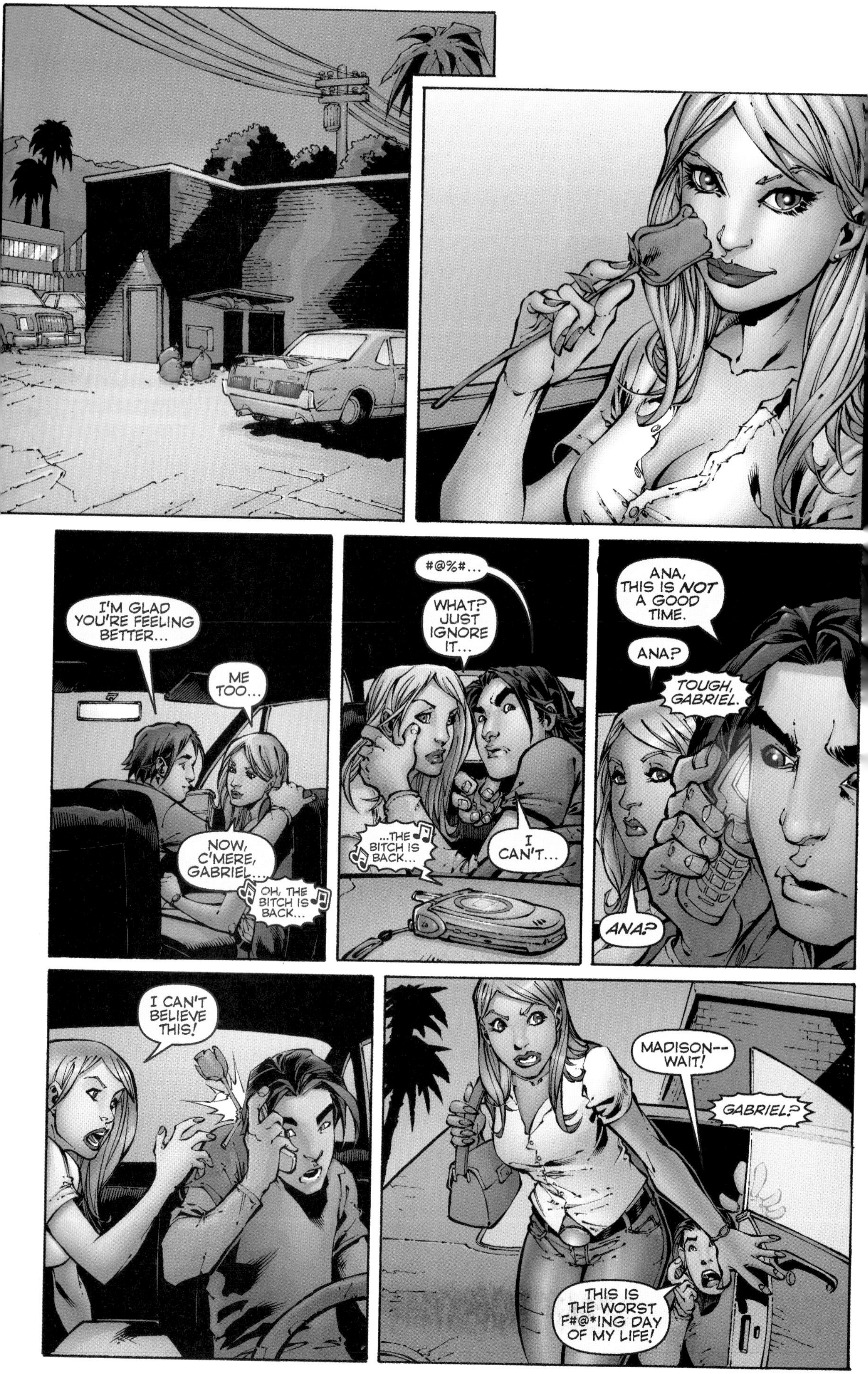

I'M GLAD YOU'RE FEELING BETTER...
ME TOO...
NOW, C'MERE, GABRIEL...
OH, THE BITCH IS BACK...
#@%#...
WHAT? JUST IGNORE IT...
...THE BITCH IS BACK...
I CAN'T...
ANA, THIS IS NOT A GOOD TIME.
ANA?
TOUGH, GABRIEL.
ANA?
I CAN'T BELIEVE THIS!
MADISON--WAIT!
GABRIEL?
THIS IS THE WORST F#@*ING DAY OF MY LIFE!

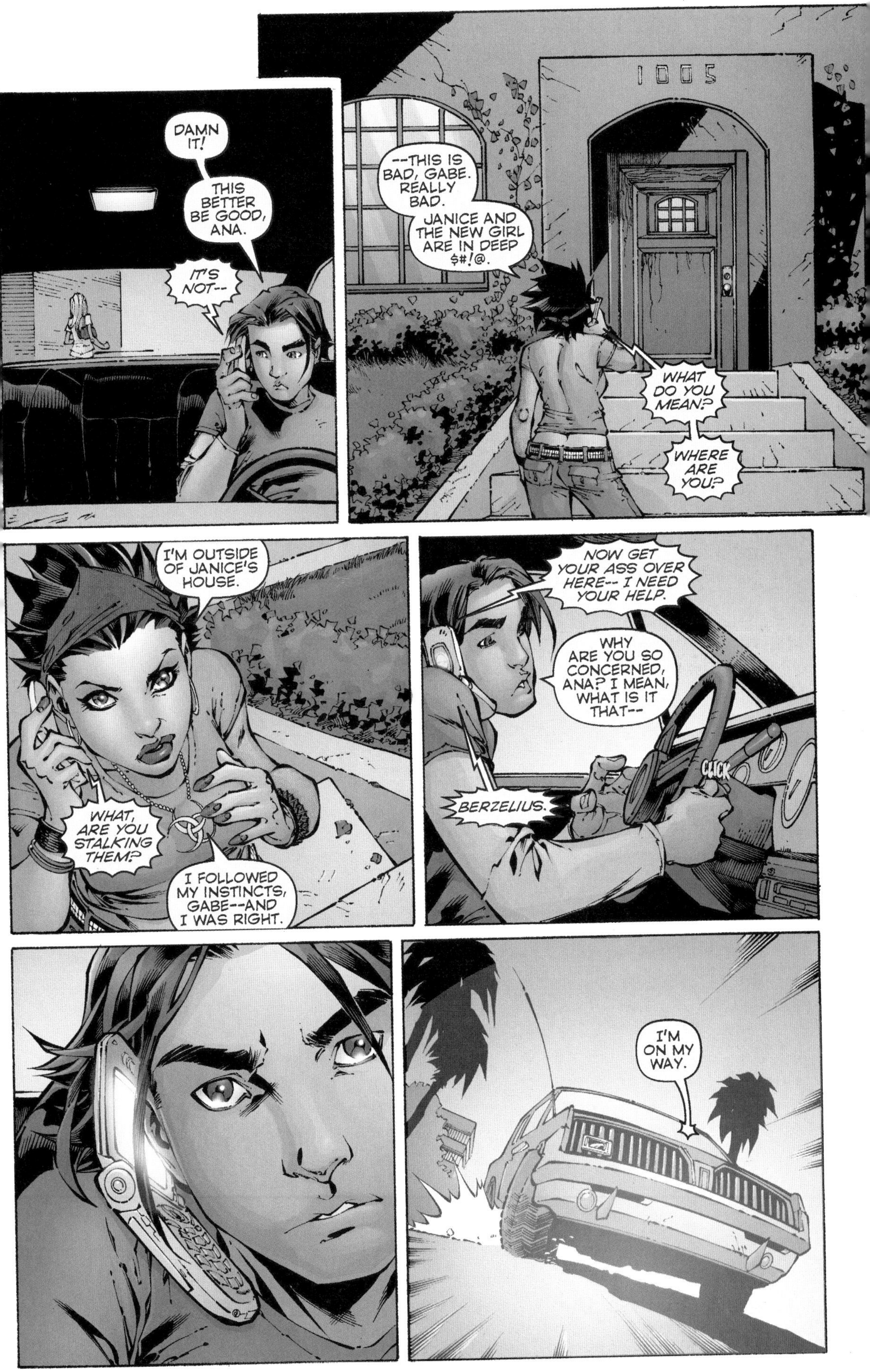

DAMN IT!
THIS BETTER BE GOOD, ANA.
IT'S NOT--
--THIS IS BAD, GABE. REALLY BAD.
JANICE AND THE NEW GIRL ARE IN DEEP $#!@.
WHAT DO YOU MEAN?
WHERE ARE YOU?
I'M OUTSIDE OF JANICE'S HOUSE.
WHAT, ARE YOU STALKING THEM?
I FOLLOWED MY INSTINCTS, GABE--AND I WAS RIGHT.
NOW GET YOUR ASS OVER HERE-- I NEED YOUR HELP.
WHY ARE YOU SO CONCERNED, ANA? I MEAN, WHAT IS IT THAT--
BERZELIUS.
CLICK
I'M ON MY WAY.

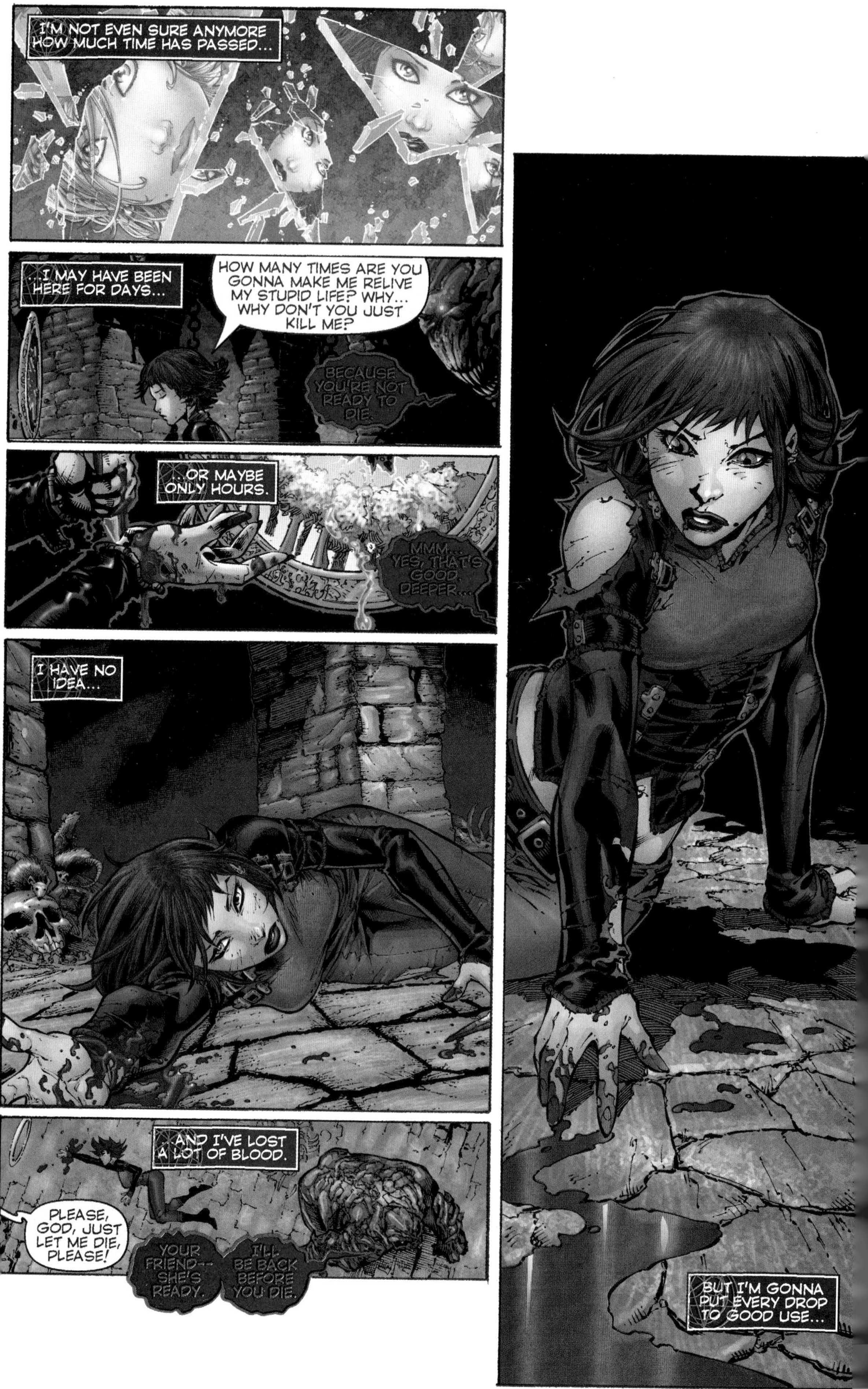
I'M NOT EVEN SURE ANYMORE HOW MUCH TIME HAS PASSED...
...I MAY HAVE BEEN HERE FOR DAYS...
HOW MANY TIMES ARE YOU GONNA MAKE ME RELIVE MY STUPID LIFE? WHY... WHY DON'T YOU JUST KILL ME?
BECAUSE YOU'RE NOT READY TO DIE.
...OR MAYBE ONLY HOURS.
MMM... YES, THAT'S GOOD. DEEPER...
I HAVE NO IDEA...
...AND I'VE LOST A LOT OF BLOOD.
PLEASE, GOD, JUST LET ME DIE, PLEASE!
YOUR FRIEND-- SHE'S READY.
I'LL BE BACK BEFORE YOU DIE.
BUT I'M GONNA PUT EVERY DROP TO GOOD USE...

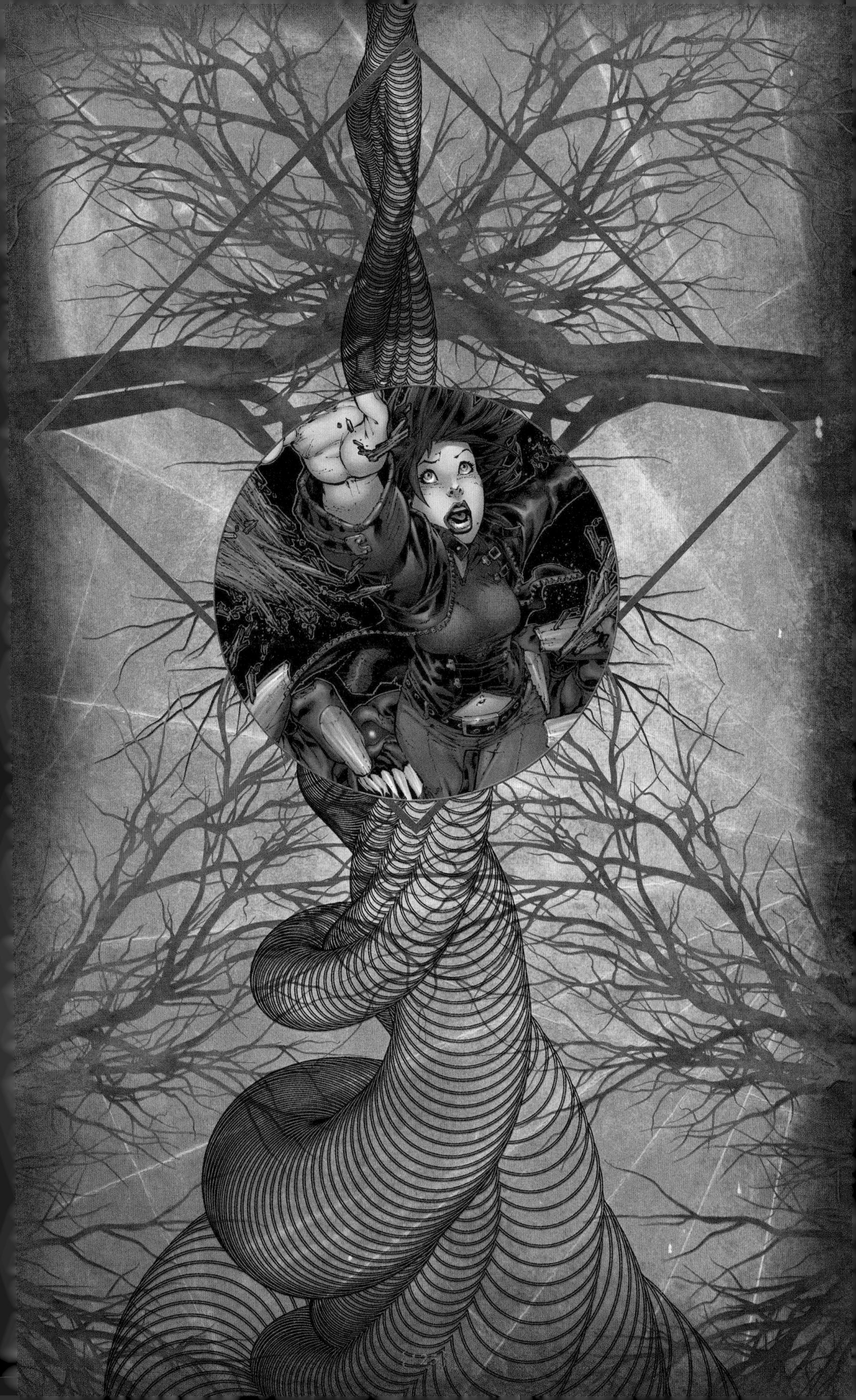

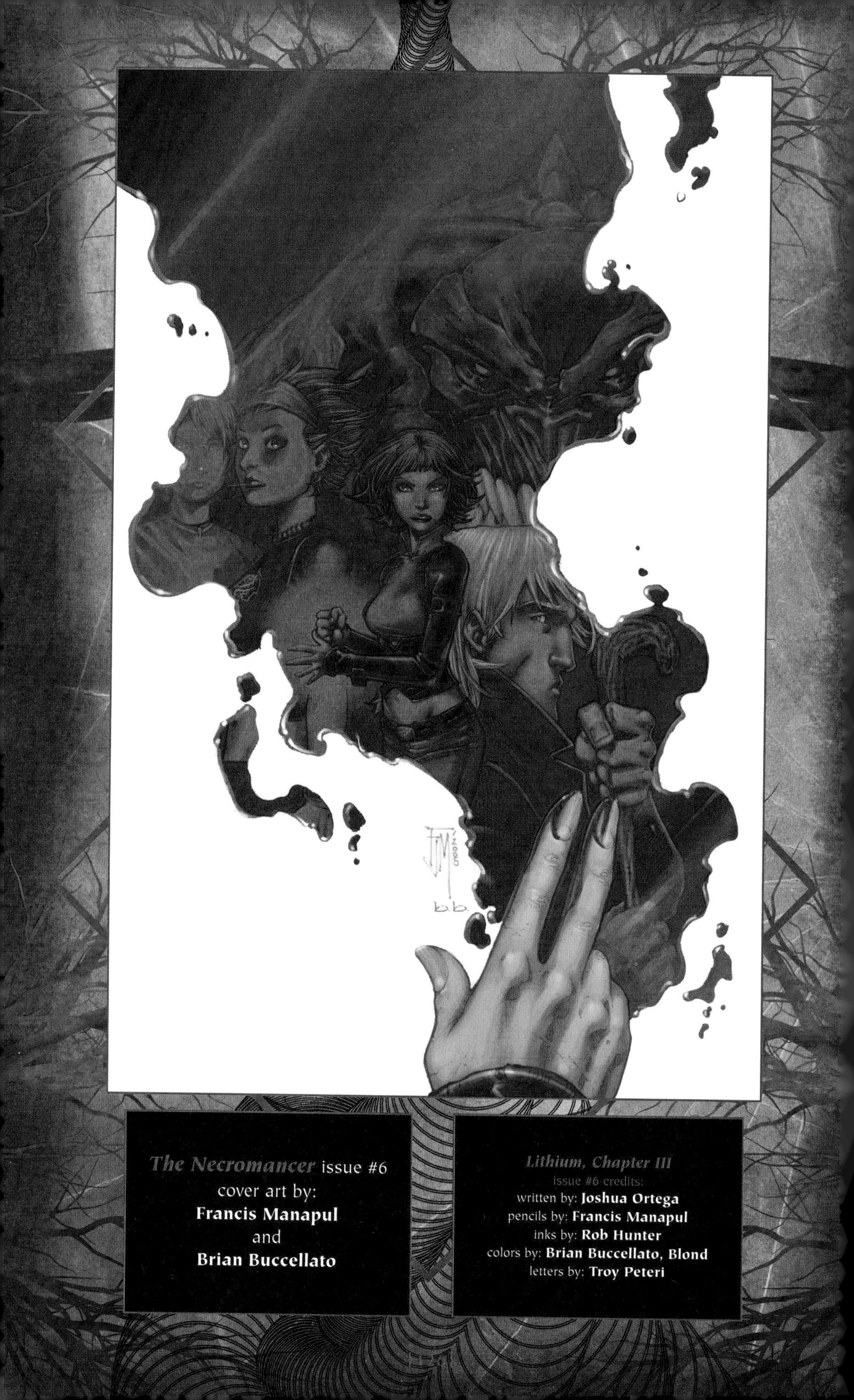

The Necromancer issue #6
cover art by:
Francis Manapul
and
Brian Buccellato

Lithium, Chapter III
issue #6 credits:
written by: **Joshua Ortega**
pencils by: **Francis Manapul**
inks by: **Rob Hunter**
colors by: **Brian Buccellato, Blond**
letters by: **Troy Peteri**

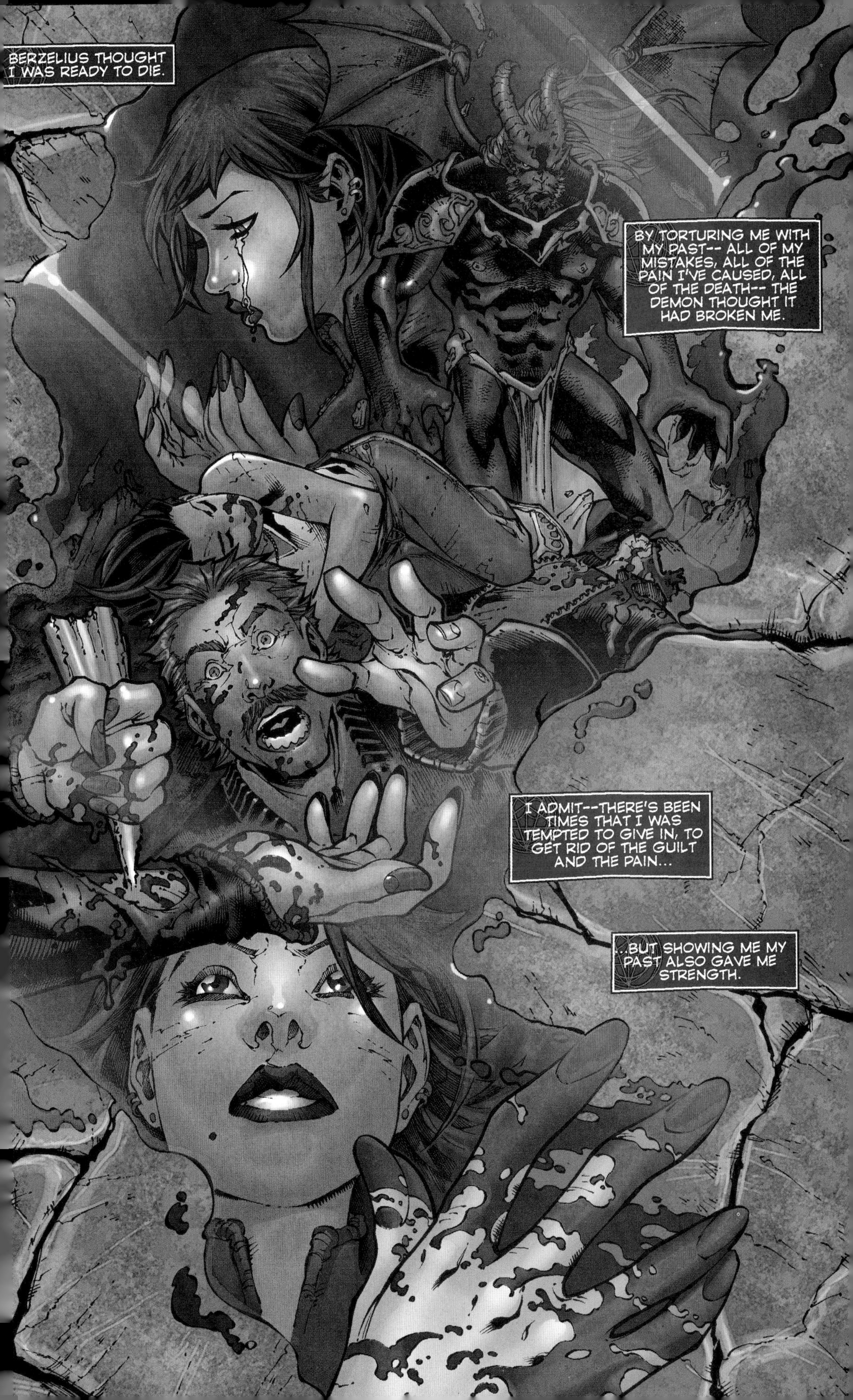
BERZELIUS THOUGHT I WAS READY TO DIE.
BY TORTURING ME WITH MY PAST-- ALL OF MY MISTAKES, ALL OF THE PAIN I'VE CAUSED, ALL OF THE DEATH-- THE DEMON THOUGHT IT HAD BROKEN ME.
I ADMIT--THERE'S BEEN TIMES THAT I WAS TEMPTED TO GIVE IN, TO GET RID OF THE GUILT AND THE PAIN...
...BUT SHOWING ME MY PAST ALSO GAVE ME STRENGTH.

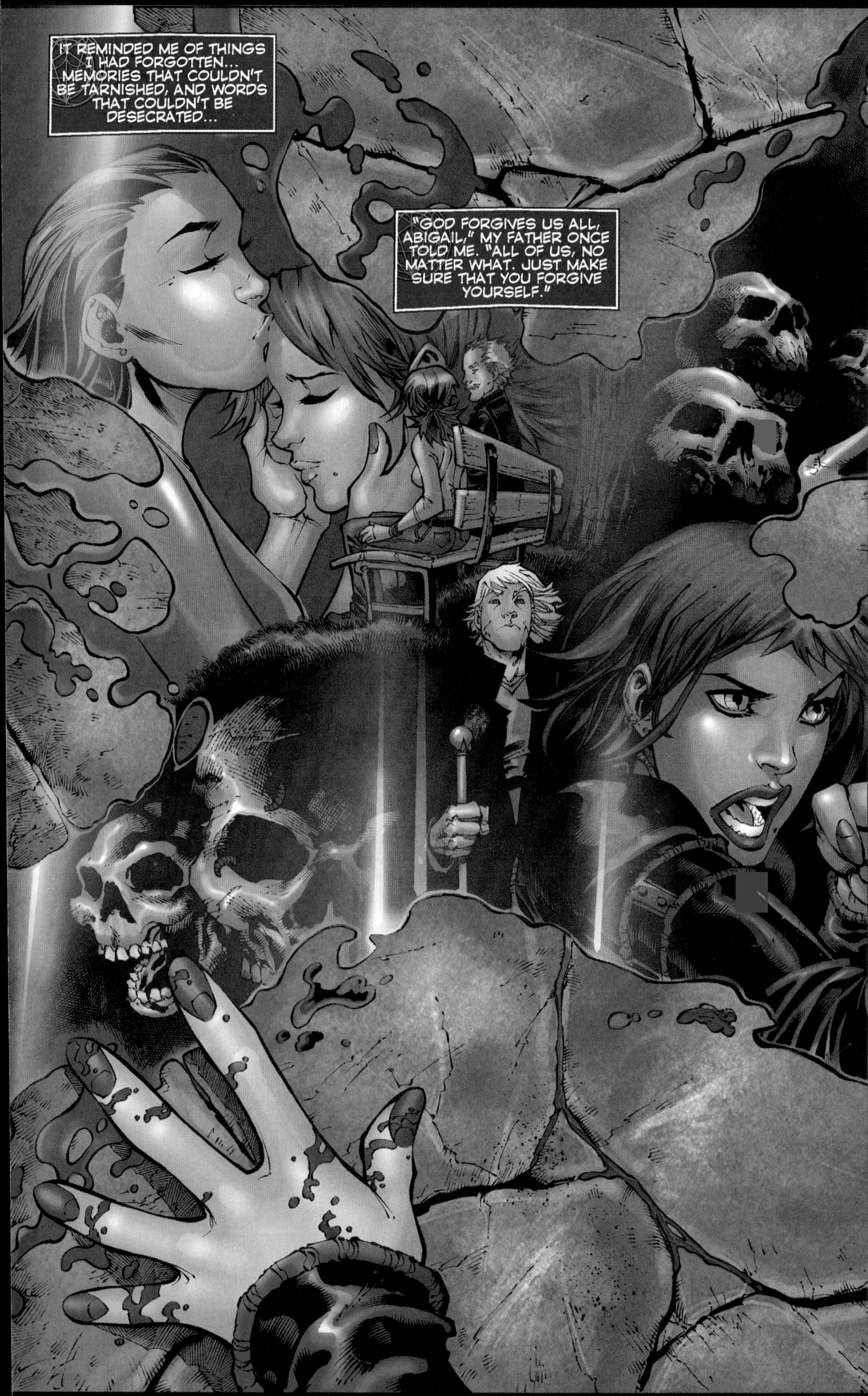
IT REMINDED ME OF THINGS I HAD FORGOTTEN... MEMORIES THAT COULDN'T BE TARNISHED, AND WORDS THAT COULDN'T BE DESECRATED...
"GOD FORGIVES US ALL, ABIGAIL," MY FATHER ONCE TOLD ME. "ALL OF US, NO MATTER WHAT. JUST MAKE SURE THAT YOU FORGIVE YOURSELF."

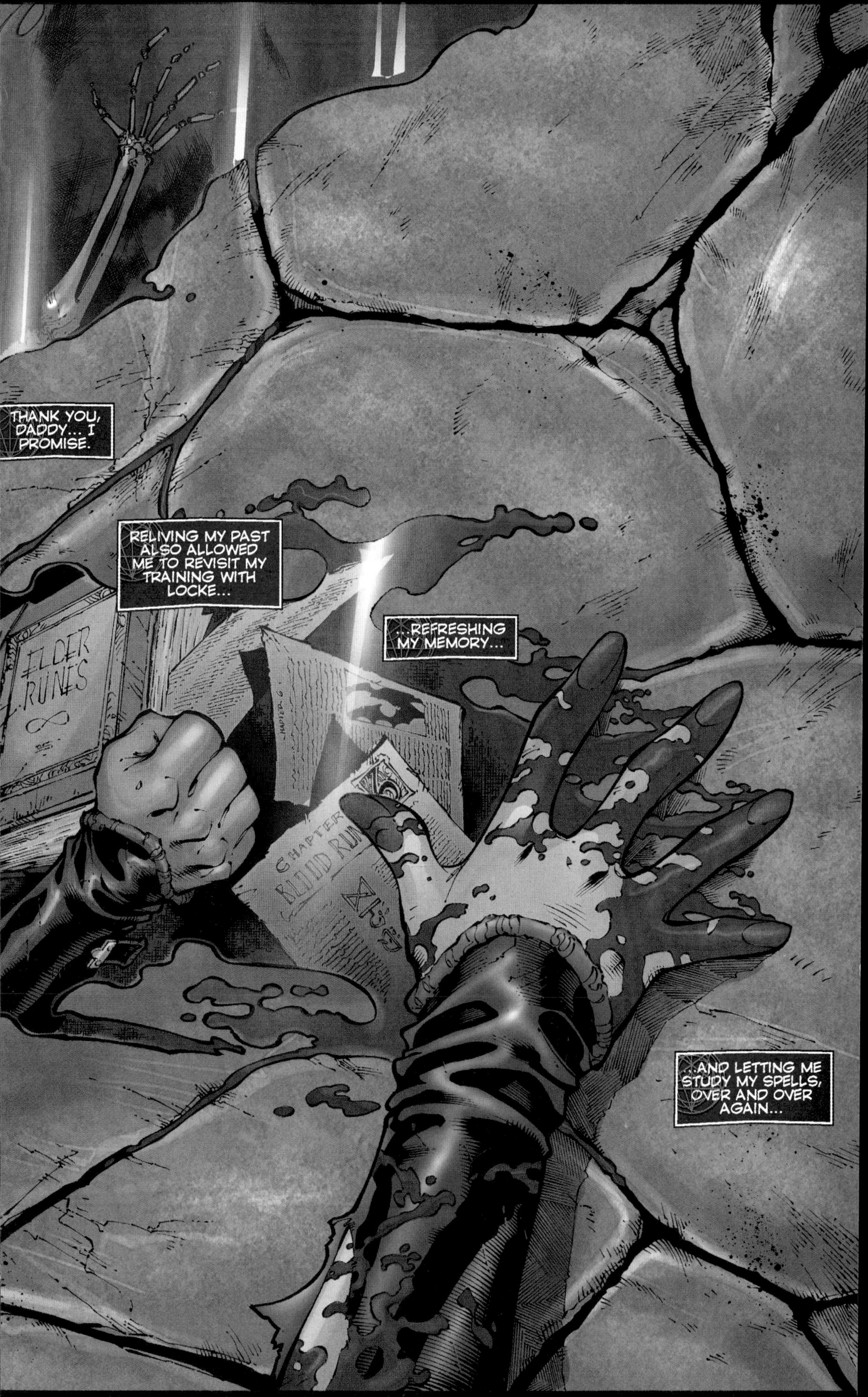
THANK YOU, DADDY... I PROMISE.
RELIVING MY PAST ALSO ALLOWED ME TO REVISIT MY TRAINING WITH LOCKE...
...REFRESHING MY MEMORY...
...AND LETTING ME STUDY MY SPELLS, OVER AND OVER AGAIN...

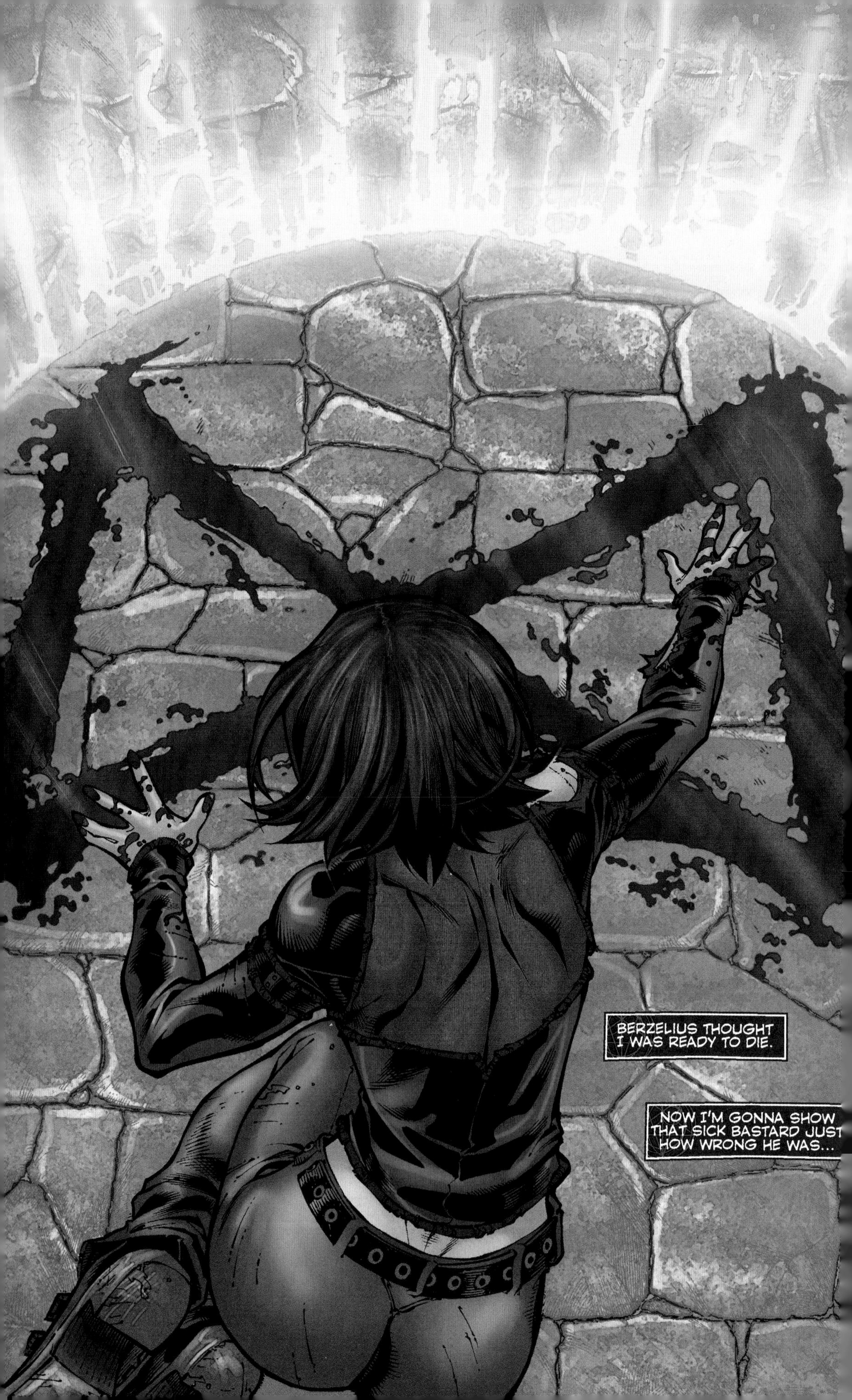
BERZELIUS THOUGHT I WAS READY TO DIE.
NOW I'M GONNA SHOW THAT SICK BASTARD JUST HOW WRONG HE WAS...

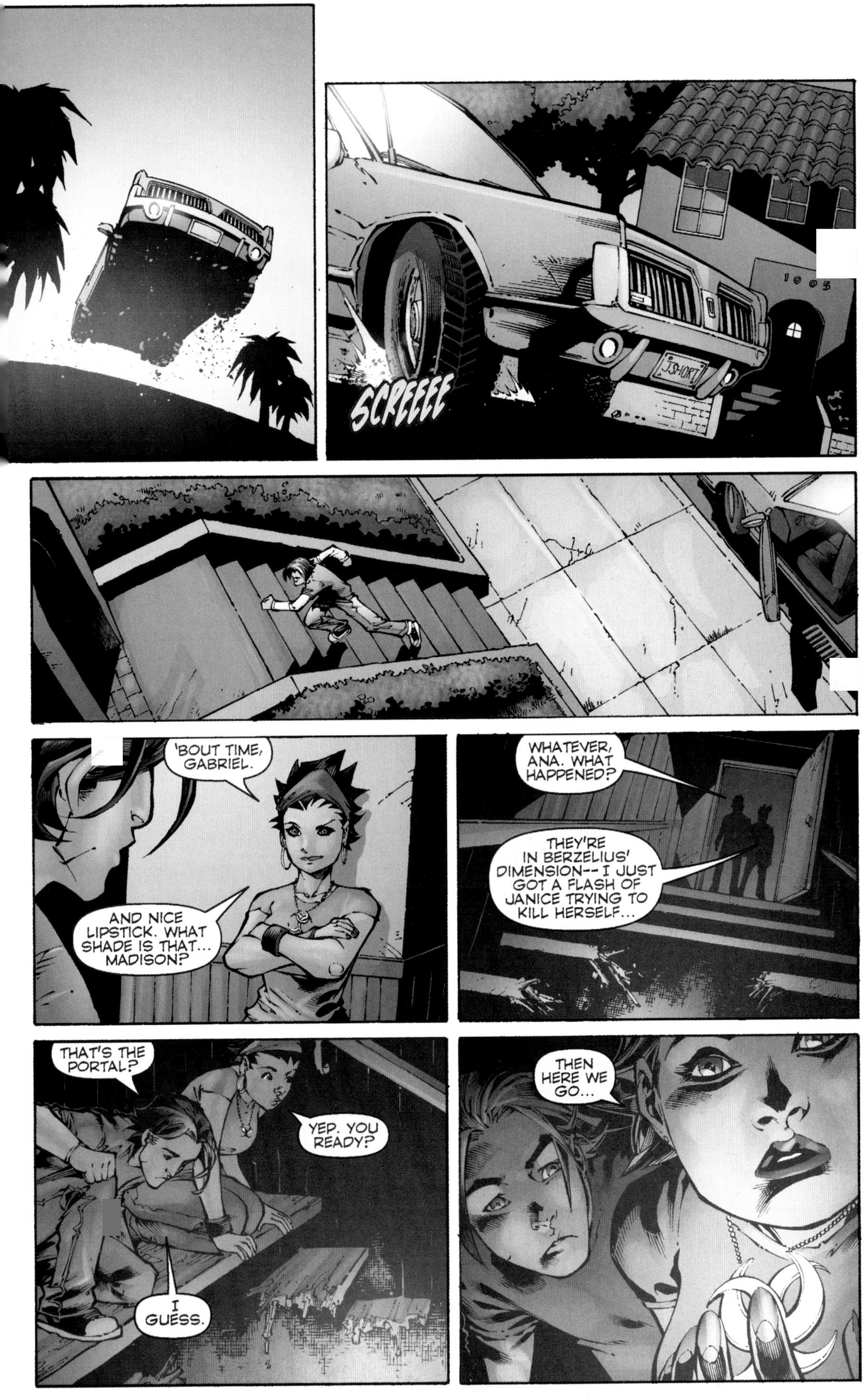
SCREEEEE
1005
J.SHORT
'BOUT TIME, GABRIEL.
AND NICE LIPSTICK. WHAT SHADE IS THAT... MADISON?
WHATEVER, ANA. WHAT HAPPENED?
THEY'RE IN BERZELIUS' DIMENSION-- I JUST GOT A FLASH OF JANICE TRYING TO KILL HERSELF...
THAT'S THE PORTAL?
YEP. YOU READY?
I GUESS.
THEN HERE WE GO...

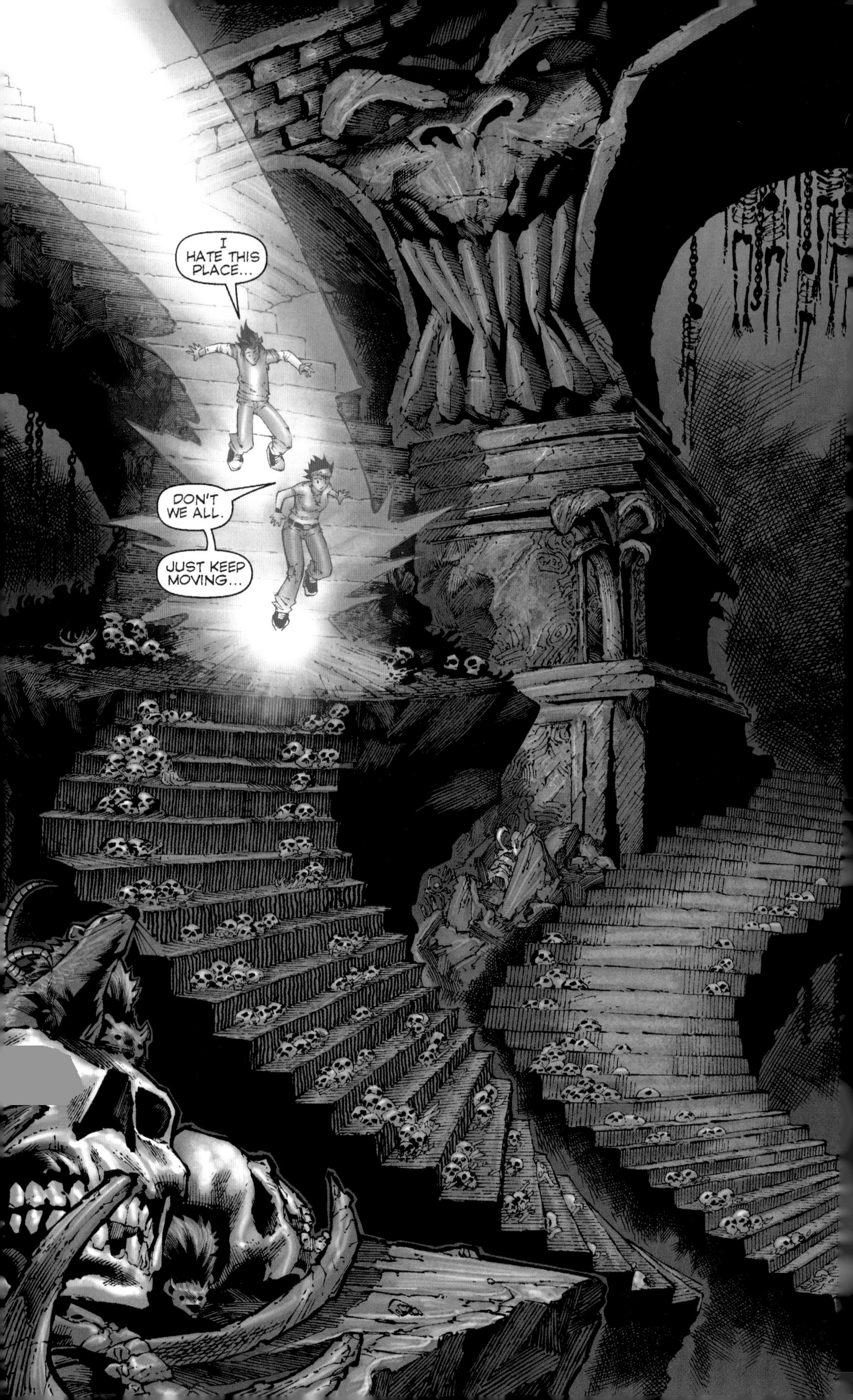
I HATE THIS PLACE...
DON'T WE ALL.
JUST KEEP MOVING...

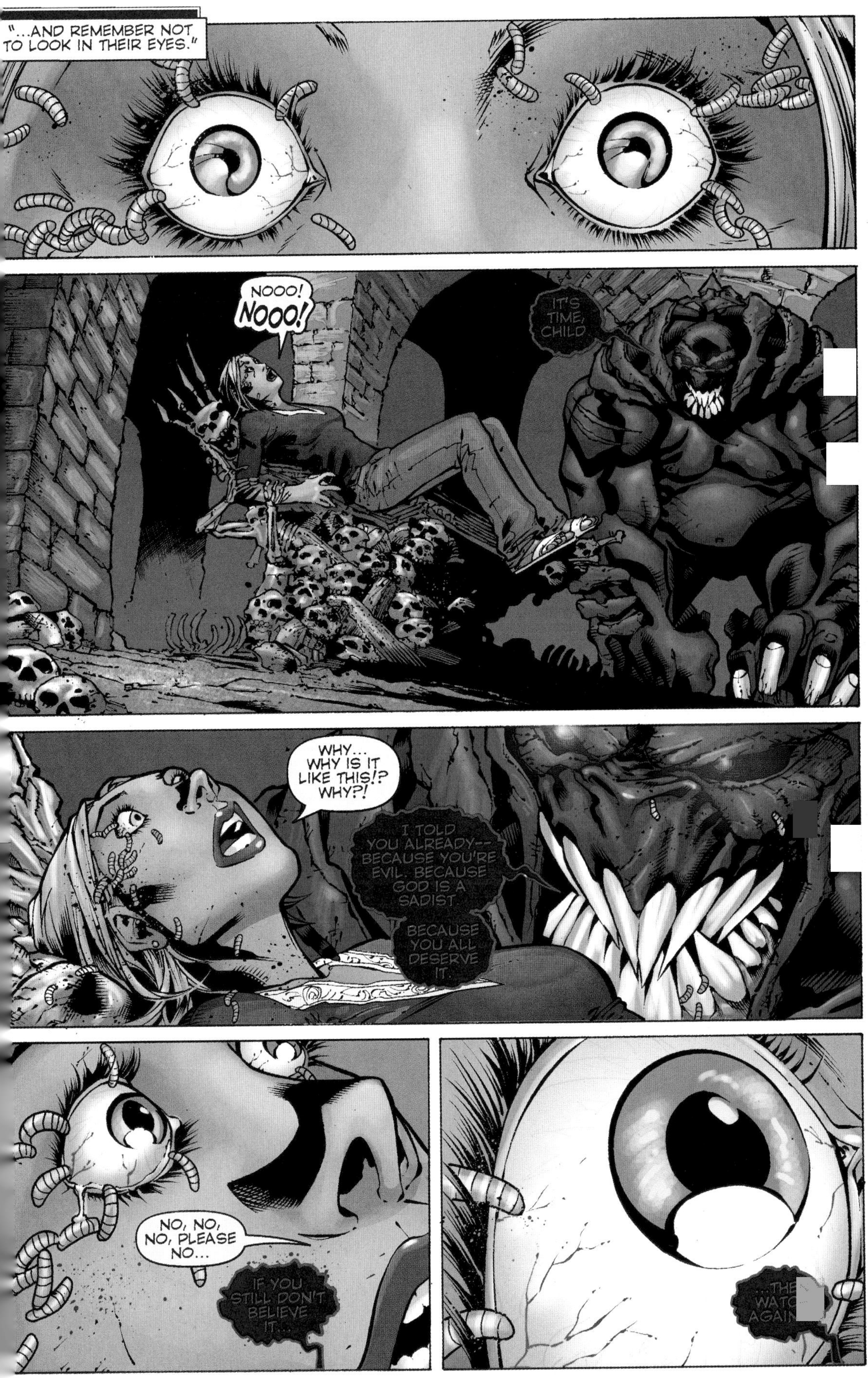
"...AND REMEMBER NOT TO LOOK IN THEIR EYES."
NOOO! NOOO!
IT'S TIME, CHILD
WHY... WHY IS IT LIKE THIS!? WHY?!
I TOLD YOU ALREADY-- BECAUSE YOU'RE EVIL. BECAUSE GOD IS A SADIST.
BECAUSE YOU ALL DESERVE IT.
NO, NO, NO, PLEASE NO...
IF YOU STILL DON'T BELIEVE IT...
...THE

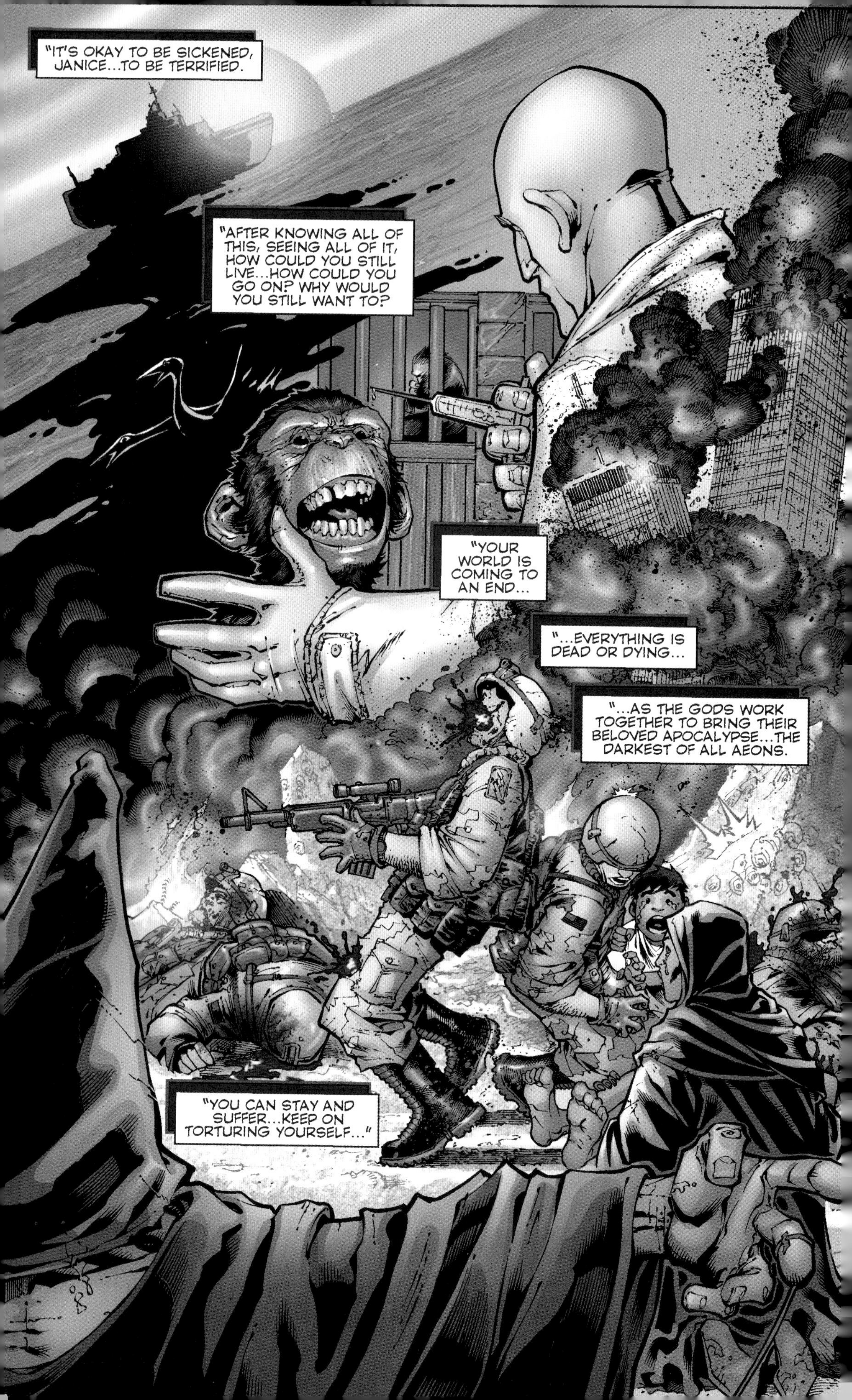
"IT'S OKAY TO BE SICKENED, JANICE...TO BE TERRIFIED.
"AFTER KNOWING ALL OF THIS, SEEING ALL OF IT, HOW COULD YOU STILL LIVE...HOW COULD YOU GO ON? WHY WOULD YOU STILL WANT TO?
"YOUR WORLD IS COMING TO AN END...
"...EVERYTHING IS DEAD OR DYING...
"...AS THE GODS WORK TOGETHER TO BRING THEIR BELOVED APOCALYPSE...THE DARKEST OF ALL AEONS.
"YOU CAN STAY AND SUFFER...KEEP ON TORTURING YOURSELF..."

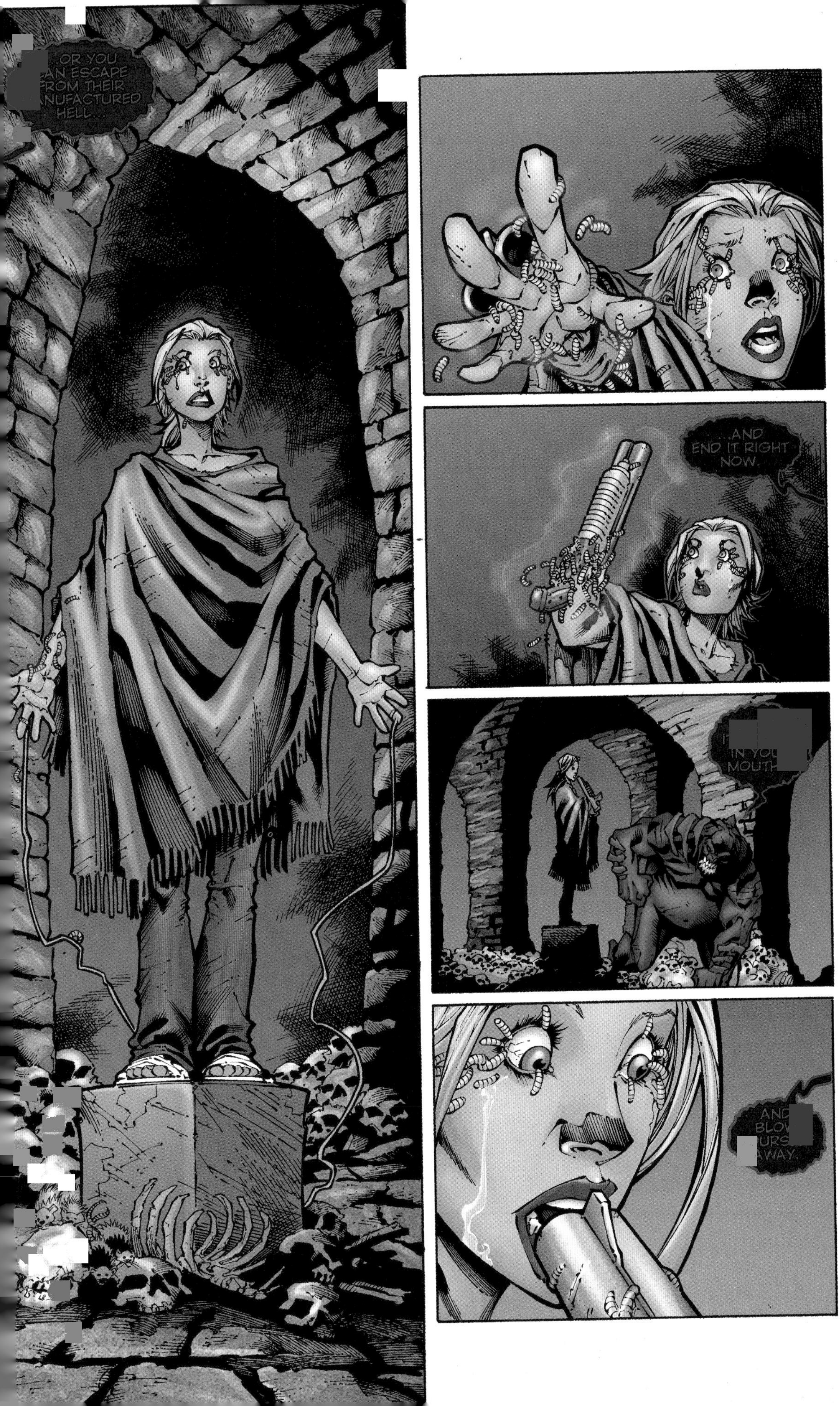
[redacted]...OR YOU [redacted]AN ESCAPE FROM THEIR [redacted]ANUFACTURED HELL...
...AND END IT RIGHT NOW.
[redacted] IN YOU[redacted] MOUTH[redacted]
AND[redacted] BLOW [redacted]URS[redacted] AWAY.

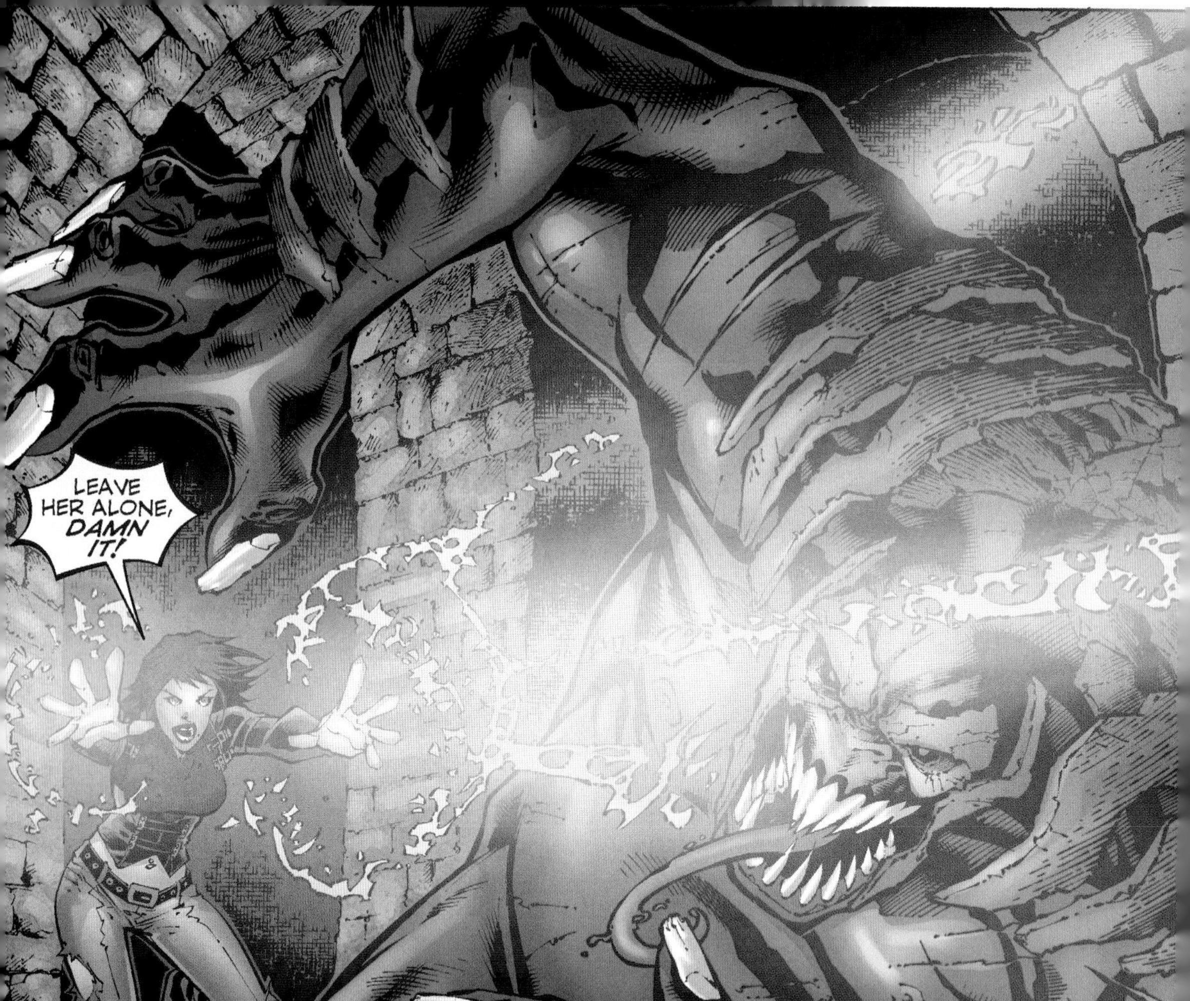
LEAVE HER ALONE, *DAMN IT!*

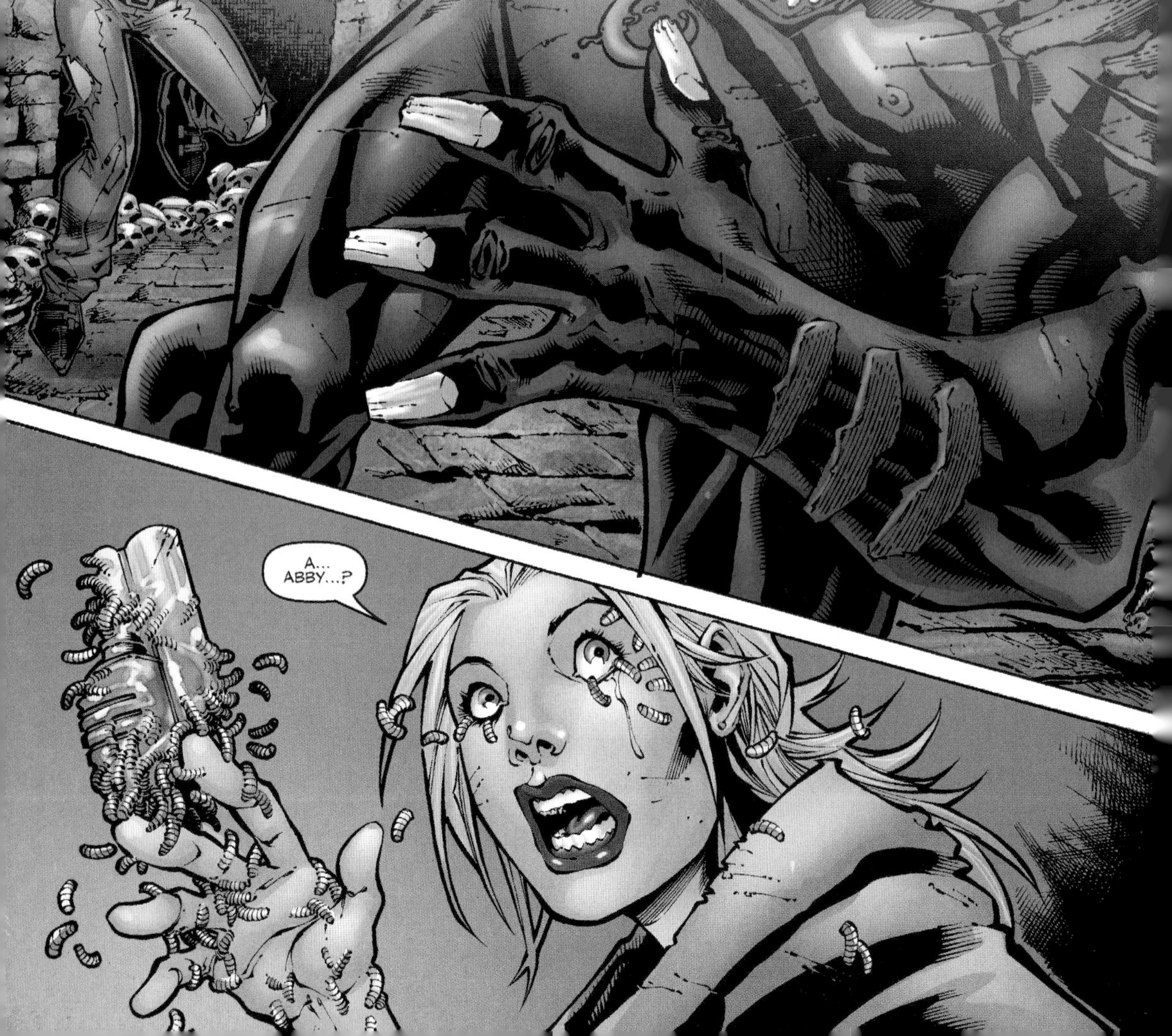
A... ABBY...?

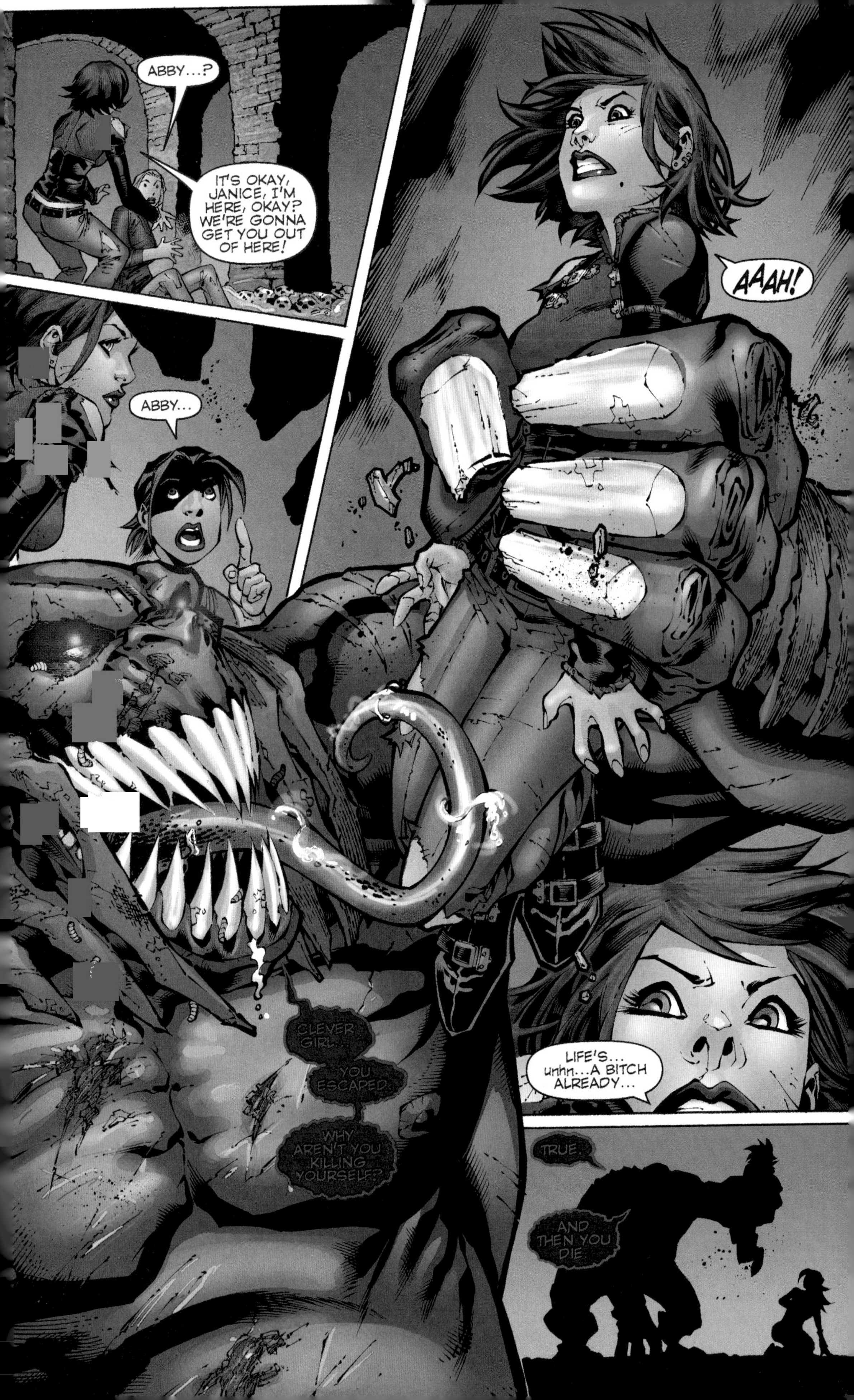
ABBY...?
IT'S OKAY, JANICE, I'M HERE, OKAY? WE'RE GONNA GET YOU OUT OF HERE!
ABBY...
AAAH!
CLEVER GIRL...
YOU ESCAPED.
WHY AREN'T YOU KILLING YOURSELF?
LIFE'S... unhh... A BITCH ALREADY...
TRUE.
AND THEN YOU DIE.

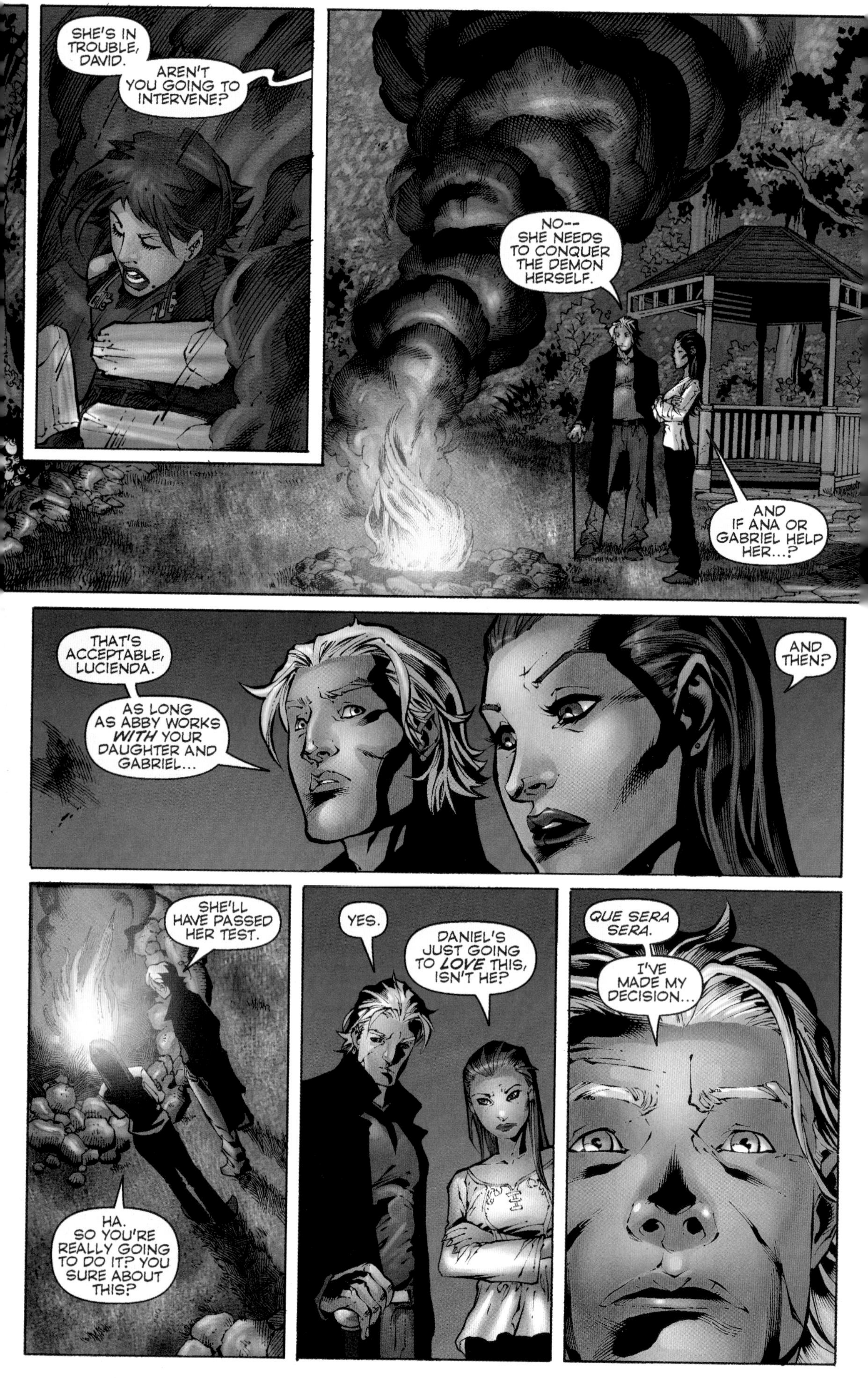
SHE'S IN TROUBLE, DAVID.
AREN'T YOU GOING TO INTERVENE?
NO-- SHE NEEDS TO CONQUER THE DEMON HERSELF.
AND IF ANA OR GABRIEL HELP HER...?
THAT'S ACCEPTABLE, LUCIENDA.
AS LONG AS ABBY WORKS *WITH* YOUR DAUGHTER AND GABRIEL...
AND THEN?
SHE'LL HAVE PASSED HER TEST.
HA. SO YOU'RE REALLY GOING TO DO IT? YOU SURE ABOUT THIS?
YES.
DANIEL'S JUST GOING TO *LOVE* THIS, ISN'T HE?
QUE SERA SERA.
I'VE MADE MY DECISION...

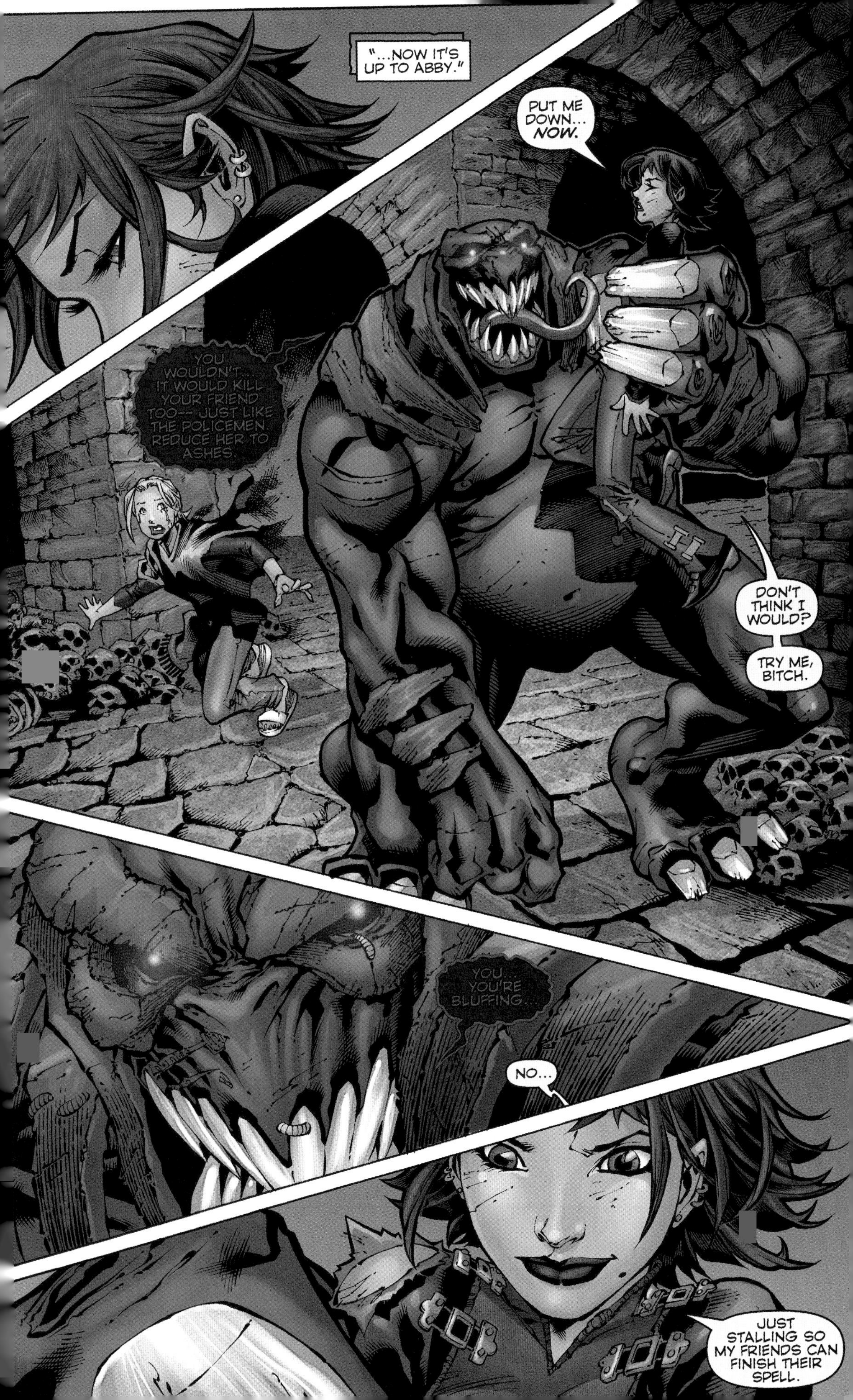
"...NOW IT'S UP TO ABBY."
PUT ME DOWN... NOW.
YOU WOULDN'T... IT WOULD KILL YOUR FRIEND TOO-- JUST LIKE THE POLICEMEN. REDUCE HER TO ASHES.
DON'T THINK I WOULD?
TRY ME, BITCH.
YOU... YOU'RE BLUFFING...
NO...
JUST STALLING SO MY FRIENDS CAN FINISH THEIR SPELL.

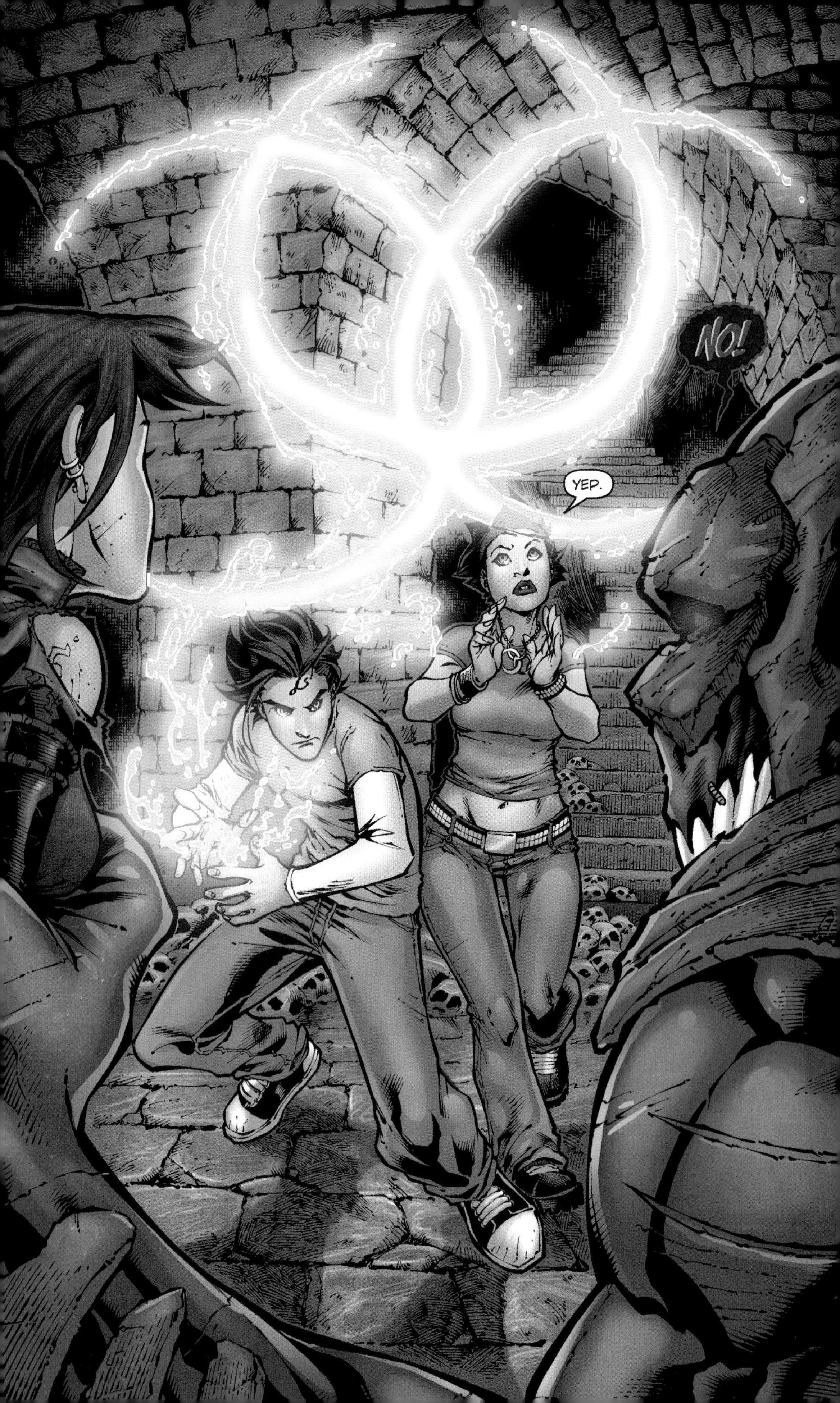
NO!
YEP.

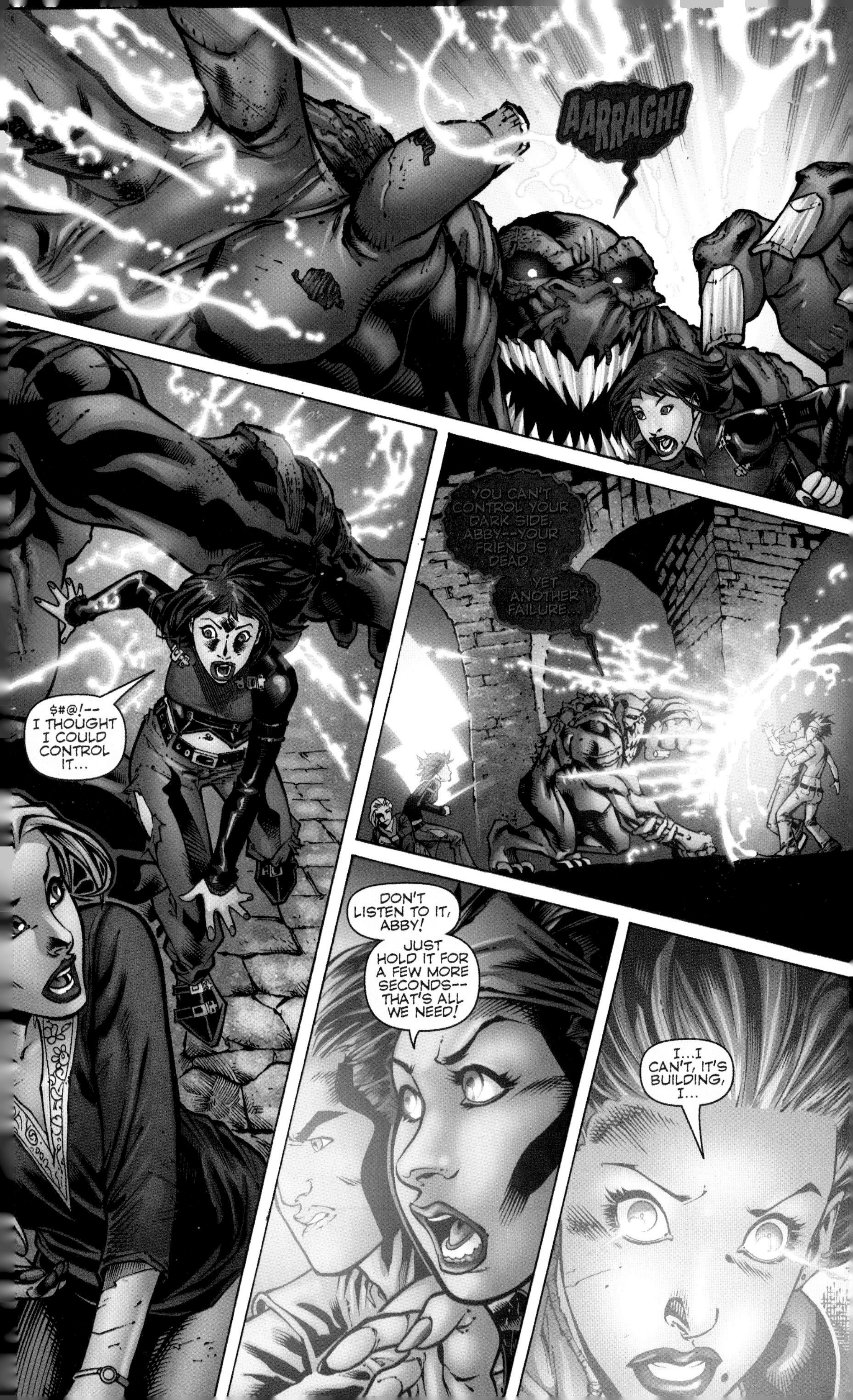
AARRAGH!
YOU CAN'T CONTROL YOUR DARK SIDE, ABBY--YOUR FRIEND IS DEAD.
YET ANOTHER FAILURE...
$#@!-- I THOUGHT I COULD CONTROL IT...
DON'T LISTEN TO IT, ABBY!
JUST HOLD IT FOR A FEW MORE SECONDS-- THAT'S ALL WE NEED!
I...I CAN'T, IT'S BUILDING, I...

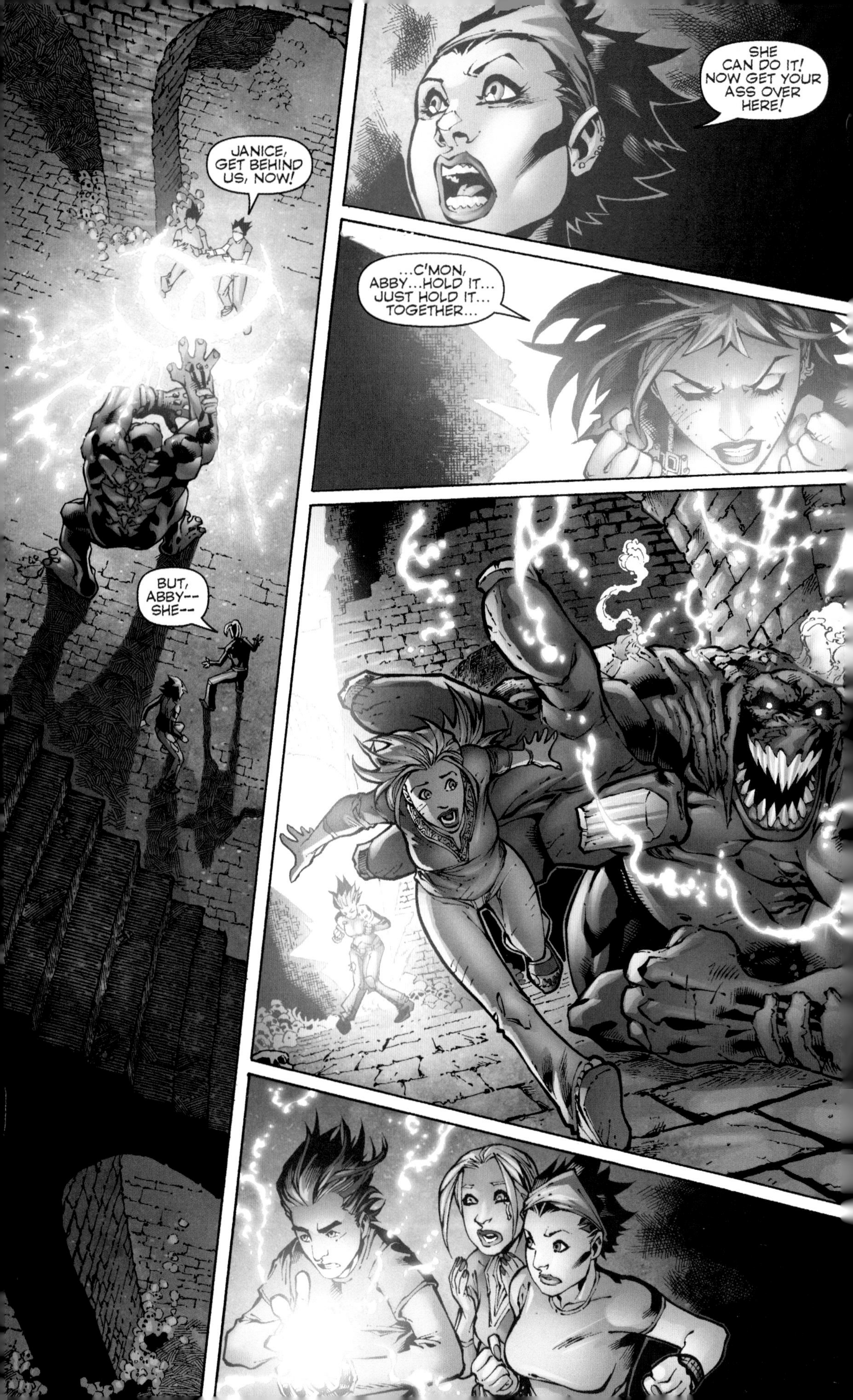
JANICE, GET BEHIND US, NOW!
BUT, ABBY-- SHE--
SHE CAN DO IT! NOW GET YOUR ASS OVER HERE!
...C'MON, ABBY...HOLD IT... JUST HOLD IT... TOGETHER...

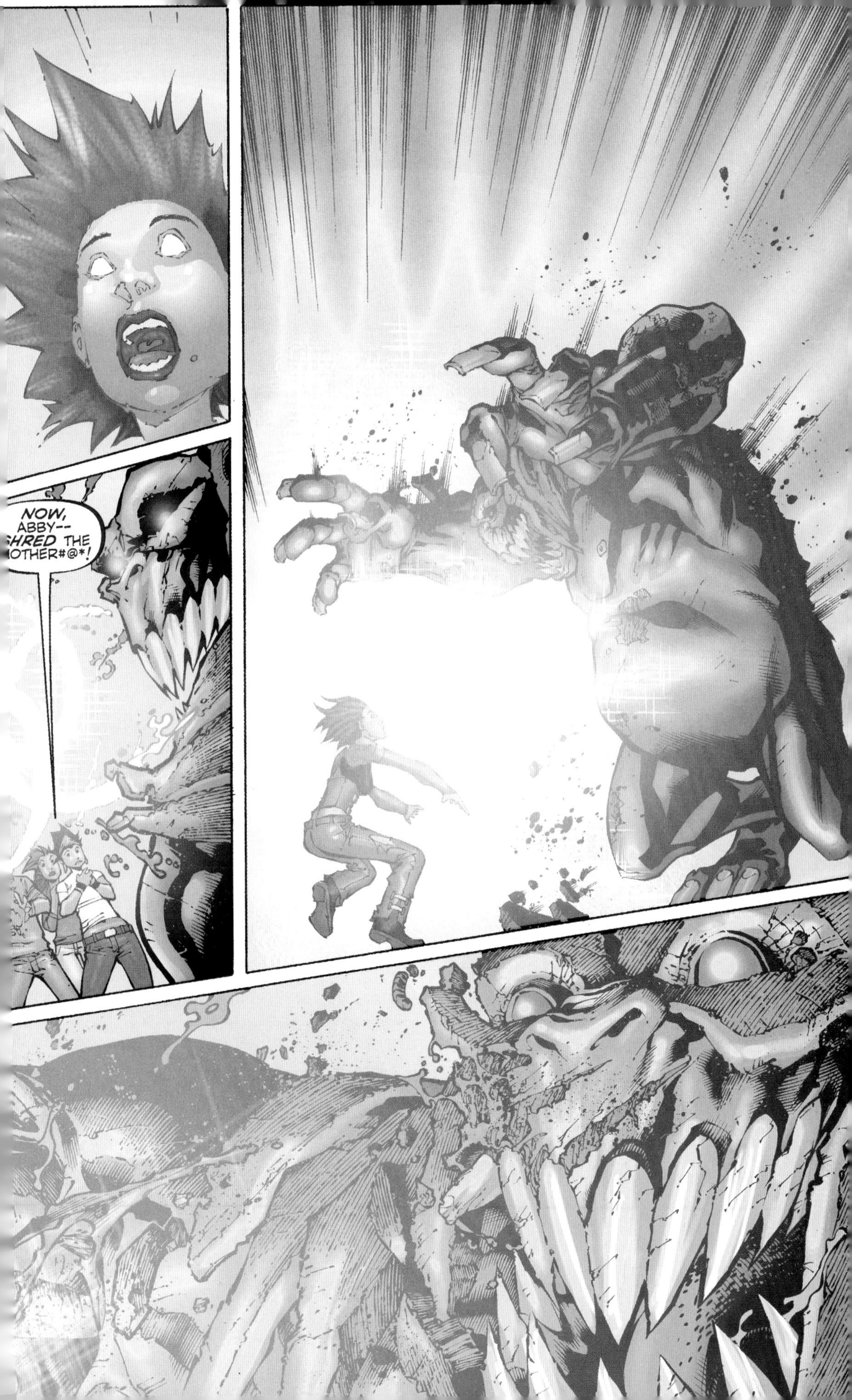
NOW, ABBY-- SHRED THE MOTHER#@*!

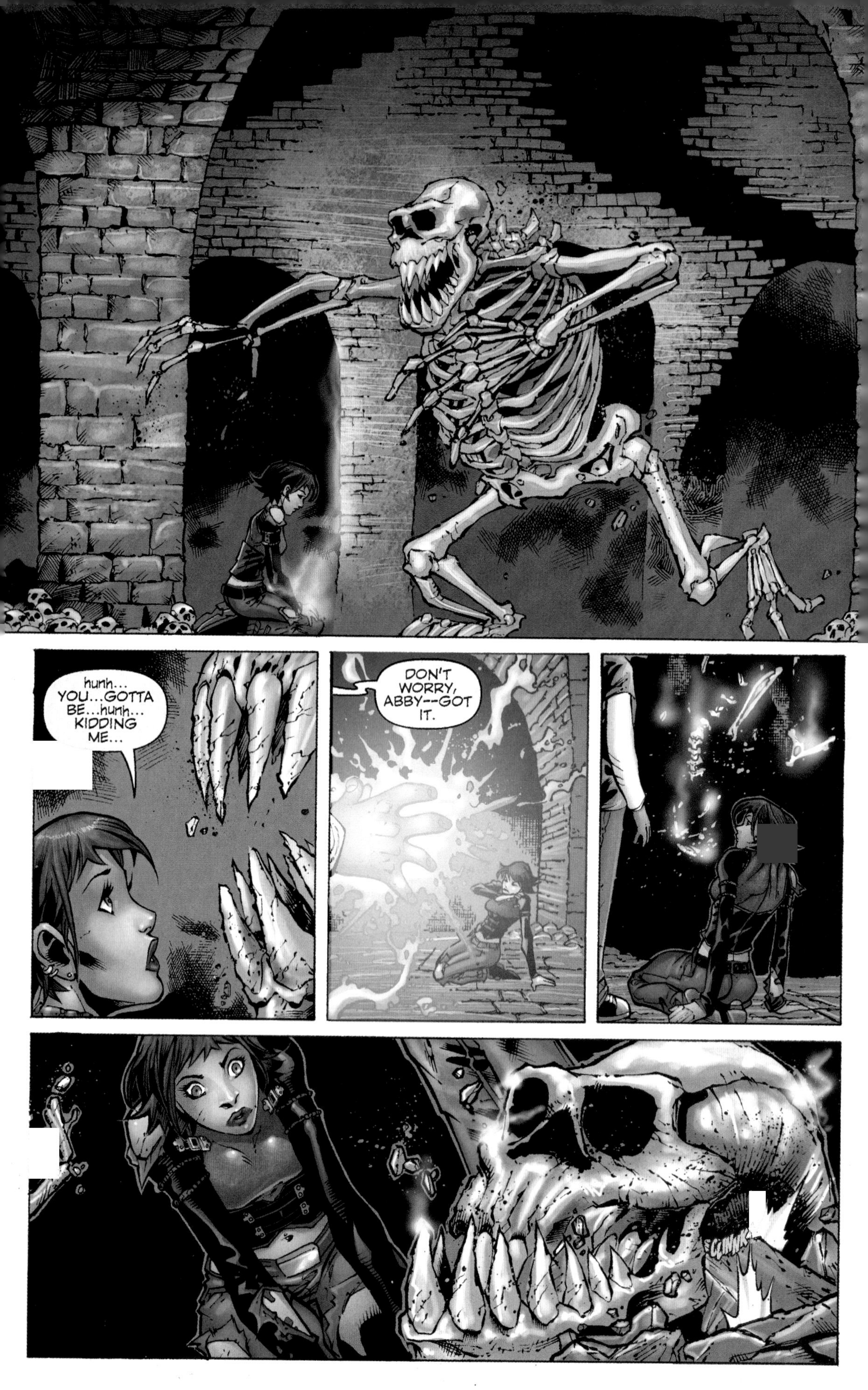
hunh... YOU...GOTTA BE...hunh... KIDDING ME...
DON'T WORRY, ABBY--GOT IT.
CLINNK

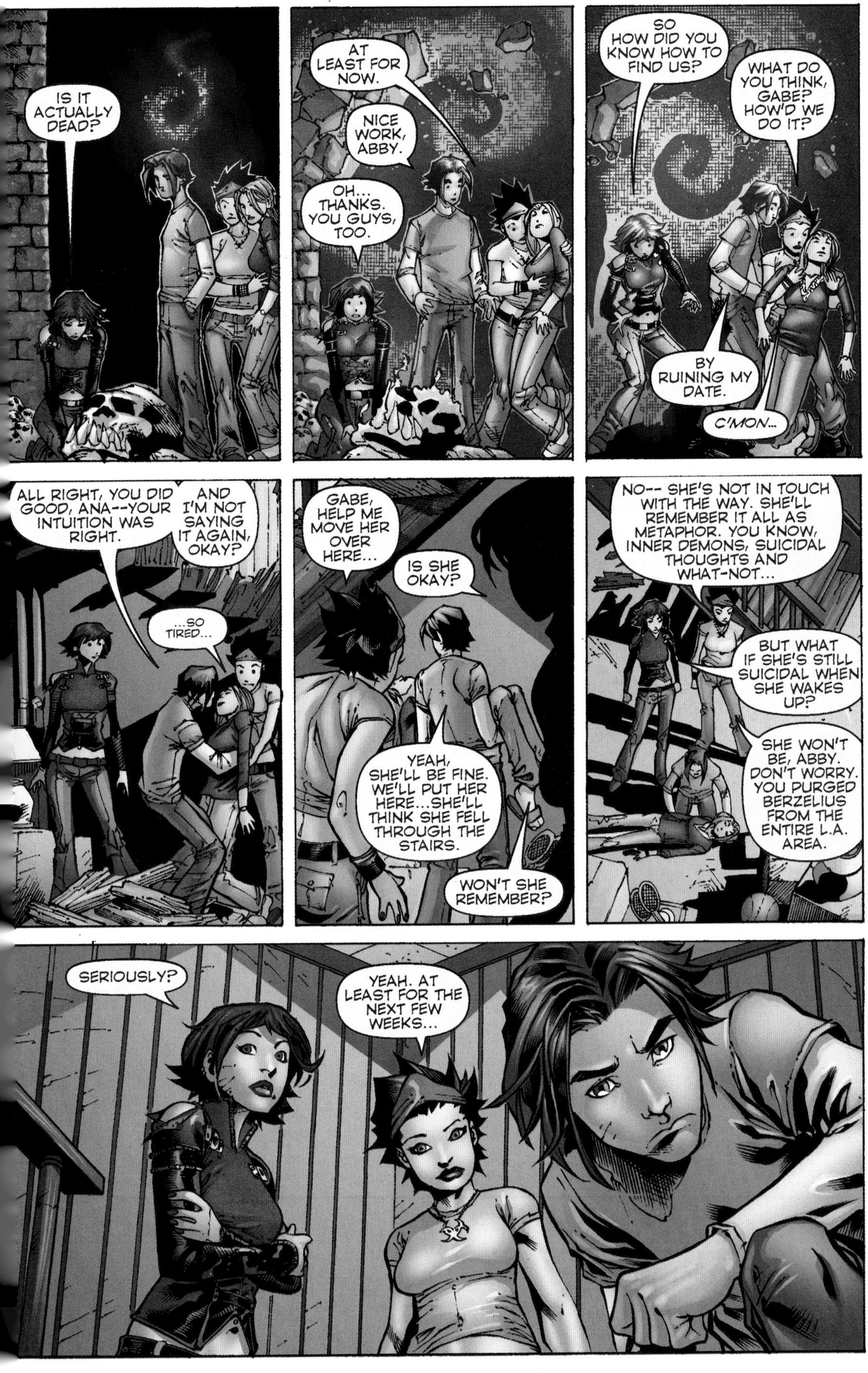
IS IT ACTUALLY DEAD?
AT LEAST FOR NOW.
NICE WORK, ABBY.
OH... THANKS. YOU GUYS, TOO.
SO HOW DID YOU KNOW HOW TO FIND US?
WHAT DO YOU THINK, GABE? HOW'D WE DO IT?
BY RUINING MY DATE.
C'MON...
ALL RIGHT, YOU DID GOOD, ANA--YOUR INTUITION WAS RIGHT.
AND I'M NOT SAYING IT AGAIN, OKAY?
...SO TIRED...
GABE, HELP ME MOVE HER OVER HERE...
IS SHE OKAY?
YEAH, SHE'LL BE FINE. WE'LL PUT HER HERE...SHE'LL THINK SHE FELL THROUGH THE STAIRS.
WON'T SHE REMEMBER?
NO-- SHE'S NOT IN TOUCH WITH THE WAY. SHE'LL REMEMBER IT ALL AS METAPHOR. YOU KNOW, INNER DEMONS, SUICIDAL THOUGHTS AND WHAT-NOT...
BUT WHAT IF SHE'S STILL SUICIDAL WHEN SHE WAKES UP?
SHE WON'T BE, ABBY. DON'T WORRY. YOU PURGED BERZELIUS FROM THE ENTIRE L.A. AREA.
SERIOUSLY?
YEAH. AT LEAST FOR THE NEXT FEW WEEKS...

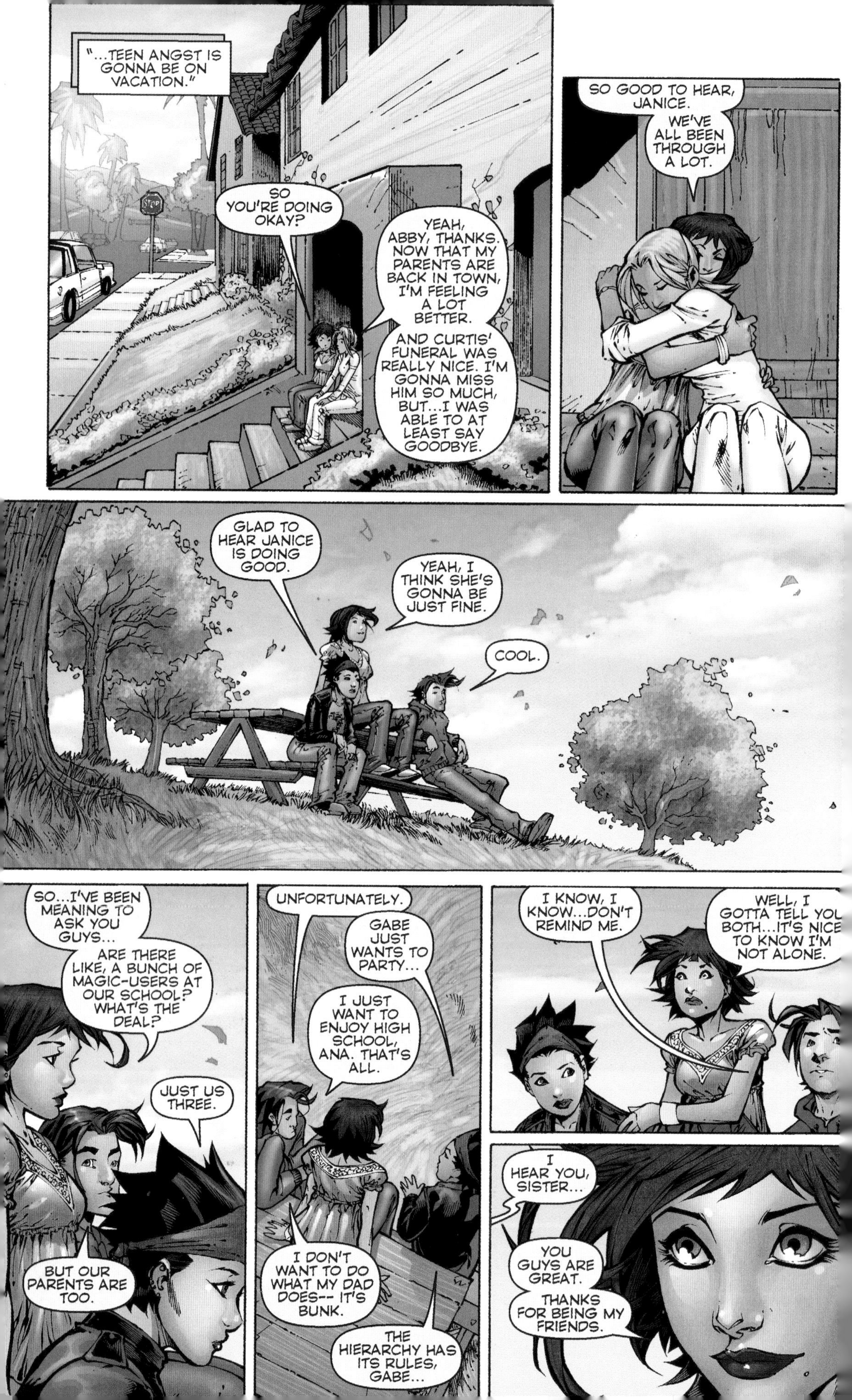
"...TEEN ANGST IS GONNA BE ON VACATION."
SO YOU'RE DOING OKAY?
YEAH, ABBY, THANKS. NOW THAT MY PARENTS ARE BACK IN TOWN, I'M FEELING A LOT BETTER.
AND CURTIS' FUNERAL WAS REALLY NICE. I'M GONNA MISS HIM SO MUCH, BUT...I WAS ABLE TO AT LEAST SAY GOODBYE.
SO GOOD TO HEAR, JANICE.
WE'VE ALL BEEN THROUGH A LOT.
GLAD TO HEAR JANICE IS DOING GOOD.
YEAH, I THINK SHE'S GONNA BE JUST FINE.
COOL.
SO...I'VE BEEN MEANING TO ASK YOU GUYS...
ARE THERE LIKE, A BUNCH OF MAGIC-USERS AT OUR SCHOOL? WHAT'S THE DEAL?
JUST US THREE.
BUT OUR PARENTS ARE TOO.
UNFORTUNATELY.
GABE JUST WANTS TO PARTY...
I JUST WANT TO ENJOY HIGH SCHOOL, ANA. THAT'S ALL.
I DON'T WANT TO DO WHAT MY DAD DOES-- IT'S BUNK.
THE HIERARCHY HAS ITS RULES, GABE...
I KNOW, I KNOW...DON'T REMIND ME.
WELL, I GOTTA TELL YOU BOTH...IT'S NICE TO KNOW I'M NOT ALONE.
I HEAR YOU, SISTER...
YOU GUYS ARE GREAT.
THANKS FOR BEING MY FRIENDS.

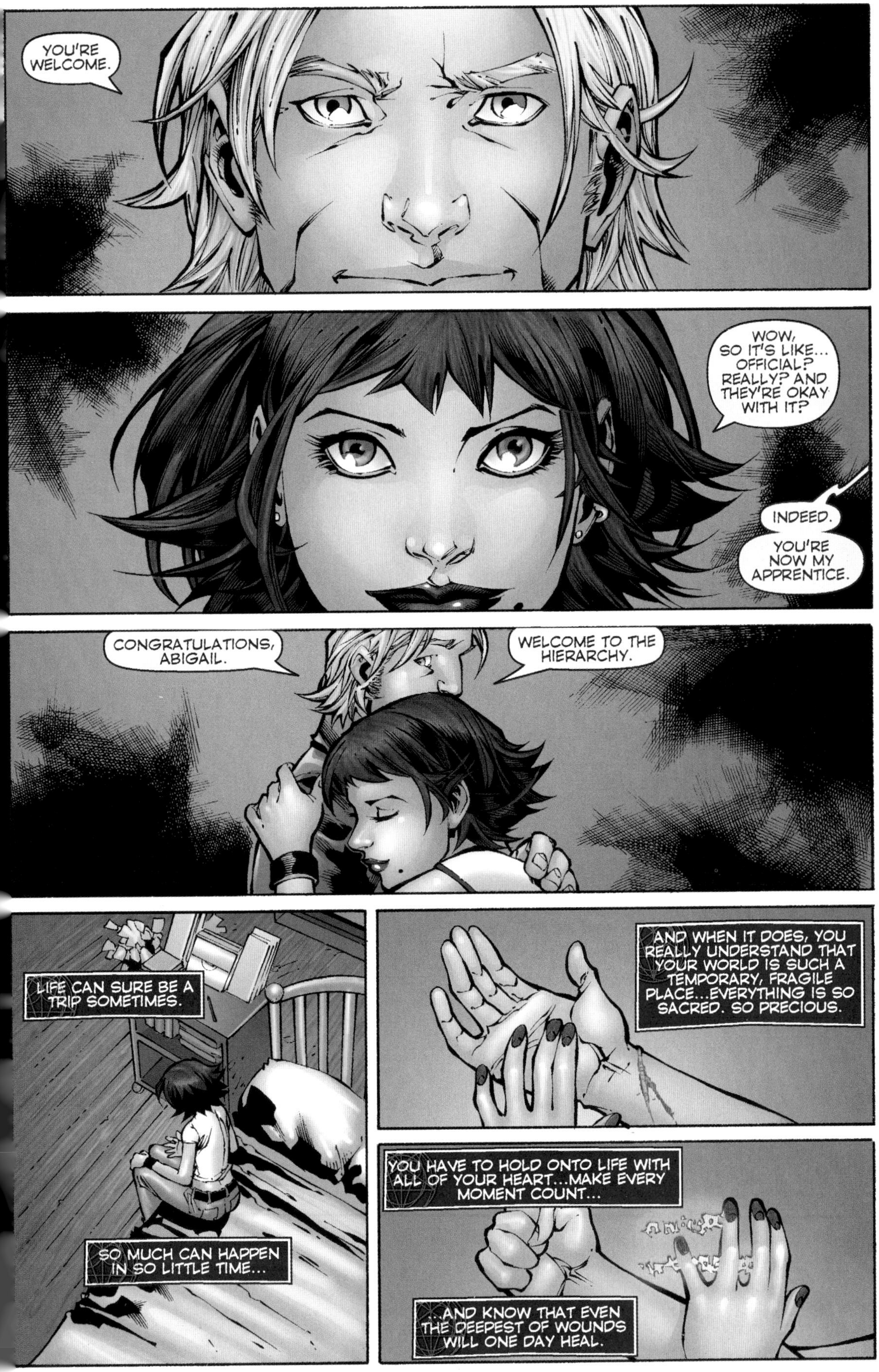
YOU'RE WELCOME.
WOW, SO IT'S LIKE... OFFICIAL? REALLY? AND THEY'RE OKAY WITH IT?
INDEED.
YOU'RE NOW MY APPRENTICE.
CONGRATULATIONS, ABIGAIL.
WELCOME TO THE HIERARCHY.
LIFE CAN SURE BE A TRIP SOMETIMES.
SO MUCH CAN HAPPEN IN SO LITTLE TIME...
AND WHEN IT DOES, YOU REALLY UNDERSTAND THAT YOUR WORLD IS SUCH A TEMPORARY, FRAGILE PLACE...EVERYTHING IS SO SACRED. SO PRECIOUS.
YOU HAVE TO HOLD ONTO LIFE WITH ALL OF YOUR HEART...MAKE EVERY MOMENT COUNT...
...AND KNOW THAT EVEN THE DEEPEST OF WOUNDS WILL ONE DAY HEAL.

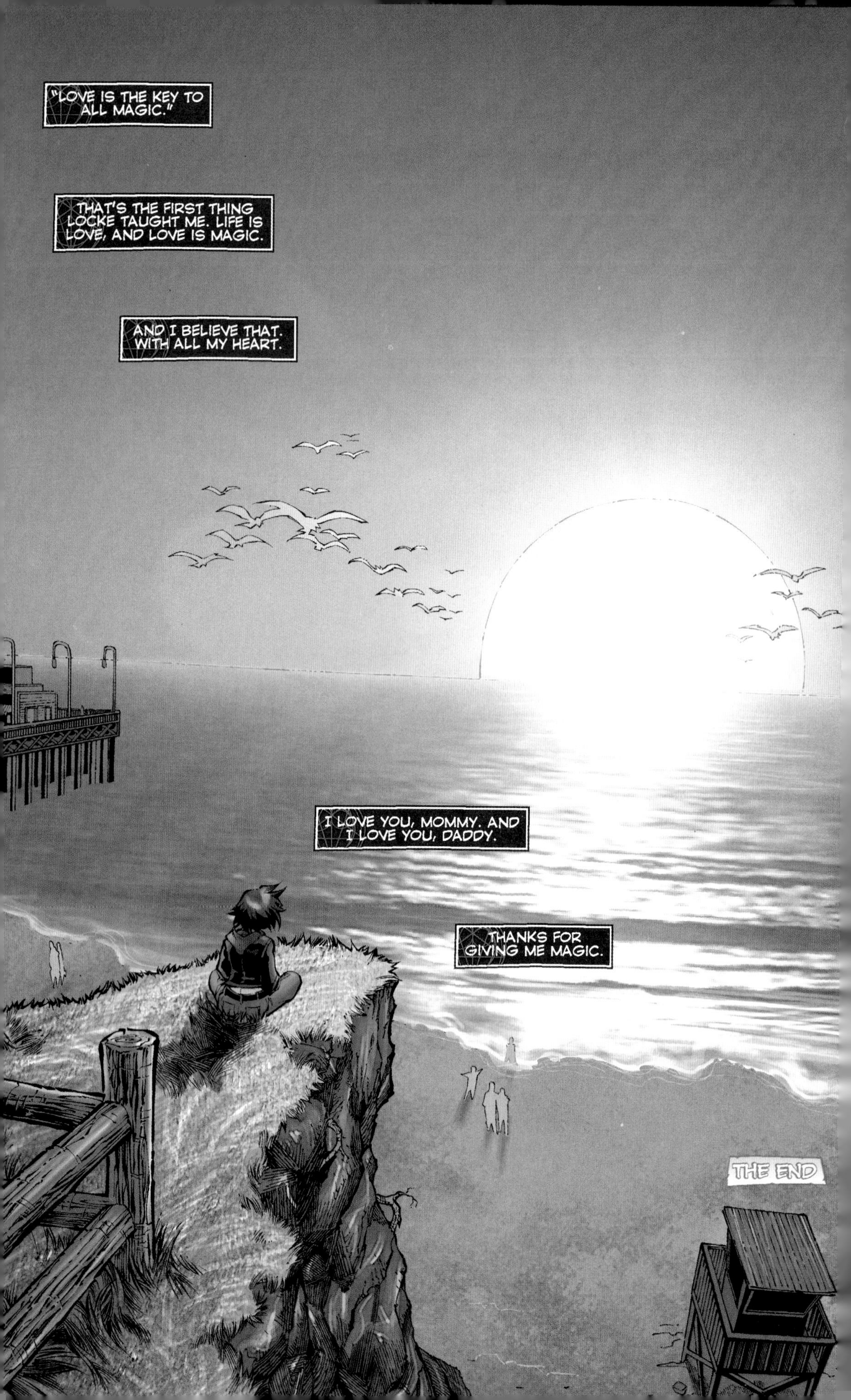
"LOVE IS THE KEY TO ALL MAGIC."
THAT'S THE FIRST THING LOCKE TAUGHT ME. LIFE IS LOVE, AND LOVE IS MAGIC.
AND I BELIEVE THAT. WITH ALL MY HEART.
I LOVE YOU, MOMMY. AND I LOVE YOU, DADDY.
THANKS FOR GIVING ME MAGIC.
THE END

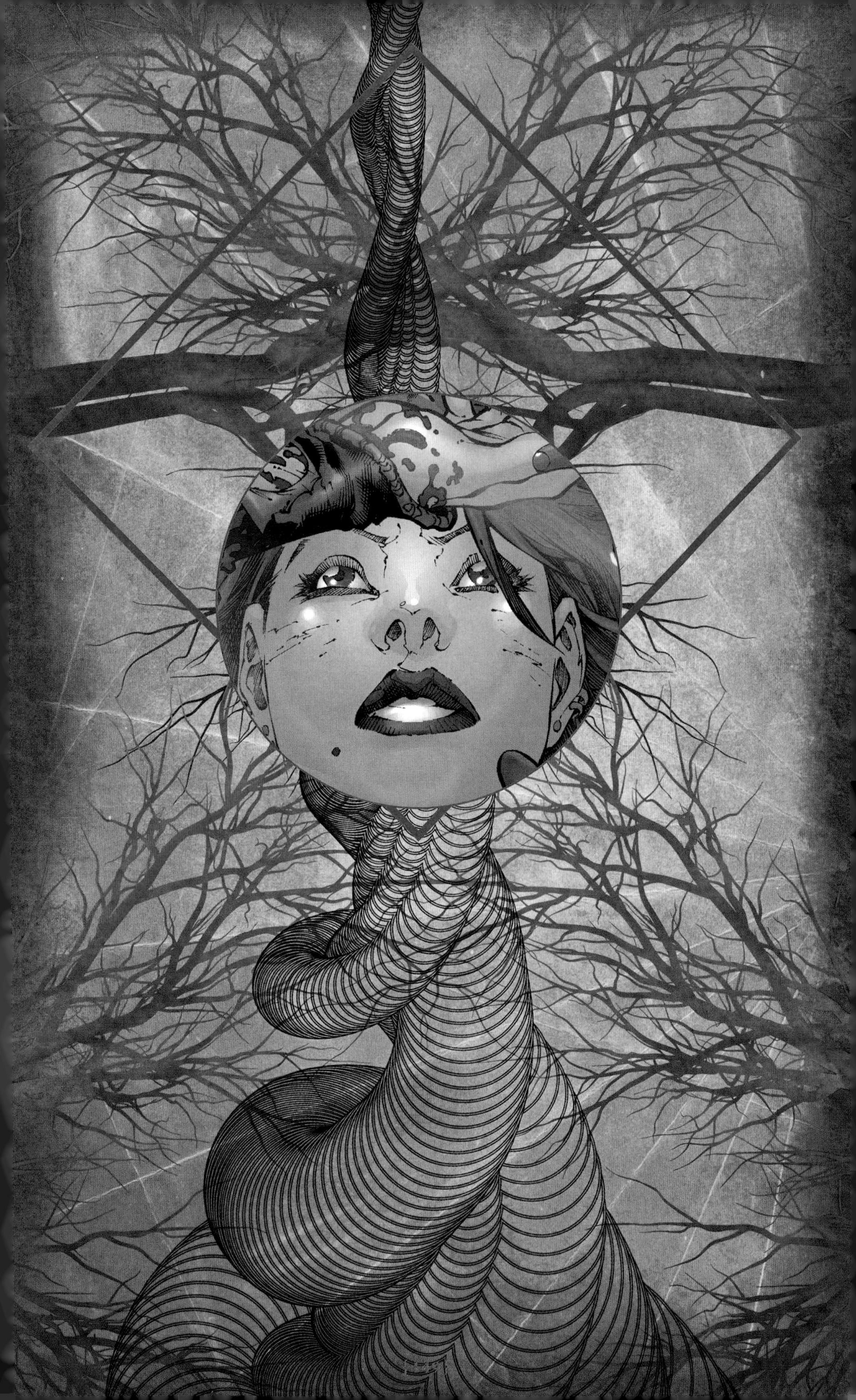

AFTERWORD

I don't recall exactly when I got the original idea for *The Necromancer*. It was around ten years ago when I was publishing *Lady Pendragon* through Image. My parents are both pretty hardcore Christians and I was raised in various Southern Baptist churches near military bases where my dad worked. I lusted after an older girl in Warrensburg, Missouri whose father was the pastor of our church. She was wild, very rebellious in a hot kind of way. I remember her telling me what an Ouija board was. I hadn't been exposed to the occult before that, so it made an impression on a future Dungeons and Dragons, Everquest and Warcraft addict. I hadn't thought about her in a very long time but she popped up in a dream of mine. Unfortunately, it wasn't some childhood erotic fantasy remembrance, but her playing with an Ouija board and summoning a demon that burned down her house and killed her family. I have some bizarre dreams, but ever since the *Lady Pendragon* origin came to me in a dream I've kept a notepad by my bed and write them down.

Flash forward about four years and I'm at Top Cow going through some of my old notebooks when I come across that scene I had jotted down. Marc Silvestri and I had been talking about new books and how the Top Cow universe had a supernatural, magic bent to it. This seemed a potential fit so I put it on my desk to think about. I was talking to Brian Ching at one point and he liked the idea so Brian and I were planning on being the creative team on it. Wizard did an article at that point with some drawings that Brian had done and interviewed me about the project. A lot of the basic ideas for what became the final book were fleshed out at that point.

I wrote a couple page treatment and Brian waited for me to finish a script so he could start drawing it. Well... life intervened. My wife and I had back to back kids, I had a pretty debilitating stomach injury and the full time day job at Top Cow just totally prevented me from writing anything, despite the desire. Brian moved onto other things and *The Necromancer* just became another project on the "to do" list.

Flash forward a few more years and Francis Manapul was at Top Cow working on *Witchblade* - talk about an amazing artist! I talked to him about *The Necromancer* a bit and he thought it was cool. So I started thinking about how much fun it would be to work with Francis and write something again, but… life intervened. So, a glorious thing happened! Then Top Cow EIC Jim McLauchlin gave me a book called *((Frequencies))* to read. I read through it and was struck by the talent of the author, Joshua Ortega, who wanted to write comics.

I told Jim we should find a project for Josh and Jim suggested *The Necromancer*. Sounded good to me! I knew it would be years before I'd ever get around to it. So Josh came on board and fleshed out the original treatment and added so many wonderful things. He gave Abby her name and gave her the power to talk with the dead. I remember him telling me he wanted to add that and when I asked why, he said that was what necromancer meant. I didn't reveal at that point that I didn't know that and just nodded and said ok.

I hope you enjoyed reading *The Necromancer*, I know I did. I'm honored to have my name on the book next to such phenomenal talents as Josh Ortega and Francis Manapul.

Thanks!

Matt Hawkins
March 2007

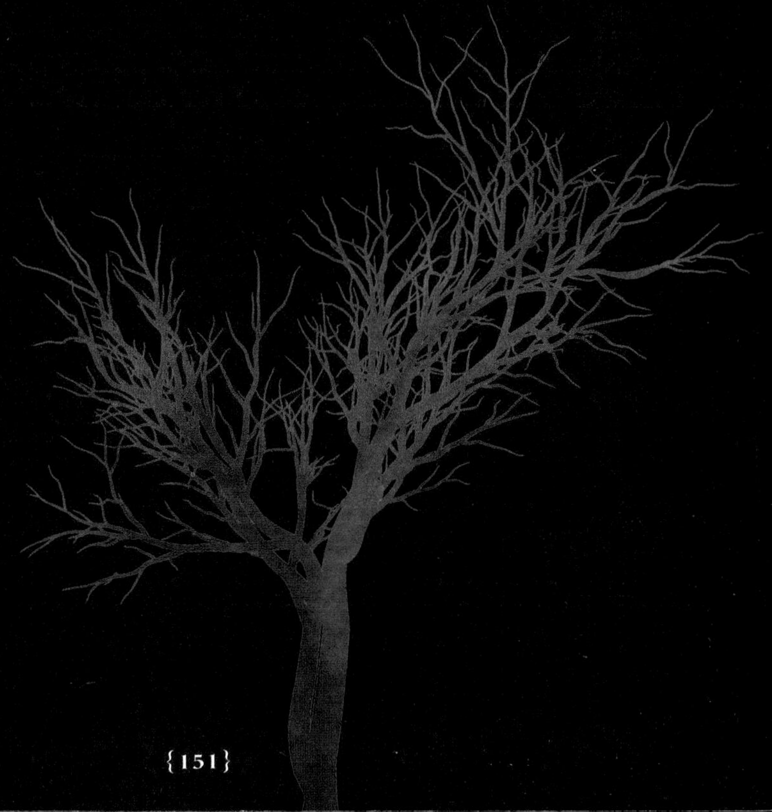

Alternate Cover Gallery

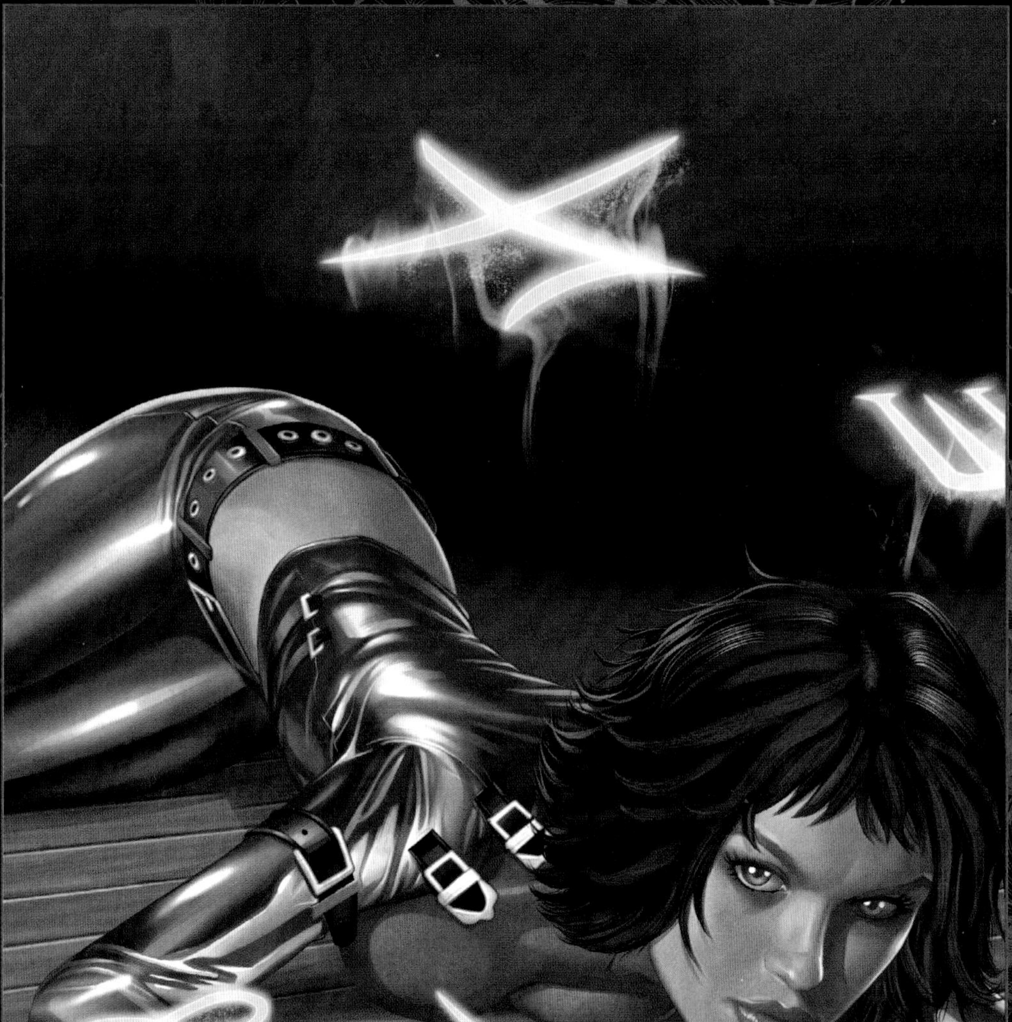
Greg Horn

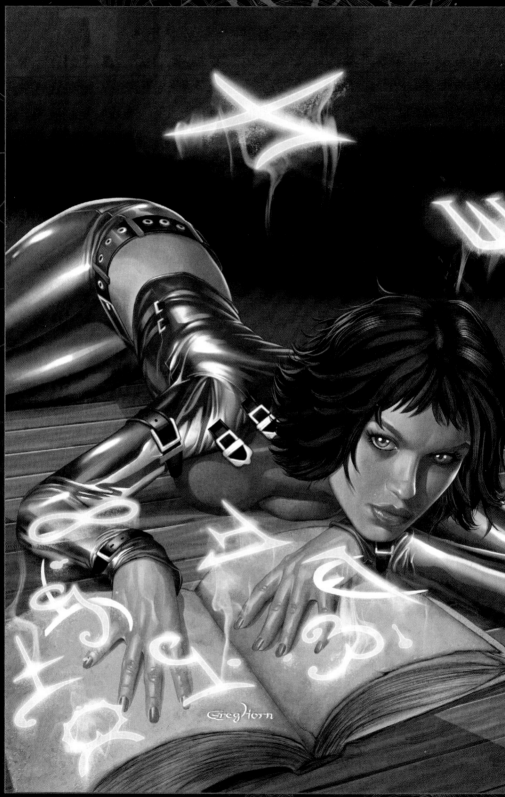

issue #1 cover B, art by: **Greg Horn**

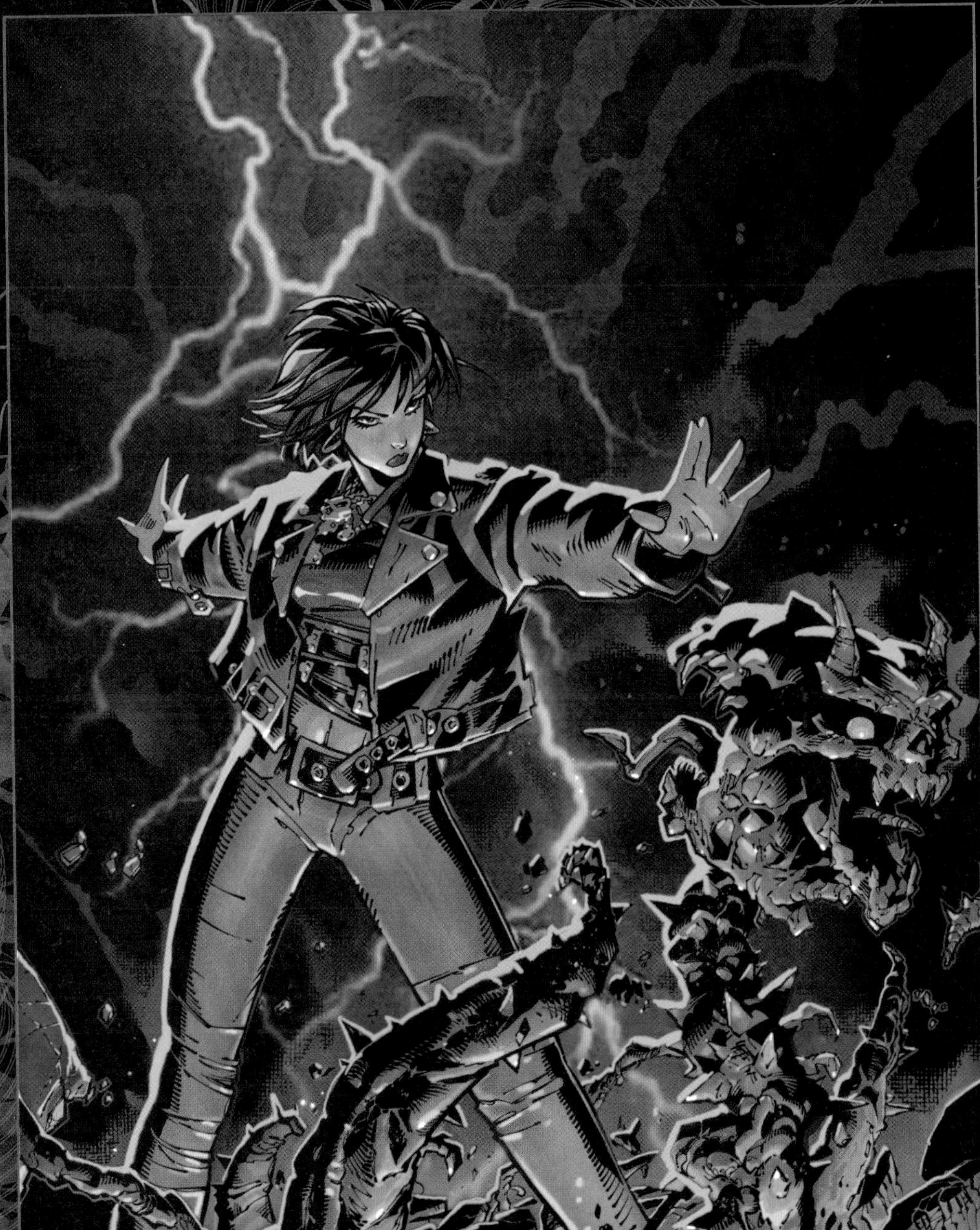

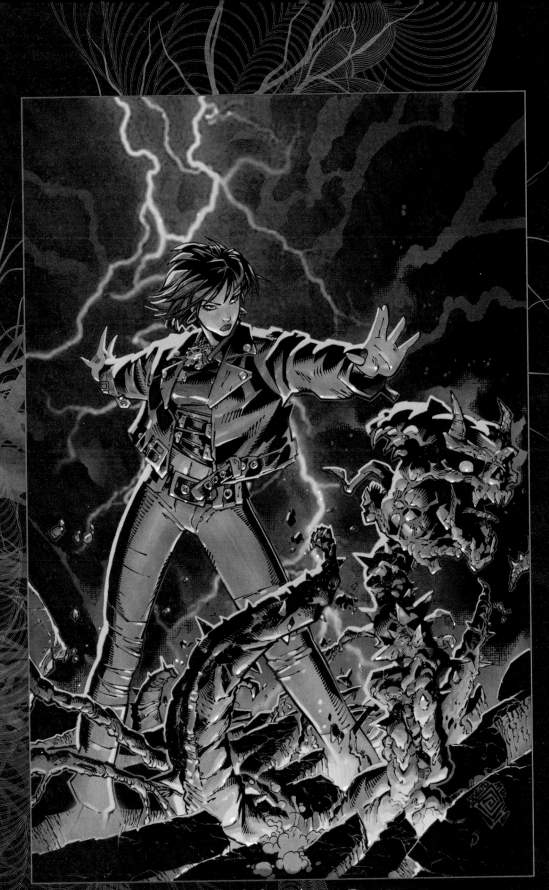

issue #1 cover c, art by: **Chris Bachalo** and **Sean Parsons**

issue #1 convention variant, art by: **Francis Manapul** and **Brian Buccellato**

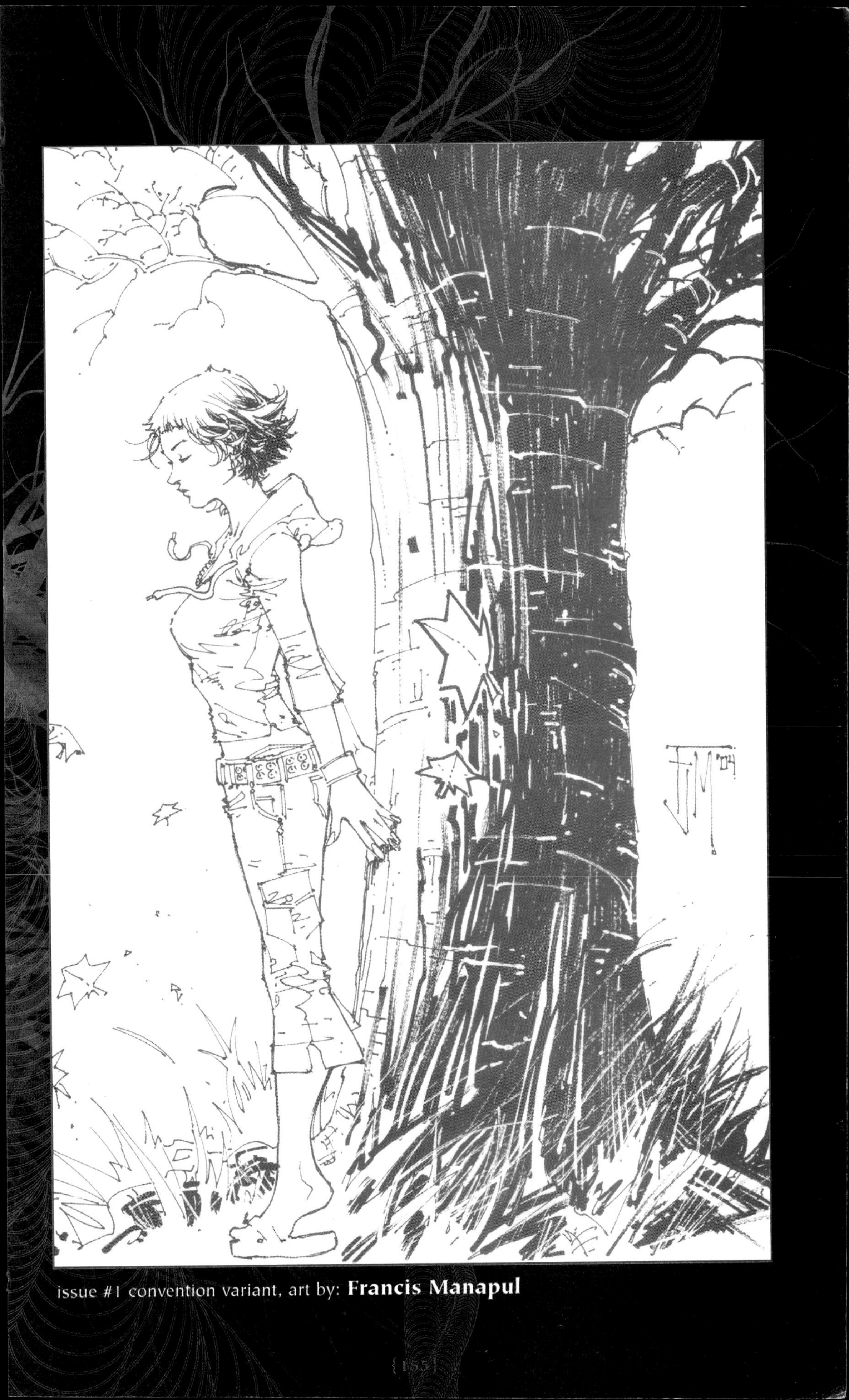

issue #1 convention variant, art by: **Francis Manapul**

Francis Manapul

Sketchbook

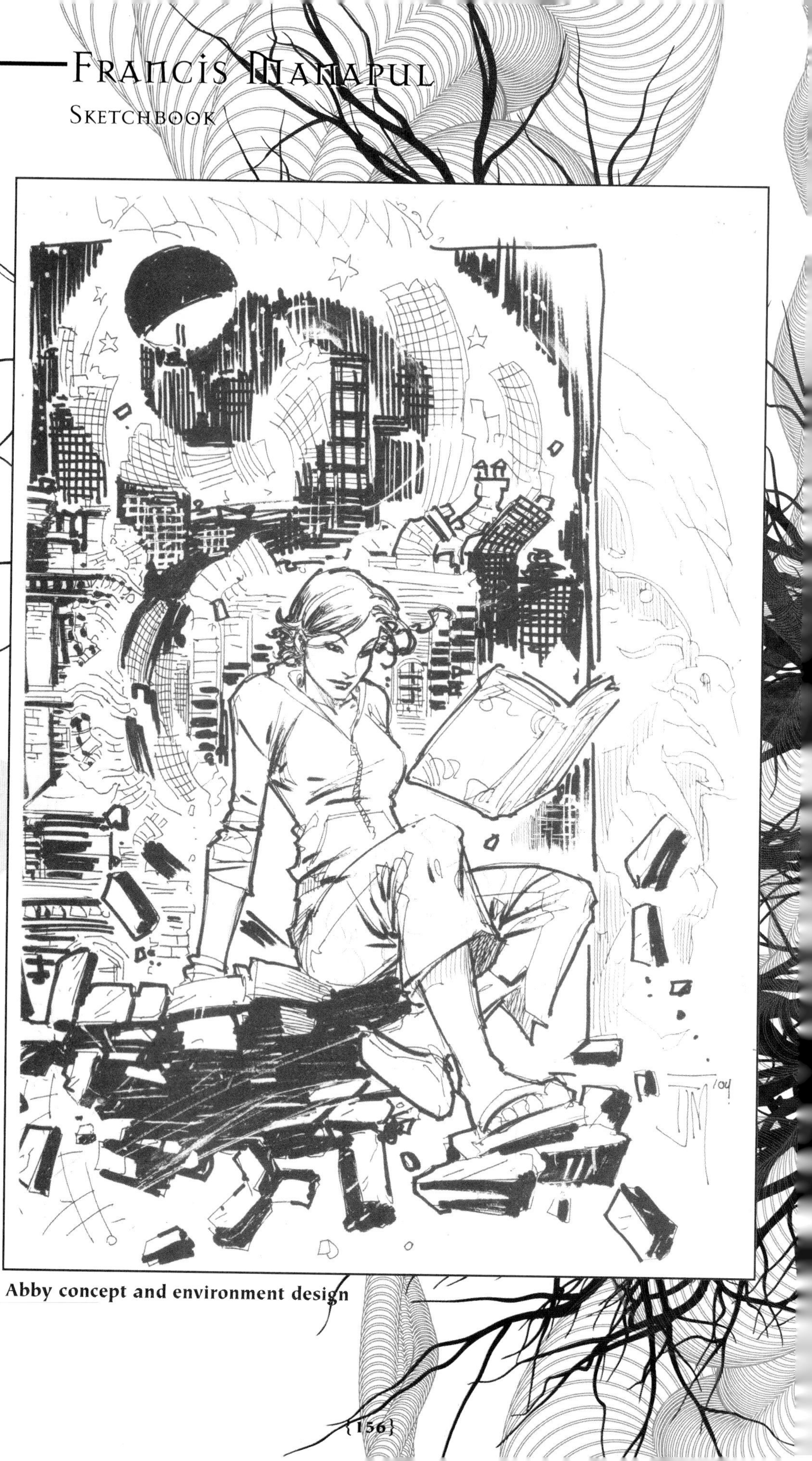

Abby concept and environment design

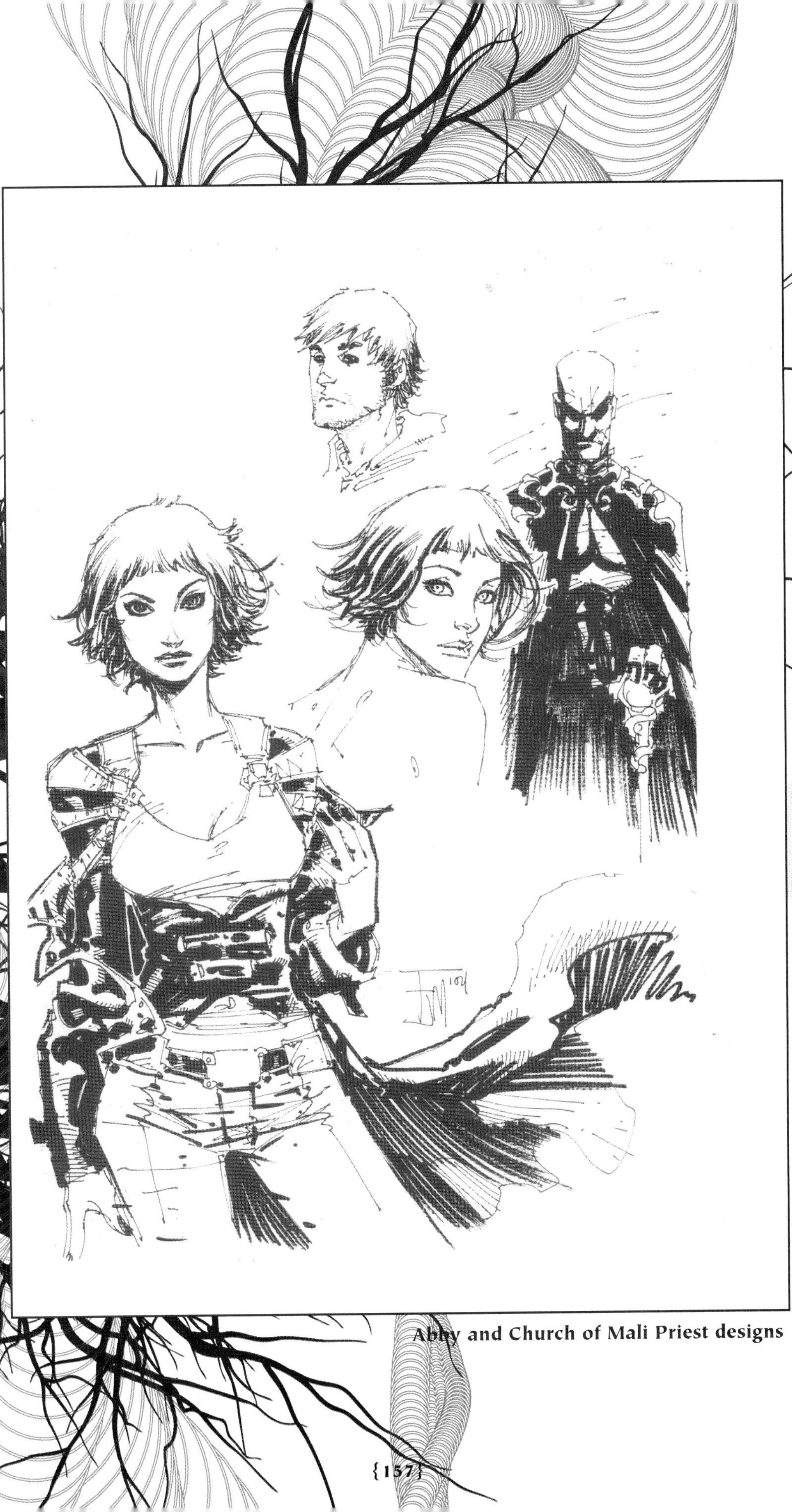

Abby and Church of Mali Priest designs

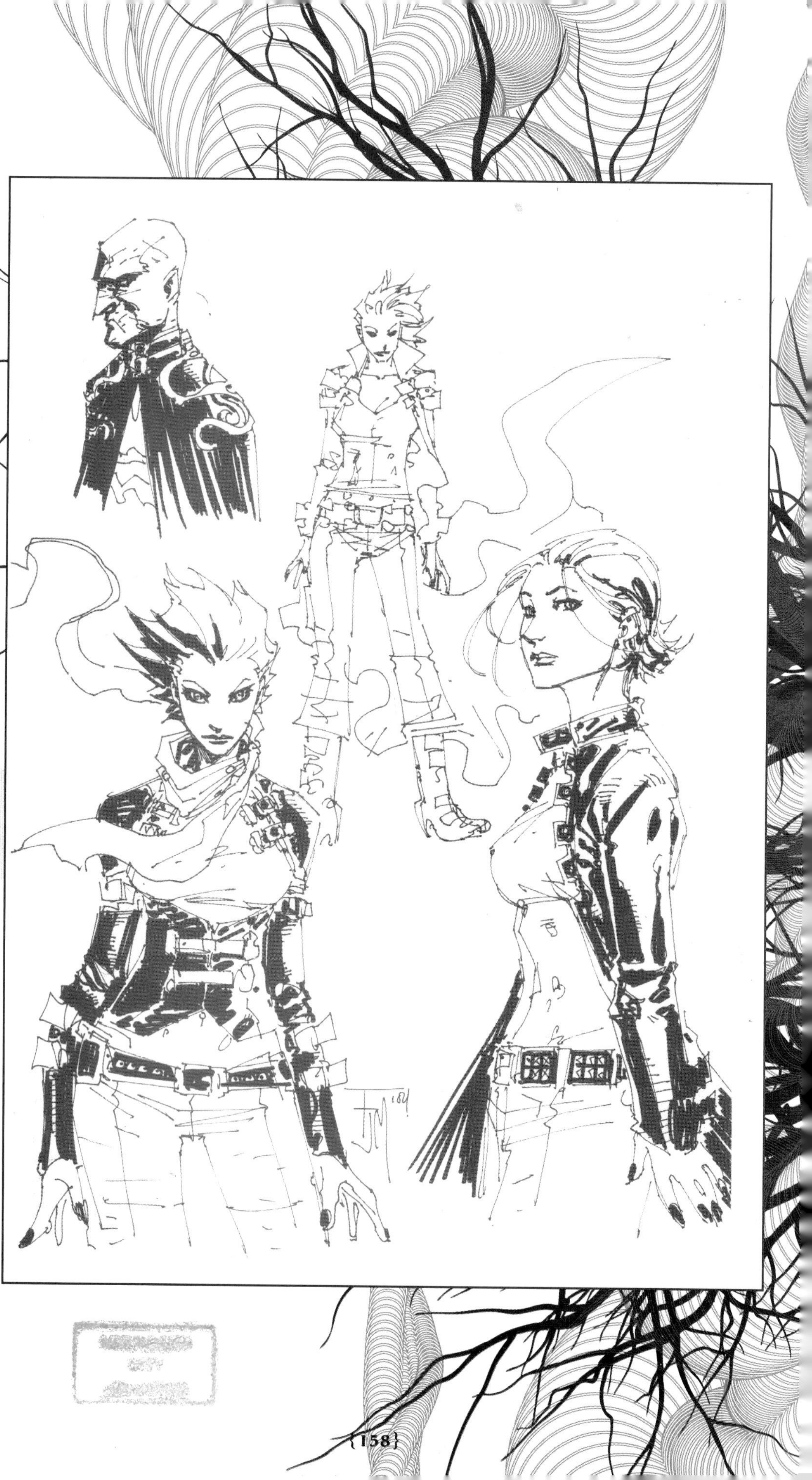

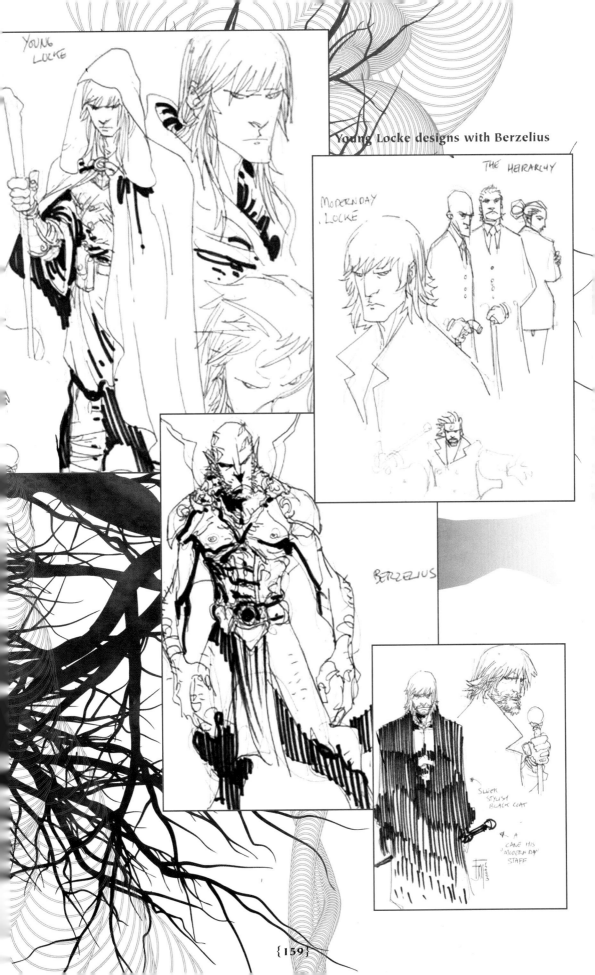

Young Locke designs with Berzelius

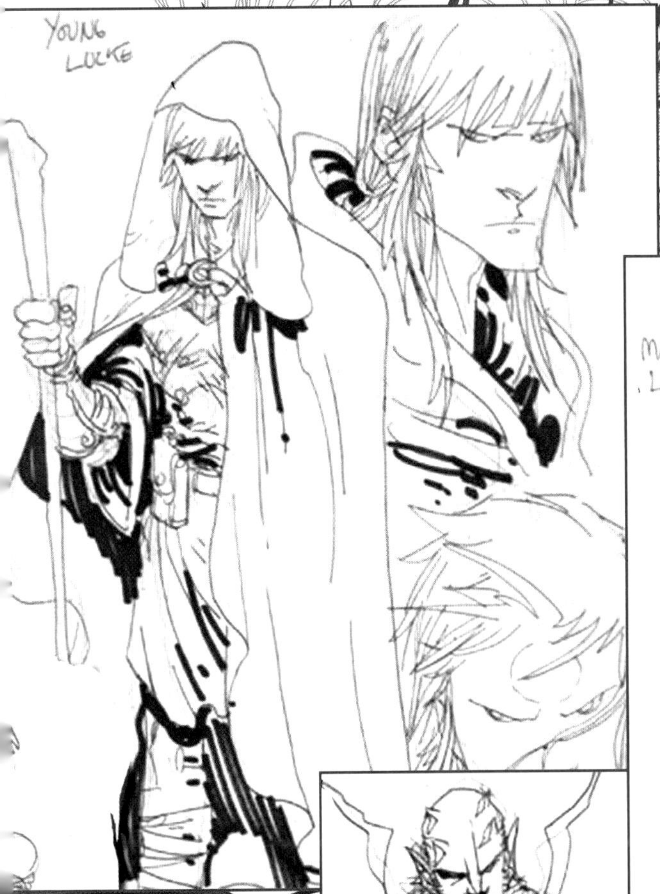
YOUNG LOCKE

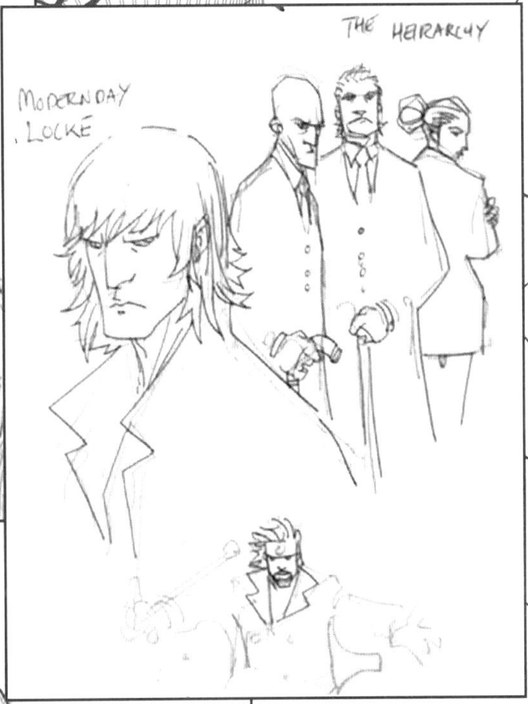
THE HEIRARCHY
MODERNDAY LOCKE

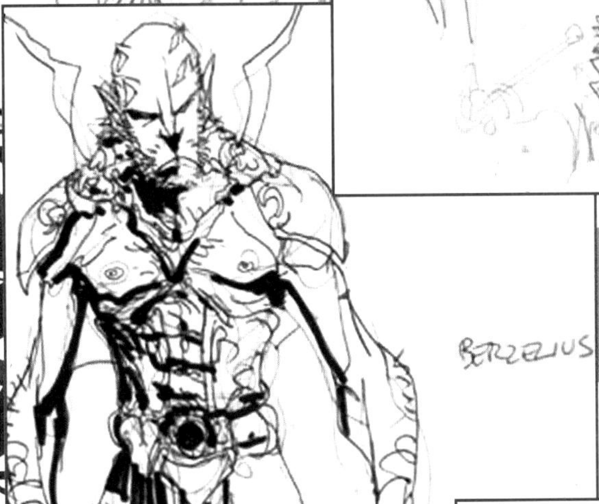
BERZELIUS

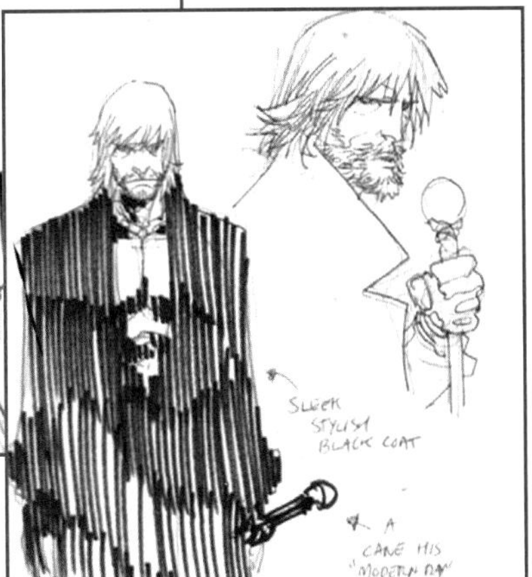
SLEEK STYLISH BLACK COAT
A CANE HIS "MODERN DAY" STAFF

Check out these other titles available from Top Cow Productions, Inc.!

The Darkness
Compendium vol.1

written by:
Garth Ennis, Paul Jenkins, Scott Lobdell
pencils by:
Marc Silvestri, Joe Benitez and more!

On his 21st birthday, the awesome and terrible powers of the Darkness awaken within Jackie Estacado, a mafia hitman for the Franchetti crime family. There's nothing like going back to the beginning and reading it all over again-- issues #1-40, plus the complete run of the *Tales of the Darkness* series collected into one trade paperback. See how the Darkness first appeared and threw Jackie into the chaotic world of the supernatural. Get the first appearances of The Magdalena and more!

(ISBN: 1-58240-643-X) $59.99

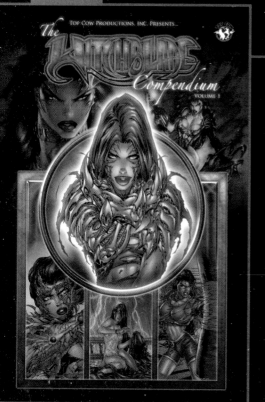

Witchblade
Compendium vol.1

written by:
David Wohl, Christina Z., Paul Jenkins
pencils by:
Michael Turner, Randy Green Keu Cha and more!

From the hit live-action television series, to the current Japanese anime. *Witchblade* has been Top Cow's flagship title for over a decade. There's nothing like going back to the beginning and reading it all over again-- issues #1-50 collected into one massive trade paperback. See how the Witchblade chose Sara and threw her into the chaotic world of the supernatural. Get the first appearances of Sara Pezzini, Ian Nottingham, Kenneth Irons and Jackie Estacado in one handy tome!

(ISBN: 1-58240-634-0) $59.99